Praise for

WARRIOR NATION

"*Warrior Nation* is intended to stir controversy, and it will. With compelling prose and abundant evidence, this fearless book punctures one of Canada's most sacred myths while challenging a complacent national narrative and warning of a deeply worrying trajectory in national life. Ian McKay and Jamie Swift have written an important work of engaged and impassioned history, and it deserves a wide readership."

— A.B. MCKILLOP, Chancellor's Professor and former Chair, History, Carleton University

"The stories that are told about Canada's past, its present, and its future are being reshaped by Canadian policymakers, the military and new warrior scholars in a way that both celebrates militarism and makes its costs invisible. . . . This excellent and timely book offers a much needed corrective to the new warrior scholarship that is becoming so pervasive. It should be on the reading list of anyone who is interested in Canadian politics, international relations, and foreign policy."

— SANDRA WHITWORTH, Professor, Political Science, York University

"Revisiting Canada's military history as a 'sub-imperial' military power of the Anglosphere, *Warrior Nation* recalls the massacre of women and children, the torture and execution of prisoners, and the true horror, lies, and prejudice that come with any war—even those 'our' soldiers fight in the name of 'civilization,' 'democracy,' and 'peace.' A welcome remedy to the 'Support Our Troops' yellow ribbon epidemic."

— FRANCIS DUPUIS-DÉRI, anti-war activist and writer, and Professor, Political Science, University of Quebec at Montreal

WARRIOR

REBRANDING CANADA

NATION

IN AN AGE OF ANXIETY

IAN McKAY
JAMIE SWIFT

BETWEEN THE LINES
TORONTO

First published in 2012 by
Between the Lines
401 Richmond Street West, Studio 277
Toronto, Ontario M5V 3A8
Canada
1-800-718-7201
www.btlbooks.com

Library and Archives Canada Cataloguing in Publication

McKay, Ian, 1953–
    Warrior nation : rebranding Canada in an age of anxiety / Ian McKay and Jamie Swift.

Includes bibliogaphical references and index. Also issued in electronic format.
ISBN 978-1-926662-77-0

1. Canada—History, Military.   2. Canada—Military policy.
3. Conservatism—Canada.   4. Canada—Politics and government—2006– .
I. Swift, Jamie, 1951–   II. Title.

FC543.M45   2012   355.00971   C2012-900792-7

Cover and text design: Gordon Robertson

Printed in Canada

Between the Lines gratefully acknowledges assistance for its publishing
activities from the Canada Council for the Arts, the Ontario Arts Council,
the Government of Ontario through the Ontario Book Publishers Tax Credit
program and through the Ontario Book Initiative, and the Government of
Canada through the Canada Book Fund.

Canada Council
for the Arts   Conseil des Arts
du Canada   Canada   ONTARIO ARTS COUNCIL
CONSEIL DES ARTS DE L'ONTARIO

To Robert and Janet
and Sister Peggy Flanagan

About the authors

Educated at Dalhousie University, Halifax, and the University of Warwick, England, Ian McKay has taught history at Queen's University, Kingston, Ont., since 1988. In 2009 he was the recipient of the John A. Macdonald award from the Canadian Historical Association for *Reasoning Otherwise: Leftists and the People's Enlightenment in Canada, 1890-1920*. He is also the author of *Rebels, Reds, Radicals: Rethinking Canada's Left History*.

Kingston author Jamie Swift's first published article appeared in *This Magazine* in 1975. It exposed Canada's corporate and foreign policy links to Brazil's military dictatorship. He has since written a dozen books of critical non-fiction and biography, including *Cut and Run: The Assault on Canada's Forests* and *Odd Man Out: The Life and Times of Eric Kierans*. In addition to the writing life, he works as a social justice advocate and teaches at Queen's University's School of Business.

It was a time of great and exalting excitement. The country was up in arms, the war was on, in every breast burned the holy fire of patriotism; the drums were beating, the bands playing, the toy pistols popping, the bunched firecrackers hissing and sputtering; on every hand and far down the receding and fading spreads of roofs and balconies a fluttering wilderness of flags flashed in the sun. . . . It was indeed a glad and gracious time, and the half dozen rash spirits that ventured to disapprove of the war and cast a doubt upon its righteousness straightway got such a stern and angry warning that for their personal safety's sake they quickly shrank out of sight and offended no more in that way.

– Mark Twain (Samuel Clemens), "The War Prayer"

To stress one's own love of peace is always the close concern of those who have instigated war. But he who wants peace should speak of war. He should speak of the past one . . . and, above all, he should speak of the coming one.

– Walter Benjamin, "Peace Commodity"

CONTENTS

PREFACE AND ACKNOWLEDGEMENTS

IN CANADA TODAY a determined right-wing elite is making full use of government power to change how we think about our country and its history. Canada, these "new warriors" declaim, has nothing to do with peaceful accommodation and steady improvement in the public good prompted by movements for fairness. Rather, it was created by wars, defended by soldiers, and kept free by patriotic support of military virtues. It is a Warrior Nation. It is a place where the horrible emotions of war are deployed for political gain, in the hopes of gaining a patriotic sense of shared purpose.

This toxic rebranding of their country demands that concerned citizens resist the war machine. But it also requires an engaged understanding of the complicated—and contested—history of Canadian attitudes towards war and peace. The following pages include scrutiny of the lives of four Canadians: Bill Stairs, a Victorian explorer and imperial emissary; Tommy Burns, a veteran of two wars who was also a leading war theorist and ultimately an ambassador for disarmament; Lester Pearson, whose famed formula for UN peacekeeping was combined with the passions of a Cold Warrior; and James Endicott, who struggled to find a path to peace and justice in a world divided into rival atomic camps. Their lives are a prism through which Canadian engagement with matters military are reflected—from African misadventures to the twentieth century's major wars to the peace-keeping enterprise. Then came the end of the Cold War and the promise of a "peace dividend," a period that Canadian militarists call their Decade of Darkness. Then came the disaster of the Afghan War, accompanied as it was by an official effort to rebrand Canada as Warrior Nation. Through all of this we explore Canada's experience of war and peace, and we insist that the enthusiasm and passion so often brought to war can energize opposition to the grim business of mass killing.

Canada's history has seen shifting phases of imperial dependency and inner disunity. It is a country ever divided and ambivalent about war. Warrior Nation, choreboy of empire, fireproof house, peace-seeker. But never solely Warrior Nation. With today's empires waning and warfare changing, Canada may have more potential autonomy to draw creatively on its rich and mixed experience of the horrors of war, and on the rigours and dangers of peace work, to help build a national and global culture of peace. Yet in seeking to reinvent imperial Canada and make the crusading soldier the epitome and essence of our history, the new warriors are not only twisting the priorities of the present, but fundamentally distorting the past.

Throughout this book, we often come back to Kingston, where we both live. It was a military town long before there was a Canada. It still touts its martial heritage. And we also believe that activists and scholars should attend closely to the everyday world around them. In Canada, to adapt an old saying, "All military politics is both global politics and local politics," and those who seek to change the country's direction need to pay close attention to the local as well as the grand manifestations of the new ethos. We would like to thank our fellow citizens and activists in Kingston, many of whom have spoken out courageously against militarism.

With thanks for research assistance from Nancy Butler, Spencer Roberts, Dave Steele, and Tena Vanderheyden. Special thanks to Jonathan Barker for diligently reviewing and commenting on the manuscript in two different stages; to Bill Robinson for reading the final manuscript in a rush; to Karen Dubinsky and Geoff Smith for providing inspiring examples of committed scholarship; to Jean Christie, Susan Gottheil, Len Prepas, and Joe Gunn for hospitality and good company; and to Robert Vanderheyden and David Wood for their photos. Audiences at activist and academic gatherings at Carleton University, Concordia University (People's Commission Network), McMaster University, University of Manitoba, University of Nipissing, Saint Mary's University, and York University provided inspiration and advice; and the excellent ActiveHistory.ca website provided a forum for our work. We are grateful to the Ontario Arts Council, the Sisters of Providence (Kingston), and the Queen's University Fund for Scholarly Research, Creative Work and Professional Development for financial support. Staff and volunteers at Between the Lines were intrepid supporters.

And, above all, Robert Clarke. As usual, this is his book as much as it is ours.

Ian McKay and Jamie Swift

A yellow ribbon on the S&R building, downtown Kingston. An American import with roots in the Civil War, the yellow ribbon would become a symbol of U.S. troops fighting imperial wars—and it all started when a pop song was performed at a 1973 college football championship as the Vietnam War wound down.

THE GREAT WAR, as it was then known, was coming to an end as Canadian soldiers approached Mons, Belgium. Germany's commander in chief had resigned. On November 4, 1918, the terms of an armistice agreeable to the Allies were announced. Kaiser Wilhelm fled to the Netherlands.

Mons was a symbolic site. This was where Britain had suffered its initial defeat at the hands of the Germans in 1914. Four years and uncountable dead soldiers later, Canadian forces under Lieutenant-General Sir Arthur Currie advanced towards the city. Currie knew the war was essentially over. But, as he cabled the prime minister, "Unless Germany is decisively crushed now and reduced to military impotency, there will not be ensured the peace and happiness of civilization."

In the negotiations at Versailles in 1919, this vengeful spirit would ensure that peace and happiness remained distant hopes. And at Mons, it meant that the killing continued until the war's final moments.

The Canadians fought their way into Mons. One general recalled the glory of it all, describing the scene as one might imagine a fine meal. According to Canada's Edward Morrison, it was all a matter of "honour," with Currie riding into the captured city "along the streets garnished with the enemy dead."

"There were men killed at the last moment," recalled Robert John Renison, an army chaplain and later a prominent Anglican bishop. During months of carnage he had often heard Canadian soldiers discussing the celebrations they would enjoy when the war finally ground to a halt. But Renison saw no rejoicing that famous day. "There were men who tried to cheer at 11 o'clock, but they seemed ashamed of their own voices."

Memory itself is contested terrain. By 2006 the dominant narrative—Vimy Fever, as Pierre Berton called it—had become politically useful in the Harper government's promotion of the military as the crucial Canadian institution, with soldiers towering over the rest of us. In 2011 Defence Minister Peter MacKay told troops withdrawing from Kandahar after years of futile struggle that they were Canada's finest citizens, bar none.

"It has been soldiers, not reporters, who have given us freedom of the press," argued a retired colonel at a 2008 Remembrance Day ceremony in Kingston, Ontario. Yet the military in Canada has often been called out to break strikes, repress democratic movements, and intimidate people. Remembrance of such dark chapters is almost always airbrushed from the official military story. Vimy Fever may infect parts of the body politic, but competing stories will never fade away.

So it has been with the memory of what happened in Mons on November 11, 1918.

In 1927 the Port Hope *Evening Guide* editorialized, "There was much waste of human life during the war, enormous loss of lives which should not have taken place. But it is doubtful whether in any case there was a more deliberate and useless waste of human life than in the so-called capture of Mons."

Currie sued the paper for libel with financial help from the president of the CPR and other wealthy Montrealers. The 1928 court case at Cobourg's Victoria Hall was a classic David-and-Goliath contest. It seized the nation's front pages and resembled war itself: there was no real winner.

The *Evening Guide* publisher faced bankruptcy and died within months of the trial's end. Technically, Currie won—the jury awarded him a modest $500 in damages. In reality, he lost. After what the general himself called a "complete nervous breakdown," he died in 1933, at the age of fifty-seven.

In the much-trumpeted new Warrior Nation, every battle Canadians fought in the Great War—every battle since the War of 1812—is bathed in glory. Of course, most of Canada's new warriors, rhapsodizing so romantically about war, have never fought in the wars they promote so enthusiastically. Nor will they fight in the many wars they envisage in Canada's future.

The veterans of Mons knew better. Many of them knew something that today's militarists like to forget. There never was, and never will be, a Great War. Lest we forget.

WARRIOR NATION

John Buchan, the former concentration camp administrator whose hugely successful career as a writer and war propagandist would propel him into a featured role in
the Conservative Party's new *Discover Canada* citizenship guide.

CHAPTER 1

WAR AND PEACE
AND PAPER CRANES

ard Rock & Heavy Metal! The advertising pitch from Kingston's Fort Henry featured a summer student brandishing a musket. He was decked out in the full regalia of a nineteenth-century British redcoat posted to the colonies. The fort, built from local limestone, bristles with old cannon, hence the double entendre of the come-on. It sits at the southern gateway of the Rideau Canal, and tourism marketers were delighted when UNESCO handed the water system the coveted designation of a World Heritage Site.

Both fort and waterway are products of Kingston's military legacy. For much of the nineteenth century the threat came from the United States, and the imperial authorities made ready for an attack that never came. Fort Henry languished as a home away from home for itinerant toffs called remittance men, the pampered sons of the English aristocracy playing soldier among the colonials.

The neighbouring Canadian Forces Base (CFB) is the small city's biggest employer. Yellow support-the-troops logos adorn the advertisements of local realtors who have done very nicely out of an expanding military constantly rotating people in and out of "the Base." In one recent year the Santa Claus parade was led by an armoured personnel carrier. City parks are dotted with cenotaphs, and City Hall—a building that dates back to the days before Confederation—boasts an ornate Memorial Room lined with romanticized First World War images in stained glass. Strippers and lap dancers can be found at a downtown watering hole that features Military Mondays.

Kingston's tourism marketing is all about selling history, particularly military history. A measure of hyperbole is to be expected: every summer Fort Henry hosts what it describes as a "world famous" joint performance by its very own Fort Henry Guard and the Battle Color Detachment of the United States Marine Corps. According to Canada's contemporary soldier-speak, the event is an example of the "interoperability" of its own forces with the forces that the officer class most envies, those of the United States.

Kingston is one of Canada's oldest garrison towns. During the War of 1812—the so-called shipbuilders' war—the outpost at the northeast corner of Lake Ontario enjoyed a brief but intense boom. Its rocky hinterland abounded with ample reserves of white pine, a strategic naval material of the day. The eminent Queen's scholar A.R.M. Lower noted that the conflict with the Americans filled the little colonial settlement with sailors, dockyard workers, soldiers, and the "other secondary human adjuncts of warfare, not least the usual female adjuncts."[1] Lower, one of the great nationalist intellectuals of his day—his general history of Canada, *From Colony to Nation*, was first published in 1946— was a shrewd observer of how the country's economy had evolved to shape its makeup. He reported that nineteenth-century Kingston had a solid coterie of wealthy citizens who mingled easily with the officers of the garrison to form "a little aristocracy" that indulged in private theatricals and musical entertainments. Without wars, Kingston would have far fewer limestone mansions.

"Kingston benefited greatly from the War of 1812," Lower concluded in 1974. "Despite occasional and ineffective American invasions, all of Canada benefited from the War of 1812. It would be possible to go further: all of Canada has benefitted (economically) from every war, first and last, in which it has been caught up. And no town has benefited more directly, positively, proudly and righteously, than has Kingston."[2]

The crusty historian, whose First World War service in the Royal Navy apparently left him with a jaundiced view of matters military, died in Kingston in 1988, just short of a hundred years of age. In his school days Arthur Lower absorbed what he came to see as a rather old-fashioned notion of history—that a country was moulded by the deeds of great men and the battles of great wars. The conventional history taught in schools and universities had intrepid European explorers pushing aside the savages, paving the way for a British Dominion. Faraway royalty and big men in Ottawa directed the affairs of state; and big battles were surely the foundations upon which a modern Canada was built. Lower's later understanding of Canada sprang from a view of history that was rather more extensive and nuanced—that Canada is the product of an intricately complex set of social, economic, and political forces, including, especially, the lives and labours of every-day people. Lower shared his revisionist view with another Canadian thinker who shifted an understanding of Canada's emergence as a nation away from an outmoded emphasis on political history. Harold Innis was, like Lower, a First World War veteran.

The academic research of these scholars in the 1920s gave rise to the insight that the economy—and particularly commodity exports or "staples" such as furs, fish, forest products, grains, and petroleum—had played a crucial role in determining how Canada emerged as a nation. Innis saw commodity exports as a springboard to a mature and independent nation. Innis came to believe that a "staples trap" could lead to a state of dependence on other countries, particularly tradi-tional imperial powers. The titles of two of Lower's works hint strongly at this view—*Great Britain's Woodyard* and *The North American Assault on the Canadian Forest*. Calling war "the greatest of economic forces," Lower was not averse to reaching back centuries for a martial metaphor to describe the capitalist's war on nature. "The sack of the largest and wealthiest medieval cities could have been but a bagatelle compared to the sack of the North American forest and no medieval ravisher could have been more fierce and unscrupulous than the lumberman."[3]

Not long after Lower's death, a group of his fellow historians began to campaign for a supposedly new, yet actually very old, understanding of Canada. In the view of this zealous cohort of conservative acade-mics—who figure prominently among "the new warriors," a term we apply to all the men and women who are actively organizing a milita-rized Canada—the writing of revisionist history had gone seriously off track in its focus on the economy and the struggles of women and working-class people and aboriginals to elbow their way into a fractious public square. The new warriors yearn for a return to the simple stories that youngsters like Lower and Innis had been told before heading off to Harvard and the University of Chicago. Indeed, according to them, soldiers forged the Canada that we know and love. The nation took shape in the white heat of battle. It was, is, and should ever remain a Warrior Nation.

In 2007 J.L. Granatstein, the doyen of the new warrior historians, brought out a new book, *Whose War Is It? How Canada Can Survive in the Post 9/11 World*. Another title for the book might be *Warrior Nation for Dummies*. The retired academic had become so popular with dial-a-quote journalists that the CBC's Peter Mansbridge even called him "Canada's national historian."

For Granatstein, to be a Canadian is to understand that the Canadian past was basically about war. The present? The country confronts grave, even existential, threats. Granatstein does not present these ideas as being open to debate. They are absolute certainties. "The simple fact is . . ." And the *simple fact* is, in the Warrior Nation, that only fools, knaves, and romantics can miss the dire necessity of massive military investment in a looming war for Western civilization. To think otherwise is to confess to ignorance and to countenance error. To argue with this thinking is to indulge in public mischief. Even people whom one might have thought to be conversant with foreign and defence policy, Liberals such as former cabinet ministers Lloyd Axworthy or Bill Graham (the latter being as much as anyone responsible for Canada's blunder into Kandahar) are ignorant. They are self-deluded proponents of a false view of history, propounders of "moralizing" views that are just "naive foolishness" and "nonsense," often anti-American purveyors of "a poison afflicting the Canadian body politic." One can but imagine new warrior reactions to Linda McQuaig's analysis of Canada's aggressive military posturing. In her book published around the same time that Granatstein came out with *Whose War Is It?* the radical journalist offered a suggestive title— *Holding the Bully's Coat: Canada and the U.S. Empire*.[4]

For Granatstein, perhaps the poison-purveyors' most odious nest can be found in "deeply pacifist and anti-military Quebec." For him, in 2003, the province played a damaging role in preventing Canada from invading Iraq beside its U.S.-led allies. Here was an abdication of our true national interests, first and foremost among which is the maintenance of good relations with the United States. Perhaps a future prime minister—or even the one elected while Granatstein was writing his book—would finally level with the child-like Canadians who cling to romantic dreams of a peaceful world. The author of hand-wringing books about the sad demise of old-fashioned history and a stalwart military imagines what such a valiant leader might tell Canadians: "Canada has a dominant cultural pattern comprising Judeo-Christian ethics, the progressive spirit of the Enlightenment, and the institutions and values of British political culture." Such a valiant Caesar would realize that "he is in a war for the soul and survival" of the country, against all who oppose these ideals.[5]

Granatstein and others have since the 1990s been attempting, recently with Ottawa's active assistance, to right what they consider to be grievous wrongs. This essentially *revanchist* struggle pits itself against ideological foes in a fight for the Canadian imagination. A revanchist is someone who wants to reverse war-induced losses, often through further warfare; and *revanchism* in this case applies to the militarist historians who are attacking not just their professional rivals but those forces that they think their rivals represent—naive and romantic tendencies excessively wedded to the ideals of peacekeeping.

What truly distinguishes this right-wing current from any we have seen since the Great War of 1914–18 is the extent to which the new warrior campaign is working in tandem with the state's propaganda apparatus to institute a new regime of truth.

In 2008 Remembrance Day fell during the middle of Canada's war in Kandahar. It was a particularly solemn occasion in Kingston, a city with a maze of nineteenth-century streets named after Crimean War battles, most notably that testimony to military incompetence, the charge of the Light Brigade at Balaclava. A street named Balaclava is around the corner from Kingston's Artillery Park, close to Alma Street and Raglan Road.

Some 150 years after the English aristocrat Lord Raglan ordered the disastrous charge at Balaclava, Canada's government was promoting a return to romantic notions of military exploits. Ottawa was working incessantly to reimagine Canada as a Warrior Nation, selling that new brand to a public conceived, not so much as a rational citizenry, but as a persuadable mass market: newly minted Loonies with remembrance poppies on them (the peacekeepers on the ten-dollar bill will simply have to go); proliferating highways of heroes (indeed, any soldier as hero); a ramped-up blood-and-soil cult of Vimy Ridge, including something called Vimy Week; a multi-million-dollar propaganda push aimed at flogging a cardboard version of history, painting the foolish, inconclusive War of 1812 in patriotic colours.

On that gloomy autumn day a crowd gathered in Kingston's City Park, site of the Royal Canadian Horse Artillery War Memorial. The pipers piped as school children freed from their classrooms mingled with grey-haired men wearing blazers and medals and greeting one another with snappy salutes. The monument itself, etched with the names of those killed in the First World War, reflected that fundamental military value—rigid hierarchy. Atop the list of the RCHA dead was a colonel by the name of Eaton. Below the colonel came the names of officers of lesser rank, and below them a list of the dead gunners who had held what the military calls "other ranks."

Bob Chamberlain, himself a superannuated colonel, addressed the crowd. He assured any doubters that Canada was at war in Afghanistan "to enable us to live in one of the best countries in the world." His patriotic message included a political angle. The veteran of the Cold War expressed the belief that Canada's military had everything to do with freedom and democracy. After declaring that it was soldiers and not reporters who had given the country "freedom of the press," Chamberlain gestured with his white gloved hand in the direction of the nearby Queen's University and proclaimed, "It has been soldiers, not campus agitators, who have given us the right to protest."[6]

The notion that the military and democracy are somehow joined at the hip is integral to the Warrior Nation message. Three years after that Remembrance Day ceremony, someone in Peterborough, Ontario, came up with the idea that cities should offer free parking and public transportation to veterans. Kingston's me-too mayor Mark Gerretsen took up the idea. "A lot has to be said for the veterans who've served to give us the freedom we have." Like the yellow-ribbon symbol, the "Love-your-freedom? Thank-a-veteran" sentiment had migrated north from the United States, where a martial mentality has far deeper roots. Still, the idea now goes beyond bumper-sticker culture north of the border, with Veterans Affairs Canada telling us that 110,000 Canadians died in war "so that we may live in peace and freedom today."[7]

The military has the luxury of employing dozens of officers working as public relations flacks to tell "the biggest story in the world," dedicated to convincing Canadians that the armed forces are "making history" and "doing fantastic things all over the world," everything from going on the Kandahar offensive to scoring a hat trick in a local hockey league game. Warrior Nation promoters do not let the facts stand in the way of a good story. Their allies are there to help. As the war to save Afghanistan from Afghans was being ramped up in 2007, one breathless Kingston radio deejay offered up a Christmas message, reminding her listeners that before they "get deep into the malls" they should take a moment to remember the troops in Afghanistan. "Remember that if they weren't there, we wouldn't be here."[8] Although this sort of logic may require a daring leap of faith, repeated often enough it can begin to sink in amidst competing advertising messages and the flash and grab of the mall.

Canadians have witnessed an effort to conscript both the distant past and more recent times in a reshaping of their country's future. The "Canada" that shimmers in the imagination of right-wing politicians, militarists, and new warrior historians is not a country offering any significant public provision to its most vulnerable. Instead it is a virtuous nation of warriors. It is one based upon blood and soil, sanctified by battle deaths and engaged in a perpetual war with the tyranny and terror championed by less-evolved peoples. We must seize the day for a new Canada, sanctified by the blood of Vimy Ridge.

When Stephen Harper, newly elected as prime minister in 2006, travelled to London to address the Canada-U.K. Chamber of Commerce, it was surely a supremely positive moment for the drum and bugle Monarchist League of Canada, long regarded as an eccentric if mildly amusing fringe group. The Canadian leader was clearly stoked about what is called the "Anglosphere"—that conglomeration of interests that is also sometimes called the "English-Speaking Peoples," sometimes the "United States and its allies" or the "liberal-democratic countries," and sometimes just "the West"—although Anglosphere is probably the most accurate and revealing term because it suggests just how much the U.S.-centred empire seeks to draw upon the cultural, political, and racial capital of its British predecessor.

"At the heart of our relationship is the golden circle of the Crown which links us all together with the majestic past that takes us back to the Tudors, the Plantagenets, the Magna Carta, habeas corpus, petition of rights, and English common law," Harper told the London business gathering on Bastille Day, symbol of quite another tradition. "All those massive stepping stones which the people of the British race shaped and forged to the joy, and peace, and glory of mankind . . . much of what Canada is today we can trace to our origins as a colony of the British Empire." In another glory-of-empire moment, the new prime minister had two months earlier welcomed Australian prime minister John Howard to Canada. Harper assured Parliament that troops from the white dominions had fought together in both world wars, in Korea, and now in Afghanistan to promote human rights, democracy, and peace.[9] So it was that we learned about the straight and glorious military line between Vimy Ridge and Kandahar. Both struggles were, it seems, all about freedom and peace.

The ideological affinity between Canada's prime minister and the former Australian leader—another militant booster of the Anglosphere—was long-standing. In 2003 a Conservative Party operative plagiarized one of the Australian's speeches, and Harper used Howard's exact words in urging Canada to join the U.S. assault on Iraq. The Harper staffer, an intellectual property expert, was forced to resign from the Conservative "war room" when the scandal came to light during the 2008 election campaign.[10]

We must apparently be ready for active service for whatever wars are necessary for Western civilization, as embodied in that great Anglo-American alliance, the Anglosphere. This is where Canadians will surely find their country's true destiny. Such a prescription for Canadian identity is consistent with a government that, more and more, comports itself like an authoritarian regime.

The word "regime" is not a rhetorical device aimed at discrediting the new warrior mentality. It is a term proudly embraced by Barry Cooper, author of *It's the Regime, Stupid! A Report from the Cowboy West on Why Stephen Harper Matters*, a manifesto for an authoritarian and militarized Canada. The Calgary political scientist, a research fellow linked to the Centre for Military and Strategic Studies, which is in turn supported by the Department of National Defence, strikes an unabashedly authoritarian tone: "A regime indicates who rules but especially what type of human being rules and is sufficiently admired that he or she has the right to enforce and coerce a specific way of life, if that should prove necessary."[11]

For new warriors, enforcement and coercion—at the heart of the military enterprise—are an imperative. Indeed, words like "must," "need," and "necessary" occur repeatedly in the manifestos and op-ed pieces that they fire out into the media with machine-gun regularity. Honour, manliness, and pride are all at stake. If necessary, the new values—and the new heroes who embody them—must be imposed from above. Democrats of convenience, they are Caesarists by conviction. As Cooper and historian David Bercuson proclaim, the task is clear— to transform Canada from a nation of "whiners" associated with a "thoroughly undignified and suffocatingly maternal" political order into a nation of virtuous warriors. As for the entire Canadian welfare state that marked the modest but hopeful beginnings of a more democratic and egalitarian society in the decades after the Second World War, they resolve to abolish it altogether. Such a welfare state is "absurd," an example of "collectivist housekeeping." Bercuson and Cooper holler, "The welfare state has created a welfare state of mind! It must go!" In place of welfare dependence, social programs, and peace-keeping, this vision looks forward to a society in which "individuals contend for prizes, honours, and recognition of their superiority."[12]

This sort of sturdy individualism appears to be particularly attractive to men of a certain age who have no actual experience of armed conflict, and it is matched by their enthusiasm for war. If the vision smacks of the war of each against all, that is because it is exactly that. At home and abroad, Canadians are urged to think like uber-patriotic hockey commentator Don Cherry and his approach that glorifies fighting as integral to the national game. It was against this background that in 2011 Canadians were treated to the spectacle of newly minted foreign minister John Baird scrawling a message on a bomb and heading off to Libya, where Canadian forces were part of a NATO effort to assist in bombing the country to freedom.

Just as Canada's contingent pulled out of Kandahar amidst escalating violence, it became increasingly apparent that the militarization of foreign policy was rivalled only by the official glorification of the armed forces. Defence Minister Peter MacKay told departing soldiers, "You are the best citizens of our country."[13] A bit of sweaty rhetoric by a politician carried away in the heat of the moment? Possibly, but MacKay's insight was that of a leading member of a government that was taking extreme pains to stay "on message." In 2007 MacKay had moved into the Defence portfolio from Foreign Affairs after the regime's first defence minister—a retired officer and former lobbyist for a leading weapons manufacturer—was demoted in the midst of the scandal over Afghan prisoner torture. The former Progressive Conservative politician had been so completely captured by the military mentality that his vocabulary became heavily inflected with the diction of soldier-speak. Military leaders were so pleased with the regime's moral and financial support that General (Ret.) Rick Hillier described MacKay as a "strong leader with a core of steel."[14]

All of which gave Paul Robinson pause for concern. A former Canadian and British army officer who had become an academic specialist in matters military at the University of Ottawa, Robinson took the trouble to survey the local landscape as Canada withdrew from Kandahar. He was particularly exercised by MacKay's proclamation that Canada itself was a much better place because of the military effort in Afghanistan. For Robinson, the most obvious domestic result of Canada's Afghan War was a "return of a militarism not seen in Canada in peacetime since before the First World War." The "shrieks" of "Support Our Troops" had contributed to a climate in which it was ever more difficult to criticize military operations. Robinson pointed with even more foreboding to the colonization of the government by a military mentality:

> When Peter MacKay is, as so often, praised for being popular with the troops, this is meant to imply that he is therefore a good defence minister. In fact, this may merely show that he is a weak defence minister, unable or unwilling to stand up to the military and prone to grant its every wish. Armed forces have bureaucratic interests in the same way as every other organization, and firm control is needed to keep them in check.[15]

Just as Canada backed away from the Kandahar quagmire, Canadians learned that all ceremonies at which new Canadians officially received citizenship would feature a uniformed soldier, preferably someone who had been in Afghanistan. Ottawa had traditionally dispatched the usual postcard symbol of Canada, the Mountie in the red serge suit and riding boots, to appear at these ceremonies. Things were changing. The RCMP would still send someone along, but the regime was attempting to position the military as central to a Warrior Nation's image. It was all part of the rebranding fervour.

Nowhere was the regime's Warrior Nation vision of a new image for Canada clearer than in the glossy pages of *Discover Canada: The Rights and Responsibilities of Citizenship*, published in 2009. Newcomers from Delhi and Taipei had to study the guide before they could qualify for citizenship and get a chance to gaze up at the uniformed figures standing stiffly at the solemn-but-happy formalities. What's more, to get to the ceremony they had to pass a test based on the new guide—which could just as well have been titled *The Beginner's Guide to the Warrior Nation*. Such guides are among the most widely circulated statements about Canada's past and present ever published. The regime's new version appears at first glance innocuous enough, with colourful tulips and happy paddlers on the cover and photos of beaming children within. But on closer inspection readers quickly discover that Canada, past and present, is centrally about *war*. Warriors are *the* significant Canadians—no one else is in the running. Of thirty images in the section on "Canada's History," twenty depict plainly military events or figures. (By contrast, not a soldier is to be found in *A Look at Canada*, an earlier version of the manual published in 2005.) The images of war are profoundly romantic, cleaned-up Victorian images of battle reminiscent of the *Boy's Own Annual*. No blood, refugees, or bombed-out cities in sight. Going to war looks like a lot of fun. Even better, we have acquired a whole new cast of Canadian heroes, fighting for the Empire long before Canada even took shape in 1867. These warriors were out in the world. They put down unruly Afghans, troublesome Russians, and misguided apostles of independence in India in 1857, where our boys helped to settle their hash in the Siege of Lucknow.

According to this spruced-up official story, "the Wars" essentially shape the entire Canadian twentieth century, with minor events like the Great Depression, the coming of the welfare state, and even the achievement of Dominion autonomy within the British Empire reduced to interwar filler. The First World War, the guide says, "strengthened both national and imperial pride, particularly in English Canada." If romantic illustrations and inspiring descriptions of the adventure of war are too subtle, the guide further promotes the military with explicit website information for those who want to make this "excellent career choice." Peacekeeping is not *entirely* overlooked. It gets an entire half-sentence on page 24—fewer words, revealingly, than those devoted to a description of some Canadians' imperial ambition to have the Dominion take over the British West Indies in the 1920s. Apparently Canada's cultural memory has been all about "a belief in ordered liberty, enterprise, hard work and fair play." This belief "has enabled Canadians to build a prosperous society in a rugged environment."[16]

That formulation, "ordered liberty"—and much else in this remarkable document—is a direct steal from John Buchan. As 1st Baron Tweedsmuir, Buchan served as Canada's governor general from 1935 until 1940, when he died after suffering a stroke and hitting his head in his Rideau Hall bathroom.

Remarkably, the Harper government's citizenship guide calls upon a British lord to tell new Canadians about the country's cultural fabric. (No twentieth-century Canadian politician receives substantial space in the entire production.) Depicted in full Native headdress, Buchan instructs immigrant groups that they "should retain their individuality." Moreover, he says, "While they cherish their own special loyalties and traditions, they cherish not less that new loyalty and tradition which springs from their union."[17] It is a messy bit of prose. To a casual reader it might seem rather unobjectionable: be your ethnic selves and relax and enjoy Canada, just like our headdress-wearing GG.

Well, not exactly. Buchan was a prolific and popular author who wrote over thirty works of fiction, including *Prester John* (1910), *The Thirty-Nine Steps* (1915), and *Greenmantle* (1916). The typical Buchan adventure story depicts a valiant male hero defending the British Empire against some conspiracy or other launched by its many anarchist, Jewish, Islamic, or dark-skinned enemies. Throughout his entire adult life Buchan saw his Empire as the bearer of enlightenment and order, with the Sovereign at its apex representing all of its noblest qualities—not just individualism but also hard work, deference to authority, and respect for property. Races "lower . . . in the scale of development" could find a place in Buchan's Empire, as long as they remained deferential, remembering their place.[18] In both his lengthy non-fiction works and his novels, Buchan put forth the idea that the blacks in Africa called out for the white men from Britain to rule over them. It was in the service of this idea that during the South African

War of 1899–1902 he administered racially segregated concentration camps and schemed to deliver the country's lands to British settlers. When serving as Canada's governor general, Buchan warned McGill University students against Slavic and "Negroid" cultural influences in Canada, a country he sometimes called a "white man's democracy," sometimes "Scotland-writ-large." Generations of Canadian school children thrilled to his tale of *Prester John*, in which one hero reflects that the "gift of responsibility" enduringly separated "white and black."[19] The novel was still on the Ontario high-school curriculum in the late 1950s.

With *Discover Canada*'s illustration of Buchan-in-headdress, the guide is showcasing a proud imperial emissary, monarchist, and racial theorist—a man taking the Empire's message to subjects he considered intrinsically, and racially, inferior to himself. Elevating Buchan to this position makes sense within the new warriors' imperial vision—Canada's deepest meaning lies within its loyalty to the Anglosphere, which, once led by Britain and now by the United States, fights for "ordered liberty" in a cosmic clash of civilizations pitting "us" against "them."

What is it that this brave new Canada is fighting for? Why, Canadians are the inheritors of a British constitution—not citizens within a constitutional order that has also been shaped by eighteenth-century treaties with First Nations, the distinct traditions of civil law derived from France, and struggles by a host of activists for a more democratic legal order. In *Discover Canada*, readers will find a Canada that means "one way of life"—just one. And this nation can be projected back far into the distant past — even before nation-states were to be found on the globe.

"You are becoming part of a great tradition that was built by generations of pioneers before you," the citizenship guide announces in its opening message. "For 400 years, settlers and immigrants have contributed to the diversity and richness of our country, which is built on a proud history and a strong identity."[20] Whatever the "great tradition" concretely entails, this four-century formulation excludes peoples who were in northern North America for millennia before the 1600 A.D. cut-off date. The "great tradition" is reserved for the history of the white "pioneers," "colonizers," and "settlers." Notwithstanding the representations of Native people, often depicted in the guide in northern territories over which the state claims sovereignty, Canadian history is discreetly racialized. History begins only when the Europeans arrive.

Discover Canada adheres closely to the scripts of many high-school history texts of the 1920s and 1930s. Although it does mention such unseemly aberrations as residential schools and slavery, the guide handles them gingerly, using a fast-forwarding technique: almost as soon as it acknowledges such troubling moments, the text quickly moves on. If you really believe that post-1945 Canada has been an unwise experiment in effete moral relativism and social-democratic softness, with peacekeeping as an unfortunate international outcome, you will do whatever is necessary to solidify the images and ideals that prevailed before Canada began its sad decline.

In *Discover Canada*, the Empire fights back. Neo-conservatives seeking a Caesarist hero in history, a man exemplifying their doctrine of a virtuous Empire under authoritative military leadership, find in Buchan an eloquent defender of the enduring mission of white, English-speaking peoples carrying civilization's burden to the far reaches of the planet. Conscious as they must have been of Buchan as the administrator of concentration camps and apostle of the White Man's Burden, the new warriors are nevertheless strongly attached to this figure. During a 1936 trip through the Canadian North, Buchan spent hours working on the index to his new book, a biography of Caesar Augustus. "It is extraordinary," Buchan wrote in March 1936, "how that great man, the only dictator who ever kept his head, anticipated so many things in the modern world."[21] Indeed.

Fear is a time-honoured political tactic, a particular favourite of authoritarian regimes. Criminals, terrorists, immigrants, Communists, foreigners, Jews, savages—the list of targets stretches back into history. In the antebellum United States a nativist Know-Nothing movement flourished, gaining traction by stoking fear of Irish Catholic and German immigrants. Canada had its Orange Lodge and Protestant Protective Association. The early twenty-first century, arguably the safest period that Canadians had ever experienced, would be marked by levels of official scaremongering the likes of which had not been seen since the Red Scare of the 1950s. Fear entrepreneurs may not be familiar with Edmund Burke's observation that despotic governments rely on "the passion of fear." Fear-based regimes seek to keep apprehension on a constant simmer, even if the odds of being assaulted by an eighteenth-century highwayman, though slim, were probably greater than of being felled by a contemporary terrorist. "When we know the full extent of any danger," said Burke, "when we can accustom our eyes to it, a great deal of the apprehension vanishes."[22]

"Friends," Canada's prime minister warned a group of his core supporters as the election of 2011 got underway, "We are living in a fragile global recovery. Yes, Canada is doing relatively well, but a sea of troubles is lapping at our shores, disaster in the Pacific, chaos in the Middle East, debt problems in Europe and of course very serious challenges south of our border. Canada is the closest thing the world has to an island of security and stability." The headline of one news article during the campaign was "Fear the Main Factor in Harper's Stump Speeches."[23] During the campaign, Sun TV, headed by Harper's former spokesperson, was running a promo spot proclaiming "The world's a dangerous place!" In 2008, gripped with a fear of his own—the loss of his hold on power in a minority situation—Harper's rhetoric was all about a scary "coalition" of socialists and separatists; government supporters assembled on Parliament Hill bearing signs that stated "Safe with Steve." Then too, the Harper government's rationale for putting offenders away for longer periods by building more jails was to keep law-abiding Canadians "safe." The entire tough-on-crime package was wrapped up in a Safe Streets and Communities Act.

The politics of fear are aimed at scaring people into supporting myopic policies. They also allow politicians the luxury of not having to map out a vision of what exactly it is they stand *for*. Fear is connected to the more widely discussed tactic of negative or attack advertising. It can lead to a form of anti-politics well suited to a broader political strategy of encouraging passivity. In this view Canadians are not citizens but a marketplace of voters who are regularly polled and at whom "messaging" is endlessly calibrated. In *The Politics of Fear* sociologist Frank Furedi argues that the effect can be ominous, transforming fear "into a cultural perspective through which society makes sense of itself. Despite appearances, such fear is not finally limited to specific issues but is about everything. The culture of fear is underpinned by a profound sense of powerlessness, a diminished sense of agency that leads people to turn themselves into passive subjects who can only complain, 'We are frightened.'"[24]

This political calculus is well suited to the vision of a Warrior Nation whose expanding military stands on guard against dark foreign threats. By 2007 the war in Afghanistan was providing what the top brass was describing as a "perfect wave"—the sort of engagement of which their predecessors in the pre-9/11 and Cold War periods could only have dreamed. Major-General Daniel Gosselin, commander of the Canadian Defence Academy in Kingston, was upbeat when he spoke to a meeting of the Conference of Defence Associations (CDA), a group of zealous lobbyists for more military spending . . . funded by Canada's Department of National Defence.[25] Gosselin waxed optimistic about the likelihood that the Afghan War would change the future identity of the Canadian military. These were "exciting times," not the least of which were equipment acquisitions during "a period of growth of [military] strength on a scale not seen since the 1950s."[26]

Back in the days of the Cold War, fear of a Soviet attack meant that Canada's army and air force assisted in garrisoning NATO's Fortress Europe while the security police amassed thick files on public figures as dangerous as Tommy Douglas. In those days the military had been able to justify its insatiable appetite. Now Ottawa was opening the public purse in a way that was unprecedented in peacetime. With the war in Kandahar escalating, General Gosselin recalled to his audience how "the air in the room was electrifying" when, soon after the Liberals had appointed Rick Hillier as head of the military, the new boss outlined the impending transformation of what was being rebranded as "Forces.ca." There would be a "prominent role for Canada's military within Canada's international policy."[27]

The principal "dominant idea" behind the great transformation was that the Canadian military would no longer face what Hillier described as "the bear," the massed divisions of the Warsaw Pact. The new enemy in a promisingly endless war would be "the snakes." NATO would, for the foreseeable future, be the scourge of the new fauna—also described as "non-state actors"—and something of the fascination with snakes even entered Operation Medusa, which the Canadians launched to rout out Taliban fighters in southern Afghanistan.[28] The gorgon Medusa was famed for the nest of snakes resting upon her head.

Yet the childish animal analogies hinted at the absence of strategic intelligence or informed insight at the heart of the Canadian endeavour in Afghanistan, where, for centuries, empires have encountered stiff resistance from indigenous peoples. Veteran *New York Times* war correspondent Dexter Filkins recalled Hamidullah, a young Pashtun Taliban from Kunduz whom he met under a mulberry tree in Kandahar. The amputee told him that he and his comrades had "seen more battles than hairs on our head." In *The Forever War*, a book that evoked the future as envisaged by Canadian and U.S. military planners, Filkins described the Afghan fighters: "The old men, the leaders, were walking junkyards, metal and bullets and shrapnel, heaped over with holes and scar tissue. . . . They'd look at you and you'd think, Jesus, they are not killable. They're from another world."[29] Still, after pulling its troops out of Kandahar in something less than glory, Canada would presume to keep military staff in the country to "train" Afghans in the art of war.

Most Canadians had long suspected that the West's invasion of Afghanistan had turned into a disaster for all concerned. By the end of the Kandahar effort, public opinion on the war had remained unchanged. A national poll funded and published by the pro-war Sun Media chain, whose Kingston outlet had long sported a yellow support-the-troops ribbon on its masthead, revealed the war's deep unpopularity. Three in five Canadians believed that the Afghan War was not worth the blood and money their country had expended. Typically, only 21 per cent of women judged the ten-year effort worthwhile, compared to 39 per cent of the men. Quebec, with the highest proportion of those holding strong doubts about the debacle in Afghanistan, maintained its historical scepticism about war.[30] While most summaries of Canada's Kandahar pullout mentioned the 157 Canadian deaths in ten years of fighting, few stories highlighted the uncountable Afghan deaths, including many civilians, for which Canada and its NATO allies must be held responsible. Typically, the blame for the abject failure of Canada's plans for Afghanistan falls upon the Afghans themselves—supposedly the recalcitrant enemies of progress and modernity—and not upon the NATO and U.S. planners whose grand strategy amounted to little more than bribing warlords and subsidizing one of the world's most corrupt narco-states.

Canada's propaganda often relied on images of Afghan poverty while claiming that the war was about helping little girls go to school. There was hope for the locals if they could only be lifted from their primitive ways by the kindly ministrations of forward-thinking Canadians. "Afghanistan is an ugly place," explained Laurie Hawn, a former colonel who went on to become a Conservative MP and parliamentary secretary to the defence minister.

> We have to work with the Afghans and build their capacity, starting from zero. It's a pretty tough climb. We've been building their capacity to handle their affairs themselves. Because ultimately when we've gone from Afghanistan, this is their business, this is their country. We're trying to get them to the point where they can handle [their affairs] properly, to something like the standards we would expect in the West.[31]

The new warrior version of the ten-year war—the longest in Canadian history—was similar to the story of many another war. It was packaged in patriotism, wrapped in the flag, and peppered with images of "ramp ceremonies" and Highways of Heroes. But as with so many other wars and so many other dead, the propaganda masked an unpalatable reality. There is another word for that reality, often still unmentionable. It starts with "D" and rhymes with deceit. Those who spent a decade promoting war with *Pravda*-like consistency portrayed it as the ultimate in "realism," as a welcome departure from peacekeeping and "Pearsonian romanticism." That was how the *Globe and Mail* described Canada's peacekeeping history in a 2010 front-page editorial that argued that Canada had to keep "using our military muscle" after Afghanistan. The paper did concede that the Afghan War "has not gone as we had hoped."[32]

Deceit is, of course, common currency when it comes to offering up the official story of war. Truth, it is rightly said, is "the first casualty" in much war reporting.[33] It is a given that the state's propensity for lies and deception becomes exaggerated during war. During Canada's Afghan War, both cover-up and double standard were evident in the contrast between how the state publicized the return of dead soldiers—

ramp ceremonies, pipers piping, cabinet ministers arriving to console grieving families—and the silence with respect to those who suffered non-lethal injuries. There were no elaborate official ceremonies or heroic highways for soldiers who returned with the physical and spiritual scars that war inevitably inflicts. Indeed, the Canadian military made a deliberate effort to downplay non-lethal casualties, treating their number and extent as a state secret, with the Department of National Defence only releasing data on the wounded once a year and withholding information about the gravity of their injuries. It used the same rationale as in its attempted cover-up of the torture of prisoners turned over to Afghan government forces—national security. Ottawa claimed that its secrecy was necessary to make sure that enemy forces remained unaware of the effect of their operations on Canadians in Kandahar—except that the United States and Britain were releasing such data on a regular, sometimes weekly, basis.[34] Apparently, little glory arises from spending months in rehabilitation programs or being quietly dismissed from the Canadian Forces.

Pat Stogran would become familiar with these dynamics. He learned of how the families of soldiers worried not just about whether their loved ones would return, but also about just who they would be when they did return. He was familiar with what had been named—with brutal accuracy in the First World War—shell shock, now dressed up clinically as post-traumatic stress disorder (PTSD). By the twenty-first century the emotional wreckage wrought by war was well recognized. Col. Stogran, who had served as a UN peacekeeper in Bosnia, was diagnosed with PTSD after working in that civil war zone. "Life was a battle drill for me," he said.[35] He went on to lead one of the first battalions that Canada sent to Afghanistan in 2002. Appointed by the Harper government as ombudsman in 2007 after its creation of a Veterans Bill of Rights and a Veterans Ombudsman Office, Stogran was fired in 2010, his contract not renewed. He had been too good at his job, describing Ottawa's penny-pinching attitude to wounded soldiers as "an insurance company culture of denial." Just before leaving, Stogran testified to a Commons committee: "Our government knowingly brought in flawed legislation. . . . The people who are suffering are the people with missing legs, missing arms and lives that have been completely disrupted." He added, speaking of the new veterans charter, that it was "clearly an attempt to unload the financial liability, the long-term financial burden that the government carries with injured, wounded veterans," and that veterans had "an overwhelming perception" of "being cheated." As complaints about payments to wounded vets mounted, Conservative MP Greg Kerr, the parliamentary secretary to Veterans Affairs Minister Jean-Pierre Blackburn, explained that the government wanted to make the payouts "more flexible."[36]

A Warrior Nation might be expected to treat its wounded warriors well. But adulation and adjectives are cheap; meaningful programs of rehabilitation and assistance more expensive. This outcome has always been one of war's tragic costs, to the extent that in the interwar years between 1918 and 1939 the cost to Ottawa of programming and pensions for veterans was second only to the cost of servicing Canada's national debt.[37]

Kingston police officer Mathew Belear was one of many who learned about the government's need for flexibility. He had been a regular forces soldier when he was sprayed with shrapnel during Operation Medusa. The wounds ended his war and his military career. He underwent three surgical procedures and had to reconcile himself to permanent nerve damage in his shoulder. It took months of appeals and paperwork before he was awarded $23,000 as a one-time payment for some of his wounds.

Soldiers set great store by honours and decorations, and Belear looked forward to the Sacrifice Medal he would be receiving for being wounded in action in an operation as highly touted as Operation Medusa. (One new warrior academic wrote an entire book on the encounter.) But he was disappointed when the higher-ups forgot to give him his wounded-in-action medal. They also neglected to invite him to the ceremony where his unit received a citation for its participation in the much-publicized battle. Although the army eventually did send him his citation, he was not impressed. As he remarked, "I feel like I got lost in the shuffle, pretty much."[38]

What did not get lost in Ottawa's fervent support-our-troops propaganda push was the relentless effort at changing Canada's national channel by promoting institutions that reflected hierarchy and authoritarianism, values that the Conservative leadership held dear. "The Liberals had medicare and the CPP and we needed to have our brand on something," a former senior Conservative official told Canadian

Press defence correspondent Murray Brewster. "We chose the military and the RCMP and poured what we had into backing them."[39]

Prior to the bracing tonic of combat in Afghanistan, Canada's military was, at least according to Rick Hillier, "risk averse."[40] This may have come as a surprise to the families of peacekeepers like Major Paeta Hess-von Kruedener, casualties in the peacekeeping operations that started in the 1950s. (The major was targeted and killed by the Israeli military in 2006.) But it was the party line. By 2011 the Vice-Chief of the Defence Staff was telling a military lobby group that in the wake of Afghanistan, "we have a force with a much higher tolerance for risk."[41] Canada's top brass and the new warriors, fighting the good fight in the public square, believed that it had been a good war for both the military as an institution and the country as a whole. A government with a pronounced authoritarian streak, concentrating ever more power in the hands of one person—a "Caesarist" regime, in short—lavished money and praise on an institution that shared its values. It did not matter that Canada's longest war, with its fuzzy and fluctuating aims, had been an expensive disaster for all concerned—save the militarists and weapons producers.

"How will historians of tomorrow characterize this war?" Daniel Gosselin asked those assembled at a meeting organized by the Conference of Defence Associations as the war in Kandahar ramped up.[42]

An important question. The answer? "In different ways." For history is more than a fact after fact chronicle of everything that happened in the past. It is an account shaped in the present. Some forms of history make up a country's hegemonic ideology, a set of dominant ideas and practices that, in encompassing many traditions and ideals from different and often opposing groups, attempts to harmonize them in ways suitable to the perpetuation of the ruling order. For militarists, Canada's Afghan War will be framed by memories of noble sacrifice, yet another contribution to that military aspect of the nation's history idealized and promoted as a selfless attempt to rescue unfortunate foreigners from barbarism. For others, it will be remembered as yet another grim chapter in the history of war, an enterprise that remains cruel to its core.

The key to Canada-at-war is to understand the country as part of a shifting imperial hierarchy, a kind of condominium arrangement in which the Canadian government's sovereignty is shared with that of another far more powerful state. Before it became a real-estate term, "condominium" had this political meaning: a territory administered by two or more states. Sometimes the denizens of the condo emerge to fight wars, but these occasions bear the mark of their subordinate status and position: Canadians are almost always part of some larger enterprise, whose supreme leadership resides with people from other countries. As if in compensation for their status in the condo they call their country, Canadians have evinced an immense fascination in things military. Many people—and they are usually, though not always, men— have written about war, although few of the most recent generation have experienced what the intrepid Soviet war correspondent and novelist Vasily Grossman described as "the usual smell of the front line—a cross between a morgue and a blacksmith's."[43]

Many Canadians—including the vast majority of the new warriors—have no such visceral memories. So, how should we who have not been to war "remember" it? And how might we imagine peace? On a languid summer evening in 2011 some seventy people gathered in a downtown Kingston park, a few metres from the hum of the traffic on Ordnance, a street named for munitions, artillery, and other means of mass killing. It was uncertain whether anyone noticed the irony, for it was a ceremony to commemorate people vaporized, burned, and poisoned sixty-six years before. Local peace activists had been organizing annual Hiroshima Day events for some thirty years. While participants, mostly women, fashioned paper peace lanterns to float in a nearby wading pool, they listened to poems, songs, prayers, and short speeches.

The organizers had moved the 2011 Hiroshima remembrance day to a park shaded with century-old silver maples that provided a canopy against the sun, still strong as dusk approached. The park, known to locals as Skeleton Park, was Kingston's nineteenth-century common burial ground, an appropriate venue given the occasion. While the participants folded paper into symbolic paper cranes, organizer Judi Wyatt told the story of Sadako Sasaki and the paper cranes. Sadako was a Hiroshima girl who died at twelve from what her mother called "atom bomb disease." Although Sadako had heard that you would be granted a wish if you folded one thousand paper cranes, she didn't make it, so her friends completed the job and the cranes were buried with her. The plaque on Sadako's statue at the Hiroshima Peace Memorial states, "This is our cry. This is our prayer. Peace on earth." Wyatt explained that the story had become a staple for teachers of peace studies.

Following the reading of a poem by Al Purdy, Pauline Lally, a Catholic Sister of Providence, recited the Prayer of St. Francis.[44] Then she told the story of the time she offended local Kingston warriors by backing a city council motion to request that the Royal Canadian Horse Artillery refrain, during their Freedom of the City days, from encouraging children to play on their equipment. The motion also called on the Artillery to not stage activities that make conflict and the machinery of war look like fun. Sister Lally told the people folding paper cranes that she could not forget the frenzied backlash from veterans and their supporters who maintained that the military was being "censored," that the memory of "the fallen" had been besmirched, and that she was being "utterly arrogant."

"All we were saying," she recalled, channelling John Lennon, "was 'Please don't portray war as a game.'"

As dusk fell the women lit candles and floated them on the water of the children's wading pool. The chain-link fence around the pool was adorned with signs. "We remember," in Japanese and English. "Bikes not bombs" and "Give peace a chance." And the longest one, a variation of a ban-the-bomb movement standby: "War is inevitable, says the pessimist; war is impossible, says the optimist; war is inevitable unless we make it impossible, says the realist."

One woman stood back, watching as the floating candles began to fade. She was wearing a yellow ribbon around her neck. It too was a variation on a theme. It did not say "Support Our Troops." Nor was the ribbon complete. Instead, it was in the shape of the familiar "?" It read: "Question War."

THE ILLUSTRATED LONDON NEWS

REGISTERED AT THE GENERAL POST-OFFICE FOR TRANSMISSION ABROAD.

No. 2494.—VOL. XC.   SATURDAY, FEBRUARY 5, 1887.   TWO WHOLE SHEETS   SIXPENCE. By Post, 6½d.

1. The twelve sections of the boat.   2. Carrying one section, weight 75 lb.
STEEL WHALE-BOAT, CONSTRUCTED BY MESSRS. FORREST AND SON, FOR THE ASCENT OF THE CONGO.

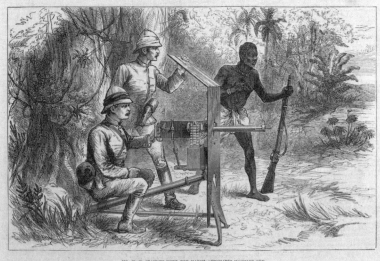

MR. H. M. STANLEY WITH THE MAXIM AUTOMATIC MACHINE-GUN.

THE EMIN PASHA RELIEF EXPEDITION.

Stanley and Stairs in Africa with the Maxim automatic machine gun. Royal Military College graduate William Stairs was treated as a Canadian hero for his African adventures.

CHAPTER 2

PAX BRITANNICA AND THE WHITE MAN'S BURDEN

THE AFRICAN EXPLOITS OF WILLIAM STAIRS

Take up the White Man's burden—
Send forth the best ye breed—
Go bind your sons to exile
To serve your captives' need;
To wait in heavy harness,
On fluttered folk and wild—
Your new-caught, sullen peoples,
Half-devil and half-child.

– Rudyard Kipling, 1899

I N SEPTEMBER 1878 a fair-haired, fresh-faced fifteen-year-old gentleman from Halifax arrived at the squat limestone railway station in Kingston, Ontario. Like so many young people who descend upon the grey city in September, Bill Stairs was in search of advanced education—not at the well-known Queen's University but at the new Royal Military College of Canada (RMC).

Young William Grant Stairs wanted to become a soldier. Soon he would be Cadet No. 52 at the school established just two years earlier across the Cataraqui River from downtown Kingston. Not long after he graduated four years later he would help to lead a famous expedition across Africa from the mouth of the Congo River to Zanzibar. Soon after that he took a second contingent into unexplored terrain in Katanga. He died young—before he reached his twenty-ninth birthday—yet his short life, commemorated in books, articles, and plaques, made him something of a Victorian hero.

Bill Stairs was born in Halifax on July 1, 1863, the sixth child and second son in the prominent family of John Stairs and Mary Morrow. The firm of William Stairs, Son and Morrow, founded by William Machin Stairs (1789–1865), was a fixture on the Halifax waterfront from 1810 to 1975, specializing in hardware, ship's chandlery, rope works, and the operation of a mercantile agency. A disagreement in 1853 between the patriarch's two sons William J. (1819–1906) and John (1823–88) meant that by the 1860s two Stairs enterprises were in competition with each other: John Stairs and Company, headed by Bill's father, and Stairs, Son and Morrow, headed by his uncle.

In many ways the Stairs were a typical Halifax bourgeois family— Protestant, proud, civic-minded (William Machin was one of the city's early mayors), economizing, hard-working, and profoundly convinced of the eternal truths of classical liberalism: equality, liberty, and above all property. They lived and breathed business. Only hard work and discipline would accomplish "the best work of man," wrote W.J., who would forever remember his mother's advice: "William, be industrious." W.J.'s son John F. Stairs was just that: he became a business titan associated with the Nova Scotia Steel and Coal Company, Eastern Trust Company, and Royal Securities Corporation.[1]

John's son Bill grew up with all the inherited privileges and propertied assumptions of a Stairs boy, yet his life was not entirely tranquil. His mother, who had given birth to eleven children, died when he was eight. The following year his father married the family governess, and in 1875, at the age of twelve, Bill was sent off to Merchiston Castle School in Edinburgh, an elite boarding school. It was a fitting move for a mercantile family whose horizons had never been bounded by North America. Parts of the Stairs clan had hailed from Ireland and the island of Grenada; one member in the extended family died en route to repressing the 1857 Indian Mutiny. The Stairs of Halifax had long been shaped by the sea, ships, and empire.

At RMC Bill Stairs was by all accounts a fine student. He had a good head for practical subjects and little taste for abstract arguments. The all-male college recruited young men from elite backgrounds, a good many of them from Maritime families.[2] In the same year that Stairs joined the school it added to its lustre by inserting the word "Royal" in its name—which evidently raised a few eyebrows in England because it had failed to secure the Crown's permission. The small school—its entering class had but eighteen students—was widely considered to be something of an affectation for an essentially rural country with no standing army. Perhaps, many believed, Canada would never even need a permanent army. The conventional wisdom, shared by the most powerful politicians, was that the British would provide any regular forces required by the country, with Canada's contribution limited to a part-time militia—the kind of force that some still mistakenly believed had saved the country in the War of 1812.[3]

Through the 1880s and early 1890s Liberal critics would lambaste RMC as a den of pampered aristocrats. In 1894 William Mulock stunned the House of Commons with information about the eleven RMC graduates who had been appointed to military positions in Canada since the establishment of the college, at a cost to taxpayers of $116,000 each. Here, he broadly implied, was a "rich man's school," with the working-class taxpayer on the hook for it.[4] RMC's founding father, Prime Minister Alexander Mackenzie—also a Liberal—saw the college in a different light. It was a matter of Canadian pride that the young country should be able to train officers for a time when it would need a professional army. Until that day arrived, though, RMC would, despite its name, devote itself not just to teaching military subjects but also to turning out civil engineers. Some graduates might be taken on by the British Army, but most could find jobs building bridges, perhaps, or designing railways, working in the mining industry, or running government departments.[5]

Still, many of the red-coated cadets, snootily dubbed "gentlemen cadets," did earnestly yearn to be soldiers, and in the 1870s and 1880s it was becoming ever-more-fashionable to do so. In days past the British army had been generally disparaged as a refuge for social misfits and the wayward sons of aristocrats. The Crimean War (1853–56), commemorated by the "Charge of the Light Brigade" and personified by Florence Nightingale, prompted a transition to a different perception—of a people's army fighting noble crusades against ungallant enemies. The Crimean War was the first British conflict to be photographed, adding to its romantic allure.

Crimea was followed by the Indian Mutiny of 1857 (also known as the Great Rebellion). The event shocked the British public by demonstrating the Empire's unsuspected fault lines but also elevated to hero status such figures as Henry Havelock, sacrificed to the cause of keeping India British. In 1885 Major-General Charles Gordon would be "martyred" at Khartoum, yet another "Christian warrior" making "the ultimate sacrifice for God and empire" and providing a sterling role model for "an imperial race."[6] Impressionable boys were surrounded everywhere with a popular culture of war and empire. The religious could see in Britain's wars the wonderful effect of a Christianizing Empire, casting, in the words of the *Illustrated London News*, "the glorious gleam of Christianity upon an almost pagan world." A politician like Viscount Palmerston could happily proclaim that the "half-civilized" governments of the world needed a "dressing down" every eight or ten years to "keep them in order." The best "peace-keepers" in the world, he suggested, were not "diplomats and protocols" but well-armed British ships.[7]

Popular illustrations routinely illustrated the unkempt, dirty, and outlandish appearance of the many peoples around the world who were crying out for British order. In the 1860s and 1870s, as Bill Stairs was growing up in Halifax, a mass market for boys' publications about war opened up. The *Boys of England* magazine was selling 250,000 copies a week worldwide and regularly featured excitingly violent stories about war. G.A. Henty, a particularly popular author, was horrified by any lad "who displayed any weak emotion and shrank from shedding blood, or winced at any encounter." He penned some eighty books on martial themes—including *With Wolfe in Canada: The Winning of a Continent* (1887)—and depicted war as an adventure especially suited to orphan boys making their way in the world. H. Rider Haggard, coming on the scene in the 1880s, was also a great sensation. *King Solomon's Mines* (1885) and its successor *Allan Quatermain* (1887) made him one of the bestselling novelists of all time, and he had a devoted reader in William Stairs. In the literature of the time war was a sporting activity, with battles written up in the language of games. Subterfuge and deception were the marks of slippery, often "Oriental," and certainly un-British enemies, who did not play fair.[8]

The same fascination with war and the romance of being soldiers permeated RMC. The cadets went to almost any length to look like soldiers, as R.A. Preston reports in his history of the college. Off duty, the cadets would lie in the sun and place thin strips of cloth across their cheeks to avoid tanning that bit of skin, thus acquiring "the mark of an old soldier" caused by "the half-inch chin strap of his forage cap." The institution's atmosphere was reminiscent of many a British public school. RMC regulations were tough on paper, but discipline was never so severe that it stifled the boys' own martial rituals. At the end of their first full academic year, the RMC cadets "marched off the end of the St. Lawrence pier into deep water in full uniform." Boys who could not take the hazing rituals were automatically classified as "weaklings."[9]

Stairs graduated on June 5, 1882. Like most of his classmates he was passed over by the British War Office, which selected just four officers from the college. Yet RMC was already developing a sound reputation within the Empire. Stairs found a job as a surveyor in far-off New Zealand with that country's Trigonometrical Survey. He spent three years there and was just about to sit an examination for his surveyor's papers when, to his great relief, he was offered a commission in the Royal Engineers and ended up in Chatham, England.

Stairs could thank a looming sense of imperial crisis for his sudden change of fortune. The British were worried about losing India to Russia, which had an enormous army and was expanding into Central Asia in the 1880s. And then there was Africa. Having occupied Egypt in 1882 and brought the Persian Gulf into their sphere of influence, the British faced stiff European competition. The Empire seemed to be militarily vulnerable. RMC graduates, a dime a dozen in 1880, were now a hot property. The War Office engaged in a "wholesale commissioning" of officers from 1885 to 1888, reaching so far down the list that it was even signing on those in their second year of military education.[10] Many more RMC cadets could realize their long-cherished dreams of imperial valour.

Even so, for Stairs, at age twenty-two, the position of lieutenant in the Royal Engineers fulfilled none of the romantic expectations of a soldiering life. He found military life in England deadening and later looked back disdainfully at that time of "eating my full, sleeping as much as I wanted, not needing to take any special precautions for my safety, not having to think or work very much." Here was a "placid" and "boring" life, one that would kill the manly spirit and dull the mind. "Such an existence is a dreadful waste, no man of action would even consider it." There spoke a young Canadian yearning for adventure—longing to experience (as one of his later compatriots put it) "the feeling of pleasurable excitement inseparable from a plunge into the unknown."[11] When would he become a real soldier?

The answer arrived soon enough, and from an unexpected source. The result was a story that can be told in three different ways.

William Stairs and his admirers would have presented the story as a heroic epic, and it is our good fortune that Stairs left an excellent diary that sets out, in his own words, how the world looked to him.

In this first narrative, Stairs is a military hero. Many of his contemporaries so judged him. In a culture that had fallen in love with reflections of the youthful warrior, Stairs really did look the part. He was good-looking, a "tall, fair, handsome, and unassuming young engineer officer" who "blushed easily when praised and told his story in an entirely unaffected way." A colleague would add "delicate-looking" to the description; the debonair Stairs was "not at all like the 'typical African traveler.'"[12]

Moreover, he was a local boy who became internationally renowned in the two countries that mattered most to Canada—Britain and the United States. It is as "52 Captain W.G. Stairs" that his name appears— the very first of all those of the cadets listed—on RMC's Memorial Arch, erected in 1923 as Kingston's version of the Arc de Triomphe. The official history of RMC praises Stairs as an adept geographer, skilled commander of small groups in difficult situations, and an adroit soldier who won "bloodless battles." In contemporary official memory, he was one of the RMC graduates who brought "honour to their *alma mater* by their courage and ability."[13]

In December 1886 Stairs caught wind of an expedition being led by H.M. Stanley to rescue one Emin Pasha. For those who loved the

British Empire, an alarming recent event had been the Siege of Khartoum and the failure of the mission to relieve Major-General Gordon in 1884–85 from Islamic "Mahdist" rebels resisting the new British sovereignty in Egypt.[14] Earlier, in 1878, one of the more unlikely figures in the colonial history of Africa, Mehmet Emin Pasha, had succeeded Gordon as governor of Equatoria (located in the extreme south of the Sudan, where the Nile flows out of Lake Albert). Born Eduard Carl Oscar Theodor Schnitzer in Prussia, Emin Pasha had been a medical officer in Turkey before travelling to Cairo and from there to Khartoum, where he took up a medical practice and made a serious study of the region's plants, animals, and birds. He quickly became Gordon's chief medical officer before taking his place as governor. When the province was cut off from the rest of the world by the Arab revolt, the British press put forth an image of this Prussian Jew as a kindly scientist and linguist, now cruelly isolated from the British Empire and threatened by the same fate that had overtaken the late lamented General Gordon. The cry went up that Emin Pasha must be rescued. Suddenly people hard-pressed to locate Equatoria on a map cared passionately for its governor—or at least the image they had formed of him—as a man menaced by Mahdist fanatics.

Anxious English attention turned to the redoubtable Stanley to head up a mission to relieve Emin Pasha. Stanley, born in Wales, had become an adventurer and journalist in the United States and was already well known as a famously intrepid explorer who had rescued Scottish missionary and explorer David Livingstone in Africa.

Here was Stairs's ticket out of tedium. He wrote a crisp letter of application, impressing Stanley with its no-nonsense air. Stairs wowed Stanley in an interview in London on January 6, 1887, and a couple of weeks later the Canadian was off on the sort of adventure he had read about as a boy: into Africa to rescue a loyal son of the empire from the clutches of an unfathomable and cruel enemy. He was joining up with a great hero, Stanley, long a darling of the press. He was taking part in a campaign against aggression—in a purely defensive enterprise for the relief of a beleaguered imperial outpost. It was a tale familiar to readers of the *Boy's Own Annual*, of explorers venturing into "Darkest Africa."

The Emin Pasha Relief Expedition had something for everyone—Christians who wanted to defy Islamic militants, scientifically minded people who favoured the growth of human knowledge, and loyal Britons who wanted to stand by a true son of the Empire. In this adventure the Empire was *performed*, in a way that many Victorians found utterly riveting. The leaders of the expedition were well aware that the eyes of the world were upon them. Several of them, including Stairs, kept detailed diaries, with the obvious intent of publishing the material. One satirical cartoon even depicted the expedition's leaders negotiating with a group of Africans for passage through their territory: the chief's leading demand is that his people receive a percentage of the royalties generated by any forthcoming publications.

One of the expedition's more unusual decisions was to reach Equatoria and Emin Pasha by way of the Atlantic side, travelling along the Congo River, rather than simply going overland from Zanzibar on the Indian Ocean. Stairs had met up with Stanley in Suez in February 1887, and from there they travelled south past Zanzibar and around the Cape of Good Hope, then north along the coast to the river, before trekking a great distance following little-known routes across treacherously difficult terrain. Supplies ran short. Even though the expedition carried abundant firearms and an imposing Maxim gun—the forerunner of the modern machine gun—it ran into staunch opposition from the indigenous inhabitants. Throughout the ordeal, Stairs was a model of patience, calm, and courage.[15] In one battle on August 13, 1887, he was struck by an arrow, probably carrying poison. It remained embedded in his flesh for fourteen months and twenty-three days. When the arrow was finally extricated, much of it, he recorded, "had become eaten away from long presence in the tissue."[16]

Stairs stoically persevered. By July 1887 he had become second in command of Stanley's mission. As he noted in his diary, "What better place to exercise a man of action's talents than under the vast open skies of Africa?"[17] Virtue and courage were what Stairs most esteemed in others, and through exceptionally trying times—marked by near-starvation, terrible fevers, and unsettling attacks—he exemplified those traits. He offered a remarkable example of physical endurance in marching 700 miles across Africa, through lands that are now part of the Democratic Republic of the Congo, Uganda, and Tanzania.

As the expedition proceeded up the Congo, it became necessary to split into two parties. One group was left behind, and the other, led by Stanley and Stairs, went on, moving far into the interior. There, helped by two other Europeans (and plainly benefiting from his RMC education), Stairs designed and constructed Fort Bodo—a name susceptible to various translations, one of which was "Fort Peace," which was probably the meaning that Stairs had in mind. His was the steadying, well-organized influence that allowed for the establishment of a fort hundreds of miles removed from European contacts: "Every single article of food that we ate was to be planted, reaped, and gathered within 500 yards of our houses—fuel, water, clay and leaves for houses, poles, ropes, everything necessary for our daily life was found in the same circle."[18] He carefully led and monitored a little garrison made up of two or three Europeans and over a hundred others—including between fifteen and thirty "Natives from various parts of the forest." He regulated the affairs of this little society for over a year. The young Canadian was plainly a determined, practical, and effective leader.

Stairs saw himself as a peacekeeper and a peacemaker. Within the expedition he settled personality conflicts and maintained order in the ranks. His diaries develop the image of Bill as patient "Canadian," the antithesis of the flamboyant, erratic, American Stanley. (Stanley, for all the showmanship that made him the darling of the media, inspired contempt among many of his followers when they dealt with him at close quarters: Stairs came to loathe the man.)

In his own mind Stairs was also a peacemaker in a larger sense. He was bringing civilization where before there had prevailed savagery, chaos, and fanaticism. As he explained to readers of *Nineteenth Century* magazine, everything he did in Africa was related to repelling a menacing enemy. The Soudan (as Sudan was then spelled in English circles) and the Congo were imperilled by a "more modern and fanatical" Islam, whose "aim shall be to preserve the country to its own uses and keep back the white man." The Mahdists sought to preserve vast territories for Islam, with its slave traders and piratical raiders, against Christian white civilization.[19] They represented all that was backward and dark, and Stairs all that was progressive and enlightened. The much-disputed sources of the Western Nile, the exact location of the "Mountains of the Moon" mentioned centuries before by Ptolemy, the intricacies of African languages: they were all phenomena to be seen, evaluated, and assimilated by this fearless explorer, who submitted his findings to learned societies and filled his diaries with detailed descriptions.

On his return to England Stairs was widely honoured as a hero. He became a fellow of the prestigious Royal Geographical Society, the Royal Scottish Geographical Society, and the Société Royale Belge de Géographie; he received £400 from the Emin Pasha Relief Committee and attended a dizzying succession of suppers and fetes—a reception at the Canada Club, a dinner with the Prince of Wales (where he received a handsome medallion), even a ball at Buckingham Palace (he pronounced himself to be most impressed by the layout of the men's washroom). Stanley, who knew that Stairs was one of his sternest critics, nonetheless singled the Canadian out for special praise in his bestselling book *In Darkest Africa*. Stairs, Stanley said, had a devotion to duty "as perfect as human nature is capable of." He was "careful, watchful, diligent and faithful," and exemplified the qualities of "ready and prompt obedience."[20]

Stairs, whose diaries documented Stanley as a man wildly oscillating in moods and capricious in his decisions, painted a far different public picture of a stalwart, inspiring leader. Even in the privacy of his diary he eulogized the expedition as though it had been a jolly good romp across the African wilderness. On taking leave of the porters recruited in Zanzibar, he wrote:

> Good-bye, boys; you have stuck to us like the men you are. Over six thousand English miles some of us have footed it backwards and forwards through the forests and across the plains of Africa together. And though now we go to the white man's home far over the sea, still, deep down in the heart of each of us will ever live the remembrance of the pluck and fortitude shown by you through so many dark and trying days.[21]

Stairs was recalling a team that had faced great obstacles together and accomplished great things. It was almost as if he were delivering a valedictory address to his classmates at RMC.

Stairs shielded the public from a more truthful understanding of Stanley because he understood how hungry the Anglosphere was for a hero. He also realized that his own reputation had come to be intertwined with that of the more famous American. The expedition paid off handsomely in book sales and lecture tours for Stanley and other participants. Stairs had material reasons to be reluctant to diverge publicly from the emergent myth of the conquering hero providentially bringing civilization and science to Africa. His descendants hesitated to publish his diaries precisely because they cast such an unfavourable light on Stanley, whose *In Darkest Africa* became durably established as *the* book on African exploration, taking its place beside the novels of Haggard and the poems of Kipling in the literature of adventure, discovery, and empire. In his *Diary* Stairs mocked those who would publish books hailing "splendid fellows, martyrs, heroes, tigers, etc.!!"—yet he made ample use of similar language in his public representations of Africa.[22]

Millions of people undoubtedly identified with Stanley's vision of an Africa freed from oppression and ushered into the civilized age. Stairs himself believed that he had helped bring white civility and British decorum to Africa. On May 30, 1889, in an uncharacteristically introspective mood, he wondered for a fleeting moment if "we" have the right to dispose of the continent, but quickly delivered an emphatic answer: "Yes! What value would it have in the hands of the blacks who, in their natural state, are crueller to each other than the worst Arabs or whites? And could one suppose for a single moment that the Arabs would leave the continent to remain unexploited?" In his mind, if the British did not intervene, the continent would be overrun by Arabs. He depicted a continent menaced by Islamic fanaticism, fanned into flames by "miserable, yellow-bellied Egyptians."[23]

Stairs saw the expedition as an exercise in defending human civilization against a legion of menacing Others—incomprehensible "brutes" and "savages," slave-trading Arabs, indolent and pampered Egyptians, evasive residents of the "Orient," and fanatical Muslims. When he looked upon Africa, he did so with an "improving eye,"[24] imagining what wonders Europeans could realize were they only in possession of the land. Railways and farms, good government, and peace would all attend the coming of the white man.

The founder of the "Peaceful Fort" and member of a mission that had made use of the good vessel *Peace*, Stairs exemplified the hope of a more pacific and equitable world, one distant from the depredations of slave traders and pirates. As Stanley put it:

> The natives of Africa cannot be taught that there are blessings in civilization if they are permitted to be oppressed and to be treated as unworthy of the treatment due to human beings, to be despoiled and

enslaved at will by a licentious soldiery. . . . When every grain of corn, and every fowl, goat, sheep and cow which is necessary for the troops is paid for in sterling money or its equivalent in necessary goods, then civilization will become irresistible in its influence, and the Gospel even may be introduced.[25]

Stanley himself claimed that he had been directly aided by God as he proceeded through the forests of Africa—so he told his chief financial backer William Mackinnon: "I feel utterly unable to attribute our salvation to any other cause than to a gracious Providence who for some purpose of His own preserved us."[26]

Back in Kingston, the religious significance of the Emin Pasha Relief Expedition was not lost upon the congregation of St. George's Cathedral, which honoured Bill Stairs with a plaque. No less a personage than Queen Victoria herself sent Stanley a congratulatory telegram, remarking on his "marvelous Expedition."[27]

In 1890 Stairs returned home to Halifax. The conquering hero was given the honour of addressing a special city council meeting graced by the lieutenant-governor and scores of the most reputable Haligonians. The band struck up, appropriately enough, "Hail the Conquering Hero Comes." A commemorative plaque was bestowed, and then Lieutenant Stairs summed up in a few words the achievements of the expedition. He underlined the immense practical benefits of the mission for all humanity, including "the expansion of English and other trade in supplying new markets for the goods of the world, the improved condition of the native that will ensue, the suppression of the slave trade through the influence of the railway and telegraph lines."[28]

Almost before his image could take off in the public imagination, and before he could bring his own record of the Stanley expedition into print, Stairs—"wedded to action and burning to excel," as one of his close colleagues put it[29]—returned to Africa for a second expedition, this time in the employ of the Belgian king Leopold II's Compagnie du Katanga, an amalgamation of European and British capitalists. In 1891 the company commissioned Stairs to venture to Bunkeya, located in the region south of the Congo, and there subjugate a native ruler named Msiri. In December Stairs arrived in Zanzibar, and this time he proceeded across Africa from east to west. Commanding an expedition of 336 men, facing down illness and wrestling with internal dissensions within his troop, he reached Katanga. There his second-in-command, Omer Bodson, shot Msiri, and Stairs exerted himself to extract a pledge of peace and submission from native leaders in the vicinity. But Stairs fell ill, and soon his expedition was experiencing severe food shortages and desertions.

On February 3, 1892, Stairs wrote to a Belgian officer in the vicinity reporting on his predicament. As he noted, he had achieved many objectives—the overthrowing of Msiri, the election of his successor, and a country now "tranquil and at peace" in which "the European is not only feared, but respected." It was even possible to "explore the country and open up its resources." Yet, now stranded for want of provisions, with many men having died of hunger and sickness, he believed he could leave in good conscience, having planted a European flag in Katanga. The trek back towards the coast of the Indian Ocean was arduous—in one forced march they travelled 120 miles in little over four days—yet Stairs apparently recovered much of his vigour and cheerfulness. At last the expedition crossed into British territory. As they neared the coast, Stairs, though not entirely well, still appeared to be "in excellent spirits, and constantly spoke of Zanzibar as the starting-point of future adventures." But, after chastising some natives for their intemperance, he fell gravely ill. Suffering from "haematuria in its gravest form"—that is, large quantities of blood in his urine, a symptom sometimes associated with acute fatigue—he was carried by steamer to Chinde, on the coastline of the Indian Ocean. "The ocean's surf could be heard rolling on the bar," his associate Joseph Moloney noted, "and the S.S. *Rovuma* appeared, ready to take us to Zanzibar in the following week." It would leave without Stairs, who died on June 9, 1892. Two missionaries helped to make the coffin, and he was buried with full military honours. A wooden cross was placed upon his grave.[30]

"Be thou faithful unto death and I will give thee a crown of life" (Revelation 2:10) is inscribed upon his tombstone at Chinde at the mouth of the Zambesi River. The Memorial Arch at his old college in Kingston commemorates Stairs along with other cadets who died "Pro Deo Et Patria" (For God and Country)—the same words uttered by the American operative right after he gunned down Osama bin Laden in 2011. Stairs is honoured once again on an imposing plaque that hails the college's first fallen soldiers. He is remembered, by some, to this day, as the staunch and loyal soldier, the true son of RMC, the intrepid explorer whose diaries have now been published and whose exploits are still commemorated.

★

Those who followed Stairs's travels and career have been disposed to apply such terms as "adventure" and "exploits" to his time in Africa. But before Stairs becomes a prime subject for a "Heritage Minute"— as the local boy who explored Africa and brought a vision of peace, order, and good government to the continent—we should consider a second way of telling his story: Stairs as mass-murderer, as directly responsible for scores of deaths and indirectly responsible for delivering a large portion of Africa into the hands of a European regime that slaughtered between six and nine million people.

This alternative approach starts with a seemingly minor detail. Why did Stanley's expedition, starting off from the east coast of Africa, take what would appear to have been a crazy route that involved circumnavigating the Cape of Good Hope, arriving at the mouth of the Congo, and then travelling across lands that were almost certain to be more difficult than those on the more direct route westward from Zanzibar?

Although Stanley offered various unconvincing explanations, from the pragmatic to the scientific, the actual answer lies in his behind-the-scenes relationship with King Leopold II of Belgium, who was orchestrating his sometime employee Stanley and the Emin Pasha project as a whole to fulfil his dream of ruling over a vast, enormously lucrative African colony. Leopold II promoted his African enterprise as the quintessence of nobility—he wanted to further the geographical understanding of Africa's interior, free the slaves, and establish a territory devoted to free trade and prosperity—but within Belgium and gradually well beyond it more and more people came to realize that the enterprise was actually about the enrichment of King Leopold II himself.

In 1885 a group of European politicians had got together to divide up those parts of Africa that their countries had not already seized earlier in the colonial era. That was when they agreed to hand a territory the size of Poland to King Leopold as his own personal colony. They recognized Leopold's supposed holding as the Congo Free State; from 1908 until independence in 1960 it was known as the Belgian Congo. Stairs may or may not have been suspicious about Stanley's Belgian connections (he did write dismissively of the Belgian enterprise), but it was common knowledge on that expedition that it was designed to safeguard Belgian claims to the gold-rich region before rival hustlers from South Africa moved in.[31] On his second expedition, to Katanga, Stairs was consciously furthering the extension and consolidation of Leopold II's fledgling imperial project—accumulation by dispossession.[32]

The Africans would increasingly be enmeshed in relations of exploitation that divested them of their capacity to benefit from their own natural resources. The hard-nosed calculations of Leopold II entered even into the fine details of the first expedition itself. It would have been relatively straightforward for Stanley, with hundreds of armed men and greatly superior armaments, including the famous Maxim gun, to march across Kenya and Uganda to Equatoria. The far more challenging route via the Congo River through the Ituri Forest to Lake Albert allowed Leopold II to develop the possibilities of annexing Equatoria to the Congo—and hence adding considerably to his future profits.

The first expedition—more, then, about business than heroism—also did not accomplish the "relief" of the beleaguered Emin Pasha from supposedly fanatical Muslims. When after thirteen months the travellers finally reached the governor, he turned out to be living in comfort. Indeed, it was Emin Pasha who rescued the incoming party, supplying them with much-needed clothing and food. As one expedition member recorded when they finally reached their goal: "The station is exquisitely clean and the houses are cool and airy—they all looked so smart and clean compared with us who had arrived in rags, we looked as if we were in want of relief more than they." One commentator remarked as early as 1889: "It is impossible not to admire Mr. Stanley's pluck and endurance. But I venture to question the use of marches like his into the interior of Africa. The plea was that Emin Pasha wished to be relieved. He does not want to be. He is only desirous to be left alone." Far from demonstrating scientific rationality over backwardness, the expedition was a badly planned and badly executed fiasco. As Stairs recorded, "Never yet has left England any expedition so wretchedly provided for as this one is."[33]

Rather than "adventure" and "exploits," more accurate terms would be "murder" and "death march." Of the expedition's 706 initial members, only 255 returned to the coast. About 44 per cent had died, and 137 deserted or were left behind. Of the 314 deaths, according to Stanley, "245 (78 percent) were due to fever, debility, starvation, ulcers, dysentery, or exhaustion."[34] An African porter was expected to carry up to 100 kilograms of goods and supplies on his head and walk as many as 30 kilometres a day. These were exacting terms under the relatively good conditions of traversing well-established paths and trade routes; they were murderous when imposed on men forced to walk through dense forests. Of the porters near the end of the expedition, Stairs would tell his readers:

> We had worked the men by this time into splendid condition; their leg and back muscles were like steel in hardness; the result was many long and fast marches. Each member of the Expedition, from its leader down to the smallest girl, was doing the best to get forward, and it was common now to find everyone in camp by noon, having done ten to twelve miles since dawn.[35]

He delicately refrained from pointing out the greater number of men who had been worked to death. How many workers Stairs was personally responsible for killing will always be unclear, since he merely annotated in general terms the numbers who died; and although he recorded with some enthusiasm the lashings and tortures he applied to upstarts, it is not always clear whether they were beaten or tortured to death.

Men were not only worked to death, but starved to death. As one painstaking scholar has established, the conventional narrative about Stanley's trip up the Congo—that they ran out of food just because they mistakenly decided to travel through sparsely populated or depopulated areas—is simplistic: the expedition provoked drastic price inflations in the territories it traversed, and its food supplies were unequally shared.[36] Food allowances were based on race, not expertise. At times whites received six times as much food as natives did, and among Africans food was also unequally apportioned, according to status and connections. Many of the porters in an expedition supposedly dedicated to stamping out slavery were slaves themselves, hired out by their masters for this purpose. These slaves were far more at risk of death by starvation than were their betters.

Stairs and his fellow officers enforced harsh discipline. In a rare moment of introspection, Stairs wrote on April 13, 1887:

> Mr. Stanley, we hear, intends taking a chap called [Herbert] Ward with us across the continent. He is said to be a very good chap at his work, namely nigger-driving. Certainly nothing I have ever seen so completely demoralizes a man as driving negro carriers. One's temper is up all the time, kind feelings are knocked on the head and I should think in time a man would become a perfect brute if he did nothing else but this.[37]

Beatings with rawhide whips, up to 100 strokes; chains applied for weeks at a time to the ankles of porters caught in the act of desertion; forcing men to stand with a heavy stone on their heads in one position for hours; the execution of expedition members, including children, for minor thefts: in all of these Stairs was complicit.[38]

The expedition brought death and destruction to many of the lands through which it passed. Certain passages in Stairs's diary are extraordinary in their quick shift from romanticizing the idyllic simplicity of village landscapes to detailing how the Europeans swiftly transformed the scenes into killing fields. On September 28, 1887, Stairs wrote:

> It was most interesting, lying in the bush and watching the natives quietly at their day's work; some women were pounding the bark of trees preparatory to making the coarse native cloth used all along this part of the river, others were making banana flour by pounding up dried bananas, men we could see building huts and engaged at other such work, boys and girls running about, singing, crying, others playing on a small instrument common all over Africa, a series of wooden strips, bent over a bridge and twanged with the thumb and forefinger. All was as it was every day until our discharge of bullets, when the usual uproar and screaming of women took place.[39]

On December 11,1887, he noted: "Out again at the natives, burnt more houses and cut down more bananas; this time we went further up the valley and devastated the country there. In the afternoon Jephson and I went up to some high hills at the back of the camp and burnt all we could see, driving out a lot of natives like so much game."[40] Inside Fort Bodo, the "Peaceful Fort," were traders, whose murderous slaving activities were integral to its survival:

> I often wonder what English people would say if they knew of the way in which we "go for" these natives. Friendship we don't want as then we should get very little meat and probably have to pay for the bananas. Every male native capable of using the bow is shot, this of course we must do. All the children and women are taken as slaves by our men to do work in the camps. Of course they are well treated and rarely beaten as we whites soon stop that. After 3 or 4 weeks with the men they get to be as happy as clams and gorge themselves with food almost to bursting.[41]

Stairs may not have personally participated in the killing and the abduction of the women and children as slaves, but he clearly approved of brutality as a necessary strategy for Fort Bodo.

The Canadian hero differentiated between the "Zanzibaris" who travelled with him—although they were "mean, low, stinking skunks, almost to a man cowards," he at least regarded them as fellow human beings—and the "mean, cunning, low-class bushman with his poisoned arrows and pointed sticks stuck in the ground."[42] But this was a question of degree. The Zanzibaris were tortured, whipped, and starved because they were thought to have violated some rule. The "bushmen"—men, women, and children alike—were murdered simply because they were in the expedition's way. Stairs's raiders even took to severing the hands of victims as a means of demonstrating their kill counts for the day—a practice that would become the infamous trademark of Leopold II's regime. Any resistance was treated harshly. On August 21, 1888, the same month in which two children were executed for alleged thefts, Stairs penned this description of a "raid" upon his party:

> At a signal we all three fired, reloaded, and gave them three rounds each. Like men possessed with the devil they ran, dropping bows and arrows, baskets half filled with tobacco and making for the bush like

deer. . . . This morning, also in the bush, we found their hiding place before emerging into the open; all sorts of wild roots and potatoes had been cooked by them and two baskets more of roots, etc., were brought in by our own men this morning.

This will be a most salutary lesson to them I hope. The sudden surprise at night when fancying we were all asleep and harmless will have great effect on the savages' brain.

This morning I cut off the heads of the two men and placed them on poles one at each exit from the bush into the plantation. This may prevent further attempts of the sort for some time and so save life.[43]

Significantly, it was precisely the use of severed heads as trophies that would later utterly condemn the African ruler Msiri in Stairs's eyes— as it has also convinced readers of Joseph Conrad that Kurtz is a devilish presence in *Heart of Darkness*.

Yet even this record of violence, deprivation, and mass death does not quite conclude the critical portrait of this Canadian's exploits in Africa. When Stairs, feted in the United States, Britain, and Canada, professed himself weary of official dinners and receptions and returned to Africa in 1891 as an employee of King Leopold's Katanga Company—in the process helping to firmly establish the king's claim to the territory—once there he attempted to purchase slaves directly for his expedition, even though the project had been widely advertised as part of the good Belgian king's campaign against slavery. Although Stairs said that he disliked slave-raiding of the type that Fort Bodo had relied upon, that did not prevent him from having his expedition indulge in its practices. Indeed, he evinced admiration for the wholesome effect that slavery had upon the people subjected to it. Of the two thousand slaves whom Stairs said he encountered after leaving the Indian Ocean coastline, many of them seized by slavers travelling close by his own expedition, he thought 90 per cent were better off—"plump and sleek"—than the poor inhabitants of Liverpool or London. On this expedition he also managed to put to one side his earlier fierce critiques of the Congo Free State: "one huge mistake," "that most 'rotten of rotten' concerns," and a "mismanaged concern" that only fools could extol were his earlier verdicts on this experiment.[44]

These crimes did not go unnoticed. Contemporary commentators noted the extraordinary death rates on such expeditions. As one sceptic remarked, "What benefit, then, is it to the cause of civilization that a white man should hire a vast number of carriers and undertake an expedition, in which half of them die of fatigue, and some are hanged for wishing to desert, in order to force his way through tribes by burning their villages and shooting them?" Even the modern editors of his diaries, who have given them such innocuous titles as *African Exploits* (published 1994) and *Victorian Explorer* (1998), appear to be somewhat nonplussed by the record of a man who, on his two African expeditions, killed scores of men and enslaved even more women and children "whose sole offence," as one of those editors puts it, "was that they resisted the entry of the European expeditions and Arab slavers into their homeland."45

Even judged by British imperial standards, the Stanley expedition was in essence a pointless exercise in media-mongering sensationalism. The Katanga expedition was more historically momentous—but because it shored up a regime that would ultimately rival those of Hitler and Stalin in mass murder. Between 1880 and 1920 the Congo's population was radically reduced by slaughter, starvation, and disease as Belgium ransacked the territory's rubber, ivory, and minerals. It was one of the great colonial holocausts of the modern era.46

A third way of looking at Stairs, as neither hero nor villain, addresses itself to the underlying structures—economic, political, cultural—of his world. Both in Africa and elsewhere, Stairs proclaimed, with a young man's earnest certainty, the convictions of his age. His view of the African landscape was coloured by conventional conceptions of property, order, and peace. He wanted to be a success—to look good in the eyes of his family and friends. Being a success, for a man in a Victorian liberal order, meant self-mastery, hard work, perseverance, enterprise, and frugality—all of which qualities Stairs had in abundance. Indeed, in his life Stairs was his own man, proudly convinced of his own free-standing independence. He was a "doer," not a "dreamer," and he regarded with ill-disguised impatience the ivory-tower intellectuals and out-of-touch bureaucrats who had no hands-on experience of the frontiers of the Empire about which they spoke and wrote so freely. Stairs admired masculine toughness. He criticized Stanley for sometimes allowing himself to be carried by porters, which for Stairs was a damning mark of the explorer's effeminacy.[47]

In the Halifax of Stairs's youth, Afro-Nova Scotians were routinely ridiculed in the press and often confined to segregated institutions. In the history books aboriginal peoples figured as bloodthirsty savages, tamed by the beneficent Anglos who planted Halifax and saved the peninsula for the Empire. Stairs did not arrive in Africa as an "innocent" unaware of racial hierarchies. The word "nigger," which he used so enthusiastically in his diaries, was a commonplace epithet on the streets of Halifax. Stairs arrived in Africa with an already well-developed vocabulary of race and a firm belief in the social evolutionary patterns that supposedly positioned one race over another.

His racism registered in different ways depending on the context. Time and again Stairs simply denied the humanity of the people that his expedition was slaughtering: "All of a sudden Stanley fired a shot into the air, when like lightning, every man, woman and child dived into the water and swam off in every direction down stream like so many wild ducks." The Africans were "so much game," or, in trying to escape from his clutches, they made "for the bush like deer." He noted, "The Zanzibari is a very dirty animal about camp, if not watched."[48] Like the early Anglo settlers of Nova Scotia affixing the heads of dead Mi'kmaq to poles as a warning to any and all aboriginal attackers, Stairs reconciled the violence of his deeds with his mission of peace.[49] He was dealing with a lower order of beings whose "thoughts do not go beyond their daily needs." They would never go far: "They are even incapable of so conducting themselves as to promote their slow evolution toward a higher level of existence. Left to themselves, one would find them in the year 3000 in exactly the same state that they are to-day . . . the level of wild, fearful animals."[50]

On other occasions Stairs thinks of racially defined Others as children, uniformly trapped in the same low level of development. On July 25, 1891, he wrote:

Unlike whites, there is no diversity among blacks. They lead the same kind of life; eat the same food, and concentrate their thoughts on the same few subjects. The result is that, little by little, they now have the same identical brain. We whites, on the other hand, learn to know so many different countries, inhabited by such varied people and we encounter so many different things that our ideas become as diverse as our characters.[51]

So convinced were Europeans that the native inhabitants of Africa had nothing to teach them that the ill-fated rear column that Stairs and Stanley left behind in 1887 suffered hunger-related deaths amidst large fields of cassava that had sustained the indigenous inhabitants for generations.[52]

As a reader of romantic imperial fiction, Stairs was critical of any forms of war that diverged from the Western pattern. "Miserable, contemptible bushmen, lowest form of man, the only weapon you can devise is one which inflicts a protracted, agonizing though certain death," he exclaimed after examining the weapons in a canoe belonging to a fleeing native whom the Europeans had just shot through the back. "You have made yourselves our enemy, so look out!" Yet afterwards Stairs himself experimented with precisely such "primitive" techniques. He tried out various poisons, surrounded his fort with stakes, and used the severed heads of his enemies as warnings to potential raiders.[53]

On other occasions Stairs shows yet another side—a side suggesting that had he lived beyond the certainties of his twenties he might have arrived at more complicated understandings of the peoples of Africa. He took considerable pains to learn enough Kaswahili to converse with some of the people he encountered. For the readers of *Nineteenth Century* he described the Wazamboni living in the vicinity of his camp as "fast friends during the whole time we were among them."[54] He acknowledged that some Africans did uphold religious ideals. He recognized a certain diversity: "Africa is an immense continent, peopled by an enormous number of tribes who differ greatly from one another in their practices, appearances, what they wear, their tribes and language." Some of them lived "like animals" and were slated to disappear; others had developed a sound conception of "justice, of what is yours and what is mine." Under a "strong government of whites," they might eventually become "competent farmers."[55]

Stairs, then, had at least three concepts of race: one in which blacks were animals, fair game for white explorers; a second in which they were one and all perpetually backward children; and a third in which a minority of them might aspire to become true individuals in a Victorian sense—property-holding and law-abiding—always provided that whites could provide them with stern counsel and wise leadership. When it came time to wield the whip or fire his gun, all three frameworks provided ample rationale for the mission to which he gave his life in Africa.

His preoccupation with class was equally that of the times—that is, of maintaining the divisions between the rulers of the expedition and the ruled, with the first exploiting the labour of the second. Like his grandfather and uncle, Stairs fairly worshipped work. He occasionally reproached himself for the zeal with which he attempted to discipline the men under his command: "Every now and then I am horrified at myself and almost driven crazy as I in a frenzy cut a man's head open with a stick. Control myself I cannot as my work would remain undone."[56] Stairs relied completely on his ability to extract the maximum amount of labour out of men, even if some of them ended up dropping dead from starvation and exhaustion. The workers often exasperated him: "Oh you infernal collection of belly-worshipping brutes!"[57] Echoing General Gordon at Khartoum, Stairs complained that when his workers were not eating they were sleeping; when not sleeping they were praying; and when not praying they were sick. In the face of such cunningly concealed class resistance he was, in his own words, forced to become "a perfect demon at using the stick." Stairs the peacekeeper sometimes felt hurt that Africans did not acknowledge that he was trying his best to be a reasonable and calm presence among them, slowly mentoring them into becoming good human beings like himself— although in private he sometimes fantasized about torturing the troublemakers in his expedition.[58]

A tempting way of erasing this painful page in Canadian history is to deny that it even is a page in Canadian history. We can say to ourselves, "Ah, such were the ways of the English overseas, at a time and in a place very distant from our own." And certainly much about Stairs was "English." When he gazed upon Africa and imagined it transformed into an "ideal existence" for himself, what came to his mind was a large estate in the English countryside, a pleasant place "far from the hurly burly of town, with great lawns soft as velvet on which to play lawn tennis under the shade of great trees." He was truly devoted to his Sovereign, Queen Victoria: "Today is the Queen's birthday. God grant her many more! I am sure that foreigners must admire her, an honest, upright woman who always acts prudently and rationally."[59] He signed an important missive to Msiri, king of Katanga, as "Stairs, the Englishman"—which may have led that leader to misconstrue what this agent of King Leopold was up to.

Stairs was also deeply attached to Canada, and particularly to Nova Scotia. In Africa, he pined for the Nova Scotia outdoors:

> Upon my word, I would sooner be back far away in the Nova Scotia bush, camping out and trout fishing, than engaged in any single sport or pleasure I know of. Look at the happy days . . . I have spent at the Sambro Lakes, at Preston, at the Magdalen Islands, Musquodoboit and scores of other places, why they are the best days of one's life and ones we all will look back on with feelings of pleasure as long as we live.[60]

Even while in the Congo, Stairs noted the anniversary of the founding of Halifax, speculating about his hometown's birthday celebrations. In his second expedition, he even named his vessel the *Bluenose*, after the name given him by many of his contemporaries. The death of his father made him worry about the breaking up of the "old home" at the North West Arm.[61]

Sometimes, then, home for Stairs was England; sometimes home was Canada; but his actual homeland was the Empire. He likened African landscapes to those in either place: certain sites on the Congo River outdid the scenic wonders of the Thousand Islands, near Kingston; other lands made him think of "one huge English scene, rolling hills divided by patches of bush in the gullies."[62] His heroes and his core narratives were those of the Empire.

As the history of RMC suggests, and Bill Stairs's diary confirms, many Anglo-Canadians like him believed that a good British subject could and should simultaneously be loyal to Nova Scotia, Canada, and the Empire, and in doing so experience no sense of contradiction. Moreover, Stairs could quite happily be an officer in an expedition headed by an American, H.M. Stanley, whose African exploits were driven by the demands of the U.S. newspaper industry, and he could even take a leave of absence from the British Army to work for Leopold II's British- and Belgian-backed company. In truth, both RMC and its graduate operated as elements in a wider world of Anglo-Saxondom, an Anglosphere increasingly unified by a shared sense of an uplifting history and shared projects that aimed to uphold the "noblest traditions of the race"—recall Prime Minister Harper's "massive stepping-stones which the people of the British race shaped and forged to the joy, and peace, and glory of mankind"—against its ignoble enemies.

Thus, both within the expedition and without, Stairs interpreted his African context and shaped his strategies according to Anglo ideals of manliness, whiteness, and industry characteristic of the golden age of Victorian liberalism. When he gazed upon Africa with his "improving eye," he might imagine an English estate, a U.S.-style railroad, or even a New Zealand sheep station. What he could not imagine was a society legitimately and permanently structured in a way that was different than his own. The Anglo framework had its universal laws of the market, property, government, and order, and it was the job of a Canadian abroad to persuade, or to force, often recalcitrant societies to appreciate their need to evolve accordingly. For this world to be truly transformed it was necessary to import styles of rule that, having proved effective in one Anglo colony, could also work for the benefit of another. Indeed, the example of the North West Mounted Police in Canada—where, it was said with great pride, only 450 men had kept over 60,000 "Indians" in order—was promoted to King Leopold II as a potential model for the Congo Free State.[63] The imaginary African landscapes could then be truly *settled*, both in the sense that they would draw European farmers and that they would be finally and decisively defined as British colonies, irreversibly under British imperial control.[64]

The world in which Stairs lived and breathed was an imperial world of individualistic values, at once liberal and capitalist. When he returned as conquering hero to Halifax in 1890, Stairs emphasized "the openings that will be offered to the expansion of English and other trade in supplying new markets for the goods of the world."[65] Still, one hitch to the full commemoration of Bill Stairs as a hero in Halifax was the small detail that at the time of his death he was acting on behalf of Leopold II, and not the British sovereign. Long before the term "transnational capitalism" was invented, Stairs was acting as its armed emissary. His activities on its behalf had an incontestably powerful effect on the trajectory of sub-Saharan Africa, consolidating the regime that combined absolutism with the purest capitalism. Unsavoury as Leopold II's reputation deservedly became, he operated in much the same predatory league as other colonial rulers in Africa, both inside or outside the British Empire. The makers of the new armaments of imperialism could look to Africa then, as they do today, as an excellent testing ground for their products. In 1893, in only ninety minutes, about fifty members of the British South African Police were able to massacre some three thousand Ndebele warriors in what is now Zimbabwe.[66] Ultimately no state save Ethiopia was able to stave off the Europeans by force of arms.

As a "peacekeeper," sailing on the steamer *Peace* and founding a fort named *Peace*, massacring countless of its villagers so that Africa might enjoy the "blessing of civilization"—Stairs reminds us that peace is a word open to a wide diversity of meanings. The peace that Stairs had to offer to Africa was, like the Roman word *pax* from which it descends, close in meaning to "domination." *Pax Britannica*—or today's *Pax Americana* or the Anglosphere—was, as Mark Neocleous puts it, "not simply an absence of conflict or the making of a pact, but the imposition of hegemony achieved through conquest and maintained by arms." In Ancient Rome, Neocleous says, some coins portrayed the goddess Pax "with her right foot on the neck of a vanquished foe."[67] Peacekeeping imposed from on high, by a militarily superior external colonizer, can often look and sound a lot like war—no matter how earnest and sincere the humanitarian rhetoric by which it is marketed to the public.[68]

★

Stairs was a loyal son of the peaceable kingdom, a Canada lacking a standing army and, unusually, with no tradition of launching wars of conquest on other states. Canada was just one part of a growing empire. Its Anglo children warmed to the *Boy's Own Annual*, the novels of Haggard, the poems of Kipling, and the rituals of the Boy Scouts and Girl Guides. When the call came to defend the Empire in South Africa, and later to defend King and Country in Europe in 1914, tens of thousands of Canadians would heed it. They were passionately convinced, as Stairs had been, that the best prospects for the planet could be found in the worldwide union and leadership of the English-speaking peoples.

The South African War of 1899–1902 was the first of Canada's "great wars," and the honoured names of its battles still figure on many a war memorial and in Remembrance Day services. In that war—popularly known as the Boer War—an empire claiming one-fifth of the world's surface and one-quarter of its population fought two small Afrikaner republics with a combined fighting force of roughly fifty thousand men. Although the precise causes of the war will long be debated, few would dispute the significance of three issues: the discovery of gold in the Transvaal; an imperial rival's looming presence in German East Africa (later Tanzania) and German Southwest Africa (Namibia), combined with the possibility of its acquisition of a powerful position in the two Boer republics; and differences between Boers and Britons over the political rights and privileges of British settlers in South Africa generally and the two Afrikaans republics specifically. The conflict was a late phase in the Scramble for Africa that Stairs was so much a part of, and it was also an early premonition of the far greater wars to come in the twentieth century.

Not even the most ardent of imperialists could argue that any Canadian interests were directly at stake in this distant African war. In Britain itself, many imperialists did not initially rally to the banner of war—Lord Minto, who was governor general of Canada through much of it, initially thought the Boers were more in the right than were their British opponents.[69] Many in Canada, especially French Canada, agreed, distrusting the motives of the capitalists involved in British South Africa. In an issue that was much closer to home, fears lingered about a possible conflict with the United States. In the winter of 1895–96 a British war with the United States over the settlement of Venezuela's boundaries seemed a real possibility. Some in the United States sensed a wonderful opportunity to live up to the full spirit of the 1823 Monroe Doctrine by invading Canada. The doctrine had declared that the U.S. government would consider further efforts by

European nations to colonize land or interfere with states in North or South America as acts of aggression fully warranting its intervention. A strict reading of the statement indicated that Canada's westward expansion provided grounds for invasion. The northern neighbour's 3,800-mile-long land frontier was hardly impregnable. In such a climate, should Canadians not be more concerned about the defence of Canada than the conquest of two Boer republics?

Wilfrid Laurier, prime minister since 1896, had been hailed as a saviour by some imperialists in Britain. His Liberal Party was in principle committed to the end of the previous government's National Policy of tariff protection and to closer commercial and diplomatic relations with the United States. In practice the Liberals preserved much of the National Policy, and Laurier himself was the star of grand imperial conferences. Like Conservative prime minister John A. Macdonald before him, Laurier basked in the pomp and pageantry of empire without wanting to pay an extortionate price for it. He had inherited much of the penny-pinching classical liberal's resistance to big military expenses—standing armies, military adventures, certainly long-running wars—on the grounds that they menaced balanced budgets and raised the spectre of increased taxation. He also had to keep his eye on a rising nationalist movement in Quebec. In the minds of determined imperialists, Laurier's caution seemed a "shabby and faint-hearted" attitude. As British statesman Joseph Chamberlain put it, Laurier was clearly "not a man with whom to go out tiger-hunting."[70]

By the time of the South African War, Laurier was confronting an increasingly powerful militarist lobby that was in control of major newspapers and enjoying substantial support within state institutions. Here was a moral crusade. To shun it was to abandon helpless women and children and condemn South Africa to a future of backwardness and incivility, tantamount to letting scumbags and murderers undermine the values of freedom and equality. It meant abandoning innocent people—British settlers—to their plight, their lives (and property) endangered by less-evolved religious fanatics. In the end Laurier appeased the Colonial Office by authorizing a one-thousand-volunteer-strong contingent, later augmented by some six thousand more. They would join a much larger British force.

A pattern was established in South Africa that has persisted to our own time. A conflict is initially seen, by key interpreters, as a toss-up between two relatively similar sides. Yet once war is engaged, the enemy is progressively demonized and racialized—even if, as in the case of the Boers and later the Germans, that enemy looks as white as most of their British opponents. The Dutch-descended Boers were described as evolutionary throwbacks, the cruel, even savage relics of another time. The British were confronting a fanatical, inhuman, and barbaric regime. In some wartime illustrations the white Boers even took on an ape-like animality.[71] They were terrorists and woman-haters, led by a fanatical dictator who drank four gallons of beer a day—something guaranteed to horrify the many Canadian advocates of temperance. The Boers were even attempting to obtain weapons of mass destruction—the Bushmen's secret poisons so detested (yet also adopted) by Stairs. As Sir Arthur Conan Doyle would tell the story, it was a case of British soldiers who "behaved like gentlemen" opposing uncivilized Boers.[72]

Canadian dissenters, as historian Carmen Miller notes, were quickly tarred with the same brush. The Toronto *Evening News* proclaimed French Canadians to be the "Canadian Boers," living in a "priest-ridden, backward community 'honeycombed with traitors and conspirators' who had been granted 'lingual and religious privileges that never should have been granted.'" Montreal men attending a special service at the Church of England's Holy Trinity Cathedral were incited to "'Stand Up for Jesus,' 'Fight the Good Fight,' and uphold 'the charter of the world's freedom' once given to the Israelites but 'now in England's keeping.'" Just as we had beaten back the fanatical Louis Riel in the Northwest Rebellion, so now must our recruits carry "the banner of civilization into the very heart of Africa."[73]

Some French-Canadian critics of the war retorted that, given the extreme uncertainties of Canada's relations with the United States, "Canada might better retain its troops at home to protect its part of the imperial estate." Some even mused that, in a battle between an overbearing British Empire and republics built by pious farm folk, their sympathies resided with the republics. The war also saw the first sustained emergence of a radical left-wing anti-war movement. In Montreal, where the socialist movement in Canada enjoyed some of its first significant stirrings, one union handbill urged "soldiers and workmen to refuse to fight, to 'Stop The War And Arrest The Murderers.'" So bitter was the polarization in Montreal that the British victory at Paardeberg in February 1900, in which Canadians played a key role, was celebrated by riots in Montreal. "No lives have been lost so far," an alarmed Governor General Minto informed the British colonial secretary. "But there is cause for anxiety and the feeling between French and English runs very high."[74]

On October 25, 1900, the "formal war" came to an end and the British annexed the two Boer republics. Many of the Canadian soldiers returned home with a proud sense that their mission had been accomplished, the empire secured. But then, having ousted the insurgent governments, the British (and remaining Canadians) confronted the challenge of an extended counterinsurgency operation in the African countryside. What Miller calls a "more mobile, dirty war" began, with "guerrilla tactics, concentration camps and farm burning." The conflict would continue for close to two years.[75]

The South African War was something of a prototype of the country's twentieth-century wars. Canada as Warrior Nation appealed to young men steeped in the romantic, war-glorifying literature of the time and yearning for adventure. It appealed to imperialists who wanted to strike a blow for civilization, businessmen who hoped to score big with military contracts, and even some socially minded "liberal imperialists" who wanted to do the right thing for the women and children of South Africa. It repelled many French Canadians who disliked imperial adventures, leftists suspicious of jingoism, and even some hard-nosed critics unconvinced that Canada's interests were really at stake. Newspapers transformed a complicated little war into a grand crusade for freedom, and many Canadians seemingly bought into their construction of events. In the end the government's compromise position—to collect volunteers and send them—reflected the balance of forces with which the centrist French-Canadian prime minister contended.

Perhaps the most enduring contributions of the South African War were its refinements of the concentration camp and counterinsurgency warfare. The British established some sixty-eight concentration camps, most of which, according to Miller, became "places of death, disease and malnutrition." Imperial soldiers devastated the Boer countryside with a scorched-earth policy that aimed to drive the Boers into submission through the destruction of their farms and crops. In joining the army of occupation, Canadians were complicit in acts of looting and (apparently) rape. To avenge the death of their leader, the "Canadian Scouts" serving under Major 'Gat' Howard—he was so named after the Gatling gun—swore an oath that they would "never take another Boer prisoner." Perhaps as many as three hundred to four hundred Boer prisoners paid with their lives for Howard's death. The concentration camps, farm-burnings, lootings, apparent rapes, and prisoner executions were then deftly excised from public memory.[76]

John Buchan—later to be Canada's governor general and even later the featured star of the Harper government's citizenship guide—was in South Africa as a protégé of Alfred Milner, who took up the post of high commissioner for South Africa in 1897. In South Africa Buchan became Milner's "fixer." As the record shows, Buchan in South Africa was willing to skirt the very edges of the law in pursuit of the Empire's, and his own, objectives.[77] Buchan administered concentration camps holding 118,000 white and 43,000 non-white prisoners. He later remembered them as "health resorts"—but thousands died on his watch.[78]

In early 1902 Buchan directed a clandestine operation through which his agents posed as private land dealers, scouting out good Transvaal properties. The agents identified owners whose family members were in the concentration camps and made seemingly private offers to buy their land. In effect, Buchan was surreptitiously pressuring prisoners menaced with death to sign land deals with agents who, unbeknownst to them, were actually in the employ of British authorities scheming to undermine the Boers' predominance in the countryside.[79] Very much like that of Bill Stairs, when Buchan's improving gaze took in the African countryside, he dreamed of a land of British settlement, dotted with farms that recalled New Zealand or Australia.[80] Even after the signing in 1902 of the Treaty of Vereeniging ending the war, Buchan was extraordinarily active in his crusade to make the South African countryside less Boer and more British. He was thrilled, on one excursion through the countryside, to see "three huge Canadians" emerging from the bush:

> They had a ramshackle cart and two mules, and the whole outfit was valeted by the very smallest nigger-boy you can imagine. It did one

good to see the way in which that child sprang to attention at sunrise, and, clad simply in a gigantic pair of khaki trousers and one side of an old waistcoat, lit the fire, made coffee for his three masters, cooked breakfast, caught and harnessed the mules, and was squatting in the cart, all within the shortest possible time.

Here was the "advance-guard of our people"—"our people" in this case obviously not including the subordinate "nigger-boy."[81]

In defence of the concentration camps and shady land deals that became associated with his name, Buchan had theories of race and empire to fall back on. Although he expressed a certain fondness for the Boers—they reminded him a bit of the rustic folk he knew in the Scottish borderlands—he did not doubt for a moment that they were biologically and culturally the Britons' racial inferiors. A backward race, they had failed to do "justice to the country." Trapped in age-old forms of religious superstition and tribalism, they exhibited "mental sluggishness" and "stagnant intelligence," not to mention sexual immorality, a tendency to systemic perjury, and other instances of "ragged and twisted ethics." Moreover—and here once more we see an evolutionary script that had worked so well for Stairs and subtly persists into our own time—his opponents were a bleakly homogeneous lot. Unlike the sophisticated Britons, the Boers were all pretty much the same as one another: the "race" was "little more than the individual writ large." Here was a grey primitive land in the grip of a people guided by a grim primitive faith. They were so backward that they did not understand that true gentlemen hunted for sport and not for food. They were "without imagination and that dash of adventure which belongs to all imaginative men." It might take years to bring these specimens up to "our" standards. And so, obviously, "The last word in all matters must rest with us — that is, with the people of British blood and British sympathies."[82]

The blacks in Buchan's imagined Africa could take their place in the lower ranks of the industrial proletariat. They could be offered limited forms of education in the humanities and religion—though one should take care not to turn out underemployed pastors and schoolmasters and to recognize that "the ground must be slowly prepared before the materialist savage mind can be familiarized with the truths of a spiritual religion. Otherwise the result is a glib confession of faith which ends in scandal." It could well be that, in any event, like the North American "Red Indian," most of the indigenous inhabitants were headed for the trash can of history. Even if they seemed civilized, even if they had somehow acquired wealth and property, they were still intrinsically prone to a disabling "instability of character and intellectual childishness" that might manifest itself at any moment. Even if he or she seemed "quick of understanding, industrious, curiously logical," the average native was, mentally, "as crude and naïve as a child, with a child's curiosity and ingenuity, and a child's practical inconsequence. Morally, he has none of the traditions of self-discipline and order, which are implicit, though often in a degraded form, in white people."[83]

Buchan's own fictional character, the charismatic African Reverend John Laputa—whose villainy in *Prester John* would thrill thousands of boys throughout the Empire (or, later, the Commonwealth) until well into the middle of the twentieth century—was merely the distillation of the writer's more prolix and less entertaining expositions of racial theory. "Get these strange, sullen, childish, dark-skinned people hammered into a peaceable and prosperous society, and you have laid the foundation of all the virtues," proclaimed yet another of his characters, Francis Carey, in the 1906 novel *A Lodge in the Wilderness*, in a direct echo of Kipling.[84] As a concentration camp administrator, theorist of the Empire's mission to make white Anglos the master race, and later as a governor general, Buchan fully agreed with him.

Increasingly the term "English-speaking peoples," which Winston Churchill would later put to masterful use, came into vogue. From the 1870s on, despite annexationist campaigns, trade disputes, and significant diplomatic tensions, the United States and Great Britain entered a long-lasting Anglo-American Accord. (It was telling that, notwithstanding fierce popular criticism of Britain's South Africa War, founded on the precepts of the republic's sworn hostility to empire, the U.S. government did not move against Britain.) The Canada that made Bill Stairs was undoubtedly part of the Empire, but it was also increasingly enmeshed in a North Atlantic triangle linking the three

North Atlantic countries culturally, economically, and politically.[85] The peaceable kingdom was always something of an illusion because its many Anglo subjects were so often captivated by quite warlike visions of the White Man's Burden. It was a vision they applied rigorously to the indigenous societies located within the Dominion's borders, and also to many racialized peoples they encountered outside them. And especially after 1885, Canadians were very much inclined to see themselves reflected in the exploits of the British Empire's soldiers, the bearers of Anglo-Saxon freedom and civilization throughout the world.

Canada was not, then, innocent of empire; it was not the peaceable kingdom exempt from the warlike passions of the world. Rather, Canada itself was an imperial project—and one designed not just to protect and defend Victorian liberal values of peace, order, and good government within the boundaries of the Dominion defined by 1867. It would also send forth Canadians to defend the greater empire in the wider world. Canadians were not the passive recipients of an imperialism nurtured outside Canada's borders. Many of them were active creators of and participants in an Anglosphere that they hoped would civilize the world.

Yet the aura of Canadian innocence and virtue sometimes seen in Stairs—of him feeling homesick when he delivered his "wholesome lessons" to Africans—would endure. The image of Canadian rectitude is rooted in the Victorian period. The Canadian peacekeeper arrives as an innocent in a zone in which the English-speaking peoples and their humane values are under siege. Churchill rhapsodized about the great Expeditionary Force—"Guards, Highlanders, sailors, Hussars, Indian soldiers, Canadian voyageurs, mules, camels, and artillery"— that struggled unsuccessfully in 1884–85 to rescue General Gordon at Khartoum from "the rising tide of barbarism."[86] In this imperial model of peacekeeping, we arrive with our superior notions of rights, freedoms, and property, seeking always to defend ourselves against backward peoples who may be primitive, yet, perversely, can be part of a happy future if they can only embrace our way of life.

We have nothing to learn from them. Even thousands of miles from home in lands we scarcely know, killing people whose cultures and languages we do not understand, we are defenders of a true faith and victims of barbarians incapable of understanding it. Canadians march to *relieve* General Gordon, to *relieve* Emin Pasha—and, more recently, to *relieve* the beleaguered citizens of Afghanistan. We are far from finished with the ideal of a *Pax* imposed at the end of our bayonets and guns—and far from comfortably distant from the assumptions and practices that shaped the world of William Stairs.

Rather than *remembering* World War I as an imperial event, new warriors have Canadianized it as the birth of a nation.

CHAPTER 3

FROM WAR
TO WAR TO WAR

THE BATTLES OF
TOMMY BURNS

Generation after generation for centuries to come will follow the Canadian way of glory over the battlefields of France and Flanders, with reverent hearts and shining eyes, learning anew the story that will doubtless always remain the most romantic page in our national history.

– J.W. Dafoe, journalist and newspaper editor, 1919

APRIL 9, 1967, dawned cold and raw on the Douai plain near Arras in northern France, much as it had on Easter Monday fifty years earlier. Thousands of French spectators broke into spontaneous applause as a column of old soldiers made their way forward singing "Mademoiselle from Armentières" and "Take Me Back to Dear Old Blighty." The Vimy Ridge killing grounds were now swathed with green, although the ghosts, the mud, and the blood still lingered in the minds of the seventy-three veterans who walked slowly towards Canada's towering white monument atop what the survivors remembered as Hill 145. This, it had often been said—and the story would be repeated more frequently as the veterans died off—was where Canada became a nation.

Leading the proud Canadian contingent in Canada's jubilant Centennial Year was a short, stubby man with a neat moustache and the demeanour of a career soldier. General E.L.M. Burns had been a young signals officer in 1917. Some ten years after the famous Vimy Ridge battle took place he remarked, "In 1914, when war threatened the British Empire, I had a powerful objection to dying for my country, or for anything else."[1]

Many of the men who charged up the hill had been weaned on the ripping imperial yarns of H. Rider Haggard and Rudyard Kipling. At least before they hit the trenches they had been taken by the notion, popular in the daily propaganda barrage raining down on the home front, that the Great War was a kind of splendid sporting match. Civilians back home learned that the artillery war that smashed soldiers into unrecognizable mush ("the Fallen") and drove many others to the point of insanity was akin to a "symphony orchestra" of effects, or a "fireworks display."[2] Boys of the Edwardian era, especially those like Burns who had attended upper-crust schools such as Montreal's Lower Canada College, were among the many who devoured *Boy's Own Annual* and its tales of plucky lads—doing this with the same enthusiasm that William Stairs had evinced years before.

As a young child Eedson Burns had, perhaps not surprisingly, adopted a different name. E.L.M. Burns became "Tommy"—after Tommy Burns, who was the world heavyweight boxing champion when Burns was a lad, and the only Canadian ever to gain the title. Tommy the soldier would look back at his own Vimy Ridge experience with a sardonic eye, free of blood-and-iron gloss. Burns was a soldier who could write. When the boys he commanded went over the top, the sky was "a cupola of lead, and the appalling uproar, reflected down from it, pressed on one like deep water." He noticed that the "insane stammering rhythm" of the Canadian machine guns was only barely audible, such was the artillery's roar. A German position, less than 100 yards away, gave him pause to reflect. "There is no more vicious noise than that of a machine gun trained directly at one: in the half-light long streaks of flame reached out like adders' tongues." Telling himself that he had at least to appear to be less frightened than the men he was leading, Burns continued uphill. He admitted later that he never knew whether he hit the enemy with his own fire. When a bullet struck nearby, sending a shower of stone splinters into his face, it made "a most demoralizing crack." He noticed a "faint clang" sound on his tin helmet. When he removed the hat he saw a neat crease made by a German bullet. Using a metaphor that echoed George Orwell, Burns recalled an enemy soldier captured by the Canadians he commanded that day at Vimy Ridge. The diminutive Bavarian was so afraid that he "hopped up and down precisely like a little boy who had wet his trousers, until he decided we were not going to slaughter him."[3] To Burns the whole affair did not seem anything like the glorious story of a patriotic battle that was recounted so often, so heatedly, that Canada's most accomplished popularizer of history, Pierre Berton, would label the mythologizing "Vimy Fever."[4]

Young Lieutenant Burns also saw action at the Somme and Passchendaele. One of the lucky ones, he avoided permanent damage, though he was twice wounded in action. He was awarded a Military Cross for conspicuous gallantry because he had "personally laid and repaired" signal cable while exposed to heavy enemy fire at the Somme, displaying "great courage and coolness throughout." But he returned from the war with a sense of tragedy. He had survived "a sad history of mud and muddle."[5] In 1967, when he marched up Vimy Ridge at the head of the column of elderly Canadians, General Tommy Burns was also sporting the Distinguished Service Order. The decoration was awarded in recognition for his role in commanding Canada's army in the bloody struggle to oust Hitler's forces from Italy.

For the fiftieth anniversary of Vimy Ridge, in April 1967, Prince Philip, Duke of Edinburgh, offered a sober assessment of what he called "a four year aberration in human conduct." It was not clear whether he was referring to his distant aristocratic relatives on the German side or all of those who enthused about the Great War. Whatever his terms of reference, the Duke had a clear enough message: "All mankind must learn from this what happens when the personal ambition, arrogance and pride of its national leaders and the nationalism and aggressive instincts of a people drag half the world into war. The first Great War was bad enough, but we did not learn the lesson and we let it happen again."[6]

Like Tommy Burns, Prime Minister Lester Pearson had experienced war, though far from the trenches. On Vimy's fiftieth anniversary he remained at home, where he reminded veterans at an Ottawa dinner of the "stupid bloodletting" that characterized so many First World War battles.[7]

"Canada celebrated its military coming-of-age yesterday in a ceremony that showed it has something to learn about the susceptibility of nations," observed the *Globe and Mail* in a story about a "hallowed Canadian feat of arms." Holy as the event may have become to some, Tommy Burns chuckled as he told reporters about how he ran up Hill 145, a bullet nicking his helmet. Burns joked to reporters, with a grin, that he never did get "his wound stripes."[8]

In 1967 Burns was serving as Canada's chief disarmament negotiator, holding the rank of ambassador at ongoing arms-control talks in Geneva. If Canada ever produced an intellectual general, Burns was the man. Some writers applied the cliché "a soldier's soldier" to him. Another more original description was "the brain that marches like a soldier."[9] As one of Canada's oldest active field commanders in the Second World War, he had led Canada's army in Italy, overseeing the breakthrough at the Liri Valley south of Rome and breaching the heavily fortified Gothic Line, Hitler's main bulwark in northeast Italy. He also commanded the first big peacekeeping force ever mounted by the United Nations, the operation that so famously won Lester B. Pearson the Nobel Peace Prize. Pearson's diplomatic demarche would also leave a mark on Canada's cultural landscape, inspiring Canadians to consider themselves a country of peacemakers and bedevilling Canadian politicians, historians, and others intent on reimagining the country's past in a rather different manner.

Today when we "remember" the First World War, in many ways what we are remembering is not so much the actual conflict in Europe—whose enduring contribution to its civilization was that it laid the groundwork for two decades of turmoil and repression culminating in a second, even more deadly world war—but an imagined Great War, one in which gallant soldiers performed great deeds for a noble cause. As in South Africa, the Empire's soldiers are depicted as struggling against a despotic enemy; and those who sacrificed their lives on Flanders Fields have become foundational Canadians.

Yet this was never a war for democracy, freedom, or "Canada," but a war fought between empires.[10] Turning this war into something sacred means sacralizing the Empire on whose behalf it was fought. It means not troubling to analyze and understand an event that cost humanity over fifteen million lives, over sixty thousand of them Canadian, without conclusively resolving any of the underlying political issues over which it was fought. In the emergent right-wing myth-symbol complex being put forward as the orthodox interpretation of Canadian history, the war was one in which individual soldiers proved their mettle and Canada somehow became a nation. Twenty-first-century Canadians are enjoined to "remember" the war as though the verities of Victorian liberalism still prevail. They are counselled to see the war as an unfolding of individual acts of valour and selfless nation-building, and not as the outcome of the world's socio-economic order.

John Buchan was one of the war's most prodigious and skilful propagandists. He undertook to write the instant history of the war as it unfolded, a task he likened to that taken up by Thucydides in Ancient Greece.[11] From February 1915 to July 1919, Buchan pushed out volume after volume of *Nelson's History of the War*, ultimately producing a series encompassing about 1.2 million words, all written by him. It was lucrative work—he earned £3,000 for the U.S. rights alone—and it was also highly significant because it led readers, and especially American readers, to see the war as a clash of civilizations, one in which they had an immediate interest. Getting the Americans onside (and combatting parallel propaganda efforts on the part of the Germans) was central to Buchan's War. Earlier, it is true, he had evinced an interest in U.S. history, but it was the Great War that really turned him into an ardent advocate of an Atlantic Anglosphere: a union of the English-speaking peoples who, though divided by an ocean, could nonetheless pursue a common racial destiny.

At the same time as he was writing those twenty-four volumes Buchan was also directly employed by the War Propaganda Bureau, where he aimed to disseminate stories that might help the Allies but resisted spreading tales he knew to be false about the Germans.[12] The prodigiously energetic Buchan also, as a diversion, began to write the Dick Hannay books—including *The Thirty-Nine Steps* (1915), *Greenmantle* (1916), and *Mr. Standfast* (1919)—that would win him a vast international public, especially among the soldiers.[13] Buchan's suave heroes, foiling the conspiracies of various swarthy non-British ne'er-do-wells, were having precisely the sort of imperial adventures that the lice-ridden, cold, and alternately bored and terrified trench-bound troops were not.

Buchan captured the romance of war. Rather than a mass slaughter, the Great War was a theatre of chivalry and honour. He caught the spirit of the age: many people in the British Empire saw the war this way. Here was a defence of "our freedoms." In 1915 and 1916 English Canadians flocked to recruitment meetings, sang lustily in their churches about vanquishing the enemy, and were thrilled by the Highland regiments with their colourful kilts and piercing pipes. Recruitment was voluntary and many men happily signed up—a large percentage of them recently arrived British immigrants returning to fight for their homeland.

Canadians quickly learned to despise the Hun. Clergymen who had spent 1914 denouncing capitalist greed spent 1915 reviling the Kaiser. Professors ransacked German philosophical texts to prove the incurable militarism of the entire German race. Universities were soon depleted of many of their male students—with Dalhousie reporting the departure of one out of three. Some patriots gave serious consideration to renaming New Brunswick, whose name had disturbingly Germanic overtones; in Nova Scotia, Lunenburgers whose families had arrived as German-speaking "Foreign Protestants" 150 years earlier found their Britishness questioned, and some took to calling themselves "Hanoverians" after the blameless (if equally Germanic) British Royal Family. Some workers were so patriotic that they refused to work alongside "enemy aliens" or, in the case of coal miners, insisted foreigners wear lamps specially designed to thwart them from acts of terrorism.

Women across Canada knit socks, prepared care packages, and pressured men to enlist. As the Halifax *Herald* explained, "The Duty of Every Nova Scotia Woman, Every Nova Scotia Girl Today is to See that the Men Folk Fight or Farm: Women Must Show the Way to Loafers, Funkers, and Pink Tea Tango Boys!" New Brunswick donated 100,000 bushels of potatoes. Working-class girls in Halifax chipped in to buy their lads a machine gun. Businessmen liked the war. One business publication exclaimed, delightedly, "It is possible to carry on war and do a profitable business at the same time."[14] At a time when competitive tendering was as rare as windfall profits were common, that was something of an understatement. There was good money to be made in this war.

Buchan deeply believed in, and in turn helped to organize, this romantic adventure called war. Now and again his million-word-plus saga ventured into dangerous terrain and he allowed himself to wonder if war on such a scale would not someday be seen as a terrible aberration in humanity's history—but then he found himself returning to *Boy's Own Annual* patriotism. For Buchan the Great War was not, could not be, a dehumanizing and cataclysmic eruption of mechanized modernity. It was, rather, really just like the inspiring and heroic battles of the chivalric past, only on a much bigger scale. It could not be the case that Germany and Britain, when one got down to it, were roughly similar sorts of societies with roughly similar political traditions, with the German universities, kindergartens, planned cities, models of political economy, and social-democratic institutions all worthy of investigation and admiration—which had been the pre-war consensus among the educated and informed in Britain and the United States.[15]

In the world imagined by Buchan, the British bore no responsibility for the origins or consequences of the war. They were fighting a morally, intellectually, and racially inferior enemy. Although both pre-war Britain and Germany had democratically elected assemblies, largely privately owned economies, and reasonably free presses, the war was portrayed as pitting a freedom-loving Britain against a brutally dictatorial Germany. Just as Buchan could persuade himself in South Africa that a struggle he had first interpreted as one in which the British were *just* in the right was really one that pitted the forces of ordered freedom against woman-beating and alcohol-abusing primitives, now he relinquished any notion of moral equivalence between the two sides. Borrowing the recently invented rhetoric of Kipling, he thought of the Germans as racially inferior "Huns." It could not be the case that the origins of this war resided in large part in the contradictions of a socio-economic system, a scramble for markets, territories, and resources, or that it was intensified and perpetuated by people who stood to make money out of it. It *had* to be a Great War pitting a Good Empire against an Evil Empire.[16] It could not be the case that the war demonstrated that the very individualistic principles that Buchan and many of his fellow Victorians brought to the world had helped to create a phenomenon in which poison gas, machine guns, tanks, and warplanes dwarfed the individual and rendered null and void the ideal of war as a theatre in which human beings could demonstrate their sense of chivalry.

Nowadays, in the Great War as the new warriors restage it, in a militarized Canada in which Remembrance Day has become Remembrance Month, plucky and valiant Canadians, fighting for our freedom, chivalrously laid down their lives for their country. This Buchan-style gloss turns the mass death of twentieth-century warfare into the romance of heroes facing down fear and foe to achieve an inspiring result.

In Buchan's romantic interpretation of war, death on the battlefield is something sacred. By mixing their blood with Flanders Fields, our soldiers performed Christ-like sacrifices, deciding as individuals to lay down their lives for their country. In Flanders Fields we find the truest, most foundational Canadians, to whom we owe our freedoms and our nationhood. In representations of the massacre of these soldiers, their deaths often receive what cultural and literary historian Paul Fussell calls the "merciful soft focus" treatment. They become, not men senselessly massacred in a mechanized war but "the fallen," soldiers giving up their lives with dignity and purpose.[17] The perpetually commemorated—if rarely actually remembered—Great War promoted within this official cult attains the solemnity of a religious sacrifice.

Remembrance Day, whose atmosphere for decades was one of solemn mourning of lives snuffed out by war, sometimes even the lives of Germans in Dresden or Japanese in Hiroshima, now becomes ever more a day to celebrate this nationalistic cult of blood and death. Those who embrace a new secular religion of militarism colour the Great War fought for Empire as the Birth of the Nation—and implicitly cast out of the Nation those many Canadians, particularly French Canadians, who steadfastly opposed it. They select out of the actual record of the war only very specific themes, and thus construct a very particular "war"—one resolutely focused on the individual and his (or more rarely her) steadfast stoicism and noble sacrifice. Questions about the causes or consequences of the war, or the intelligence with which it was waged, or the lessons it can suggest about the speed with which human beings can dehumanize each other, both literally and figuratively—these are not only unwelcome: they are becoming dangerous, heretical, even anti-Canadian.[18]

In his voluminous history Buchan offered moving descriptions of the "desperate gallantry" of the Canadians, charging "magnificently" to their deaths, or, in the case of the British soldiers, of the "gallant individuals who managed to break the Germans' positions." But it pays to remember that the author of these words did not see anything first-hand about the battles he was glamorizing. He was safely in the rear, along with the generals who had generated what many hold to be inanely conceived and executed plans that held murderous consequences for average soldiers. On the evening of July 1, 1916—when Canadians and especially Newfoundlanders were dying in the hundreds—Buchan was so far removed from the event he purported to describe in detail that he could write to his wife of the "perfect summer day," with the "larks . . . singing above the bombardment."[19]

With the encouragement of the Canadian state and a vast apparatus of museums, monuments, and films, Buchan's romantic war has become official truth. It makes some room for the horrors of the soldiers' suffering, but only en route to the religious exaltation of their sacrifice. The devastated landscape of death in France and Flanders figures, not as an indictment of the social and political order that produced it, but as the sublime backdrop against which heroic individuals perform their acts of self-sacrificial chivalry.

Among the many who constructed the Great War for Canadians and Americans, Buchan was highly influential but did not stand alone.[20] Canadian-born Gilbert Parker, in *The World in the Crucible: An Account of the Origins and Conduct of the Great War*, noted, "Physically and morally . . . the German of to-day is the same as the German that . . . conquered in the Teutoberger forest in the dawn of our era. He is still in most essentials a primitive man." Kipling, always keen to pound the war drum, told the London *Morning Post* in 1915, "However the world pretends to divide itself, there are only two divisions in the world to-day—human beings and Germans." That Germans were monsters was substantiated by esteemed historian James Bryce's *Report on Alleged German Outrages*, apparently based on shocking first-hand testimony, little of which could subsequently be confirmed. Many such atrocity stories, and the sad case of Edith Cavell, executed by the Germans as a spy in 1915, were gendered: it was a telltale sign of the enemies' lower rank in the evolutionary order that they were predisposed to harm women and children, whose rescue became our chivalrous obligation. Drawing on secret-service funds, the Bureau de la Presse disseminated so many atrocity stories, historian Peter Buitenhuis remarks, that the French press "simply ran them week after week under the same headline: Les Atrocités Allemandes." As Bonar Law, the Canadian-born colonial secretary, put it, speaking of British patriotism, "It is well to have it properly stirred by German frightfulness."[21]

Perhaps the most explosive of all the stories about such frightfulness was the tale of the crucified Canadian. It was based on the testimony of two British soldiers who said they had seen the body of a dead Canadian soldier fastened with bayonets to a barn door. Subsequent investigations, by such figures as the legendary and much-loved Canadian Expeditionary Force chaplain Canon F.G.S. Scott and by Canadian Corps Commander Sir Arthur Currie, failed to corroborate the story.[22] In his memoir *Goodbye to All That*, distinguished British writer Robert Graves likewise maintained that the "atrocity had never been substantiated." But many Canadian soldiers believed the story and apparently took revenge where they could. The result, according to Graves, was that "the troops with the worst reputation for acts of violence against prisoners were the Canadians (and later the Australians)." But, Graves admits, "How far this reputation for atrocities was deserved, and how far it could be ascribed to the overseas habit of bragging and leg-pulling, we could not decide. At all events, most overseas men, and some British troops, made atrocities against prisoners a boast, not a confession."[23]

Graves told the story of a "Canadian-Scot" who narrated a story about how he had treated German prisoners entrusted to his care: "They sent me back with three bloody prisoners, you see, and one started limping and groaning, so I had to keep on kicking the sod down the trench," the Canadian remembered. "It was getting dark and I felt fed up, so I thought: 'I'll have a bit of a game.' I had them covered with the officer's revolver and made 'em open their pockets without turning round. Then I dropped a Mills bomb in each, with the pin out, and ducked behind a traverse. Bang, bang, bang! No more bloody prisoners."[24] Sir Arthur Currie called it a mere "yarn." For Currie the novella *Generals Die in Bed* (1930), by former machine gunner Charles Yale

Harrison, was even worse. Harrison told of Canadian looting and prisoner-killing ("We are to take no prisoners. We say this on all sides. It has become an unofficial order"). Currie responded: "His book is a mass of filth, lies and appeals to everything base and mean and nasty. . . . He talks of nothing but immorality, lice, and other not only disgusting but untrue things."[25] Yet, as historian Tim Cook's research in primary sources has shown, Canadian infantrymen "regularly executed prisoners on the battlefield." Cook provides documentary evidence for a story of prisoner-killing remarkably similar to the one told by Graves. At Vimy, soon to be immortalized by Canadian militarists as the birthplace of the nation, at least as they imagine it, "Archie McWade of the 13th Battalion testified that his platoon officer informed the men: 'Remember, no prisoners. They will just eat your rations.'" In April 1917, when German prisoners emerged from honeycombed underground dugouts, they advanced towards the Canadians' advancing line, "hoping to be taken alive. Many of them were not."[26]

In today's Warrior Nation, we are invited to commemorate some of the hardships of war, all the better to glorify the stalwart heroes who fought for it. "In Flanders Fields" has become the country's most famous poem and the memorial at Vimy Ridge the destination of many a state-subsidized excursion for the young and the epicentre of a vast but improbable cult that attributes to this one fairly insignificant battle a world-historic significance that nobody, including Buchan, sensed at the time.[27] The glorification of the Great War rescripts Canadian history by turning a war fought for empire into one that speaks of Canadians' most fundamental values. As it comes to be treated as "Canada's myth,"[28] indeed the nation's founding moment, the Great War, cleansed of all moral ambiguity and transformed into a crusade against a primitive and barbaric Other, symbolizes the new warriors' pivotal claim: that Canada was and is a nation formed by war. The important events in its history were military events, and its priorities should continue to be military priorities.

And so the Great War, as recounted by Buchan and many others of his ilk, becomes an ever-purer and ever-more-unrealistic copy of something that never actually existed, at least not in the stark purity and moral clarity that the new secular religion of the extreme right demands of it. Rather than *remember* the Great War as a complex historical event, we are enjoined to *commemorate* it as Canada's finest hour. There can be no room in it for Canadians who shot prisoners or who mutinied at war's end or detested their officers or came to question the war's very purpose, because in the "war-as-birthplace-of-the-nation" myth, Canadians' motives must be pure, their actions unsullied.

Ironically enough, such hyper-patriotic commemoration silences the very voices of many of the soldiers whom we claim to be celebrating. Many actual soldiers of 1914–18 remembered a completely different war. They remembered a hypocritical class system, senseless and horrific violence, official incompetence, corrupt profiteering, and moral ambiguity.[29] Many returned home with revolutionary ideas, unfocused but powerful, of changing a hidebound Victorian order from top to bottom, and building a Canada whose independence would forestall any recurrence of such mass murder. Theirs are complicating, discordant voices in the hymn of praise to the chivalric romance of war that Buchan helped bring into the world, and which is now becoming a potent element in Canada's new far-right religion— the religion of war.

A couple of years after the battle of Vimy Ridge, returning from a battlefield tour in 1919, the influential journalist and newspaperman J.W. Dafoe urged Canadians to study the story of the war. He wanted them to think about the lessons in patriotism that it offered. Myth-makers were afoot, and ninety years later some of them would claim as a given that the battle was surely "a turning point in Canadian history," a time in which "Canada entered as a British dominion, but emerged with a much stronger identity."[30] One 1996 documentary film was unabashedly titled *Vimy: The Birth of a Nation*, with the flimsy saying repeated often enough that it would find its way onto ball caps sported by grey-haired men at the *Royal* Canadian Legion.

The Great War did shake English-Canadian society to its core. Something so devastatingly difficult to comprehend provided fertile soil for the growth of mythology. So many dead, so many more maimed in body and crushed in spirit in what was then a very small country. Vimy Fever, a condition unknown in French Quebec, was

amply stoked by patriotic clerics and politicians in English Canada.
That most popular warrior trope, the Christian concept of "sacrifice,"
was much invoked. Prime Minister William Lyon Mackenzie King
himself would refer to Vimy as "one of the world's great altars."[31]

Yet the 1917 battle was neither a turning point in the Great War
nor a strategic breakthrough in Canada's push for independence from
Great Britain. At the time the war itself was advertised as a great imperial undertaking; and it is said that the 10,602 casualties at Vimy, including 3,598 dead in a few short days, "contributed to the most divisive
political debate in Canadian history."[32] The official story of something
as intangible as national identity jostles uneasily with facts just as
incontrovertible as the 60,661 Canadians who went to their deaths in
what Tommy Burns called the "mincing machine" of the Great War.
The conflict that launched Burns's half-century-long military and
diplomatic career also gave rise to scars and splits at home. Patriots
scorned those who did not fight as white-feather "slackers." British-
born Canadians had joined in greater numbers than those who hailed
from other lands or indeed from Canada itself. Most importantly, the
war divided English from French, not just in Burns's home province of
Quebec but also across the country. In the West, no less an opinion-
maker than Dafoe called Vimy Ridge "holy ground" on which "men
by the tens of thousands died for mankind." He disparaged French
Canadians as the "only white race of quitters."[33] Department of
National Defence historian Jean Martin explained in 2011 that although
the birth of a nation idea was coined (predictably enough) by a First
World War general, the notion that the battle was in some way formative for Canada has been "a relatively recent invention." Martin,
hardly a new warrior historian, described the war dead as "victims"
and concluded that the battle had "nothing to do with the birth of the
Canadian nation."[34]

When wars end, as they must, turbulent times often accompany
the tales of glory. The patriotic tub thumpers had to compete with dis-
senting voices who were not confined to the malcontents of another
Canadian historical milestone, the Winnipeg General Strike of 1919.
The Reds replaced the Hun as the enemy *du jour*. Within weeks of the
guns falling silent on the Western Front, French-Canadian conscripts
of the 259th Battalion of the Canadian Siberian Expeditionary Force
mutinied in Victoria. The government of Prime Minister Robert

Borden was preparing to dispatch the troops to crush Russia's dreaded Bolshevik revolution. Officers fired their revolvers in the air and ordered the obedient troops, mainly from Ontario, to remove their belts and whip the French into line. The Royal Bank of Canada was preparing to open a branch in Vladivostok, destination of the SS *Teesta*. Some among its cargo of four thousand Canadian soldiers were clearly reluctant to give their lives for the empire, or at least its latest manifestation.[35]

Better known are the Easter conscription riots of 1917 in Quebec City: soldiers gunned down four protesters. Then there was the savagery unleashed on the men who had fought at places like Vimy and the Somme but now found themselves still languishing far from home well into 1919. Riots at Kinmel, North Wales, claimed the lives of five Canadian soldiers. They were among the survivors who would be known in the aftermath of the war as "returned men"—it would be a while before the term "veteran" became popular. Unlike the Québécois conscripts at Victoria, they *wanted* to board ships to cross the ocean and were increasingly angry at delays in returning to civilian life. They had volunteered while most other men had given the war a pass. Despite the much embroidered memory of Canada's Great War, most men of military age gave war a pass. When conscription did arrive, seven of ten eligible men filed for exemption.[36]

Demobilization is the predictable aftermath of any major war, and the Great War accelerated the eclipse of the empire that had so inspired patriotic English Canadians. Less than a century ago many English Canadians were proudly calling themselves "imperialists." Yet the tragedy of the Great War had tarnished imperialism's polish in English Canada while further discrediting it in Quebec. Moreover, Canadians had never shared that national mythology so widespread in the United States—the mythology of a distinctively North American people who, as clear-eyed defenders of their freedoms, always defeated their enemies and gained strength and unity through war. Although to an extent many had once seen the Empire in this exalted light, fresh memories of elitist British officers and an emergent drive for Canadian autonomy changed the image of Britain held by many Canadians. Even in the United States, the Great War did not give birth to the ideal of a permanently militarized society: in the mid-1930s the U.S. military was judged the *sixteenth* largest in the world, and in 1938 one journalist could rejoice that Canada and the United States, with a combined population of about 140,000,000, harboured only 200,000 people in their armed forces. These two countries provided a model of an informal "League of Nations" that unlike the actual League could actually stand as an example of disarmament and "defensive democratic peace" for the entire world. Vast armies under the sway of potentates were held to be symptoms of the Old World, not attributes of the New.[37]

After the Great War Canada's military drifted without clear purpose or public support. As an institution it fared poorly as Ottawa demobilized. Imperial defence demanded little of Canada's treasury in the 1920s and 1930s. Mackenzie King, the fussy obfuscator who dominated national politics from 1920 to 1948, was a politician who had no great love for the drill hall mindset. The prime minister was a shrewd political tactician, and in the immediate postwar period his government depended on the support of western Progressives and Quebec members of Parliament. The influential *Farmers' Sun* captured the spirit of prairie populism: "The people of this country do not propose to submit to the god of militarism. We have just fought a five years' war to make wars cease."[38]

Like so many of his contemporaries, Tommy Burns learned enough about the mechanized warfare of the twentieth century that he understood, in a way most of today's new warriors cannot, how little romance and how much callous calculation is involved in industrialized killing. Like Canada's famous flying ace, Billy Bishop, he had left RMC to fight in 1914, though he would never be as famous as the official war hero. Unlike another fighter pilot, scion of a Montreal brewing dynasty and one-time owner of the Montreal Canadiens, Hartland de Montarville Molson, Burns would not become a member of the Hockey Hall of Fame. Nor would he be as influential as Walter Gordon, an RMC graduate who became federal finance minister and an influential Canadian nationalist.

But Burns would emerge, in an understated and largely unrecognized way, as one of the most important soldiers in Canadian history. His career path wandered from combat officer to wartime general to leading UN peacekeeper. He was also a fascinating, iconoclastic thinker. His plaque inscription on RMC's Wall of Honour (along with seven others including Bishop, Molson, and Gordon as of 2010) reads: *Decorated WW I Soldier, WW II Canadian Corps Commander in Italy, pioneer UN peacekeeper, professor, author.*

Burns became a career soldier in an era in which few ambitious young men were choosing a military career. He had enrolled at RMC at age seventeen, placing second in the entrance examinations that admitted fifty-four very young men who arrived in Kingston as the guns of August began to rumble in 1914. The lad with the Irish Protestant heritage had been in the militia in Montreal, as had his father. When the Great War ended Burns returned to complete his studies at RMC. He had been marked by war in ways that went beyond his physical wounds. In 1919 his mother Louise, who had herself just returned from an overseas job at a staff headquarters, told the RMC commandant, "They say he looks more like 35 than 21."[39]

Upon finishing his RMC courses, Burns joined the permanent force. After spending a short time overseeing the restoration of drill halls in the backwoods of New Brunswick, he set sail for the British School of Military Engineering, where he became adept at surveying and map-making. He soon became an instructor back at RMC. The 1920s (famously "Roaring") and 1930s (equally famously "Dirty") were, Burns recalled, a "melancholy" interlude for Canada's small cadre of professional soldiers. The government had limited interest in the military, and provided scant funding.[40]

Burns turned his hand to writing in the early 1920s, telling himself that if Field Marshall Douglas Haig (the British commander-in-chief who oversaw the 1914–18 slaughter) could write a book on cavalry tactics on the eve of an industrialized war, then a young Canadian who had recently added military theory to direct personal experience in the trenches might also give it a go. He knew that among the British officers who still served as role models for their Canadian counterparts, placing an article on rugby football or travel in the venerably conservative *Blackwood's Magazine* brought considerable cachet. Burns, an aspiring fiction writer who would eventually co-author a novel, turned his sights in another direction: the new and hugely successful *American Mercury* magazine. The literary and current affairs magazine, edited by the celebrity writer H.L. Mencken and founded in 1924, had an impressive stable of authors who included F. Scott Fitzgerald, Dorothy Parker, James M. Cain, and William Faulkner.[41] Burns wrote the magazine a letter protesting an article that took up "the recurrent theme" of how Canada would one day inevitably be absorbed by the United States. Mencken replied that the soldier wrote clearly and well. He invited him to contribute to his magazine. The great man's encouragement, Burns wrote later, "really sent me up on a cloud."[42]

Mencken's magazine was soon running a story by one Arlington B. Conway under the general heading of "Military Science." A look at the history of the recent war, it was the first of many contributions that Burns would make to *American Mercury*. He became the magazine's de facto military correspondent. The editors described "Conway" as having seen active service "in the World War," after which he had "devoted himself to the study of military science." In his following contributions Burns often elected to use his own byline for technical articles such as "Artillery in the Next War," reserving the Conway pseudonym for more acerbic pieces that he no doubt worried would turn his permanent force career path into a cul-de-sac.

The first item, "The Training of the Soldier," reflected a sardonic style. Morale, important to any group undertaking, had been boosted by the romantic flash of the new war in the air, with the victories of aces like Billy Bishop on the Allied side providing "a great effect on the elevation of the tail of the man in the trench." The men he had led through the mud and blood of Vimy Ridge and the Somme seldom thought well of the generals in their faraway chateaus. "Propaganda may do its best, but it will probably be impossible hereafter to make the private cowering in the shell-hole believe that the fat brass hat, ten or a hundred miles back, sympathizes with him or understands anything about war." (It was not only brass hats but also zealous propagandists like Buchan and Canadian-born newspaper tycoon Maxwell Aitken—Lord Beaverbrook—whom the rank and file might well have had trouble imagining as being intimate with the stench, terror, and cacophony of the trenches.) For Burns, patriotism seemed a mug's game, "obviously moonshine." The glory-of-war propaganda had faded. Burns was clear enough about the conventional appeal of arms.

> The flash and flare of flags and uniforms and the barbaric rhythm of martial music may work a man up to enthusiasm while his feet are yet

on the asphalt, but let him spend five minutes in a trench listening to the blurred wailing of a comrade shot through the belly, and if he thinks of patriotism at all it will only be to curse it.

Burns reflected the elitism of his class. In the "manufacture of soldiers," the best raw materials were primitive, honest men "uncomplicated by elaborate thought-machinery." He quoted Conrad and Shaw to the *American Mercury* readers, sketching a lurid portrait of the British Director of Bayonet Fighting. The colonel in question could take a handful of sheepish young men and "rapidly strip away the coverings of civilization from them and turn them into fighting animals." According to "The Training of the Soldier," the bayonet instructor did not rant or holler but spoke rapidly, in a "low, confidential, compelling tone. . . . That's where the liver is . . . two inches of steel . . . He's a dirty, greasy German waiter . . . He's raped your sister . . . in the throat . . . right there . . . two inches."[43]

Burns went on writing through the 1920s and 1930s, anticipating future wars. But he held no romantic notions. The young officer was well aware of the corrosive nature of martial values. One incident from Vimy Ridge stood out in his memory. He was overseeing a nighttime pick and shovel party as the men under his command dug trenches for communications cable.

> "How long have we got to dig tonight, sir?" asked the sergeant in charge. . . . "About half-an-hour," I replied facetiously, and was immediately reproved by a war-shaken boy's melancholy voice coming out of the darkness. "Don't kid the troops; you mustn't never kid the troops!" But that is what we did, and that's what we'll have to do in the next war. We'll kid them with the news that they are to die for the Glory of the Flag, for the defense of democracy, for their wives and firesides, to keep God's country inviolate, to save humanity from militarism . . . kid them with pictures of Christ on the Cross and a dead soldier at his feet . . . with the promise of forgiveness of their sins and the hope of a glorious resurrection.[44]

Clearly, six years after the Great War's end "Arlington Conway" was permitting himself to cut through the cant of patriotism to get at the war's futile tragedy. Other more scorching critiques of the war would soon emerge as a veritable canon of anti-war literature developed, including R.C. Sherriff's drama *Journey's End* (1928) and Erich Maria Remarque's *All Quiet on the Western Front* (1929). Canadian veterans' groups, in response to stories of the shooting of prisoners and looting of cities, urged the government to ban Charles Yale Harrison's acerbic classic *Generals Die in Bed* (1930). One critic called Harrison a "degenerate minded fool," while Canadian commander Sir Arthur Currie denounced it with equal vehemence.[45] Harrison's lurid description of a gurgling German being stabbed would, however, surely have warmed the heart of Burns's Director of Bayonet Fighting.

The flap over Harrison's book hinted at perennial disputes over how Canada would remember war. George Orwell, who wrote memorably of the ways in which language could be distorted by politics, would in the middle of the next war describe the "systematic lying of 1914–18." War was and would remain the cockpit for messy struggles over political language "designed to make lies sound truthful and murder respectable."[46] In his *Propaganda and Censorship during Canada's Great War*, historian Jeffrey Keshen notes that for five years after the Great War "the stupendous qualities of and critical role played by Johnny Canuck in garnering worldwide esteem went unchallenged" due to press corps patriotism and harsh censorship. Despite novels like Harrison's and war memories like Burns's that did focus on mud, rats, and death, romantic notions of combat would remain as part of the core explanation of what Canadians did in the war and what the war did for Canada. Keshen writes of the persistent "picture of soldiers who, through their extraordinary bravery, won the hardest and most important battles—particularly Second Ypres and Vimy Ridge—and thus emerged as a singular and heroic force in transforming Canada from colony to nation."[47]

While writing for *American Mercury*, Tommy Burns became a mainstay of another new publication, the rather more obscure *Canadian Defence Quarterly*. He continued his RMC teaching, establishing himself as an independent thinker and an up-and-coming military intellectual with an interest in how changing technology would alter warfare. The long history of horses as a weapon of war was finally at an end, he argued. Their role on the Western front had been "a melancholy one," and if war were ever "to be an art again, armies must be put on wheels."[48]

As a military engineer Burns was an early booster of the use of aerial photography, although he was aware of the complexities brought on by weather and camouflage. Similarly he wrote about tanks, saying they were "destined to influence profoundly the tactics and organization of armies."[49] By 1937, when both he and Leon Trotsky were speculating in the pages of *American Mercury* about the next war, Burns (writing as Conway) was foreseeing "a first class war." (Trotsky also had an abiding interest in a class war, though in a rather different sense than Burns imagined it.) That comment came just as Hitler's Condor Legion carried out its famous terror bombing of the Basque town of Guernica during the Spanish Civil War. The attack killed hundreds on market day and left Burns wondering about "the next great war, to which the events in Spain are but a crimson prologue." He had no doubt that air power would come into its own. Anticipating the controversy about the mass bombing of civilians that would begin immediately after that next war, he weighed in on the effectiveness of terrorizing people by bombing them into submission, sapping the will to wage war. "It has been shown," he wrote, "that armed resistance will not collapse because cities are bombed from the air." He would go on to develop a "low opinion" of the Royal Air Force as the Second World War unfolded.[50]

In the late 1920s Burns spent two years studying for the entrance examinations to the British Indian army's staff college in Quetta, then a garrison town in British India. He placed first among all the Empire applicants. Quetta was an exotic locale, some 1,800 metres above sea level, just across the border from Kandahar in Afghanistan. The so-called Durand Line, established thirty-five years previously, was named for British civil servant Sir Mortimer Durand—though it had been negotiated with Afghanistan ruler Abdur Rahman Khan after the British had once again failed to conquer the Afghans. It was part of the famous Great Game played by the contending British and Russian empires that treated Central Asia as a chessboard. The locals, however, were of independent mind. Always resentful of intrusive foreigners, the Pashtun proved adept at insurrectionary gamesmanship.

For a thirty-year-old Canadian, even one who had attended an upper-crust Montreal private school, the life of a colonial military man in remote Quetta came as a surprise. Each officer had at least half a dozen servants, including a gardener, two grooms, two personal servants, and "one untouchable for menial tasks."[51] There was polo, tennis, golf, and, perhaps inevitably, riding to hounds. Burns recalled that the various exercises were well suited to "ward off myopia and the scholar's stoop," although "in Quetta society we did not meet Indians."[52]

The social apartheid of colonial life excluded Quetta's many Pashtuns, who had long given the imperialists fits during periods of what was usually described as "tribal unrest." These warriors were familiar enough to Winston Churchill, then Britain's chancellor of the exchequer. Having trained for the officer corps a generation before, Churchill recalled how he and his Sandhurst chums lamented that they had little chance of putting their military instruction to good use because in 1906 it seemed that the age of war between "civilized" peoples was at an end. Churchill was aware, however, that out there on the imperial fringe lurked "savages and barbarous peoples" like the Afghans. "Some of these might, if they were well-disposed, 'put up a show' some day." The Canadian soldiers who found themselves in Kandahar a century later would no doubt agree, although the men who sent them there were more circumspect than Churchill, who had observed, when fighting the Pashtuns in 1898, that Islam was "as dangerous in a man as hydrophobia in a dog."[53]

After his sojourn in Quetta—a happy time, Burns noted—he spent six years in charge of map-making in the Geographical Section of the Department of National Defence, receiving the OBE for designing a new machine to make maps from aerial photographs. While helping to pioneer air-photo mapping was heady work, a move to Montreal to work on volunteer militia training reminded him of the realities of military life. "We weren't exactly drilling with broomsticks, in the classic tradition of patriotic volunteers," he later wrote, "but we sometimes thought we were not far away from it." Burns, for one, understood where the soldiers stood: "The politicians . . . merely reflected the Canadian public's lack of concern with things outside the ambit of its own municipality or employment—or lack of employment, for the depression still lay heavily on the country."[54] As was the case for many another veteran of the trenches, the prospect of war held no romance for Burns.

In 1939 Burns moved to England to study at the Imperial Defence College. Given that much of the research literature on the science of photogrammetry—the production of maps from photographic images—was in German, he had decided to learn the language and began to read *Mein Kampf* in the original German—"a feat of endurance of which I have always been rather proud." When Hitler moved the Wehrmacht into Danzig in 1939, Burns and his wife Elinor were enjoying the sights of Paris at the end of a long-planned road trip through France. It was obvious that Canada would declare war, but a brief delay occurred while, as Burns later put it, "Mr. King had determined to submit the issue to Parliament."[55] He was between terms at the Imperial Defence College, having gotten to know Lester Pearson, then the number-two Canadian diplomat in London after High Commissioner Vincent Massey. Pearson decided—with Burns's prodding—that Canada needed a senior military attaché at Canada House and requested his services. Burns remained in London for a year, assisting Harry Crerar, the staff officer who would become Canada's overall commander in Italy and later northwest Europe, Canada's key "theatres." Like Burns, Crerar was a private-school boy (Upper Canada College) and an engineer from RMC. For several weeks they comprised the entirety of Canada's wartime expeditionary force.

In the spring of 1940 the so-called phony war was coming to an end. The Germans called it the period of inactivity—it ended with their devastatingly successful May blitzkrieg on the Western front. In his memoir Pearson recounted how two months before the German attack Burns was asked to join a party of officers to do a "Cook's tour" of the French and British defences. The official report of that mission reflected the optimism of their hosts, but Col. Burns gave Pearson a notably different private account, which both "impressed and depressed" the diplomat. According to the official report, the French considered their defences impregnable, but Burns, a keen student of changes in technology, particularly air power and more efficient tanks, told Pearson that the dependence on the static Maginot line, the terrain, and Dutch and Belgian neutrality "would soon be exposed as foolish and fatal." Burns pointed out exactly where the German attack would take place, and his analysis proved prescient. Pearson said he "learned to respect the independence and wisdom of 'Tommy' Burns's military judgement."[56]

Burns was clearly on the road to a top wartime job, destined for big things as a top commander. A 2011 history of Anglosphere generals described him as "a star of the Permanent Force." He briefed the Cabinet War Committee, and Crerar, like Pearson, thought he had a "keen analytical brain." But by 1943 Ralph Allen, the influential *Globe and Mail* war correspondent, was reporting from London that Burns had twice been reassigned to Canada, far from the action in Europe. Allen sensed that Burns had crossed swords with the wrong people. When the *Globe* correspondent went through channels to request an interview, Burns apparently told the army public relations go-between, "Until the war's over I'm not saying another word."[57]

Allen knew that something was up, but did not know the half of it. Burns's rise to the top as one of Canada's leading generals had stopped abruptly in the fallout from an affair with a married woman. The two had met when Burns was back in Canada, and they began corresponding after Burns returned to England just as the heaviest German air raids hit London in 1941. Burns was slated to be the principal planner for the Canadian Corps under Andrew McNaughton, then Canada's most prominent soldier. Within weeks a letter from Burns to his mistress in Montreal was intercepted by post office censors and passed to McNaughton, and Burns was quickly dispatched back to Canada. The letter included a reference to cabinet heavyweight C.G. "Chubby" Power as being in a "disgusting state" during a visit to London. Power, who did drink heavily, was a family friend and it was unseemly for Burns to be slurring him in what may have been an attempt to impress his lover. More importantly, Burns put in writing his feeling that British generals had not been aggressive enough in the war so far and maintained that he had advised McNaughton not to sacrifice Canadian lives in "minor operations." He wrote that he understood Mackenzie King shared his view. "But the urge to take some action may be too strong—and the contrary view may win the day. Don't blame me too much if this occurs." In the end Burns was busted back to colonel, sent back to Canada, and suspended from duty. Defence Minister J.L. Ralston personally informed Burns of his "grave displeasure."[58]

In retrospect Burns was again eerily prescient given the disastrous Dieppe raid that in a few hours cost five times more Canadian lives than would ten years of counterinsurgency in Afghanistan sixty years later. Military historian Desmond Morton explained that there was plenty of blame to go around—Canadian generals were "easy marks" for calling for the 1942 raid on France, and "more than most Canadian battles, Dieppe has been clothed in myth and scapegoats' skins."[59]

Burns, angered by the depths of the Dieppe debacle, did manage to survive this crisis and make his way up the promotional ladder. Even though he had blotted his copybook in a dramatic fashion, he had one of the sharpest minds in the Canadian military.[60] By the middle of 1943 he was well on the road to redemption, promoted by Crerar and McNaughton to the rank of major-general in command of a division. He was on the way to a first-class war.

In early 1944 Burns took over command of a single armoured division in Italy and then, a few months later, the entire Canadian Corps. The Italian government had capitulated within a few months of the Allied invasion of Sicily the previous July, but Canada's forces continued to face determined and well-organized German resistance.

When Burns learned in 1944 that he had gotten the job of top Canadian military man in Italy, he found it hard to believe. Other candidates had been managing battles for months, and he acknowledged that they "might possess more dominating personalities." His new subordinates had been at it since the invasion of Sicily and "took a dim view" of him. "I had been given a job by my superiors with the approval of the Canadian Government, and it was up to me to do it as best I could."[61]

Although Burns went on to command Canada's forces during two of their most important Italian battles against the Wehrmacht (the Liri Valley and the Gothic Line), he would in the end be forced from his job by what military historians regard as his personality defects.[62] Ralph Allen had hinted at Burns's demeanour just before the invasion of Sicily. "In the classroom," he wrote, the RMC cadets "knew him as a grim, stocky little man who gave brilliant lectures in a dull monotone walking up and down with his hands in his pockets and staring at the floor to hide his nervousness."[63]

Burns was not a natural leader in the conventional sense. Soon after arriving in Italy he acquired the nickname "Laughing Boy." One of his hard-swearing division commanders, the bombastic Chris Vokes, remarked that his manner was usually akin to that of "a funeral director." Unlike Vokes and most of the other officers serving under him, Burns had faced artillery and machine-gun fire in the First World War. Combat had affected him dramatically, to the extent that he later explained that battles have to be planned to succeed "without paying a heavy price in blood."[64] He was aware that his role as overall commander would indeed be very much like that of an undertaker. After taking the top job he had but six weeks to prepare the massive Canadian corps for its biggest battle of the campaign. "The grim business of war," writes Mark Zuehlke in his account of that campaign, "seemed even grimmer after Burns took command."[65]

Burns used familiar jargon—the "butcher's bill"—as the fight in the Liri Valley ("the Battle for Rome" in Canada's official military history) totalled 789 killed, 2,463 wounded, and 116 listed as "missing." The troops experienced high levels of what was then called "combat fatigue." Not far from the ruined Benedictine abbey at Monte Cassino is a cemetery where Canadians were buried in what Zuehlke describes as "undoubtedly the most forgotten of the large battles Canadians fought in World War II." The family of George Amos chose the inscription "Went the day well? He died and never knew, well or ill, Freedom, he died for you." The epitaph of Calgary's Edgar Harris stands as a reminder of how many in his generation thought they were fighting for a better, more egalitarian existence: "Died that fascism be destroyed, and that workers might build a new world."[66] Both soldiers were thirty-one years old when they were killed, older than most of their comrades in arms.

Despite the victory, all had not gone well—particularly due to traffic jams that clogged the narrow road through the Liri Valley. Within days of the capture of Rome on June 4, 1944, splits emerged at headquarters. Commanded by swashbuckling English cricketer Sir Oliver Leese, the Eighth Army included British, Canadian, and Polish Corps along with troops from Greece, New Zealand, and India. Leese had initially preferred Burns over his predecessor Harry Crerar, but went on to demand that Burns be replaced by "the best British officer." Or, if that were not possible, that the Canadian Corps "be broken up and the divisions placed under the command of a British Corps."[67]

Leese's demand was not well received. Burns suggested to Leese that without a Canadian leader it would appear that the British were using Canadians as "colonial shock troops."[68] It was a clear political no-no for Canada's high command and its government. The British brass, it seems, was often patronizing about Allies who were bankrolling their war effort as well as supplying troops and materiel. Crerar responded with explicit reference to imperial attitudes. "No other Canadian, or American, or other 'national' commander, unless possessing quite phenomenal qualities, is ever rated quite as high as an equivalent Britisher," Crerar stated. "It also means that to a British army commander such as Leese the cohesiveness created by the existence of a Canadian higher formation, such as a corps, is a distinctly troublesome factor."[69] Crerar remarked that the notion of dissolving the Canadian Corps was "not a prospect even worth discussing." Leese was in search of a scapegoat and insisted on blaming Burns for the Liri Valley shortcomings, complaining that giving Canada's top soldier in Italy a second chance was "rather like a second helping of suet pudding." In the event, as military historian C.P. Stacey noted, Burns was left in a kind of probationary limbo, "a devilish situation for any commander."[70]

During the summer of 1944 the Allied armies in Italy ground their way north from Rome towards Florence and the Wehrmacht's heavily fortified Gothic Line, constructed by Italian slave-labour gangs. Late that summer, even though they enjoyed air superiority, the soldiers who broke through the line found the German defences formidable. The month-long battle produced the highest Canadian casualties of any engagement in Italy, significant in light of the overall casualty rate of over 28 per cent—of the 92,757 Canadians who served in Italy, total casualties were 26,254. According to the official history, "The men who wore on their shoulders the name of Canada were identified with the costliest struggles of the entire campaign."[71]

Tommy Burns did not see the end of that campaign, nor did Leese, who was dispatched to East Asia. When the Allied northward push stalled that autumn, the new Eighth Army commander, British general Richard McCreery, decided that Burns lacked "dash and verve."

Moreover, Burns's immediate subordinates also thought that the boss was not up to the job.[72] His own chief of staff later recalled that he did not joke or socialize with his fellow officers.[73] As the Italian campaign began to get bogged down in the autumn mud of northern Italy, "General Mud" headed for an office job in northeast Europe. One of Burns's harshest critics, his subordinate Chris Vokes, would rise to the highest levels of the Canadian army. Bert Hoffmeister, another celebrated commander, resumed his career in British Columbia's forest products industry and succeeded H.R. MacMillan as chair of MacMillan-Bloedel.

In contrast, Burns was an intellectual and a theorist with a noticeable lack of bravado. The prevailing wisdom pegs him as an exceptionally bright, well-meaning chap who, in the end, got fired because he was not a go-go leader with people skills. In his book about Second World War corps commanders, RMC historian Douglas Delaney describes Burns as a "tragic figure" who would "criticize without decapitating," as someone who lacked the "cold-bloodedness . . . to put one or two 'heads on sticks' as examples to others." The commander was at times "like an old lady unhappy with how a picture had been hung." Delaney, a former colonel, concluded that Burns, unable to either inspire or intimidate, was "vulnerable to enemies from above and below."[74]

For his part, Burns evidently felt that he had successfully focused on the enemy that was the Wehrmacht. He wrote to Crerar at the time that, "whatever the defects of my personality," the Canadian Corps, "acting on plans I made, fought two successful battles, breaking through the very strong Hitler [Liri Valley] and Gothic lines." They "defeated the best German divisions in Italy" and "advanced farther and faster than any British Corps." Later admitting that he had bitterly resented his dismissal from the Italian campaign, he added that it eventually allowed him to "serve the country in ways in which I may have been more useful than I could have been had I gone on."[75]

In 2006, just as Canadians headed for Kandahar, a young Canadian officer who would soon join them offered a revisionist look at Burns's role in Canada's war in Italy. According to Lt. Will Lofgren, Burns was "one of the most successful Canadian corps commanders in the entire Second World War," and his Gothic Line success "should have guaranteed him a more distinguished place in Canadian military history." What historians have got "hung up" on, Lofgren said, was "that Burns was not an archetypal leader, in terms of leadership style and interpersonal skills." According to Lofgren, Burns ended up being "pilloried" even though "he was a winner."[76]

★

It would be nine years after the end of the Second World War that Tommy Burns would again don a khaki uniform. In the interim he was charged with administering one of Ottawa's more ambitious new post-war programs of public provision. So profoundly did the Second World War influence Canada's historical memory that for those who endured it, and for the baby boom generation that it so famously spawned, "postwar" became a commonplace adjective. "The war" marked a watershed period. It was the end of sixteen years of Depression and bloodletting and the beginning of extraordinary changes in the character of a country taking determined, if hesitant, steps in the direction of a welfare state. Labour unions officially took hold, and in the record strike year of 1946 helped working-class Canadians hang onto their wartime gains. Their country was making a halting withdrawal from the embrace of a fast-fading empire and contemplating the growth of an American superpower.

Countries fortunate enough to lack fervid martial traditions and imperial aspirations tend to demobilize after major wars, particularly when politicians who do not identify with the military as a cherished patriotic institution are in office. Yet such resistance to permanent militarism risked being undercut by military alliances. King and his undersecretary of state for External Affairs, O.D. Skelton, were wary of adventures in British militarism. Skelton, notes historian Adam Chapnick, "shared his prime minister's suspicion of British political leadership and had never forgotten that following the British blindly into battle in 1914 had nearly destroyed his country."[77]

Despite the government's initial intention of leaving 25,000 troops to help occupy Germany, sit-down strikes by servicemen and a wave of protest at home brought Canada's occupying forces back to Canada in 1946, much to Britain's disappointment. Canada's own military brass was equally disappointed. Still feeling their wartime oats, they actually called for peacetime conscription ("perfectly outrageous," responded the prime minister) and requested two aircraft carriers, 56,000 regular soldiers and 156,000 reservists, and 30,000 air force personnel. They got less than half of what they asked for.[78]

Those who returned could not wait to shed their uniforms and get back to civilian life. "The war" had been total war, waged with all the resources the state could muster. In Europe the equivalent of the entire population of France—36.5 million—had died in six years of fighting. Guernica had been a mere bagatelle compared to the mass incendiary bombing campaigns and nuclear attacks that followed. Over half of the dead were non-combatant civilians—starved, shot, gassed, and bombed to death.[79] Although not as many Canadian military personnel were killed as perished in the four years of the First World War, casualties had been immense, and the war shook life on the home front to its core. Canadians had been rationed, admonished, cajoled, and propagandized just as they had been a generation earlier. Conscription had, once again, been potently divisive. Many Quebecers saw the conflict as a European, and especially a British, affair fought by a homegrown military led by English Canadians.

It was a testament to the political myopia of Canada's officer class that it could promote peacetime conscription. In his first book on matters military, Tommy Burns pointed out that even during the war "only the most obtuse" among the military failed to recognize that the political problems of conscription far outweighed any of its military advantages. The military, like any large bureaucracy, tends to the top-heavy. Burns's analysis of Canada's wartime personnel headaches began with a précis of Churchill's famous 1942 metaphor about back-office and front-line soldiers: "The tail kept growing vastly, the teeth little." The wily political fixer Chubby Power, who had been badly wounded at the Somme, was suspicious of "brass hats" and virulently opposed to sending conscripted soldiers overseas.[80]

The Second World War would live on in popular memory as what the American broadcaster and popular historian Studs Terkel dubbed the "Good War." Canada's academic historians concurred, labelling it "Canada's Swell War" and "The Good Fight." Others thought of it as the "People's War."[81] The war was just, the enemy demonstrably evil. The war's cultural fallout stands in contrast to that of the First World

War, remembered (at least until recently) as a grinding war of attrition triggered by shifting imperial rivalries, as one mass slaughter that would give rise to yet another.

Canada's new warriors, steeped in the glory of war, tend to promote the notion that the world wars were somehow similar struggles for similar values. Their ideology depends upon reading Canada as a nation founded and nurtured by war and warriors. In their myth-symbol complex, the Great War, which Canadians fought for King and Empire, is thus transformed into an ideological precursor of the Second World War—with Vimy and the trenches also imagined as a struggle for freedom. (This sort of thinking recalls the Great War propaganda retailed to Canadians, who were told that the Kaiser was a threat to their way of life.) Magically, what this ideological manoeuvre also accomplishes is the erasure of all that the new warriors find most objectionable about the 1940s, which in their view marks the beginning of the Bad Age of Canadian history precisely because it meant the coming of unemployment insurance, family allowances, and some measure of central economic planning—that is, the modest beginnings of the Keynesian welfare state, with many of the policies heartily supported by returning veterans. By blending the two wars together, the historians simultaneously exalt the first as the Birth of the Nation and the second as the Defence of the Nation—and erase all the profound differences between the two conflicts, not least the factors identifying the second war so clearly with the coming of the welfare state that so disgusts many of them.

The end of the Great Depression and the events of the Second World War did indeed give impetus to the creation of a far more comprehensive social provision than Canada had ever known. Within a generation public pensions and unemployment insurance would give rise to public health insurance. A consensus developed based on a new faith in government as an agent of the common good. The postwar period and the stirrings of Canada's welfare state are synonymous. If the Canadian state could plan a war, surely it could develop universal programs that moved, however tentatively, in the direction of wealth redistribution and social justice.

The new sense of public responsibility was clearly evident in the provisions made for those who had marched off to war. Rather than the "returned men" who arrived back from the Great War trenches, those who had fought under Burns were now called "veterans," a label hinting of gritty determination. Except for the disgraceful neglect of merchant marine veterans, the veterans of the Second World War returned to programs that were in good measure designed by public officials who had themselves experienced war. Policy-makers also knew that the benefits furnished by a conventionally Liberal government in Ottawa after 1918 had been woefully stingy. Indeed, so conscious was the King government of the need to assist war veterans that planning for their return started within weeks of the German attack on Poland. As the war ground on, the planning accelerated, spurred not only by the earlier wartime experiences of the planners but also by the realization that legions of unhappy veterans could spell political trouble. In spring 1944, just as the Liri Valley battle was about to be joined, Ottawa created a Department of Veterans Affairs (DVA), which two years later had twelve thousand employees. The programs it administered became the Veterans' Charter. By 1948 the DVA was running thirty-four new hospitals. The King government spent over $500 million on programs to provide veterans with farms and university educations, and between 1944 and 1948 $1.8 billion—fully half of all federal social welfare costs—were going for DVA pensions and benefits. "Servicemen may have distrusted and even despised Mackenzie King," writes Jeffrey Keshen, "but his government provided what likely still stands as the most generous welfare and benefit package in Canadian history."[82] These new forms of public provision would overshadow the demands for a large peacetime military force.

One of the men hired to administer these programs was Tommy Burns, who had decided by war's end that getting sacked as a Corps commander had not marked him for a spot at the summit of the military hierarchy. By the end of 1945 he was the DVA's director-general of rehabilitation; five years later he was its deputy minister. While running the department, Burns made at least one foray into the field, dressing in rags and posing as a down-and-out veteran in order to find out how front-line DVA staff treated their clients. "I looked after the boys during the war," he told his daughter, "and I should look after them postwar, too."[83]

The postwar period would also mark the start of another new era for Canada. The seeds of Canada's internationalism were evident in 1945 just as the United Nations was taking shape. Paul Martin Sr., who would be a leading Canadian foreign policy figure in the twenty-five years to come, told the Commons that Canada was "one of the leading middle nations." His Liberal colleague J.J. McCann was somewhat more exercised. He described Canada as it emerged from the war as "one of the most important nations of the world" and even "a fighting world power."[84] UN peacekeeping forces began to be deployed in conflict zones, initially as observers. Lester Pearson and Defence Minister Brooke Claxton nominated Lt.-Col. Harry Angle to serve in India and Pakistan with the UN Military Observer Group, which arrived in Kashmir in early 1949. As with so many of the early peacekeeping operations carried out by the United Nations, it was basically an attempt to mop up and mediate conflicts that had arisen with the end of European colonialism. Within eighteen months Angle was Canada's first peacekeeping casualty, killed in a plane crash.

Canadians insistently romanticized the new United Nations and, in hazy retrospect, made Lester Pearson one of its great architects. But he and Canada actually played a minor role in founding the organization, and as early as 1946 Pearson, now deputy minister of External Affairs, despaired of its playing much of a role in the world. The United Nations had severe limitations—such as the veto powers bestowed upon the great powers in the Security Council and the absence of any effective policing power—and soon enough, for Pearson, the UN Security Council had become a divided, almost futile body.[85] Pearson and the Liberals instead turned much of their attention to the ideal of the "pooled sovereignty" of the North Atlantic states, all technically partners in a grand alliance to save the West from the Communists. They explained to Canadians that their true destiny and purpose now lay in building a grand peacekeeping and civilizing alliance; and indeed, the North Atlantic Treaty Organization was formally established in 1949, with Pearson rightly considered one of its fathers.

Canada's most famous diplomat hoped, vainly as it turned out, that the Atlantic pact would be more than "an instrument of unimaginative militarism." He promoted Article 2 of the NATO treaty—the "Canadian article"—emphasizing cultural, social, and economic co-operation among the European and North American signatories. Secretary of State Dean Acheson, an ardent Cold warrior, wanted a straight military alliance and no part of what he saw as "sentimental and empty Canadian moralizing." He would not be "talking Canadian" in selling the NATO treaty to the U.S. Senate. In selling Article 2 to the Americans, the Canadians also had an eye on Quebec's anti-militarist traditions.[86]

Pearson would relinquish that position—that NATO was much more than a military alliance—only after a stubborn struggle. NATO in itself represented a striking retreat from the internationalist optimism surrounding the foundation of the United Nations to an Atlanticist (and U.S.-centred) vision of world order. Pearson himself had once proclaimed the urgent necessity, above all in an atomic age, of transcending the old limits of conventional diplomacy. The new weapons called out for international governance through something like the United Nations. Yet now he became a key figure in establishing a treaty that returned the world to conventional balance-of-power diplomacy, placing standard armies and alliances once more at the centre of world affairs. "In short order," historian Robert Teigrob observes, "the high-minded rhetoric of 'One World,' global cooperation, and collective security gave considerable ground to ideas that had recently been declared anachronistic, even suicidal: nationalism, power balancing, counter-subversion, and regional defence arrangements."[87]

For diplomat Norman Robertson, an Atlantic pact would provide "a providential solution" for many of Canada's key issues—such as "how to assure American commitment to European defence, how to avoid a bilateral Canadian-American commitment, and how to escape being 'orphaned' by a purely American-European entente." For Pearson the emergence of NATO offered a wonderful opportunity "to promote the economic well being of their peoples, and to achieve social justice, thereby creating an overwhelming superiority of moral, material, and military force on the side of peace and progress." The "inferior" side, it almost went without saying, were those "Slavs" who had organized a "cold-blooded, calculating, victoriously powerful" empire.[88]

Polls suggest that an overwhelming majority of Canadians supported this militarized version of "peace, order, and good government" throughout the second half of the twentieth century, even though they might not have been fully briefed on all its details.[89] For

Pearson, NATO exemplified the "safety-in-numbers" approach that came to be a hallmark of Canadian foreign policy.

By contrast, the Americans, whose 1948 Truman Doctrine declared it their right and duty to shield countries from communist movements, both external and internal, were poised to become the policemen of the "free world"—a term that, along with "free enterprise," they did much to popularize. In July 1949 Truman revisited a doctrine he had rejected with a shudder in 1946—announcing that Americans should be prepared to fight the Soviet Union with atomic and biological weapons if necessary—and decided that the United States should attain the ability to fight communism in a prolonged atomic war. In January 1950 he declared that his government would develop the hydrogen bomb, a thousand times more powerful than the atomic bombs dropped on Hiroshima and Nagasaki. By 1952 Washington had articulated a goal of overwhelming world military preponderance that it has preserved to this day. Official rhetoric and private bonhomie notwithstanding, the British seemed to understand that the Americans were replacing them as the world's hegemonic power. Behind-the-scenes hard-knuckle battles took place, centred on control of colonies, bases, trade routes, international organizations, and the Americans' new weapons of mass destruction. Most of those battles would be lost by the British, culminating in their humiliation in the 1956 Suez Crisis.

From the Pearsonians' long, sad crusade to make of NATO something more than what it transparently was—a military coalition of the willing centred on the United States, and not a benevolent agency for the elevation of the world—comes a telling indication of the pressures they faced. In part, attempting to brand NATO as a peacekeeping and civilizing alliance was an attempt to forestall criticism from Quebec, where the Liberals continued to worry about their nationalist critics, who could now cite two conscription crises in which Quebec's viewpoint had been marginalized. It was also an attempt to reach out to the many Protestant, and especially United Church, peace-lovers who might be compelled by the message that war preparedness was really the best way to build peace. For Pearson, as for Canadian diplomat Escott Reid, there might be "economic and even spiritual defences against Communist attack which should not be overlooked." The Americans had little patience with such preachiness. As Reginald Whitaker and Gary Marcuse remark, "Once Americans had assumed the driver's seat in the Western alliance, they developed a steely resolve in regard to the Soviets that Canadians seemed unwilling to maintain."[90]

In a curious sense, membership in an "Atlantic Alliance" substituted for the achievement of Canadian independence, providing an imagined community of free democracies, the English-speaking ones at their head. This ideal transcended the older ideal of the British Dominion; and for that reason NATO attained a heavy permanence as a body that would prove "exceedingly difficult" to opt out of.[91] Even left-centre parties, like the Parti Québécois of the 1970s or the New Democratic Party in the 1980s, encountered massive scepticism and opposition when they tilted towards abandoning NATO. Atlanticism was structured on the ideological pre-1940s legacies of British imperialism. The Slavs, against whom Buchan and Pearson had so eloquently warned, inherited the mantle of Kipling's "sullen peoples, half-devil and half-child." In Pearson's hands Atlanticism was something new: a great crusade in which Canadians could find their identity in working to build a transformed postwar world. Tellingly, Article 2, upon which Pearson and the Canadians had banked so heavily, became the deadest of dead letters.

Yet, thanks to Pearson, NATO was seen by many Canadians, as was the United Nations, as an almost moral force for the reordering of the world—one in which they should take deep pride. Paradoxically, Canadians vested much of their newly intensified nationalistic pride in an alliance perpetuating, indeed accentuating, their subordinate status within the American empire and sacrificing much of their newly acquired (post-1931) sovereignty. For Pearson, NATO was "a forward move in man's progress from the wasteland of his postwar world, to a better, safer ground . . . a sane and moral world."[92] Many bombed-out citizens in the former Yugoslavia or today's Afghanistan—people subject to the violence implied in the script of the alliance from the beginning—might respectfully beg to differ.

Canadian ambivalence about matters military was reflected in the career of a quintessential Liberal of the period. Brooke Claxton was an Anglo-Montrealer and classmate of Tommy Burns at Lower Canada

College. He, too, joined the army as soon as he could and was decorated for bravery on the battlefield while still a teenager. Certainly no pacifist, he was aware of the reality of war. Claxton biographer David Bercuson explains that the former soldier saw war as "a base, dreadful and dirty business, without glory. He rejected the romanticism expressed on war memorials and in Armistice Day speeches about the 'glorious dead.'"[93]

Claxton, a close associate of Mackenzie King, was a key Liberal organizer and an early devotee of the new science of poll-based politics. The prime minister appointed him minister of national health and welfare in 1944 just as Canada's welfare state was getting established. Some two years later King handed the savvy politico the Department of National Defence portfolio, landing him in a job he would hold for eight crucial years of rapid decline and equally quick escalation in military spending—manifesting a delicate Liberal balancing act between the need to avoid excessive military budgets and the task of managing the transition to a Cold War *Pax Americana*. Claxton's paradoxical position reflected a Liberal ambivalence that, in the final analysis, most always ended up with Canada acting as a junior "partner to behemoth," dressed up as helpful fixer and middle power. "Claxton strongly supported and believed in NATO and all that it stood for," Bercuson writes, "but he still could not reconcile himself to a large, costly, peacetime military establishment." Even though Canada would soon boost its military spending dramatically, a theme emerged that would recur in the decades to come: "This was still not enough for the Americans."[94]

Claxton's tenure at Defence ultimately marked the consolidation of a permanent military establishment in Canada. The process began with a massive cut in military spending in 1946–47,[95] followed by rapid rearmament spurred by the intensification of the Cold War and the outbreak of war in Korea. Within a few months Canada went on a massive military spending binge that would total $5 billion over three years. By 1953 Canada's military budget had jumped to $1.9 billion, a tenfold increase over the postwar low of 1947. Canadian forces had returned to Europe under the aegis of NATO, with the army an affiliate of the British Army of the Rhine and Canada's air force serving under the Americans.[96]

The Korean war, lasting from June 25, 1950 to July 27, 1953, was fought by the West under the official auspices of the United Nations but the de facto command of the United States, with NATO as the ostensible overseer—thus foreshadowing the conditions of the Afghan War fifty years later. The Asian war was a brutal confrontation between the dictatorships that shared the Korean peninsula and served as client states to the respective superpowers. Protesting the Security Council's refusal to seat Mao's China after the "Reds" had pushed the West's Koumintang allies onto the island of Taiwan, the Soviet Union and its veto had been absent for the Council vote authorizing the so-called police action that Pearson, who became External Affairs minister in 1948, publicly described as a "high act of courage."[97] Pearson worried privately about the risks run by the United States and its allies when U.S. commander Douglas MacArthur (subsequently fired by President Truman) pushed ever closer to the Chinese border.

Truman made it plain that, while the Americans hoped to build a broad international coalition to defeat the Communists, he was perfectly willing to see the United States go into Korea alone. It was the clearest manifestation that within the Anglosphere the Americans were now the leaders—distinguished, writes Teigrob, by notions of "exceptionalism, unilateralism, chosen-ness, and national destiny."[98] Canadians began to pick up disquieting signals that senior U.S. figures thought the basic purpose of the Korean War was not to defeat a totalitarian enemy in a strategically important peninsula, but to score points in domestic politics. It was a realization made all the more sobering as some U.S. military men took to musing about dropping atomic bombs on Korea and China.

Weeks before the Chinese army crossed into North Korea to engage MacArthur's forces in the fall of 1950, Pearson—who cast Canada's UN vote for the U.S. resolution to approve the war in the North and condemn China—sat at his room at New York's Biltmore Hotel and penned a remarkable letter to Arthur Lower. The prominent historian and Great War veteran was distressed by the UN vote. Pearson told Lower that what was said publicly and what was said in a private conversation might not be the same. He assured Lower that he did not agree with those Americans who equated victory in Korea with a time when that country would be "blessed" with "Western capitalism and free enterprise." At the same time the future prime minister was clear about the shifting winds of imperial power and how Canada should be thankful that the United States had stepped in "to assume the leadership and exercise the power that formerly lay in Western Europe."[99]

For Canada the Korean War marked the unprecedented step of the Dominion following the United States, rather than Britain, into war. The conflict, branded as a struggle for humanitarian liberalism, was generally supported by a Canadian public, although some serious doubts were expressed. Among the major dailies, only Montreal's astute *Le Devoir*, then as now easily dismissed by Anglo-centric Canadians, opposed the participation of ground forces. For Canada's Cold warriors, Christianity and Canadianism were at stake in the peninsula. It was crucial to Canadians that, from the outset of their involvement, this was a UN and not just a U.S. struggle.[100]

The war's many supporters could even present Canada's participation as confirmation of their nation's new-found stature. For here was a multilateral peacekeeping enterprise, a project that was simply an extension of the civilizing efforts mounted through the centuries by the British Empire to deliver the benighted peoples of Asia from their bondage in Oriental sloth and superstition, in a land so primitive that "men had hardly caught up with Galileo"—where one found subservient women devoting much of their lives to washing clothes, where life's chief purpose was simply to procreate.[101] Should one allow such simple people to be the victims of a Moscow-orchestrated conspiracy? Did not the oppressed women of Korea call out for rescuing?

Initially Pearson believed that the Korean conflict offered a tremendous opening for a troubled United Nations to demonstrate its utility as the world's peacemaker—to demonstrate the effectiveness of "collective action through the United Nations for peace," as he told the House of Commons. Cold War social democrats, such as writers in the *Canadian Forum*, thought they saw the first beginnings of a permanent UN military peacekeeping force.[102]

The dream soured almost immediately. Like turn-of-the-century imperial federationists who imagined parlaying Canada's status as the senior dominion into honour and respect in the counsels of empire, these internationalists aspired to be recognized by the Americans as respected colleagues. They discovered that their voices were even less appreciated within *Pax Americana* than within *Pax Britannica*. Pearson in particular developed early and acute doubts about the legality, wisdom, and, finally, the very sanity of the Korean exercise. Even if one concluded that the North had indeed invaded the South, was the conflict not in essence a civil war? Could the U.S.-led campaign really be reconciled with the UN Charter?

Pearson's July 1950 discussions with Secretary of State Acheson were deeply disturbing. He found Acheson "inspired by the highest motives," with "no trace of warlike excitement or boastful imperialism in his attitude." Yet Acheson made it plain that the struggle over Korea, "of no military significance," was primarily about U.S. domestic politics—the prospect of a Communist victory "had made it politically possible for the United States to secure congressional and public support for a quick and great increase in defence expenditures." Rather than being the wise leader of nations united in a pact, Acheson seemed to be signalling a kind of "interventionist isolationism," an American willingness to crusade against communism whenever and however they chose.[103]

Pearson struggled to find a diplomatic solution to the crisis, one that entailed having the UN forces stop roughly at the old frontier between North and South, near the 38th parallel—only to find the Americans intent on surging northward, almost to the Chinese border. When the Chinese counterattacked and pushed the UN forces back southward of the 38th parallel again, the Americans succeeded in having the United Nations declare the Chinese the aggressors. Soon there was talk of dropping atomic bombs on Chinese cities and, it was later revealed, dropping as many as fifty atomic bombs on Korea itself. In 1952 and 1953 the mandarins in External Affairs often expressed their .acute discomfort with the war's seemingly mad escalation and urged Pearson to take a stand. Sometimes he did—in a brief quietly critical of the tactical use of nuclear weapons, for instance, and in a 1952 bid with India to craft a diplomatic settlement, an effort intensely resented by the Americans. But through most of the Korean conflict he was trapped in the contradictions of quiet diplomacy.

In 1950, when his Ottawa colleagues had warned him of the dangers of the UN resolution paving the way for the advance of UN forces north of the 38th parallel, he pleaded with them to understand the situation in New York: "You have no idea what the pressure is like here. I can't possibly oppose the resolution." After his top colleagues in External had advised him of the folly (not to mention counter-factualism) of the resolution branding China as the aggressor, Pearson seemingly agreed with them. The resolution was "premature and unwise," he said. Then he voted for it.[104]

The on-the-ground realities in Korea, insofar as they came to be known in Canada, further complicated the good-vs.-evil story that Canada's internationalists had told themselves in 1949. Only a few ideologues persuaded themselves that the corrupt and repressive South Korean regime exemplified the values of the "free world." The carnage in Korea was stupefying. Terror bombing of the cities was paired with the calculated destruction of rural dams and irrigation systems. So massive was the bombing that one intelligence report claimed that in all of North Korea no building over a storey high had been left standing. Canadians themselves were complicit in violations of the Geneva Convention on Prisoners, and credible reports appeared citing a lack of discipline and documenting rampant prostitution, drunkenness, and sexual assaults upon Korean women. Even Claxton was taken aback at the brazenness with which the Americans, using techniques later perfected in Vietnam, lied about the war.[105]

The Korean War stalemate was finally confirmed with a 1953 armistice—leaving the boundary separating North from South at the 38th parallel, more or less where it had been when the fighting started.[106] At what cost? In three years 312 Canadians perished. The Americans, who ran the show, lost 33,629. Over 400,000 South Koreans died, and the North Koreans and their Chinese backers lost some 1.5 million military personnel. Pierre Berton covered the war and later described it as an exercise in futility tempered by racism and military arrogance. "In its headlong rush to follow the American lead and get into action as quickly as possible, the Canadian Army had made no effort to tell the troops who signed up anything about the Koreans, their history, or their society." One Canadian soldier, having seen Hollywood movies about the 1941–45 jungle war on the Pacific islands, told Berton that at first he believed he was going to the tropics. Berton spent time with a university-educated corporal who had thought it was "a great thing that the UN was sticking its neck out" but soon changed his mind about the idealistic rhetoric. "It seems that you've got to take somebody's word for it that the Korean people are 'liberty loving.'

I haven't met a gook yet who was."[107] The use of "gook" by North American soldiers did not, apparently, start in Vietnam.

"Have we been able to convince the Koreans themselves that the phrase 'our way of life' is something more than a slogan?" Berton asked rhetorically as the war raged. "In Korea we have given very little thought to anything but the military expediency of the moment, whether it encompasses the breaking of dikes in a paddy field, or tacit support of a government that is about as democratic as Franco's. . . . You can't burn away an idea with gasoline jelly, but can only destroy it with a better idea."[108]

Tommy Burns understood Cold War complexity, the need for each side to put aside propaganda to understand the ideas that animated the other. The world, he realized, faced a highly polarized political situation compounded by "attitudes of fear and hostility" that generated a dangerous arms race. It was always threatening to erupt into war, as it did in Korea. Perhaps, he noted, the Americans really did think that theirs was a defensive posture. And maybe the Russians were convinced that they were being threatened by imperialist encirclement. Burns had not bought the Cold War package. He believed that it was up to political leaders and those being led to understand that their fears were "not really justified." He concluded that, when defence budgets and arms buildups increase, it simply "reinforces the impression of implacable hostility, the implied intention to destroy and thus degrades conditions of trust and good faith."[109]

Two sons of the Methodist manse: Lester Pearson would come to be remembered as a Canadian saint of peace; peace activist James Endicott would become Canada's "Public Enemy Number One."

CHAPTER 4

PEARSON, ENDICOTT, AND THE COLD WAR

PEACEKEEPING AS PASSIVE REVOLUTION

Earth is sick
And Heaven is weary, of the hollow words
Which States and Kingdoms utter when they talk
Of truth and justice . . .

  – Wordsworth, 1814

T wo sons of Methodist ministers, both born in the waning years
of the nineteenth century. Both became representative figures for
the cause of peace in the middle of the next century. They would
come to know each other well, and through the decades their lives
would overlap in peculiar ways.

One—undoubtedly the more famous of the two—was Lester Bowles
Pearson, born on April 23, 1897, in Newtonville, Ontario, not far up
Yonge Street, a place later (as Pearson himself put it) "engulfed" by the
city of Toronto. "Mike" Pearson, the winner of the Nobel Prize for
Peace in 1957, is remembered as a master diplomat, a father of the
United Nations, a self-deprecating man of peace, and the prime minis-
ter who helped usher in medicare, bilingualism, and Expo '67.

The other, James Gareth Endicott, was born on December 24,
1898, in China, to James and Sarah Endicott, Methodist missionaries.

He would become de facto head of the mid-century peace movement in Canada. He would also become "Public Enemy Number One," as his own father described him (with a touch of hyperbole), a figure publicly reviled for raising thorny questions about foreign policy. He was the "Taliban Jack" of his day.

Oddly enough—though perhaps not so oddly because Canada is in some respects a small place—the two men, early on, were linked together in many ways. They were shaped by the same religious milieu and knew and interacted with many of the same middle-class people. They both entered the Great War as young men and later went to the same college, where they first got to know one another. Until the 1930s they shared many of the same ideas. Early on they were both attracted to the same woman—though Jim Endicott ended up marrying her.

The lingering paradox of Pearson was that Canada's pre-eminent peacekeeper was also one of its most ferocious Cold warriors; and in the 1950s the unresolved contradictions of Endicott's peace movement—many stemming from Endicott's wholehearted identification with the Chinese Revolution—would leave it wide open to the violent attacks of the most ardent proponents of Canada's place in the Anglosphere.

Peace activists had been busy organizing for the cause in Canada since at least the early part of the century. During the South African War the country's first cross-Canada left organization (the Canadian Socialist League) and dissident Québécois who saw no value in British imperial ventures both opposed Canada's involvement. During the Great War the Social Democratic Party of Canada organized in solidarity with the anti-conscriptionists in Quebec, and historic peace sects—Quakers, Mennonites, Doukhobors, Jehovah's Witnesses—voiced their anti-militarism. In the wake of the Great War more and more Canadians became disillusioned with militarism and opted for the idea of peace. Some United Church members after 1925 expressed profound disgust with the devastation wrought by mechanized war; others argued that there was no evil more profound than war itself.[1]

In the interwar years, members of Parliament J.S. Woodsworth and Agnes Macphail pressed hard for a peace agenda in the House of

Commons—up to and including the abolition of cadet training (progenitor of a "bombastic military spirit of toy soldierism," in Macphail's memorable expression) and, more audaciously, the dissolution of the Department of National Defence itself.[2] The League of Nations Society in Canada put peace on the agenda of high-school curricula and mounted campaigns on behalf of the Kellogg-Briand Pact, signed by sixty-five nations in Paris in August 1928 and condemning any further recourse to war. In the early 1930s the Society organized world disarmament conferences. With memories of the mechanized carnage of the Great War fresh in their minds, many Canadians flocked to a diversity of large anti-war groups. The Women's International League for Peace and Freedom and the Fellowship of Reconciliation were inclined to outright pacifism, but their members often worked with others, such as members of the Canadian Institute for International Affairs, whose opposition to war, though firm, was not absolute. Middle-class English Canada, and especially the large portion that was Protestant, provided a congenial home to such peace-loving liberal Canadians.[3]

Some, especially in French Canada, were inspired by isolationism and the image of Canada as a peaceful "fireproof house" far removed from European conflagrations. Others wanted to see the League of Nations develop the capacity to enforce a system of "collective security," a structure in which all nations would come together to preserve the peace and deter any would-be aggressor. They pushed for world disarmament and were critical of capitalists who profited from arms. This peace movement encompassed the likes of the Conservative George Drew, later the scourge of all things left-wing when he became premier of Ontario, but who in 1932 was so sharp a critic of arms manufacturers that he wanted them all to be nationalized. The movement included women in the Imperial Order Daughters of the Empire, which denounced arms profits in 1934, and many members of the League of Nations Society.

The anti-war views ran deep enough that the Liberals fretted about the public reaction to their modest rearmament of the Dominion in the 1930s. In 1936, when plans for training Commonwealth air crews at Canadian bases were being hatched, Prime Minister Mackenzie King warned English diplomats to keep the entire thing quiet. Any publicity, he said, would "certainly force an issue in Canada at once which would disclose a wide division of opinion, something that would do the Empire more harm than good." He was right to worry: the plan was blasted in *New Outlook*, the United Church publication, as a dangerous step.4

Many Canadians, repulsed by war and horrified at the drift of events in Europe, hoped the Munich Agreement of 1938 would indeed bring "Peace in Our Time," and when the *Winnipeg Free Press* criticized the deal about twelve thousand readers cancelled their subscriptions in protest. The response was an indication not only of how "unmilitary" was mainstream Canadian opinion, but also of how intensely the public followed foreign affairs. Canadians agitated for effective "collective security" against aggressor countries, and some of them eventually went off to fight for Republican Spain. The "men in Ottawa" who made foreign policy paid close attention: the editorials in the *Free Press* from Dafoe, the "Pope of Prairie Liberalism," were studied in Ottawa with the intensity that Catholic priests devoted to the examination of encyclicals.5

One of the Canadians navigating these churning waters of war and peace in the interwar years was Lester B. Pearson. Pearson's image as a Canadian nationalist and peacemaker diverges from a more complicated historical record that shows him also to have been a loyal son of the Empire.6 Young Pearson's world was a British imperial world. Like William Stairs and many others, Lester loved the books of G.A. Henty and the poems of Rudyard Kipling. For him the British were the best; the non-British, and especially those whom the British had colonized, were simply not of the same quality. As his biographer John English points out, when Pearson went off to the Great War he saw the Macedonians he met near Salonika as a "treacherous, deceitful lot." When his military service took him to Alexandria in Egypt, he wrote of the city's "very low specimens of humanity" and speculated about whether such a race could ever be regenerated. By contrast, Canadians were "easily the best as well as the most civilized."7

These certainties were little unsettled by his later studies at Oxford University—from whence, young Pearson wrote, came men "well equipped to govern the Empire—aye, the World." For Pearson, the Great War, which for him consisted mainly of a stint in "the forgotten front" of Macedonia, was relatively uneventful, full of "disease, boredom, and mounting frustration" during a time in which his "college friends were falling in France." Returning home, he finished his undergraduate degree at Victoria College, later enrolled at Oxford for further studies, and eventually found a job in the History Department at the University of Toronto. There he found men who thought the meaning of Canadian history lay in the country's peaceful accession to a position of leadership as the senior dominion within the British Empire. Although he formed friendships with some of the young social-democratic iconoclasts and nationalists of the day, Pearson never shared their conviction that post-1918 Canada called out for a social and cultural revolution. Not for Pearson the ideal of a comprehensive planning state championed by some of his socialist friends; he even doubted whether "planning is possible anywhere, except in a cemetery, without destroying more than it creates."[8] He abandoned, it seems, his formal attachment to Methodism, but he never lost the emotional tie to Britain or the missionary zeal to make the world a better place, as a Victorian Methodist from small-town Ontario might reckon it.

Pearson in his youth was a self-described "British-Canadian Conservative." In important respects he remained one long after he officially became a Liberal. In the one scholarly piece he wrote during his time as a university professor, he extolled the "westward march" of an Empire in which the "recognition" of cultural differences would provide a basis for a "deeper unity." Pearson praised an Empire in which all manner of people, even the "low specimens" of humanity, might be wisely governed and slowly civilized, as they gradually assimilated the culture of their imperial betters. Like many Depression-era Canadians, Pearson was not convinced that Jewish immigrants, supposedly unconditioned to agrarian life, were the most suitable candidates for membership in the Empire.[9]

Pearson took his slender portfolio of scholarly achievements to the Department of External Affairs in 1928. Yet he had many other gifts. One was an extraordinary affability and cheerfulness. People simply liked Lester Pearson (calling him "Mike"). His two-volume memoirs, very much a 600-plus-page love letter to himself, are replete with beguiling stories, gentle humour, and unpretentious folksiness. He loved to tell self-deprecating tales of Mike the provincial innocent, coping with the intricacies of getting in and out of court uniforms for coronations and smoothing the ruffled feathers of the Empire's many awkward personalities. Vincent Massey, his old university teacher, senior diplomat, and eventually governor general, found there was "something curiously loose-jointed and sloppy about his mental makeup."[10] So there was, and it helped Pearson flourish within a Canada in which, it so often seemed, the rewards went to the accommodating, the compromising, and the ingratiating. Like Canada itself, Pearson was a masterpiece of studied ambiguity.

Was this Dominion of Canada a country or a colony—and, if the latter, whose colony? The Statute of Westminster of 1931 declared it the equal of any self-governing country in the Commonwealth. Until then Britain had been vested with final say over many questions regarding Canada's foreign policy. British citadels (like Kingston's Fort Henry), naval stations, and the famous redcoats testified to this reality—as did, more subtly, the absence of any discussion of foreign policy in the British North America (Constitution) Act of 1867. With the Statute of Westminster Canada acceded to more independence, as shown by the formation of the Department of External Affairs, the creation of a foreign diplomatic corps, and the country's seat at the League of Nations. Pearson's boss, O.D. Skelton, the undersecretary of state for External Affairs, often seemed convinced that Canada could and should chart its own course in the world—taking positions well removed from the whirlpool of European politics. Canadians, said one witty official memo about Italy's 1935 invasion of Ethiopia, "are immensely more interested in Alberta than Abyssinia."[11] Yet no sooner had Canada acquired this measure of independence than it began to qualify it. Rising tensions in the world posed a particular threat to a land whose vast extent and small population made it, in some ways, impossible to defend.

To an extent isolationist Canadians were following the lead of the United States, which had rejected the Treaty of Versailles and the League of Nations, and along with them the prospect of further immersion in Europe's seemingly endless quarrels. Prime Minister Mackenzie King himself could often sound this note. Canada was, of course, deeply interested in the welfare of peoples in "the Orient, Spain, or in any part of the world," King intoned at the time when the Japanese were invading China and Fascists were overrunning Republican Spain—but it was "particularly concerned with the welfare of the Canadian people."[12] King and the government memo about Ethiopia were oversimplifying—as the cancelled Winnipeg newspaper subscriptions and general public interest in international affairs showed.

Yet he had identified a major current of Canadian opinion, especially pronounced in Quebec. To an extent not fully conceded in his memoirs, Pearson largely agreed with him. Canada, after all, still seemed to be separated by a wide ocean from the storms and travails of Europe. As governor general, John Buchan himself, keen to build a North Atlantic alliance of the United States, Britain, and Canada, thought that most of the Canadian "isolationists" he encountered were, in contrast to many Americans, well informed and intensely interested in the League of Nations.

Excepting the explosion that in December 1917 destroyed much of Halifax—the result of the collision of two Allied ships—no Canadian city had ever been devastated by war; and since 1814 no significant invasions of Canadian territory had taken place. King could starve the military because Canadian territory seemed to face no real and present danger. Even the imperial attachment could give Canadians a sense of being insulated from the conflicts of the modern world. Should Canadians, in Pearson's mind "easily the best as well as the most civilized" people on the planet, get mixed up in the affairs of lesser peoples? Yes, but only if the call came out that the Empire was in danger. Canadians would then once more rise up—"education and tradition and sentiment," Pearson mused in 1938, "would make for that inevitably."[13]

Pearson yearned for the world to move into a new order of peace. He wanted a permanent disarmament commission. He called for "a new world" in which "each nation is part of an organic whole, respecting the rights and sharing the duties of others."[14] He was moved by the opening session of a disarmament conference, in which ordinary people were brought forward to testify to the horrors of war. Yet much of the optimism of the movement behind the Kellogg-Briand Pact renouncing war was dissipated by Japan's attack on Manchuria in September 1931 and on Shanghai in 1932. The League of Nations, in which Pearson had vested considerable hope, was a model not of a new system of collective security but of old rivalries between great powers. Like Mackenzie King, Pearson wanted an orderly international world engineered through an international regime of collective security; he did not want any entanglements that might draw Canada into a series of distant wars. Also like King, despite many misgivings Pearson remained deeply attached to Britain and tended not to back any measures that were critical of the motherland.

Despite a massive and mainstream movement to repudiate war in the 1920s and early 1930s, by 1936 the League's weakness, the coming of the Spanish Civil War, and the collapse of a Naval conference designed to limit the militarization of the seas all suggested the imminence of another major conflict. Pearson himself dallied with isolationism. He had come to view with a shrewd cynicism high-flown talk about peace that did not translate into effective measures: "It was the same old stuff—why cannot everybody be as highsouled and peace-loving as we are?"[15]

★

Although Pearson's sense of Anglo-Saxon superiority outlasted the Second World War, he was forced in the 1940s to reckon with a world transformed. A "fireproof house" an ocean away from the conflicts of Europe was changed, suddenly, into the superpowers' prospective battlefield. The United States and the Soviet Union might well resolve their differences over Canada, sandwiched in the middle. Still, for years the idea that the British Empire was fading fast, and that Canada had to rethink its fundamental position in the world, would remain highly contentious.

As it turned out, Canada was being swiftly integrated into a *Pax Americana*. Canadians were subject, without public consultation, to a far-reaching change in their geopolitical identity. The country was undergoing a revolution of sorts—not a bottom-up transformation but a top-down imposition. It was a "revolution" in the sense of a significant change in the country's alignment and politics; but it was a "passive revolution" that, like Confederation itself, did not entail any fundamental change in social structure or political ideology (of the sort, say, that might have told the "Canadian people" that they were sovereign within their own state).[16] Nobody, for instance, put Canada's realignment to anything like a popular vote, just as Confederation itself had never been given a popular mandate.

The upshot was that Canadians were now effectively—and not entirely unsuspectingly—occupants of a new condominium. The senior power was now located not in London but in Washington. From the late 1940s on, Canadian foreign policy would be shaped, decisively, by the U.S. fact. Within this condominium structure the Canadian government was obliged to share its sovereignty even over questions of criminal justice, road-building, and defence installations. A bit like the holders of a humble condo in today's real estate world, the Canadians might exult in their proud ownership of a slice of prosperity—but tremble at its annual costs and blanch at the prospects of changing their residency, even if sharing the same roof as overbearing and more powerful owners had become unendurable. Any breakout from this ambiguous structure—one entailing a de facto sharing of sovereignty with another state—would mean changing their ingrained habits of passive revolution into the far more difficult challenges of radical democracy.

It was a paradoxical time. Having long encouraged the Americans to leave isolationism behind, by the late 1940s Mackenzie King and Pearson must have felt a bit like farmers standing in a flooded field and regretting the day they ever prayed for rain. Once U.S. isolationism was brought to an abrupt and savage end with the Japanese attack on Pearl Harbor on Dec. 7, 1941, they began to feel a tender nostalgia for the good old days of the British Empire. Pearson tellingly described a Canada suspended "somewhat uneasily in the minds of so many Americans between the position of British Colony and American dependency." One of his colleagues at External wrote with unprecedented bluntness of "American imperialism": how ironic it was, Hugh L. Keenleyside remarked, that Canada, having "acquired our rightful place as a free and separate nation in the British Commonwealth," was now confronted with the prospect of accepting "something less than the equivalent of that position in our relationship with Washington."[17] Pearson understood intuitively that Canada had greater status in London, as the "Senior Self-Governing Colony," than it was ever likely to attain in the United States.

Canada's diminished status became evident in wartime negotiations in which British-American plans treated Canada as a negligible quantity. Pearson himself would worry in 1942 about the "very definite and discernible tendencies" in Washington "to consider us either as a part of the British Empire to be dealt with through a British Empire spokesman from the United Kingdom or as a North-American colony." On a question related to the status of Saint-Pierre and Miquelon he said, "There is very little we can do to influence American policy on this matter," though he added, "I am, also, afraid that we have ourselves partly to blame for this."[18] Pearson viewed with especial alarm the coming of the Alaska Highway, built by the U.S. Army Engineers, which he saw as "one of the fingers of the hand which America is placing more or less over the whole of the Western Hemisphere." Likewise, the imperially minded Vincent Massey complained in 1943 about the Americans: "They have apparently walked in and taken possession in many cases as if Canada were unclaimed territory inhabited by a docile race of aborigines."[19] At the two important wartime conferences in Quebec, in August 1943 and September 1944, King played the odd role of the non-participating host. In visual representations of the event, he looks very much like an equal player. In reality, as everyone knew, he was little more than the head waiter. Perhaps, historian C.P. Stacey mischievously remarks, that was the whole point of having King there at all—to generate the photographs in which he at least appeared to be operating on the same level as the leaders of the great powers.[20]

The basic contradictions of the 1940s were dramatic. In the aftermath of the Great Depression and now in the midst of a new world conflict, Canadians were fighting a "People's War" against totalitarianism, an engagement in which they were incessantly reminded of their democratic rights. All around them were signs of a state doing new things—not just innovations in social welfare, but transformations of the economic base itself through a massive program of state capitalism. Renovated or entirely new industrial complexes—shipbuilding in Thunder Bay, petrochemicals in Sarnia, aircraft manufacture in Montreal—were ushered into being at the behest of a state that had suddenly found itself with a capacity to do things that an earlier generation would have regarded as both impossible and impermissible.[21] Ideas of social and economic planning had penetrated the Liberal Party.

Perhaps somewhat predictably among people who had been so immersed for so long in war, nationalism flourished in this climate. Leftists resurrected the old slogan, "conscription of wealth as well as manpower." They derided the capitalists who wanted, in the expression of the radical Co-operative Commonwealth Federation (CCF), to "take the widow's last son to protect the millionaire's last dollar."[22] Novels, historians, paintings, and manifestos all proclaimed the advent of a new Canada. Historian after historian brought out a version of "Colony to Nation," and for once the books were widely read. And so, especially among the troops overseas, was *Make This Your Canada*, the CCF's iconoclastic manifesto that laid out, in great detail, how the new democracy was going to work. In this book, one of the bestsellers of the 1940s, David Lewis and Frank Scott saw in the extraordinary efflorescence of state enterprise the harbinger of a socialist future. Even in linguistically divided Montreal the RCMP kept picking up distressing signals that workers of various nationalities were uniting in an unprecedented wave of union organization, strikes, and political activism. Social democracy was on the march—for a short time the CCF headed the polls, and it came to power in Saskatchewan in 1944. Many working-class Canadians felt something they had rarely experienced before, certainly not in the worst days of the Depression: a sense of ownership of their country. This Canada was experiencing something of a popular uprising, and Mackenzie King, finely attuned to the merest tremor in the political landscape, fully realized it as he brought in his various welfare measures, all carefully constructed to pacify and contain the left.

As Robert Teigrob shows, even the dropping of the bomb on Hiroshima and Nagasaki prompted, along with comments regretting the loss of life, nationalistic celebrations of the country whose uranium deposits and scientific know-how had created such a marvel. The *Globe and Mail* exclaimed, "Japan rocked today under the most devastating destructive force ever known to man—the atomic bomb—and Canadian science and Canadian uranium played a large part in this epochal achievement." Here was an "Anglo-American-Canadian" achievement to be proud of.[23]

The extreme irony is that this Canadian democratic nationalism—the radical intuition that these currents portended a kind of revolution from below, a new sense that the "Canadian people" could make a difference in the world—arose precisely at the moment when making that difference was least possible, for it was also the time of the rise of the United States to the status of global superpower.

In November 1946 Lester Pearson wrote a stirring memorandum for Mackenzie King. Exceeding even Winston Churchill in his grim evaluation of the Soviets, Pearson argued that without "fundamental change in the Soviet state system and in the policies and views of its leaders, the U.S.S.R. is ultimately bound to come into open conflict with western democracy." And, he added, "We should not make the mistake we made with Hitler, of refusing to take seriously the words these leaders utter for home consumption." Deftly equating Nazis and Soviets, Hitler and Stalin, Pearson made it known that he was anticipating a next war, "short, nasty and brutish." In the age of "atom bombs, bacteria and guided missiles," Canada had no choice but to join with the United States to defend itself against Soviet domination.[24]

This crucial memorandum revealed his deepening sense that Canada's future would be inextricably linked to the great powers. Canada was excluded from the 1944 discussions of these powers at Dumbarton Oaks, in Washington, D.C., to sketch out the shape of the organization of the postwar world (namely in the form of the United Nations). The Pearsonian response to this situation was consistent: seeking to enmesh powerful countries in a new global fabric that would constrain their aggressiveness—perhaps restrain the dropping of those "atom bombs" and the use of those "bacteria and guided missiles"—and teach them the "habit of co-operation."[25] For all their crudity, the Americans had inherited the mantle of defending the values of "the English-speaking peoples." They were, necessarily, the vanguard of the Anglo-Saxons to whom Pearson had pledged his deepest loyalty.

Pearson enthusiastically supported a Cold War against any Canadians suspected of viewing the world outside the newly hegemonic framework of the American imperium. He deplored Joe McCarthy (in part because the insane logic of McCarthyism threatened to envelop even him because of past associations with leftists). Yet much of the Golden Age of Pearsonian diplomacy was also the Golden Age of cultural and political repression. Even before the coming of the Red Scare in Hollywood, and in alliance with the greatly beefed-up security apparatus of the RCMP, the Liberal government commenced a brutal purge of dissidents within the National Film Board (NFB). More than forty employees were terminated for political reasons.[26] Pearson could profess his disdain for McCarthyism and add in his next breath: "Canada had given to the FBI the names of 163 Americans. . . . The FBI in turn gave the RCMP Canadian names."[27]

The Liberal government also launched a furious campaign of denunciation and fear against homosexuals in the civil service, scores of whom lost their jobs. Much of the campaign was orchestrated by the interdepartmental Security Panel, which, as Gary Kinsman and Patrizia Gentile detail in *Canadian War on Queers*, "brought together a section of the political and bureaucratic elite, including the Privy Council and members of Cabinet, the military hierarchy, and the RCMP, and extended into the management of the federal public service." The secretiveness and brutality extended to at least one death under interrogation. "To battle totalitarianism," Reg Whitaker and Gary Marcuse say, "Canada itself became a quasi-totalitarian state."[28]

In Pearson's framework, the Soviet Union, bent on world domination, was solely responsible for the new tensions, and the United States, Canada, Britain, and Western Europe responded "slowly and reluctantly" to create the necessary defensive alliance. But, as the record shows, critics, policy-makers, and pundits of the time were radically exaggerating the capabilities of a devastated Soviet Union whose national income was approximately 15 per cent that of the United States.[29] They grossly mischaracterized the supposedly monolithic character of world communism. Despotic and irrational as Stalin's regime was, world conquest was beyond its capacity.

The construction of a Soviet demon was an important component of the profound realignment taking place in world affairs, and it happened with breathtaking speed. With Russia's entry into the Second World War, the Soviets had been described as heroes that every Canadian should admire. "We are both northern peoples, we are both pioneer peoples of the frontier," urged one prominent barrister.[30] Toronto adopted the city of Stalingrad, and over the entrance of Toronto's city hall hung a large banner with a portrait of Churchill on one end and Stalin on the other. Yet step by step the revered allies of 1943 became the reviled monsters of 1947, all in the absence of dramatic changes in the Soviet Union itself. (If the only criterion had been the awfulness of Stalin's regime, it was demonstrably less rabid in 1945 than it had been in 1937.) Much to the chagrin of those who still saw the Soviets as the spear carriers of the world revolution, the trademark of their diplomacy, at least until the 1979 invasion of Afghanistan, was self-interested and defensive caution (with notable exceptions in Hungary and Czechoslovakia). Stalin recognized Chiang Kai-shek's regime as the sole government of China, agreed that the old European empires should regain Asian colonies recently lost to Japan, and publicly defended the doctrine that democratic European countries required no communist revolution. In essence, Stalin, czar in all but name, defended much the same boundaries as the last czarist foreign minister.[31]

When cipher clerk Igor Gouzenko defected from the Soviet Embassy in Ottawa in September 1945, carrying the names of supposed Canadian spies, the event appeared to provide further evidence of the need for Canadians to accede to the Americans' senior management of their affairs. In this case—a decisive moment in Canada's Cold War—the foreign media transformed a humdrum affair into a world-class sensation. As one bemused British commentator noted, most of the supposed "secrets," many of them in the public domain, could have been obtained simply by having military attachés make inquiries of the relevant agencies.[32] Soon, as the Cold War took hold in Canada, the population could be taught to despise a vast new crowd of despicable villains—trade-union organizers, day-care activists, Ukrainian folk dancers, and anyone with the temerity to question the new alignment of power in North America.

A climate of fear and repression gripped Cold War Canada. An important memorandum by Arnold Smith of the Department of External Affairs, "The Russians and the Rest of Us," employed the metaphor of the "fifth column," which had its origins in the Spanish Civil War and was applied to anyone from Fascist sympathizers to Canadian Communists. "Most members of Soviet fifth columns are relatively unconscious of the real objectives which they serve," Smith advised. "Most members of communist parties are themselves unconscious suckers, sincere in a sense, but severely misguided." From the perspective of this influential memorandum, circulated broadly within the External Affairs community, communism could be accurately described as a form of psychopathology.[33] In both the United States and Canada, Cold warriors used anti-communism to fight health insurance, undermine trade unions, regulate wayward youths, and persecute homosexuals—all vital "moral crusades" against the Soviets. Any reservations about these campaigns could be likened to "appeasement" of a global enemy. At a time when many Canadians saw the world through lenses provided by *Time* magazine or *Reader's Digest*, a concerted effort to rebrand Canada as a stalwart member of an Anglo-led crusade against world communism could prove efficacious. Again and again Nazis were equated with Communists, who were supposedly lurking in universities, city halls, trade unions, and especially within government. Canadians like Pearson privately viewed elements of this right-wing rebranding campaign with a certain wry scepticism, but they backed it solidly in public.

Canada could hardly, in the minds of men like Pearson and King, remove itself from the troubled affairs of an increasingly bipolar world. The country's uranium, nickel, and air space had suddenly become strategically important. Canada could also not afford the stupendous costs of building the radar stations and jet-interceptor bases in the North that might satisfy U.S. strategic planners. In the eventual continental compromise formula, Ottawa was permitted to maintain its apparent sovereignty in the North, provided it assented to U.S. plans for continental defence.

Pearson also viewed with scepticism U.S. claims that the American monopoly on atomic weapons would safeguard world peace. He was nervous about bombing North Korea back to the Stone Age with atomic weapons (and later expressed similar reservations about North Vietnam). Yet he did not make his underlying reservations about Korea widely known and later heartily approved the bombing of North Vietnam, provided the action did not involve atomic weapons.

At home it fell to the Liberals to simultaneously preserve, cancel, and contain the widespread grassroots movements of mid-1940s Canada. Unions would be preserved in collective bargaining legislation, cancelled as radical or revolutionary movements (mainly by purging their leaderships), and finally contained in industrial relations regimes. Plans for a transformed planning state would be preserved in limited pieces of legislation, cancelled as overarching schemes for the reorganization of Canadian society, and contained in a form of Keynesianism that, in its commercial Canadian manifestation at least, made the world safer for businessmen. The same logic applied to foreign policy. Plans for an independent Canada were preserved in a succession of nation-building moments—the acquisition of Newfoundland as the tenth province in 1949, the gradual extension of de facto Canadian colonial institutions into the Arctic, the country's presence in the United Nations. They were cancelled in the actual working out of NATO, wherein Canadian dreams of a "North Atlantic Commonwealth" were cruelly dashed and Canadian control over questions of war and peace was more fundamentally compromised than ever before; and they were contained in the emergent doctrines, preserving the semblance but not the essence of sovereignty, of quiet diplomacy. The Orwellian logic of Peace = War would be pursued to its logical conclusions in Korea. Canadians conditioned to their place in the Anglosphere learned to accept, instead of the peace movement's exalted vision of a world without war, the restricted, partial version of that vision in UN peacekeeping.

The post-1939 realignment of Canada from British Dominion to American Dependency did not occur without controversy. Churchill for one sensed the magnitude of the takeover. In his own way, so too did a hesitant Mackenzie King, who ended his political career by recoiling in something like horror from the new realities. King was far from alone: postwar Canadians were sharply divided by questions of peace and war. A "Cold War consensus"—with its implications for Canadian sovereignty—was never uncontested, total, or permanent. In Pearson's day, one of its most visible critics was his old friend Reverend James G. Endicott.

Although Jim Endicott was born in Szechuan, China, his family returned to Canada in 1910, when he was twelve, and Toronto became their permanent home. His father, James Endicott (1865–1954), was one of the most important figures in Canadian Methodism, serving as the general secretary of the Board of Foreign Missions. Later on Endicott Sr. became equally prominent in the United Church of Canada, but he was also a renowned Canadian missionary in China. As Stephen Endicott observes in a penetrating biography of his father, the ideals of British imperialism shone with special brilliance for the missionaries spreading the Gospel in distant lands. One day in 1900, Endicott Sr. had startled an American colleague in China by shouting out excitedly: "Take off your hat! Mafeking has been relieved! Mafeking is free!"— in response to a British victory in the South African War. In 1901, "a year after 231 missionaries had been killed during the Boxer uprisings in northern China," Endicott Sr. endorsed British gunboat diplomacy, which was aimed at dampening the insurgency and rescuing Christians. He passed those same values on to his son. "We sang 'God of our fathers, known of old, Lord of our far flung battle-line . . .' as if the Empire were guided by God," Jim Endicott would later reminisce. "We were taught that it carried a white man's burden—we had gone out to the corners of the world with the best of goodwill to help the natives who were backward and ignorant and stupid."[34]

Jim Endicott enlisted in the Great War as a private; and after the war, like Pearson, took up studies at Victoria College at the University of Toronto. The Great War worked subtly on Endicott. Unlike Pearson, he did not distance himself from the church but went into the ministry, being ordained by the United Church of Canada. Yet like Pearson, father and son, Endicott experienced the Great War as a warning to humanity. Pearson's father could easily have been mistaken for one of the Endicotts when he wrote in 1927 that it would be possible to end war within "this generation" if only Christians would be earnest about it by embracing the imperatives of a new co-operative social order, nurturing the pervasive "sentiment of horror regarding war."[35]

Yet, for all their similarities, Pearson and Endicott came to view the interwar world in very different ways. Pearson's British liberalism was never fundamentally shaken by the Great Depression, and his world view remained fundamentally centred on Europe and Britain. For Endicott, "applied Christianity" meant, when he was a Methodist circuit-rider in Saskatchewan in the early 1920s, supporting the organization of the Wheat Pool—gleaning dramatic insights into the on-the-ground realities of capitalism. Even more transformative was Endicott's direct exposure to social and cultural conditions in China.

In the mid-1920s China was in turmoil. In one of a series of attacks on missionaries a Canadian was beheaded in a public street, her head tossed into a nearby latrine. Hundreds of Chinese were machine-gunned at Wanhsien in a dispute between British shipping companies and the local warlord. The British press in Shanghai explained that the Chinese had been taught a good lesson and "put in their place." As a missionary, Endicott denied being particularly "pro-Chinese," but came to the realization that many Chinese were simply demanding elementary rights. After the Wanhsien tragedy, powerful manifestos denounced the English as "perverse barbarians" and "always fierce and naturally cruel."[36] Endicott was particularly shaken by the missionary response. He estimated that, out of two hundred British missionaries in West China, perhaps six were critical of the British action.

Near the end of his first term as a missionary in the early 1930s, he taught English in the local prison, where he found "university teachers, middle school students, Chinese men of literature and common coolies" all under sentence of death: "As I stand before them and discuss the life of Jesus, I am often overwhelmed with the sickening feeling that the Christian Church as it exists on the average has very little to offer to a keen young spirit that has tasted of death for a Cause."[37]

In summer 1933 Jim and Mary Endicott returned to Canada with their four children. The mass suffering of the Hungry Thirties appalled them, providing evidence of capitalist irrationality. In China Jim Endicott had served as a member of an international famine relief commission and witnessed first-hand the horrors of food shortages and natural disasters. In Canada he heard professors and right-wing politicians pronouncing on the need for more austerity. In the company of numerous middle-class Canadians, many of them from backgrounds similar to his, he was drawn to the radical social democracy of the Co-operative Commonwealth Federation and the revolutionary Christianity of the Fellowship for a Christian Social Order. Like many liberals and socialists of his generation, Endicott was deeply impressed by Russia. Its new system of production, many argued, was making the most important contribution to world progress since Lincoln freed the slaves.[38]

In August 1934, speaking to members of the Chatham, Ontario, Rotary Club, Endicott traced his pilgrim's progress from an imperial romantic to a radical democrat. Having acquired on-the-ground experiences of what empire meant for its subject peoples, he defined it as a group of predatory interests seeking "to expand and enrich themselves by the conquest and exploitation of other countries so that the common people are separated from their natural resources and robbed of their economic security." The local newspaper found Endicott's address startling and cynical. His mother-in-law deposited newspaper clippings containing accounts of the talk in the garbage.[39]

Jim Endicott's radicalization continued after he and his family returned to China in 1934 for a second stint of missionary work. Affronted afresh by the staggering poverty and suffering he saw, he engaged in new forms of missionary work. He started a weekly newspaper, designed partly to help students learn English and partly to cover the country's upheaval and present a critique of imperialism. The Endicotts opened their home to young reformers and revolutionaries. Endicott became an adviser to opposition leaders. He endured the air raids launched by Japan against China, condemning the Western countries for complicity: one downed bomber had U.S. engines and British machine guns.[40]

Back in Canada from 1941 to 1944, he introduced a national radio audience to the unfolding situation in China and received honours from Victoria University, the United Church's Missionary and Maintenance Fund, and Timothy Eaton Memorial Church. His contemporaries found it startling to hear a missionary from a solid middle-class family advocate a wholesale change in the economic order. The once-friendly CBC began to censor his radio talks. He was banned as a supposed "Communist" from the airwaves, but not before attracting a vast coast-to-coast audience.[41]

When Endicott returned to China for the third time, he was even further drawn into the daily lives of the radicals, many of whom had been educated in mission schools. In the following decade he became a committed revolutionary. A Christian, said Endicott, was obliged to side with the Communists and denounce a corrupt regime that starved its people while serving foreign interests. Partly under the guidance of Chinese Christian scholar Wu Yaotsung, he started to see Marxism as a "philosophy and method of social change" compatible with a more all-encompassing Christianity. Neither he nor his wife Mary ever joined the Communist Party; they believed that step would be an empty gesture that might cut them off from their constituency, "the middle class Christian community."[42]

Yet he could not pretend indifference to a people's movement demanding a better world. Nor could he idealize Canada as a force for peace, having experienced first-hand the opportunistic waffling of its diplomatic representatives during a time in China when support for Chiang's corrupt regime was fast decaying. As of February 1946, Canada's "friendly support" for Chiang's regime included a $60-million credit to finance purchase of Canadian munitions and consumer goods—"the first post-war loan given to China by any country," Stephen Endicott points out. By 1948, 150 Canadian Mosquito planes were bombing northern Chinese villages.[43] Yet Ottawa stated blandly that Canada had no intention of taking sides in China's civil war.

By 1947, after returning to Canada once again, Endicott was determined to rouse Canadian opinion against the hypocrisy of preaching peace and making war. Endicott was approached by two Toronto United Church ministers who in turn had been in touch with Dr. Harry Ward, a prominent American theologian and pacifist, and with Rev. James Finlay, president of the pacifist Fellowship of Reconciliation. With enthusiastic backing from many in the United Church, the charismatic Endicott emerged as a key leader of a major current in Canada's political life. His sermon-like speeches swept people up with visions of a new world, with an appeal that went far beyond the ranks of already committed radicals. He packed auditoriums for his talks on peace. He combined the unchallengeable authority of a man who had been at the epicentre of the Chinese Revolution with the spiritual *gravitas* of a renowned missionary.

The peace movement blossomed. A few small Vancouver and Toronto peace rallies in 1948 morphed the next year into a Canada-wide Canadian Peace Congress, with Endicott as leader. The organization's subsequent campaign attracted widespread attention. Volunteers mounted a door-to-door campaign, collecting signatures on a petition calling for nuclear disarmament. By May 1950 a national peace conference had 1,706 registered delegates and culminated in a mass rally of twelve thousand people in Toronto's Maple Leaf Gardens. The Peace Congress estimated that some three hundred thousand Canadians had signed its "Ban the Bomb" petition. Here, the government worried, was precisely the "fifth column" that Arnold Smith had warned them about. The U.S. consul in Montreal reported to Washington, "It is obvious from the reception given to Dr. Endicott that the so-called 'Movement for Peace' is receiving a considerable amount of support from people in different walks of life."[44]

The Canadian Chamber of Commerce responded with a militant campaign against "crypto-Communists" who were contaminating public discourse in Canada. The authorities mobilized an effective campaign of harassment and surveillance against the Communist Party of Canada. In May 1951 police raided a Montreal meeting and seized the group's literature, provoking Mary Endicott to telephone her old friend Lester Pearson in protest. Pearson had first met Mary Austin, the future Mary Endicott, in Chatham, Ontario, when his father was the Methodist pastor there; she was, reportedly, one of his first loves.

An increasingly Cold-War-oriented CCF refused to renew Endicott's membership in 1948, and party leader M.J. Coldwell would not sign the ban the bomb petition. Yet other prominent CCFers stood by him, and Premier Tommy Douglas invited Endicott to address the Saskatchewan legislature.[45]

Endicott focused on practical demands. The three hundred thousand signatures on the ban the bomb petition supported two propositions: "1. Canada stands for the unconditional banning, by all countries, of the atomic weapon as an instrument of aggression and extermination of people, with strict international controls over the fulfillment of this decision. 2. Canada will regard as a war criminal that government which first uses the atomic weapon against any country."[46] The Ottawa mandarins confronted not only what they saw as a treasonable fifth column, but also an emerging mass movement that directly questioned their foreign policy and indeed their right to set it. These were demands being made in the name of "Canada"—and implying that decisions about war and peace should belong in the hands of Canadians, and not the Prime Minister's Office and Department of External Affairs. The people, if mobilized, could prevent a recurrence of war: "War is not a natural calamity like a tempest or an earthquake; war is man-made and man can prevent it."[47]

Red-baiters quickly mobilized, painting the Peace Congress as a Communist front. It was undoubtedly true that promoting peace was in the Soviet Union's hardboiled interests at a time when its capacity to resist any aggressor was severely impaired. Communists were involved in the campaign, yet they neither initiated nor ran it. Endicott never joined the party. The Peace Congress officially disapproved of the Soviet invasion of Hungary in 1956. Such facts did not alter the mass-media campaign against the organization's leader. Endicott was slurred as a credulous "stooge." The respected journalist and editor Blair Fraser delivered an incendiary attack on Endicott in *Maclean's* magazine—referring to his target as an opponent of God (others even called him the Antichrist), while downplaying Endicott's criticisms of the Soviet record on civil liberties in general and the Soviet invasion of Finland in particular.[48]

The peace movement potentially incorporated many of those horrified by the mass slaughter of the Second World War and anxious about the menace of a global nuclear confrontation. Communists figured that these sentiments might lead people to question capitalism as well. When they worked within this broader movement without seeking to control it, acknowledging that its credibility hinged on the independence of its non-Communist leaders, they were effective players. When they actually did strive to dominate the movement—a pattern Endicott noticed by the early 1970s—they dwindled to irrelevance. He left the World Council of Peace in 1972.

★

That Pearson and Endicott would have a violent falling out over peace and its prospects in the post-1945 world seems, in retrospect, inevitable. Endicott was making many of the same arguments about the necessity for world control over atomic weapons that Canada's top diplomat had himself made in the mid-1930s. Yet Pearson had become an ever-more-aggressive accomplice in government attacks on dissidents. Endicott was, Whitaker and Marcuse suggest, "an unwelcome *alter ego* to the liberal consciences of the policy makers in Ottawa as they were drawn deeper into the military side of the Cold War." Pearson took it upon himself "to become a kind of one-man scourge of the Peace Congress."[49]

The trouble with Endicott was that his solid credentials as a Christian missionary and informed observer made him difficult to marginalize. As diplomat Chester Ronning told Lester Pearson on May 13, 1947: "What Endicott says about the possibility of an agrarian revolution is worth noting. I know of no foreigner in China who is in closer touch with the common people and who has wider contacts outside of official circles."[50] Endicott had been sufficiently respected by the Americans to be used as a liaison with the Communists; under code name "Hialeah," he became a part-time member of the Office of Strategic Services (OSS), forerunner of the Central Intelligence Agency. He submitted detailed reports analysing the complicated state of play in Chinese politics in 1944 and 1945. Ironically, it had been at least partly his intelligence-gathering operations, which required him to go out among the people and acquire an in-depth knowledge of their situation, that had further radicalized him.[51] In November 1946 Pearson, as undersecretary of state for External Affairs, wrote warmly to Endicott, thanking him for information sent and asking him to keep sending his reports to the department. Pearson made special arrangements to help Mary Endicott sail to China in late 1946, arranging to advance payment for her passage and describing her as a "nursemaid" who was helping to take care of the Ronning children.[52]

Endicott realized that, especially after 1950 and the start of the Korean War, anyone who expressed sympathy with the Communist revolution in China would be stigmatized; and indeed, during the course of that war a smear campaign against him began. But for many Cold warriors, Endicott was an extraordinarily frustrating figure because he resisted being pigeonholed as a communist. Some United Church members believed that Endicott was morally obliged to declare himself. The virulently right-wing *Toronto Telegram* conducted a mini-campaign to force the issue. Yet it seemed that just as many people sympathized with him. The legendary Salem Bland, whose life and work had animated much of the Social Gospel earlier in the century, hailed Endicott's writing as a force for introducing people to "a reasonable, practical, brotherly and scientific Christianity."[53] Well-regarded academics defended his right to express his views. Most importantly, from Endicott's point of view, even his father, hitherto cool to his son's radical politics, warmed up. Introducing his son to ten thousand peace supporters in Maple Leaf Gardens on May 11, 1952, the Very Reverend James Endicott lamented that although Canadians in general might have been expected to hail his son's acclaim in China, they instead had transformed Jim—"an ex-soldier of His Majesty, a man who's given his life to good causes"—into "Public Enemy Number One."[54]

Indications of a Pearson-Endicott rift had surfaced in 1950, when Endicott visited the World Council of Peace in Moscow. There he spoke movingly of the case of Glen Shortliffe, a Queen's University professor of French literature and public commentator who had taken it upon himself to comment on his country's descent into the maelstrom of militarism. Although Shortliffe was critical of the Soviet Union's "brutality" and "cruel stupidity," he was also an opponent of the "hysterical hate-fest" gripping his own country. He wanted Canada to pursue a role in the world independent of the United States, "seeking routes towards peace and reconciliation, cognizant of the legitimate revolutionary aspirations of oppressed peoples, and mindful of the dangers of bullying by the great powers even in the name of democracy."[55] Why couldn't Canada develop an independent perspective in the world and offer its insights, competence, and power to the pursuit of peaceful solutions, not preparations for war?

The principal of Queen's advised Shortliffe that the university's Board of Governors was displeased. Could he not see that his opinions put the university's fund-raising drive at risk? RCMP agents appeared on campus, questioning students and colleagues. "In an atmosphere of unreasoned fear," Shortliffe wrote, "the god of 'national security' becomes an insatiable monster who knows no frontiers, and a social organism in a convulsion of terror is the very fabric of totalitarianism in itself."[56]

In his Moscow speech Endicott denounced Quebec's notorious Padlock Law of 1937, whereby the provincial government could shut down any institution or private residence deemed to be a place where communist meetings were held or communist literature disseminated. A furious Lester Pearson warned Canadians to "be on guard" against any individual who "wearing the mantle of the Peace Congress has knowingly or unknowingly sold his soul to Moscow." A man who maligned his country with "this kind of falsehood" was "beneath contempt."[57] As Whitaker and Marcuse note, Pearson "even incited Canadians to attack the Peace Congress directly, praising the action of fifty engineering students who had swamped the membership of the University of Toronto peace council for the purpose of destroying the organization: 'If more Canadians were to show something of this high-spirited crusading zeal, we would very soon hear very little of the Canadian Peace Congress and its works. We would simply take it over.'"[58]

Pearson was invited to the May 1950 national gathering of the Canadian Peace Congress, but declined, instead sending a written message. Yet he agreed to meet a small Endicott-led delegation in Ottawa, and cooled down his rhetoric—"I have read your reports [from China] with pleasure," he told Endicott. It was a richly suggestive climb-down hinting that Pearson, more and more a Cold warrior, was also well aware that his old friend spoke for a significant constituency. After all, in the face of a hostile press, on a continent increasingly enveloped in the toxic language of McCarthyism, the 1950 Peace Congress had still drawn huge crowds to the Maple Leaf Gardens peace rally. Publicly Pearson did whatever he could to marginalize the Canadian Peace Congress—an "agent of foreign aggressive imperialism"— and drew a fine British-imperial parallel between the struggle against Communists and those waged by "our forefathers in their struggles with any savages lurking in the woods."[59]

Others launched less genteel assaults: peace activists were assaulted, the Endicott home was firebombed, and Canadian radicals were hounded from their jobs. In 1951 the justice minister introduced amendments to the Criminal Code that made it treasonable for Canadians to say or do anything while outside the country that might be considered as helping any armed forces against which Canadian forces were engaged in hostilities. The strict application of this law could have meant the death penalty for peace activists questioning Canada's new international alliances.

On a visit to China in 1952 Endicott came across evidence that the Americans had experimented with germ warfare in Korea. The response when he spoke out on this issue was ferocious. "The only germ warfare going on is being waged by you and your kind," thundered the Winnipeg *Tribune*. "The germs and maggots and crawling things are the products of your warped mind. You carry pestilence with you and breathe it on clean things. You were called to lead people to God. Now you are trying to lead them into the pit, to betray them into the hands of the godless, sneering men of the Kremlin." Pearson declared his department ready to interrogate Endicott and if necessary impound his passport. The government sent Endicott a questionnaire demanding details about statements he had made in China. Although privately persuaded that the Korean War was neither legal nor rational, Pearson publicly excoriated Endicott, accusing him of a "clumsy hoax" with respect to the Americans' weapons of mass destruction on the peninsula.[60]

Endicott's other opponents were themselves armed with eggs, tomatoes, firecrackers, and stink-bombs when he arrived at Maple Leaf Gardens to attend a rally of supporters. Montreal gatherings of the Peace Council were broken up by club-swinging policemen, some also wielding blackjacks; reporters who wrote stories on the police violence were accused of harming the "common cause."[61] Even the octogenarian scholar W.E.B. DuBois, an Afro-American identified with the struggle for civil rights, was detained by Canadian agents at the border. Newspapers across the country repeated the epithet of Endicott as "Public Enemy Number One." He was strip-searched when he tried to re-enter Canada from a trip abroad. Soon there would be attempts to expel him from the United Church of Canada. "What is treason," demanded the Owen Sound *Sun-Times*, "if Endicott is not guilty of it?" It was his public visibility that probably made the federal cabinet, debating the "Endicott issue" on May 15, 1952, reluctant to assent to an RCMP recommendation that he be tried for treason.[62]

To be sure, the contradictions of Endicott's peace movement left it open to the Cold warriors' violent attacks. Many criticisms stemmed from Endicott's wholehearted identification with the bloodstained Chinese Revolution. For him, those corrupted by power would not yield unless they were compelled to do so.[63] The Chinese Revolution, and by extension China's support for revolutions in other countries, could thus be seen as a necessary stage in the development of human freedom. The Soviet connection with the peace movement was also problematic. Although ordinary Soviet citizens, or the Soviet state itself, were not necessarily hypocritical in the advocacy of peace, over time the official Communist factor became a burden, rather than a resource, for the peace movement. The Communists' modus operandi—the building of a popular front made up of disparate groups promoting "peace"—worked to create a movement that often seemed a mile wide but an inch deep, a movement that state forces could easily infiltrate and disrupt. For Endicott, the more difficult challenge came in reconciling two distinct anti-war positions: activists oriented mainly to Europe and North America, people who thought in terms of the peaceful co-existence of rival social systems; and others oriented mainly to the global South who, particularly by the 1960s, were often thinking in terms of armed struggle against colonialism. On the one hand, the peace movement reached middle-class Canada in an unprecedented way—in the depths of the Cold War Canadians by the hundreds of thousands were signing peace petitions. On the other hand, it meant the dilution of the argument that the causes of war lay in capitalism. "The paradox," argue Whitaker and Marcuse, "is that the Communists did much for the peace movement, by providing a core of experienced activists, while the peace movement did very little for the Communists."[64]

Certainly the state used every opportunity at its disposal to red-bait and persecute peace activists. But over time, as nuclear weapons proliferated, a worldwide public was aroused as never before to the dangers. As Communists became ever more indistinguishable from mainstream social democrats, red-baiting lost much of its traction. Moreover, anyone paying close attention did not have to be steeped in the work of John Stuart Mill to understand that the Cold War reflected anti-liberal militarist values and ideas. Classical republicans and liberals were often suspicious of permanent standing armies. "Of all the enemies of public liberty," wrote James Madison in 1795, "war is perhaps the most to be dreaded, because it comprises and develops the germ of every other. War is the parent of armies. From these proceed debts and taxes. And armies, debts and taxes are the known instruments for bringing the many under the domination of the few. . . . No nation could preserve its freedom in the midst of continual warfare." Many recent immigrants to Canada from war-torn Europe, and later Asia, arrived with no appetite for further warfare. Scripturally-minded Christians could call to mind that it was the "peacemakers," not the warriors, who were "blessed." All those who had upheld the ideal of Canada's transit from colony to nation might chafe at the restrictions on the country's freedom of action. Anti-racists linked their analyses of the capitalist roots of war to a critique, in Teigrob's words, of the "moral bankruptcy of the Anglo-Saxon world, 'which had, since the dawn of colonialism, extended and maintained domination over people of colour through superior weaponry.'"[65]

Endicott believed that war veterans themselves made up one of the most important constituencies of the peace movement. As a veteran himself, he sensed that "there was no meaning to their sacrifices unless it came to pass that democracy, peace, and brotherhood became the bonds that linked the races of man together."[66] Women drew upon well-established traditions of maternal feminism in pitting "Mothers" against "War," and—as Frances Early shows—in the Voice of Women created one of the most impressive of the links between peace activism in the 1960s and 1970s.[67] Anyone with a powerful interest in human survival might well fear for the fate of the species in a future in which one superpower used atomic weapons to bully others into submission.

None of these currents made Canada a peaceable kingdom. Yet, combined, they did provide a large potential constituency for a Canadian stance independent of belligerent superpowers. The idea of the country as a peaceable kingdom was, then, not wholly an invention: it was more a plausible extrapolation from long-standing Canadian tendencies.

★

The image of Pearson as "Canada's peacemaker general," the epitome of Canadian civility in a disordered world, stands in contrast to his activities as a fierce Cold warrior, willing to countenance extreme measures abroad and ham-handed tactics at home; it also stands in contrast to much of the subsequent record of the peacekeeping tradition with which he is so closely identified. Pearson was a central figure in persuading his colleagues, especially Prime Minister Mackenzie King, that the fight against Soviet Communism—that vast octopus with tentacles reaching deep into Canadian society—might entail drastic measures, perhaps even bacteriological warfare. On the domestic front, Pearson evidently had no qualms about the massive purge of the NFB in the name of rooting out supposed Communists—an exercise in state power that discreetly echoed the harsh anti-communist zealotry flourishing in the United States.[68]

Still, there remained a *potential* within the Pearsonian framework for a measure of sophisticated analysis of Cold War realities. "A moral approach to problems," Pearson once argued, "does not require that we should see all of them in simple terms of challenges to righteousness, or of black and white. Indeed the contrary is true, and gray is the prevailing shade."[69] Pearsonian internationalism was ambiguous and evolving, and it is always possible for interpreters favourable to independence in Canadian foreign policy to interpret it as at least a slight improvement on the belligerence of the United States. Rather like a Czechoslovakian Communist who loved the Soviets to bits but felt a bit queasy about the sight of Russian tanks churning up the streets of Prague in 1968, Pearson truly adored the idea of the Anglo-American partnership. He savoured the cozy tête-à-têtes he had with Churchill. In his memoirs Pearson recalled meeting with Churchill on a Sunday morning at the British Embassy in Washington, with the Great Man in bed in his pyjamas, propped up by a couple of pillows, "with a big cigar in his mouth and a glass on the tray that evidently did not contain water."[70] But Pearson recoiled before the naked expression of imperial power in Asia and its bullying tactics in North America. He had, after all, received a rude education from the likes of Dean Acheson and General Douglas MacArthur in the realities of global power. He had learned that powerful Americans had been tempted to use the atomic bomb in a pre-emptive strike against a world Red Menace. The Korean War was something of a turning-point for him as he confronted the reality of Washington pursuing its regional objectives, even considering a possible nuclear attack on China.

In many respects the Korean War, conducted under UN auspices and sold to the public as a peacekeeping war, was a transformative experience for the Pearsonian doctrine. It was the Pearsonians' last moment, as Whitaker and Marcuse put it, of "first fine careless rapture."[71] Here was collective security, humanitarian intervention, and (perhaps) the robust beginnings of UN peacekeeping. Here was a world saved from the Red Menace. Yet it looked to Pearson distressingly like Armageddon.

In Churchill's famous "Iron Curtain" speech of 1946, personally vetted by Pearson and envied by King, the Great Man described that portion of humanity that deserved to win the next world war: "If the population of the English-speaking Commonwealth be added to that of the United States with all that such co-operation implies in the air, on the sea, all over the globe and in science and in industry, and in moral force . . . there will be an overwhelming assurance of security. . . . If we are together, nothing is impossible." As he explained in his sonorous multi-volume *History of the English-Speaking Peoples*, Anglos had been the world's great successes—in war, commerce, and politics—because they remained true to the individualistic insights of liberalism. Now, confronting a communist world conspiracy, Anglo-America, uniting the "two branches of the Anglo-Saxon race," constituted a "special edition of humankind."[72]

From the 1880s to the 1960s, Anglo-Canadians had felt themselves to be part of this select circle. In the nineteenth century, William Stairs and his many admirers encountered an Empire that offered them extraordinary opportunities for heroism and discovery. Canadians enlisted and died in the thousands in the South African War and Great War. The notion that they shared a civilizing mission with the United States grew slowly, given the legacy of conflict between the two empires in North America. But by the 1930s a new political unity was emerging—witnessed by a trend towards economic integration and, most tellingly, by defence agreements, including those achieved at Ogdensburg and Hyde Park—veritable "ties that bind," to cite an apt phrase of Robert

Cuff and J.L. Granatstein.[73] The Truman Doctrine of 1947 declared the U.S. resolve to free all the world's countries (with special reference to Greece and Turkey) from the threat of Communist infiltration and subversion. That U.S. declaration and Canada's entry into NATO in 1949 both intensified the sense of the Anglosphere partnership. It was not entirely the same as the "Greater Britain" of which nineteenth-century imperialists had dreamed, for the Americans had, often in bare-knuckle fashion, edged the British from their hegemonic position. Yet, as Pearson demonstrated so clearly, it was also not so very different: Canadians could hope to find in NATO and kindred institutions a defence of the classical liberal values they so cherished.

The "Ottawa men" who constructed Canadian foreign policy always did so with a close eye on British and especially on American reactions. They became expert in floating ideas and then modifying or even withdrawing them in the face of imperial displeasure. They also had to bear in mind that the relations between Britain and the United States were important to Canada. Finally, as severe conscription crises in both world wars had warned them, they had to construct foreign policies that would not tear the country apart. Such policies should not alienate either Canadians who continued to see themselves as Britons abroad or francophones who had no emotional investment in an Empire that had conquered their ancestors in 1710 and 1759.

If, as Pearson once remarked, foreign policy was just domestic policy with its hat on, liberal internationalism was also a form of Canadian nationalism. Divided, marginalized, and even occupied, Canadians could nonetheless take pride in supporting and even inspiring institutions such as NATO that could be represented as embodiments of liberalism's finest values. Lacking many of the necessary ingredients to forge a strongly imagined community within Canada—a common language, shared myths and symbols testifying to the necessity and goodness of "the nation," and a tightly integrated economy—the Ottawa men developed a nationalist myth-symbol complex about an imagined community outside Canada in which Canadians played an indispensable, indeed world-reshaping role, placing them at the heart of a great crusade for peace and democracy.

★

The coming of the Cold War in the crucial decade of the 1940s shook, but did not fundamentally transform, Canada's status in the Anglosphere. Canadian nationalists, inspired by Canada's evolution "from colony to nation," envisioned a country that belonged to its citizens and that could take up its own post-imperial position in the world; some also dreamed of a grand reconciliation with Quebec, with its fresh memories of the imposition of the detested policy of conscription. There was an almost palpable yearning for a prosperous, peaceful, and settled society. If the Liberals did not respond to that yearning, there were, as Mackenzie King knew only too well, left-wing forces that would. Already in 1944, Saskatchewan had elected North America's first socialist government.

For his part, Jim Endicott endured much to keep the peace movement afloat in the treacherous 1950s, but saw the Peace Congress slowly shrivel as a result of repression and, later, Soviet meddling. His fellow Christians, some of them swayed by the Red Scare, still hesitated before stripping him of his status as minister. "Peace" would often be a gateway word to systemic opposition to the irrationality and cruelty of a world dominated by capitalism and policed by aggressive superpowers: from the Student Union for Peace Action grew some of the New Left movements that helped change the face of Canadian politics in the 1960s. Much later, in the 1980s, Endicott had the satisfaction of witnessing the birth of the successor to the Peace Council in a mass movement that contested the further testing of the massive weapons of war.[74]

The great danger of militarism remained. Indeed, as Pearson warned, the more distant people were from actual war-fighting, the more they could come to romanticize war. In Ottawa and across the country a keen and earnest realization came into play: the international order required a democratic transformation; the great power diplomacy of the 1920s and 1930s had led to catastrophe. Many of the same Canadian social democrats and left liberals who were pushing for the new democratic state were also crusaders for a more rational and peaceful new United Nations, whose charter would lay out a vision of universal human rights and whose agencies might bring about a worldwide regime of welfare and peace.

Major-General E.L.M. Burns, CC, DSO, OBE, MC, CD, in Italy, 1944. A Vimy Ridge combat veteran and World War II Corps Commander, Tommy Burns later oversaw the creation of the first major United Nations peacekeeping force before becoming Canada's Ambassador for Disarmament.

CHAPTER 5

PEACEKEEPING
AND THE MONSTER
OF IMPERIALISM

Whoever battles with monsters had better see that it does not turn him into a monster. And if you gaze long into an abyss, the abyss will gaze back at you.

– Friedrich Nietzsche, 1886

AT AGE FIFTY-FOUR, settling into life in Canada's sleepy capital after the trauma of fighting in his second European war, Tommy Burns evidently found the job of running the burgeoning Department of Veterans' Affairs a bit anti-climactic. His restless energy, combined with politics that were heretical for a former brass hat, led to his involvement as a central player in an event that would prove crucial in shaping Canada's postwar attitudes to matters military. General Burns became Canada's first high-profile United Nations peacekeeper. It was a shift brought on by what he had seen during the Second World War.

As Burns later explained it, he had long been sustained by the soldier's conventional philosophy that war—however regrettable—is also inevitable. Moreover, despite his sometimes curious apostasies in the pages of *American Mercury*, he still believed that "peoples who refused to contemplate the possibility of war, and, indeed, to prepare for it, would be likely pushed off the world's stage by those who still thought of war as a means of settling differences not otherwise reconcilable."[1]

Then came Hiroshima and Nagasaki; and, Burns added, the desolation that he had seen being spread about by the "conventional" high-explosive bomb. "I had seen the destruction of countless years of human effort which had been wreaked by the airmen in their blitzes, in London, in many of the smaller cities in Italy, and above all in the Ruhr." He was now convinced—in the company of many others—that no dispute "between the so-called civilized nations" was worth the risk of an "atom war."[2]

Burns had been reflecting on the nature of war for a decade when he met with External Affairs Minister Lester Pearson in 1954. The recently appointed UN secretary general Dag Hammarskjöld had contacted the Canadian government with a request: he wanted an officer who had been a wartime commander to serve as chief of staff of the United Nations Truce Supervision Organization (UNTSO). The UN body, founded in 1948, had the task of monitoring the 1949 armistice between Israel and its Arab neighbours. Pearson figured that Burns would fit the bill.

Burns jumped at the opportunity. The Vimy veteran was a staunch supporter of the United Nations. Immediately after returning from the Second World War he had joined the United Nations Association (UNA)—formed to promote a culture of peace in Canada—and was quickly "shanghaied into the hierarchy of the organization." An alternate member of Canada's General Assembly delegation, Burns became national president of the UNA in Canada. He regarded the United Nations pragmatically, as an imperfect organization at a time when "war was something to be avoided at almost any cost." War prevention was central to the UN Charter, and for Burns, "Everyone who believed in that ideal . . . had a duty to do what he could to make this aspiration into a reality." His years at the United Nations would broaden his horizons. "I learned something about the attitude of Asian, Middle Eastern and South American peoples towards the monster of the age, Imperialism."[3]

When Burns headed off for the Middle East in the summer of 1954, imperial power was waxing and waning. Britain and France watched as a string of setbacks signalled the gradual evaporation of their colonial empires and the rise of a power that was extending its imperial reach beyond its Latin American backyard. That June the U.S. State Department and CIA had orchestrated a coup that overthrew the elected government of Jacobo Arbenz in Guatemala and installed a local colonel whose policies would be less offensive to the United Fruit Company. The Arbenz government attempted to take the matter to the United Nations, calling for a Security Council investigation of the U.S.-sponsored invasion. Britain and France, the old imperial powers, seemed inclined to support the request. An indignant President Dwight D. Eisenhower complained that his country had all along been "too damned nice" to its European allies when it came to their overseas affairs. Eisenhower instructed his ambassador to the United Nations, Henry Cabot Lodge, to issue a warning: "If Great Britain and France felt that they must take an independent line backing the present government in Guatemala, we would be free to take an equally independent line concerning such matters as Egypt and North Africa." The Europeans dutifully abstained from taking a stand on the matter.[4]

Eisenhower was uttering his threats against a background of what might delicately be called "unrest" in the colonies. A year earlier the CIA had seen fit to intervene in Iran, a traditionally British sphere of oil-rich influence. The problem in Iran, as seen through American eyes, was that London had failed to dispatch the elected nationalist government of Mohammad Mossadegh, who was threatening to take control of a resource rather more strategic than bananas. The Americans finessed the 1953 overthrow of Mossadegh under the conventional pretext that communists were threatening to take over.

The Eisenhower administration was more equivocal when, just as plans for its Guatemalan coup were taking shape, one of the most important events of the era's anti-colonial struggle unfolded on the Vietnam-Laos border at Dien Bien Phu. Although U.S. pilots conducted napalm attacks against the Vietnamese forces besieging the French garrison, Washington rejected desperate French requests to implement "Operation Vulture," a plan approved by the chair of the U.S. Joint Chiefs of Staff that included the option of dropping three nuclear bombs on the Vietnamese.[5] The Viet Minh (in this case they really *were* communists) defeated the French, putting an effective end to France's Asian empire.

Although few nationalist anti-colonial struggles prompted UN peacekeeping action, independence movements in the Third World were gaining momentum. The British used air strikes and attacks by twenty thousand troops against Kenya's Kikuyu Mau Mau insurgents starting in 1952. Once the rebels had been overwhelmed, the British herded the Kikuyu people into concentration camps in a campaign described by historian Caroline Elkins as "domestic terror." The Mau Mau, demanding "land and freedom," had been armed largely with homemade weapons. Unlike the Vietnamese guerrillas, the African peasants lacked outside support. "During the Mau Mau war," Elkins points out, "British forces wielded their authority with a savagery that betrayed a perverse colonial logic: only by detaining nearly the entire Kikuyu nation of 1.5 million people and physically and psychologically atomizing its men, women, and children could colonial authority be restored and the civilizing mission reinstated." Along with widespread torture and summary execution, the British used rape as a deliberate tactic. They destroyed most of the records of their crimes, staging massive bonfires on the eve of their 1963 withdrawal from Kenya.[6]

In North Africa the French were conducting a campaign against Algerian nationalists even more brutal than the British terror in Kenya. Some one million Algerians died in a war of independence that began in 1954 and ended eight years later in independence for their country and a crisis that shook French society to its core.[7] The British were having troubles of their own in the Mediterranean hot spots that Eisenhower had warned them about, and particularly on the island of Cyprus, a long-time British colony that was being torn apart in an increasingly militant and violent conflict pitting Greek, Turkish, and British forces against each other. But the British headaches over Cyprus soon paled in comparison to big problems in the most important country in the Middle East.[8]

Egypt, nominally ruled by the decadent King Farouk until 1952, was in good measure run by the British, with Whitehall's ambassador in Cairo rivalling Farouk in terms of effective power. British troops occupied a large swath of territory along the west bank of the vital Suez Canal, placing the area beyond Egyptian control. Until the end of the Second World War the British also maintained bases at Cairo and Alexandria. Egyptians have long historical memories. They launched the remarkable revolution that dispatched the regime of Hosni Mubarak on January 25, 2011—Egypt's Police Day holiday. It was on that day in 1952 that British forces demanded that the police in Ismailia, a town midway down the Suez Canal, abandon their posts and surrender their weapons. The British massacred forty-one policemen that day, and within a month a revolt by a military clique who called themselves the "Free Officers" had ousted Farouk, catching the British by surprise—although the U.S. Embassy was aware of the plot because a number of Free Officers had trained in the United States. The military men, including Col. Gamal Abdel Nasser and Anwar Sadat, were convinced that corruption had led to Egypt's defeat in the 1948 war against Israel. By 1954 Nasser was president and, at the start of an anti-colonial push that rivalled the recent Vietnamese victory over the French, had forced the British to pull their forces from the Canal Zone.

All of which made the Israelis nervous. The new Zionist state was, along with the newly installed Shah of Iran and the Saudi royals, an increasingly important U.S. client in the region. In the face of the violent conflict between Israeli settlers and local Arabs the British had cut and run from their original League of Nations mandate to administer Palestine. At the end of the first Arab-Israeli war (known to proud Israelis as their victorious independence struggle, and to embittered indigenous Arabs as the *Nakba*, or catastrophe), the settlers had their own state and the Palestinians a six-decade (and counting) refugee crisis. The United Nations, having watched as its 1948 mediator was murdered by Zionist militants—terrorists to some, freedom fighters to others—was left to try to superintend Britain's colonial legacy, offering aid to angry Palestinian refugees and monitoring the uneasy ceasefire.

Tommy Burns may have known something of what he was getting into when he took up Pearson's offer of the job as chief of staff of the UN Truce Supervision Organization. The Canadian diplomat had backed the partition of Palestinian lands and the birth of the state of Israel. Now the United Nations was trying to prevent the conflict from turning into a major Cold War confrontation, or, indeed, from turning cracks in the new NATO alliance into a gaping split. It all came to a head in 1956 in what became known as the "Suez Crisis," or, simply, "Suez."

If Suez was indeed a defining moment for Canada-as-peacekeeper and a high point for Canadian foreign policy, it was, to say the least, controversial at the time. It would remain so as Canadians squabbled over peacekeeping and its legacy. Those who view the 1956 crisis through a Cold War lens see Canada acting as geopolitical realist, doing the right thing by calming NATO's turbulent waters. Idealists see it as the start of a long and honourable tradition of peacekeeping by a middle power uniquely suited to the task. But how did an "unknown, faceless, forgotten warrior" like Burns view it?[9] For five crucial years after 1954 Burns was an eyewitness to events from Jerusalem to Gaza to Suez, negotiating with Nasser, David Ben-Gurion, Golda Meir, and Moshe Dayan while keeping Dag Hammarskjöld up to date. He was the main organizer and first leader of the United Nations Emergency Force (UNEF), regarded as the pioneer UN peacekeeping mission.

For Burns the Suez crisis was a conflict between Egyptian nationalism and imperial control of the canal. But the Canadian general also realized that Suez and the broader regional conflict was a clash between imperialism and another potent force: "In the Palestinian drama, which is now a tragedy for its former Arab inhabitants, and may yet become a greater tragedy for the present Jewish inhabitants, where does the blame lie? Is there a villain to be condemned? Is there a crime to be expiated? In this drama the conflict is of nationalisms, Zionist and Arab."[10]

After the 1948 war and the creation of the Israeli state, a volatile truce settled over the borderlands of a region deemed holy by three Abrahamic faiths. The five states involved (Lebanon, Jordan, Israel, Egypt, Syria) had more in common than the belief of many of their citizens in a single creator. By the time Burns arrived in 1954 all of them had recently emerged as independent states after decades of domination by a succession of Ottoman, French, and British rulers. Added to the mix were the stateless people, the exiled inhabitants of the lands recently occupied by Israeli settlers who had waged the sort of campaign that, a generation later, would be termed ethnic cleansing.[11] It was a recipe for disaster, and it was up to the United Nations and, after 1953, its Secretary General Hammarskjöld, to try to keep the peace. Upon their arrival the peacekeepers found themselves arranging prisoner exchanges, playing quasi-judicial roles among short-tempered men, and negotiating the return of lost or stolen goats.[12]

After taking command of the Truce Supervision Organization Burns quickly twigged to something that would become an article of faith in the peacekeeping enterprise: when UN Blue Helmets find themselves on former battlefields that are on the verge of once again erupting into violence, there is often little peace to keep. Instead of tanks and machine guns, the tools of Burns's new trade were maps, binoculars, radios, jeeps, light side arms, and the power of personality and persuasion.

People on both sides of the issue were equally convinced that they had been wronged, and equally determined to right those wrongs. "The Israelis," Burns observed, "were particularly vociferous about their sovereignty, which occasionally reminded one of men who are always protesting their virility." The Israeli leaders had cut their teeth fighting the British and had not gotten rid of His Majesty's forces only to find themselves with "another parcel of foreigners" to deal with in the form of the "rather exiguous authority of the United Nations." The Arabs, it seemed, had more or less the same attitudes, having just escaped foreign domination. Moreover, since the UN observers were pretty well all Westerners, the Arabs were quick to resent infringements on their recently acquired independence. They suspected that Burns and his colleagues "sympathized with the Jews rather than the Arabs, as the Jews were more western in their outlook, and Israeli propaganda was so influential in most Western Countries." Burns also noticed that Israel was acquiring a militarist hue—as "a society whose young elements have passed their most formative years in an atmosphere in which the military virtues and especially aggressiveness are given the highest values, and where the Arab is always the enemy, to be made to submit to Israel's demands by ruthless force." It was a society "less inclined to the solving by negotiations of external problems."[13]

Burns negotiated with Israel's top leaders for five years. He believed that General Moshe Dayan and the rest of the Israeli leadership had a strategy that recalled the smack of firm colonial administration. They reasoned that once the Arabs realized their helplessness in the face of massive Israeli retaliation, they would come to their senses and make peace. The Canadian had seen numerous Israeli reprisals for real or imagined infiltration and attacks. But rather than forcing the Arabs to sue for peace, the Israeli policy produced the opposite effect—more resistance. Burns believed that the Israeli policy "gravely miscalculated" if it really was intended to force a lasting and meaningful peace with neighbouring nations, not to mention the Palestinians.

In February 1955, within months of Burns taking over command of the UN's monitors in the Middle East, Israeli paratroopers staged an attack on the Egyptian-controlled Gaza strip, administered by Egypt and filled with Palestinian refugees packed into "a vast concentration camp."[14] The first night raid killed fourteen Egyptian or Palestinian soldiers and two civilians. Another Israeli force prepared an ambush nearby, killing another twenty-two Arab soldiers. That night eight Israeli troops died in the most serious clash since the truce had been signed just over six years previously. The Israelis called the attack "Operation Black Arrow," reflecting the military compulsion to dream up the adventurous names that, in some minds at least, add further allure to war's high drama.

The Gaza attack was, Burns noted, a minor episode compared to what he had seen in the Second World War, "with the wiping out of cities and the decimation of their population," but it had, he thought, a decisive effect on Israeli-Egyptian relations. The raid was planned by Israeli hard-liners Ben-Gurion and Dayan in reprisal for Nasser's execution of two Israeli saboteurs who had been part of a scheme to bomb British and U.S. facilities in Cairo, the aim being to escalate tension between Cairo and the West. Israeli historian Benny Morris concludes that the Gaza raid was a catalyst for violence along the Egyptian-Israel border and a "turning point . . . in the history of the Middle East." The attack shook the Nasser regime's prestige. When Nasser went to Gaza for the first time since taking power, the visit drastically altered his views on the likelihood of peace with Israel.[15]

The day after the raid Egyptian troops killed four Palestinian refugees in Gaza during protest riots. Within a month raiders from Gaza launched a grenade attack on a wedding inside Israel, killing one and wounding twenty-two.[16] It was against this background of tit-for-tat retaliation in an unstable region that Burns and his fellow UN commanders set out to establish fixed observation posts in hope of determining who was fighting whom and reducing the number of such incidents. The UN observers could do little to stem the tide. As violence escalated and the border situation deteriorated, the great powers were increasingly implicated, cementing alliances and arming their allies.

The flood of weapons into the region intensified after the Gaza raid. The U.S. government terminated aid for the construction of the grand Aswan Dam megaproject, which was intended to furnish Egypt with electricity and irrigation. Nasser retaliated by nationalizing the operations of the Suez Canal Company, a Paris-based firm that ran the vital waterway. The move drove the British leadership into apoplexy, with Prime Minister Anthony Eden anxious to seem as hawkish as the aging Winston Churchill, whom he had recently replaced. Members of a right-wing backbench faction, encouraged by Churchill, were braying that Nasser needed to be brought to heel. The prime minister denounced Nasser as "Hitler on the Nile"—just as, over forty years later, the West's former ally Saddam Hussein would morph into "the Hitler of the Tigris." Chancellor of the Exchequer Harold Macmillan, not to be outdone, called the Egyptian an "Asiatic Mussolini."[17]

The bellicose rumblings were of grave concern in Ottawa. U.S. secretary of state John Foster Dulles, impatient with multilateralism, declared that NATO "had reached a critical moment in its life," while Pearson was still insisting that it had to be more than a military pact. Pearson was stunned to think that the British might unilaterally attack Egypt. "Surely," he told Ottawa's man in London, "the UK government will not do anything which would commit them to strong action against Egypt until they know that the U.S. will back them." Pearson was emphatic that the United Nations was the proper forum for addressing such a dispute. Although in the House of Commons he "disingenuously" (according to his sympathetic biographer) denied any split with the mother country, he told his cabinet colleagues that any attack by the British and French would damage those allies and that this "was clearly not in Canada's interest." What was in Canada's interest was to play both ends against the middle. As the crisis came to a head, Ottawa, at Dulles's quiet urging, agreed to sell twenty-four F-86 jet fighters to Israel. It also signed a deal to sell wheat to Egypt.[18]

The Israelis, French, and British made an agreement under which the Israelis would attack Egypt and the Europeans would intervene in an ostensible police action to separate the combatants and protect the Suez Canal. The ultimate goal was the destruction of Nasser and his regime. On Oct. 27, 1956, the Israelis mobilized their forces. The timing was, to say the least, awkward. Soviet tanks had just entered Budapest, and an enraged Eisenhower, facing an election the following week, sent an urgent protest note to Ben-Gurion. It was too late. The Israelis attacked and the French and British quickly followed suit.

Burns met with Foreign Minister Golda Meir to no effect and subsequently concerned himself with evacuating the dependants of UN personnel.[19]

The Israeli Defence Force crushed Egypt's conscript army. Although eventually forced to withdraw from Gaza and the Sinai, the Israelis could claim a clear victory of arms and a new access to the Straits of Tiran, their only Indian Ocean seaport. The Suez Crisis also marked a massive setback for British and French foreign policy and an ignominious end to Eden's leadership. Hammarskjöld was rumoured to be threatening to resign, and, for their part, the Soviets were threatening to attack Britain, France, and Israel. Yet Nikita Khrushchev's government sided with the United States just as its Hungarian satellite declared its intention to withdraw from the Warsaw Pact and sought UN protection. In the end, the U.S.S.R. invaded Hungary and brutalized the upstart rebels while gaining inroads in the Middle East, where its arms, money, and advisers gave it new influence.

The legacy of Suez is frequently framed in terms of how great men performed and how the crisis shaped relations between great powers. The effect on Arab and particularly Palestinian nationalism was profound. The Israeli historian Morris points out that his country's 1956 takeover of Gaza and the Sinai was "characterized by a great deal of unwarranted killing." The Israeli army killed some five hundred Palestinian civilians during and after the Gaza takeover, with suspected *fedayeen* (irregular resistance fighters) being summarily executed. On October 21, Israeli border police massacred forty-nine Israeli Arabs who had unwittingly broken a curfew.[20] The incidents only stoked the Palestinian bitterness that Burns noticed when he began his posting in the region. While the governments involved were rapidly transforming themselves into garrison states extolling martial virtues, the Palestinians had no state of their own. They were inexorably transformed into a people in desperate search of redress, by any means necessary.

The U.S. government wanted the waters calmed, and Pearson was the man for the job. In addition to the possibility of providing useful service to the United States, the Canadian government and especially its most famous diplomat wanted to restore good relations within the Anglosphere, particularly between the United States and Britain. It also sought to avoid splits in the Commonwealth (Australia and New

Zealand were zealous British backers, while India was decidedly not), keep NATO united, and promote the United Nations as an effective instrument of peace.

At the UN General Assembly a U.S. motion calling for an end to the fighting in Egypt and an immediate Israeli withdrawal was backed by the Soviet bloc, most of Western Europe, and the entire non-aligned world. It was opposed only by the invaders (Israel, France, and Britain) and their Australian and New Zealand loyalists. Canada, with Pearson on the scene, pointedly abstained, appearing to be neutral. In the wake of the passage of the U.S. motion, Pearson rose in the Assembly to propose a "United Nations force large enough to keep these borders at peace while a political settlement is being worked out."[21] Hammarskjöld was sceptical, but with the French and British bombing Egypt, the Israelis pushing further towards Suez, and Hungary pulling out of the Warsaw Pact, anything that promised stability was worth considering. Even before British and French forces landed in Egypt in early November, Pearson introduced a motion to the General Assembly to create a UN peacekeeping force. The motion was drafted by the U.S. ambassador, Henry Cabot Lodge.[22] "Pearson agreed to sponsor the U.S. draft resolution," notes the British diplomatic historian Michael G. Fry in his overview of Canada and Suez. "Thus a Canadian concept and draft proposal had produced an American draft resolution which became the 'Canadian' resolution (A/3276) that Pearson skillfully introduced. . . . The Assembly (subsequently) endorsed on November 4 the resolution (A/3290) sponsored by Canada, Colombia and Norway creating a UN command structure for the proposed force under General Burns."[23] Prime Minister Louis St. Laurent vowed that Canada would stand tall in the peacekeeping effort.

What eventually became the United Nations Emergency Force in the Sinai saved the British and the French from their own failure to realize that the sun was setting on their geriatric empires. Canada's two mother countries were running amok in league with the new and aggressive nationalism that had just "reimagined an ancient religious community as a nation."[24] Pearson knew this—and Canadian Conservatives of the day, still sentimentally attached to Great Britain, regarded "Mike" with disdain. Progressive Conservative member of Parliament Howard Green, who would within three years succeed Pearson as External Affairs minister, derided the man who had deftly worked the halls at the United Nations in 1956 as a "choreboy" for the Americans. Long after Suez, historian Donald Creighton—of a nationalist bent and habitually critical of the Liberal Party—wrote that Pearson was "invariably reluctant" to go along with any international undertaking not supported by Washington. "Pearson's alarm at the possible British use of force" in Suez, Creighton wrote, "was notably strengthened when he learned that any such move would be regarded with stern disapproval in Washington."[25] The Diefenbaker Conservatives harped on the alleged betrayal of the mother country when they defeated the tired Liberal government in 1957. St. Laurent had lost his temper in the Commons and sarcastically labelled Britain and France "the supermen of Europe" who would no longer have their way with the world. Pearson, not to be outdone by Green, stoutly countered that Canada was no "colonial chore-boy."[26]

In 1956 Pearson knew that the imperial bus had an aggressive new driver, but would never have said so publicly. The official story that won him the Nobel Peace Prize was different. For Pearson, John English writes, "the romance of empire had given away to a vision of a system of international rules and organizations that would restrain the bandits and bullies of the world more effectively than British gunboats ever had."[27] The biographer does not pause to reflect that the British imperialism upon which Pearson drew so liberally was itself a form of bullying—of the kind, say, of rebels tied to cannons and blown apart during the Indian Mutiny.

The day after the passage of Pearson's UN motion, Burns received a message from Hammarskjöld. The Swedish diplomat needed Burns's ideas on how to get things going. At the dawn of the UN peacekeeping enterprise the Canadian war veteran responded in typical military fashion. In the face of a war featuring tanks and air power, any peacekeeping force would need some muscle of its own, "capable of carrying out operations of war." Burns wanted armour and combat aircraft. "I stated that I thought the force should be so strong that it would be in no danger of being thrust aside, pushed out, or ignored, as the UN Military Observers had been in Palestine—mainly by the Israelis, but on occasion by the other parties."[28]

It was not to be. The United Nations Emergency Force—Burns had come up with the name for the force—lasted eleven years. Burns could not hide his disappointment when he learned that his force was to be "something much less potent" than he had hoped for. The recurring lament of military men trained for war and sent to keep the peace—particularly "when there is no peace to keep"—is that they have neither the equipment nor the authority to get tough with the warring parties. But peacekeeping, like war, is refracted through the prism of politics. In 1956 the aggressors had their collective arms twisted by the dominant superpower. Britain and France fell into line, as did the harder-to-convince Israelis.

The peacekeeping mission had offers of troops from Scandinavia and Colombia as well as Canada, but no one consulted Nasser. As it turned out, the Egyptian president had serious reservations about Canadian troops. The reluctance to have Canadian soldiers patrolling the canal zone sprang from nationalist resentment—a history of occupation by British forces. Egypt had no use for soldiers of the Queen and their royalist trappings. Burns got "a considerable shock" when he learned that it might not be acceptable for Canadian troops dressed like British soldiers to be on the front lines for UNEF. He protested to Nasser that Canada's line diverged from the British position and that of the other white dominions. He also speculated that if Canadian soldiers were excluded from UNEF he would have to withdraw.[29] Both Pearson and Burns later recalled being shocked when they learned that the Canadian military intended to dispatch elements of the unfortunately named Queen's Own Rifles, a force "wearing essentially a British uniform with UN badges" that would be moving "into territory that had been Egyptian and from which the British army was about to be thrown out (or retired as gracefully as possible)." Pearson admitted that the uniforms were a problem, but told Egypt that Burns could not command a UNEF that excluded Canadian troops, especially given that Canada had proposed the international force in the first place.[30] Nasser's position on the use of Canadian troops turned out to be something of a blessing in disguise. In the hastily cobbled-together initial UNEF effort, the Canadian contingent took up crucial transportation and communications functions, providing administrative and support expertise that was crucial to UNEF's successful launch.

Although the Canadian military had already been involved in truce supervision along the India-Pakistan border and in Indochina, UNEF marked the beginning of an era termed "classical peacekeeping"—the positioning of UN forces between two warring parties that have agreed to a ceasefire—or, hence, "interpositional" peacekeeping. It has been the image of lightly armed Canadians doing this dull but often dangerous work that, in the decades that followed, came to have such wide appeal in Canada. Just over six thousand military personnel from various countries served, with 106 losing their lives, in the United Nations' first extensive Blue-Helmet peacekeeping operation. Indeed, the headgear would come to symbolize UN peacekeepers. Hammarskjöld told Burns, the first commander of a major UN peacekeeping force, that he wanted a recognizable uniform for the new force. UNEF dealt with the problem of quickly coming up with distinctive headgear by taking plastic liners from U.S. steel helmets and painting them UN blue. Pearson was aware of the ambivalence of Canada's position when Nasser nixed the Queen's Own Rifles. "What we needed was the First East Kootenay Anti-Imperialistic Rifles!" The whole affair helped spur the push for Canada to at last adopt a national symbol that did away with any trace of the British connection, and after Suez Pearson began to openly suggest that his country needed a distinctive flag.[31]

Burns and the officers who followed in his footsteps from the Congo to Bosnia had trouble getting used to the politics of UN peacekeeping. Soldiering under the command of a world body comprising every nation and guided by veto-wielding great powers was—and remains—a tricky business. The United Nations, the sum of its complex and conflicted parts, would grow into a byzantine, often inefficient and sometimes corrupt bureaucracy, and peacekeeping immediately came to mean different things to different countries with different international agendas. Any peacekeeping mission was subject to conflicting political goals, including the primary goal of trying, in highly volatile environments, to keep the peace between people who often despise each other. For military people trained in the ways of war, accustomed to a clear chain of command, the project is invariably complex. Peacekeepers try to maintain neutrality, using force only in self-defence—a policy that runs contrary to military training and culture. The experience can be especially fraught when soldiers are outgunned by better-armed fighters who kidnap peacekeepers, accusing them of spying for the other side. Brian Urquhart, an adviser to Hammarskjöld in 1956, explained that peacekeepers had no enemies, simply "a series of difficult and sometimes homicidal clients."[32]

Burns soon found that "someone in the position of a diplomatic agent cannot persuade those he is negotiating with to act in accordance with their obligations under agreements they have made, or decisions given by a body in authority." The question became, "What can be done?" Parties breaching their obligations might be persuaded to honour them "either by promise of some benefit if they do, or by the threat of the imposition of some penalty if they do not." But Burns, as commander, and the United Nations, as the key authority, did not have the necessary "carrot or stick." The great powers had both: they could provide, as carrots, "the provision of arms, economic assistance, and various subsidies," or, as sticks, they could withhold assistance, or even set in place economic sanctions. "In the last resort," Burns wrote, "they would be able legitimately to use military force under the UN Charter, if the Security Council so decided."[33]

If Burns had not figured out the *realpolitik* of peacekeeping in his two years of running the UN's military observer teams along bitterly contested borders, the experience of commanding the much bigger UNEF effort brought the frustrating limits of the initiative into clear focus. He described as "flattering" the notion that he could induce the belligerents to adhere to the armistice agreements. The actual situation was sobering. His pragmatic analysis of the situation faced by UNEF after 1956 would ring true in the decades to come, and especially as peacekeepers headed off to the brutalities of Bosnia or Rwanda.

A Cold War affair: that is how Western international relations academics and military historians tend to see the conflict long known to the Vietnamese as the American War. Similarly, Canada's role in supervising a truce that never was—all the while working as an accomplice to U.S. crimes—is conventionally regarded as normal. Although the project was not an official UN peacekeeping mission, Canadian historical surveys of the peacekeeping enterprise most often list it as one of the country's first forays into the field. Few events illustrate more plainly the moral and political contradictions of Canada's relationship with the United States: throughout the Vietnam War, Canada proclaimed peace and abetted war.

After the French colonial forces had fled in the wake of their defeat at Dien Bien Phu, Vietnam was divided along the 17th parallel as a result of the 1954 Geneva Conference Agreement on the Cessation of Hostilities. The Viet Minh controlled the North, with the South held by the corrupt regime of Ngo Dinh Diem.[34] With a ceasefire arranged but no treaty set in place, a three-member International Commission for Supervision and Control (ICC) was established in 1954 to supervise the peace process. Canada, Poland, and India made up the Commission. Canada was a staunch U.S. ally; the Polish delegation, like Ho Chi Minh's Viet Minh government, was communist; India was to be the neutral ICC member.

Soon after appointing Burns to head the UNTSO in the Middle East, Pearson chose Sherwood Lett, a former soldier turned corporation lawyer, as Canada's first representative on the ICC. Canada's instructions to Lett as he headed to Vietnam and the ICC were clear. He was to promote what would eventually become the U.S.-inspired anti-communist alliance in Southeast Asia while trying not to offend the "neutralist" ICC member, India. Historian James Eayrs later described the strategy as an effort to "buy valuable time" for the Diem regime as the U.S. client prepared for the looming fight with Ho Chi Minh's Democratic Republic of Vietnam.[35]

Pearson was clearly hampered by Cold War blinkers in his understanding of Vietnam. His was also the view from the affluent North. A telling moment in this regard, as Pearson himself admitted, came during a 1950 trip to South Asia to launch the Colombo Plan, a foreign-aid effort inspired by anti-communist geopolitics. Pearson's reflections on his time in India show that "the politically conscious part of the population" in newly independent Asia was "extremely sensitive" about "any form of imperial or outside control." This was particularly true of Indian leader Jawaharlal Nehru, a champion of Third World solidarity and non-alignment. Pearson learned that Nehru "loathed and abhorred colonialism in any form in any part of the world. There were a great many in Asia who would, in fact, have preferred communism to colonialism, if they had to make a choice."[36]

Ottawa instructed Lett not to be surprised by his dealings with his Indian counterparts on the ICC. Their opposition to colonialism, could, he was told, be "irrational." For his part, Pearson was naive when it came to the U.S. war in Vietnam. As early as 1948, soon after being appointed minister of External Affairs, he opined, "It is inconceivable to Canadians, it is inconceivable to me that the United States would ever initiate an aggressive war. It is also inconceivable that Canada would ever take part in such a war."[37] Significantly, the titles of two of the most important analyses of Canada's role in the war in Vietnam contain the word "complicity," with all its connotations of being an accomplice in a criminal act. Those Canadians who took to the streets in the 1960s and 1970s to protest their country's role as, according to Eayrs, a "chore boy to Moloch," would chant *Hey, Hey, LBJ! How many kids did you kill today?* In Quebec the cry was *John-son, ass-ass-in! Pear-son, complice!*[38]

As popular opposition to the war mounted, a young Professor J.L. Granatstein was taking a different position. Writing of the charges that Canada was using its position on the ICC to spy on North Vietnam (then being subjected to an intensive aerial bombing campaign), he wrote:

> That such charges could be made illustrates the increasing emotional involvement felt by many Canadians—and many Americans, too—about the course the Viet Nam war is taking. In many ways the war has become *the* moral issue of the 1960s. There have been reports, however, that most members of the Department of External Affairs concerned with Viet Nam agree that the American position is justified.

Granatstein quoted Canadian diplomat John Holmes, who explained that the issue of U.S. escalation was "complex" but that the administration of President Lyndon Johnson should not be charged with unilaterally violating the Geneva accords. Granatstein concluded, "Stated so well, this position is impossible to refute."[39]

Such deference to the official story of the day would not stand the test of historical scrutiny. Canadians associated with the ICC gathered intelligence and submitted it to an interdepartmental Joint Intelligence Bureau of three military representatives and an External Affairs official. The Bureau selected the material that should be furnished to Washington and passed it to External for final permission. Eayrs could find "no evidence that [permission] was ever withheld." External Affairs sent the material to Canada's Embassy in Washington, which was "told to turn it over to the U.S. State Department or Central Intelligence Agency."[40] Canada, led by Pearson and his External Affairs minister Paul Martin, clearly played a duplicitous role, denying that Canada's ICC representatives acted as spies for the United States. In his foreword to *Quiet Complicity: Canadian Involvement in the Vietnam War*, military affairs analyst Gwynne Dyer described the evidence marshalled by Montreal activist and scholar Victor Levant as demonstrating "with overwhelming proof and meticulous detail" a crucial point:

> From the start in 1954 right down to the end, Canada's supposedly impartial representatives on the International Control Commission and its successor used their position to further the West's, and specifically Washington's, aims in Vietnam. We ran errands for the Americans; we lied for them; we spied for them—not once or twice but continuously for almost two decades. . . . We were not pushed; we jumped of our own accord.[41]

Canadian diplomat Blair Seaborn visited North Vietnam on several occasions as an ICC observer. Before the first aerial bombing of the North, Ottawa and Washington regarded Seaborn as both a go-between for the Johnson administration's threats and its eyes and ears in Hanoi—a contribution that came to light with the publication of the Pentagon Papers in the early 1970s. The first Canadian to comprehensively chronicle what he described as Canada's "two decades of frustrated peacekeeping, misguided diplomacy and uneasy complicity in an especially nasty and unnecessary war" was Charles Taylor, son of Toronto business magnate E.P. Taylor.[42] His book *Snow Job: Canada, The United States and Vietnam* made extensive use of the Pentagon Papers and his on-the-ground experience as a *Globe and Mail* reporter in Asia in the 1960s. Taylor noticed that Canadian officials failed to understand that "the Vietnamese communists were not puppets imposed by an outside power but veteran revolutionaries who had seized the leadership of a genuine war of national liberation." In the key

years when the war was about to heat up, External had no senior officials "who could have interpreted the turmoil in terms of Indochinese
history, rather than the sterile patterns of Cold War demonology."[43] In
an April 1964 meeting in a New York hotel room, Taylor writes, President Johnson told Prime Minister Pearson of plans to bomb North
Vietnam. The Canadian journalist assumed that Pearson approved
of the plans and the use of Seaborn as a diplomatic interlocutor on vis-
its to Hanoi. One Pentagon Papers document included the report of
a 1964 State Department cable to Ambassador Lodge. Canada was
being asked to warn Ho Chi Minh's government about U.S. carrots
and sticks. Pearson expressed a "willingness to lend Canadian good
offices" to the Seaborn mission—though he was somewhat concerned
about the nature of the "stick" being brandished: "He stipulated that
he would have great reservations about the use of nuclear weapons, but
indicated that the punitive striking of discriminate targets by careful
iron bomb attacks would be 'a different thing.'"[44]

Pearson's support of what became Operation Rolling Thunder,
couched in delicate hedging about the need for careful bombing, was,
Taylor concluded, a classically Pearsonian approach. Avoiding "antag-
onism, confrontation and especially impasse . . . was the key to [Pear-
son's] diplomatic style."[45] Defenders of the Pearsonian legacy invariably
cite his Temple University speech of April 2, 1965, in which Pearson
broke with diplomatic convention and criticized the host government
for its bombing campaign in Vietnam. They recall conversations in
which Pearson called the bombing of the North "obscene." What they
overlook, notes political scientist Mark Neufeld, is the rest of the
speech. Pearson's overwhelming focus was to reiterate and reaffirm
"the Cold War tenets and precepts that underlay US intervention in
Vietnam." His supporters like to remember Johnson's reported physical assault on the Canadian prime minister and the U.S. president's
shout: "You don't come here and piss on my rug!" They tend to ignore
the revealing and somewhat obsequious note that Pearson wrote after
the assault: Pearson thanked Johnson for his hospitality and declared
that he would be understanding if, after the North Vietnamese did not
respond to a bombing halt, the Americans simply resumed it, whether
it was "obscene" or not.[46]

With every escalation of the war Canada's peace movement gained
momentum. In his book Levant reflected on the scale of popular

revulsion with the war and Canada's involvement in it: "Hundreds of thousands of Canadians marched, sat in, attended teach-ins, wrote their Members of Parliament, signed petitions, shouted obscenities, sang, spraypainted walls, walked for peace, worked on draft resister support committees, harboured U.S. Army deserters in their homes, prayed, fasted, and wept over the senseless slaughter of the Vietnamese civilian population."[47]

As early as 1966 Canadians got a sense of the U.S. war when the CBC aired Beryl Fox's film *The Mills of the Gods: Vietnam*. It was unfiltered, early television war coverage by unembedded reporters. Fox's camera recorded footage from the rear cockpit of a Skyraider as it attacked a village in densely settled Mekong Delta farm country. The aircraft was deploying what Canada's prime minister had described as "iron bombs," much to the excitement of the pilot: "Oh! [excitedly] Look at it burn! Look at it burn! . . . Ok! Good hits! Good hits! Real fun! Real fun! That was an outstanding target all right. We bombed first of all and we could see the people running everywhere . . . It's very seldom that we see Victor Charlie run like that. . . . we know we're going to really hose them down."[48]

By 1967 Canadian opinion had shifted dramatically against the war, and Pearson was backpedalling. The prime minister, customarily adept at deploying public blandishments, discussed the matter in terms usually described in diplomatic circles as "frank." In an interview with *Maclean's* he admitted to the *realpolitik* that governed Canada's position on the war in a way that foreshadowed Canadian involvement in Afghanistan. "Any open breach with the United States over Vietnam," he explained, would result in "a more critical examination by Washington of certain special aspects of our relationships. . . . It's not a very comforting thought but, in the economic sphere, when you have 60 percent or more of your trade with one country, you are in a position of considerable economic dependence."[49]

Canada's peace movement and the economic nationalists of the day were making the same point. Canada, the activists argued, was up to its elbows in blood. The Defence Production Sharing Agreements with the United States (though continuing a pattern dating back to the buildup for the Second World War) had been negotiated by a Diefenbaker government generally seen as antagonistic to the United States—and certainly to the Kennedy administration. By 1972

McGill University peace researchers had identified 431 Canadian and Canadian-based firms that received contracts from the U.S. Department of Defence between 1967 and 1972.[50] The Dorothea Knitting Mills contract had, perhaps, the most acutely symbolic value, with its stitching of green berets for the U.S. Army Special Forces; but corporate Canada was represented in everything from predictable branch-plant death merchants like Colt Industries (Canada) and Litton Systems to Spar Aerospace and Bata Shoe.

The Nixon administration subsequently tried to beat an orderly retreat from Vietnam after several years of "Vietnamization"—a failed attempt to build up South Vietnam's military that would be repeated in the NATO counterinsurgency in Afghanistan forty years later. By 1972 Canada was being pressured to provide troops for the multilateral group—the International Commission of Control and Supervision (ICCS)—intended to superintend this late phase of the war. The Pentagon Papers had by this time exposed the details of Canada's role in the ICC, and the Trudeau Liberals were anxious to distance themselves from that record while still co-operating with the United States. External Affairs Minister Mitchell Sharp argued that Hanoi was open to Canadian participation on the new ICCS. "They positively want us. They rely on our objectivity." At the same time the fig leaf dropped again—the Montreal *Star* reported what it called a "somewhat disastrous" interview with Sharp. "He said that Canada had never acted as a stooge for anyone and never would again. The 'again' must rate as a classic in political slips of the tongue."[51] Lewis MacKenzie, who later became known for his role as a UN peacekeeper in the former Yugoslavia, was among Canada's ICCS personnel. The young officer described the undertaking as "a little ludicrous," maintaining, without any apparent irony, that the Polish and Hungarian officers on the ICCS were not objective. The ICCS—as a non-UN peacekeeping mission—"made the most basic mistake of employing officers from countries who had a natural and overt affiliation with one of the sides in the conflict."

Sharp's inadvertent admission and MacKenzie's disingenuous assumption reflected the ambiguity of a country whose nationalism had come to centre on a peacekeeping image wholly at variance with its subordinate position vis-à-vis the United States. The accommodation of the demands of empire was dressed up as a kind of benign objectivity. The hard realities of Canadian involvement, from arms sales to spying, were a good deal more sordid. In his final days in Saigon, MacKenzie recalled, he had to spend time removing Canadian flag decals from the mirrors of the numerous brothels where his comrades had stuck them.[52]

Roger Beauregard joined the army to see the world. The nineteen-year-old private soon saw some Korean hills, where his platoon took 175 Chinese mortar rounds in a single night. Terrified most of the time, the Saskatchewan native survived the Korean War and worked his way up through the ranks of the Canadian army. In 1961 he found himself working as a peacekeeper in the Congo. The Canadians were in charge of communications ("signals" in soldier-speak) for the United Nation's massive seventeen-nation peacekeeping operation. Lieutenant Beauregard, a francophone in a newly independent African country whose lingua franca was French, had just become a combat officer. His job was to keep the Canadian signallers out of harm's way.

Beauregard came away from his first UN operation disillusioned with the peacekeeping enterprise and holding the Most Excellent Order of the British Empire—the coveted MBE. He had also acquired an understanding of African history—"Borders here, there and everywhere," he said, speaking of how Africa was divided up by the Berlin conference of 1885.[53] The names of places he encountered there still reflected decades of Belgian rule over one of Africa's biggest and potentially richest countries: Elizabethville, Leopoldville, Albertville, Stanleyville. This had been, almost a century earlier, the Congo of King Leopold II and Canada's William Stairs.

Lt. Beauregard was stationed at Kamina, a military outpost that the Belgians refused to vacate after the Congo became independent in 1960. The base was situated in the mineral-rich province of Katanga, run as a virtual fief by Belgian mining firms. The Canadian officer soon gained an understanding of European rule in this corner of Africa. "When they ruled the Congo the Belgians had a very well organized way of keeping the Congolese in line," he said. "They had bases like Kamina with an airfield and paratroopers and communications with the major centres. If they heard of a rebellion in, say,

Kivu province, they flew paratroops in and killed all the able-bodied men. So there would be no problems in that area for another twenty years."[54]

No surprise, then, that Belgians were not popular in a country that became fertile ground for the nationalist agitation that swept across Africa in the 1950s. In the wake of the French defeat at Dien Bien Phu, a spirit of "positive neutralism" emerged from the 1955 Bandung Conference of non-aligned nations, described by Richard Wright, the African-American writer who travelled to Indonesia for the event, as "a conglomeration of the world's underdogs."[55] The one Congolese leader who did emerge with a national constituency, Patrice Lumumba, proclaimed a militant pan-Africanism. After meeting Nasser, Frantz Fanon, and Kwame Nkruma of Ghana at the All-Africa People's Conference in Ghana, Lumumba was fired by a deeply anti-colonial passion.

Lumumba had a vision of the Congo, a huge territory that grouped an almost uncountable number of ethnic groups, as a unitary, socialist state. Although he was popular—his Mouvement National Congolais won more seats than any other party in pre-independence balloting—the severely divided country seemed poised for chaos when it gained its independence as the Democratic Republic of the Congo in June 1960. Lumumba became prime minister while a rival, Joseph Kasavubu, took the position of president. The government, as one scholar sympathetic to Lumumba's radical nationalism hypothesizes, "was an unwieldy coalition of contradictory political forces. A number of key ministries were in the hands of politicians sharply opposed to his nationalist, pan-African ideas." Representatives of the mineral-rich province of Katanga were particularly at odds with the new administration. Soldiers in the former colonial army, resenting the continuing command by Belgian officers and what they saw as a denial of the fruits of independence, mutinied immediately after the formal end of Belgian rule.[56] Lumumba was deposed in September and assassinated in early 1961, murdered with the help of the CIA and a Canadian accomplice (otherwise known as a peacekeeper).

In the face of the mutiny Lumumba made a fatal error. He appointed Joseph Mobutu, a junior minister, as chief of staff of the mutinous Armée Nationale Congolaise. At the same time Belgium, international mining companies, apartheid South Africa, and an army of white mercenaries were backing the efforts of another Congolese leader, Moise Tshombe, to separate Katanga from the Congo. Belgian forces soon returned to the country, ostensibly to save white lives and stabilize the situation. The new state was in total disarray. The Canadian press overflowed with tales of cannibalism, witchcraft, and the dangers faced by white people in the former colony. A typical Canadian editorial, published in 1959 just after the Belgian authorities had massacred fifty nationalist demonstrators in Leopoldville, proclaimed, "Forces are loose in Africa that even the enlightened Belgians could not control." The Toronto *Star* added that Belgium was "an example to all other colonial powers on how to civilize a backward, savage people and make them industrious, prosperous and contented."[57]

Tshombe unilaterally declared Katangan independence on July 11, 1960. A day later Lumumba and Kasavubu appealed to the United Nations for assistance. The result was a four-year peacekeeping operation that, unlike UNEF in the Sinai, operated in conditions more akin to civil war than a formal positioning of forces between armies of states that had agreed to a ceasefire. Unlike the 1956 Suez crisis, when Canada very much wanted to send infantry and had to settle for technical specialists, the Diefenbaker government was explicit in its determination not to send combat soldiers. Nonetheless, Canada had technical expertise, French-speaking personnel, and a rapidly emerging predisposition to peacekeeping. The country was a logical candidate for participation in what became the Opération des Nations Unies au Congo (ONUC). The Congo was but one of a handful of African countries with which Canada had diplomatic relations. The Diefenbaker government was well informed about the situation, and Howard Green, the secretary of state for External Affairs, was a strong UN supporter. He was also anxious to cement Canada's links to the newly independent states swelling the UN membership. In the immediate aftermath of the mutiny and the Katangan secession, Norman Robertson, the former ambassador to London and Washington, offered Green some advice:

> Any white troops involved in the proposed law enforcement role of the United Nations would be in a most difficult situation, since it would be difficult to persuade the Congolese masses that the United Nations

force was not another form of white domination.... We should have to look very carefully at any request involving a Canadian contingent for the force and the Secretary-General should be made aware of our hesitation to become involved in this way.[58]

Robertson's sense of caution proved to be justified. On several occasions Canadian peacekeepers would be attacked by Congolese soldiers, although the reasons for the violence remained obscure. The situation was fraught with peril. Lumumba's radical nationalism had earned him the tag of "another Castro"—Congo achieved independence six months after the start of the Cuban revolution. Belgium portrayed Lumumba as a Communist, something the United States quickly picked up on, and the leader's period in office was as turbulent as it was short-lived.

Just as Bill Stairs had framed his Katanga conquest on behalf of Belgium's Leopold II as a campaign against a bloodthirsty tyrant, so too did twentieth-century Belgians proclaim Lumumba a dangerous tool of totalitarianism. They reinvaded their former colony. For this they were vigorously condemned by most of the international community—but not by Anglosphere-dominated NATO, an alliance reluctant to alienate a member with whom it shared a civilizing script. As Kevin Spooner, the leading scholar of Canada's Congo peacekeeping effort, notes, "To the Congolese the arrival of the [Belgian] paratroopers was tantamount to a reversal of decolonization." Still, Belgium was disappointed with what it regarded as Canada's tepid support throughout the crisis, arguing that the West had a "moral responsibility" in the Congo because "it was necessary to face Communist-Afro-Asian unity with Western unity." The Belgian foreign affairs minister would go on to tell Canada to "reconsider her attitude" in light of "common interests that would be best served by supporting Belgium more openly and fully."[59]

This frustration reflected Canada's attempts to be seen to be playing a middle-power role in which peacekeeping featured prominently. Official opinion in Canada was mixed. Charles Hébert, Canada's ambassador at Brussels, bought his hosts' line. He told the diplomat Escott Reid about Belgium's wonderful achievements before independence among "backward peoples" supposedly inclined to cannibalism.

Warning that self-determination would lead to chaos and tribal warfare, Hébert insisted that the change would produce a government
that would either "exploit their fellows for their own benefit or for
the benefit of some other foreign power, possibly the U.S.S.R."
Reid, serving as Canada's high commissioner to India at the time,
responded by informing Hébert that although progress might be
slow in the Congo, India had managed to achieve self-rule despite
its diverse society. He also sardonically challenged the claim that the
Congolese were incapable of meeting Western standards of justice
and responsible government, listing European luminaries who had
not quite fulfilled these exalted criteria: Franco, Hitler, Stalin, and
Mussolini. Spooner concludes that Canadian officials generally "held
the Belgians partially responsible for the Congo crisis for not having
enough faith in the Congolese to assist them fully in preparing for
independence. . . . In this sense, later views and attitudes had more in
common with Reid than Hébert."[60]

The events in the Congo in the early 1960s remain subject to
intense scrutiny, with controversy surrounding the violent deaths of
two key players. After his overthrow, Lumumba was murdered in
Katanga in January 1961 by a hit squad composed of Belgians and
their secessionist allies in Katanga. Within months Hammarskjöld
died in a mysterious plane crash in Northern Rhodesia (now Zambia)
while en route to mediate a ceasefire in Katanga. Although not as
famous as the controversies surrounding the assassinations of U.S.
president John F. Kennedy and Swedish prime minister Olaf Palme,
Hammarskjöld's death has also not been completely explained.

Kasavubu's dismissal of Lumumba in early September and
Mobutu's subsequent coup gave rise to charges that the United Nations
had taken sides in the Congo conflict. Attention focused particularly on
the machinations of Andrew Cordier of the United States. Cordier,
serving as Hammarskjöld's special representative, had ONUC occupy
the crucial Leopoldville radio station, preventing Lumumba from
speaking to the population at the same time that Kasavubu had access
to the airwaves from across the Congo River in Brazzaville, capital of
the newly independent Republic of the Congo. Hammarskjöld (who
had a testy relationship with Lumumba), Cordier, and ONUC deliberately facilitated Lumumba's overthrow. Cordier decided that a

change of leadership would be the only viable solution to the problem.[61] After an August briefing on the Congo, President Eisenhower asked in reference to Lumumba whether "we can't get rid of this guy." Some three weeks later Belgian foreign minister Pierre Wigny wrote that "responsible authorities had the duty to render Lumumba harmless." Wigny's colleague in African Affairs, an aristocrat named Count Harold d'Aspremont Lynden, signed a document stating that Belgian interests required "the final elimination of Lumumba."[62] Lumumba was placed under house arrest on October 10, protected from hostile Congolese troops by a ring of Ghanaian Blue Helmets.

With Lumumba out of power, the U.S. government quickly took steps to legitimize Kasavubu's government with a seat at the United Nations, which would grant de facto international recognition to a regime that owed its existence to the intrigues of foreign powers. Washington expected support for this measure from Ottawa. The Diefenbaker government demurred, even though it preferred the Kasavubu option, and in any event its vote was not needed to carry the day. Spooner sums up the logic of the position: "Canadian policy attempted to strike a balance: there was a need to appear neutral or detached and, at the same time, not jeopardize Western interests in the Congo."[63]

Ottawa continued to urge ONUC to refrain from supporting any faction in the Congo while maintaining the facade of neutrality in the continuing tension between the United Nations and its NATO allies. After Lumumba's death the Security Council passed an ambiguous resolution urging the United Nations to take all measures, including the use of force, to prevent civil war in the Congo and requiring all foreign mercenaries, military personnel, and advisers to leave the country.

The UN motion had serious implications for the remaining Belgian operatives in the country, and in March 1961 Belgium approached Canada with what officials described as an "embarrassing request." The former colonial power asked Canada to give it confidential information on the proceedings of the UN secretary general's Advisory Committee. The committee majority included Asian and African states that were hardly sympathetic to Belgium. Officials in the Asian and Middle Eastern Division at External Affairs noted that any leaked material would probably be traced back to Canada, the sole NATO member on the committee. But Canada's man at the United Nations, Charles Ritchie, went along with the scheme, apparently agreeing with a Belgian diplomat that "it was possible at times to be 'too objective.'" Green concurred, agreeing to provide Belgium with general information.[64] Again, Canada was trying to play both ends against the middle, hoping to be able to influence Belgium without losing its public face as a major UN backer.

Splits in the peacekeeping operation were emerging, with the Third World contingent led by the Indian officers who had supported Lumumba and the NATO members from Europe who supported Mobutu. The divisions in ONUC mirrored the differences between NATO and Western peacekeeping participants and their governments and the representatives from Indonesia, Ghana, India, Morocco, and Tunisia. The countries that had recently freed themselves from European rule did not view the Congo through a Cold War prism. Like Nasser of Egypt, they were highly suspicious of an alliance dominated by colonial powers and the United States. The Indian leaders of ONUC, notably the former Bengal Lancer I.J. Rikhye, who had served under Burns in the Sinai, were not as quick as NATO-bred soldiers to pass harsh judgments on the popular Lumumba while backing the Belgian favourite Mobutu. Rikhye had been inspired by Gandhi's philosophical tactics of non-violent social change and Nehru's doctrine of *panch sheel*, or non-alignment.[65]

One Canadian military man ostensibly acting as a peacekeeper while serving at ONUC headquarters in Congo, Lt.-Col. J.A. "Johnny" Berthiaume, accused "the Indian coterie" of "running the whole show" with "no intention of allowing other nationals to interfere."[66] Berthiaume, chief of staff for ONUC's first commander, the Swedish general Carl von Horn, charged Rikhye and Indian diplomat Rajeshwar Dayal with favouring Lumumba, who had managed to escape house arrest. But Berthiaume was involved in intrigues of his own. He was complicit in the conspiracy to arrest Lumumba, an event that led directly to the murder of Congo's elected prime minister. Some thirty years later Berthiaume gave his version of the story. He said he had phoned Mobutu and said, "Colonel, you have a problem, you are trying to retrieve your prisoner, Mr. Lumumba. I know where he is, and I know where he will be tomorrow." Mobutu asked what he should do. "It's simple, Colonel," Berthiaume said, and proceeded to tell the future dictator to use "the core of your para-commandos" and fly them to the small village where the nationalist leader had taken refuge. "There is a runway and all that is needed. That's all you do, Colonel." Mobutu arrested Lumumba as suggested, Berthiaume said, "and I never regretted it."[67]

External Affairs was aware of Berthiaume's sympathies, and in the end the officer failed to keep his ONUC job. It remains uncertain as to whether External officials knew or approved of an event that Spooner describes as one in which the Canadian "gravely crossed the line of impartiality and neutrality expected of all peacekeepers."[68]

Roméo Dallaire, Canada's most famous, if tragic, peacekeeper, would learn about Africa's postcolonial realities in another former Belgian colony. The genocide in Rwanda would show the world the complicity of Western nations and the impotence of the United Nations in the face of a land regarded as a geopolitical backwater. Dallaire, son of a Dutch war bride and a Canadian soldier, had a historical memory extending back to the Second World War. "As Canadian soldiers fought tooth and nail against the Germans, King Leopold III of Belgium and his ruthless lackeys kept millions of black Africans in Rwanda and all of the Great Lakes region under subjugation, raping these countries of their natural resources," he would write in his memoir. His assessment of Rwanda applies equally to the tragedy of the Congo—"A crime against humanity that the Belgians had unwittingly laid the spadework for."[69]

Canada has a national monument to peacekeeping called "Reconciliation . . . At the Service of Peace." It stands in the nation's capital between the U.S. Embassy and the National Gallery. One of its more subtle features, overwhelmed by the tall bronze figures of Canadian soldiers sporting UN headgear, is a pile of stylized rubble symbolizing the Green Line that divides Nicosia, Cyprus. The actual Green Line is a snarl of nettles, weeds, and cement-filled oil drums marking the place where the Republic of Cyprus was attacked by one NATO ally and partitioned after a nasty little war with another. According to Christopher Hitchens, the protracted conflict was an example of "the way in which small countries and people are discounted or disregarded."[70]

The eastern Mediterranean island was annexed by the British as the ruling Ottomans watched their empire collapse in the wake of the First World War. Cyprus had already passed to de facto British control at the 1878 Congress of Berlin, when the great powers reorganized things in Southern Europe, ostensibly bringing peace and stability to the Balkans after the Ottomans lost a war to the Russians. By hoisting its flag at Nicosia, Britain got an important naval base close to the Suez Canal and the seaway to India. The British said they would use their new base to protect the Turks from the Russians, though by the time war came in 1914 the Russians were allied with the British against the Turks. During that conflict and again in 1939 many Greek Cypriots believed that the British would grant them *enosis*—their much desired union with Greece—after the war ended. Greeks form the overwhelming majority of the island's population, although on a clear day Cyprus is within sight of mainland Turkey.

As it turned out, British control of Cyprus helped to furnish a legacy of conflict similar to the strife that the British mandate bequeathed to nearby Palestine. In the face of increased demand for *enosis* and the end of Crown colony status in the 1950s, the minority Turkish population launched a demand of their own, *taksim*—partition of the island. In this sectarian cauldron both the Greek and Turkish Cypriots organized their own paramilitary organizations, inevitably labelled terrorist by the British and by each other. As with the Ottomans before them, the imperial authorities watched their fortunes fade, with the Suez debacle constituting the crucial watershed. The British wanted to rid themselves of the responsibility of having to put down the proverbial "warring factions" while simultaneously maintaining control over what they called their Sovereign Base Areas in Cyprus. The strategically located island had become an important Cold War listening post and nuclear weapons staging base, effectively a British aircraft carrier in the region. Although the loitering British were open to some form of home rule, particularly due to the island's increasing violence, they and their NATO allies insisted that their eastern Mediterranean bases at Akrotiri (home to British nuclear devices) and Dhekelia remain firmly under the control of the Defence Ministry as "overseas territories" under the sovereignty of Her Majesty. By the 1960s Cyprus had become a well-established sanctuary for retired Col. Blimp types with a fondness for gin at sundown and an aversion to the locals, be they Greek or Turk.

Here was the postcolonial rub. In 1960 Cyprus became a republic as well as a United Nations and Commonwealth member under president Archbishop Makarios III. It had been a curious colony, with two ancient motherlands that long predated the arrival of the British. What's more, and more important with respect to the Cold War dynamic that animated Great Power concern, both Turkey and Greece were NATO members situated on the alliance's southwestern flank. Every time Greece and Turkey (themselves each home to U.S. nuclear weapons) threatened to go to war in defence of their Cypriot brethren, the generals at NATO headquarters shuddered. Not only would the stability of their Mediterranean enclave be at risk, but even more horrific to contemplate was the likelihood that two members of their alliance would declare war on each other, ignoring the clear and present danger posed by the Russian Bear. The Soviets, for their part, were keen to stoke the fires of communal tension on the island.

As a result, over the course of three decades Canadian troops found themselves stationed near the sun-soaked beaches and spectacular medieval ruins of a vacation island. Their colleagues languishing in the chilly confines of NATO bases in Germany waiting for the Soviets to attack—or for orders to attack the Soviets—were not amused by mess-hall reminders of the attractions of Cyprus. Canada's longest peacekeeping mission was not, however, a series of strolls in the park. Canada would suffer twenty-four fatal casualties over the course of endless six-month rotations in Cyprus. The total UN dead after 1964 came to 180 personnel.

After 1960 Makarios found himself doing a delicate political dance, pressured by domestic ethnic and religious pressures, the looming shadows of Turkey and Greece, the ever-present arm of the British, and a local left backed by the Soviets. Canada's high commissioner noted in 1962 that many onlookers foresaw a "Middle East Cuba" in the making.[71] The Israelis, quick to take advantage of their Western patrons' Cold War angst, pitched in by organizing anti-Communist trade unions, while Makarios declared Cyprus part of the non-aligned movement and began treating with his neighbour Nasser. Cold warriors looked on with jaundiced eyes. The irony of a neutral nation with nuclear weapons on its soil was not lost on Western geopolitical strategists.

By 1963 violence in Cyprus was on the rise as bombings and drive-by shootings threatened the country to the extent that the British made regular forays outside their bases to guard their own nationals. Things were threatening to spin out of control, with Turkish ultimatums and aggressive Greek responses. The British initially rejected the idea of a UN peacekeeping force, instead suggesting a NATO contingent. In such situations, military men and politicians with little stomach for UN-style multilateralism often urge action by NATO; the politics of a superpower-dominated alliance are less complex, the lines of command more efficient. Makarios was having none of it. He rejected the NATO idea in January 1964. Cyprus was, after all, an independent nation despite its tumultuous situation.

With its growing experience in peacekeeping Canada was an obvious candidate for any such undertaking in Cyprus, with domestic political considerations coming into play. Nationalist sentiment was growing rapidly in Quebec, and Pearson's Quebec ministers were sensitive to the thorniness of sending troops to help the British out of a jam—or, as External Affairs Minister Paul Martin put it, for "English purposes." Pearson decided that francophone troops should be included in the standby force. The military declared itself ready, having studied British doctrine and gained experience in the Middle East and the Congo. The army underlined the need for a ceasefire and the agreement of "responsible leaders" on each side so that "any fighting . . . should be ascribed to terrorist and irregular forces."[72]

In early March Pearson got a call from an anxious Lyndon Johnson. The president, preoccupied with Vietnam, was keen to have the deteriorating situation in Cyprus calmed down. The United Nations was not acting quickly enough for him, and it was well known that Makarios wanted no Americans or Moslems in any peacekeeping force. Could Canada move before the UN approved a peacekeeping force? Pearson wanted to help but was unwilling to act unilaterally. He told

Johnson that as soon as the United Nations approved the mission, Canada would send its troops even before other nations sent theirs. "I said not to worry; we knew our duty to the UN; we knew the danger of war breaking out there very, very quickly between Greece and Turkey. . . . The President seemed reassured and very grateful." Canada had its airlift ready and troops on the way to Cyprus before Parliament authorized the effort, though Pearson said that they would have been called back if the mission had not been approved.[73]

The Canadian forces arrived to supplement British troops already on the ground but little trusted by either side. Eventually joined by Irish, Finnish, and Swedish forces, the UN contingent would be called the United Nations Peacekeeping Force in Cyprus (UNFICYP), with its base becoming known as the Blue Beret Camp. Its years of peacekeeping resembled war, if only to the extent that they were characterized by long periods of boredom punctuated by short episodes of terrifying violence. As with many other peacekeeping undertakings, one of the dangers was the presence of young men with guns, little discipline, and an ethnic nationalism fuelled by hormones and, often, goodly amounts of alcohol.

Just as the United States dispatched another contingent of five thousand troops to Vietnam in summer 1964, the crisis in Cyprus was still threatening to boil over. Pearson scribbled a few notes-to-self in light of a call from U.S. secretary of state Dean Rusk asking the prime minister to travel to New York to "stiffen up" UN secretary general U Thant on the Cyprus issue. Makarios was, Rusk believed, playing footsie with the Soviets as well as with Nasser. "We know that a small conventional war in any place—Cyprus or Vietnam—can lead to a nuclear global war. We have a duty to do what we can as human beings to prevent this." Ever the multilateralist, Pearson worried that the failure of peacekeeping would be a threat not just to peace but also to both the North Atlantic alliance he had done so much to build and the world body in which he still placed much hope. "The League of Nations received its death blow in Ethiopia [with the non-action surrounding the 1935 Italian invasion there]. We must prevent the United Nations from suffering the same fate through failure in Cyprus. Furthermore, armed conflict between two NATO members will end NATO in its present form."[74]

Finally, the prime minister's ponderings foreshadowed the wrenching dilemmas that would come to bedevil peacekeeping operations in the post–Cold War world.

"UNFICYP's method of peacekeeping," explained Arthur Andrew, Canada's high commissioner in Cyprus, "starts with the assumption that the parties concerned want the peace kept. This is sometimes true of one or the other parties, and even, on occasion with both, but it is not always true everywhere."[75] UN peacekeepers quickly realized that their blue helmets, military training, and light side arms did not make them immune from gunfire from either side of the Green Line that lurched erratically through settlements, zig-zagging like a drunken soldier. In the end the success of the mission in settling the differences between Greek and Turkish Cypriots remained open to question. In 1974 UNFICYP's blue helmets could not stop the Turkish invasion that led to the permanent partition of the island. Yet the ethnic cleansing that occurred in Cyprus never did reach the scale of horror and continuing turmoil experienced in Israel/Palestine or later in the Balkans or Rwanda. If the mission was a partial UN failure, for a quarter-century it was a NATO success, keeping Greece and Turkey more focused on the Soviets than on each other. Veteran Canadian peacekeeper Roy Thomas, who served in UN operations in Cyprus, Afghanistan, Haiti, and the Middle East, underlined how the United Nations' extended Cyprus peacekeeping operation helped Pearson's other multilateral priority: "The apparent effect for NATO staff was that another international organization with someone else's money helped ameliorate a possible alliance-breaking confrontation."[76]

In 1958, while still serving as commander of the peacekeeping force UNEF at its Gaza headquarters, the sixty-one-year-old Tommy Burns had a visit from John Bassett, who had served under his command in Italy in 1944. Bassett, now a prominent Toronto Tory, had run unsuccessfully for the party that had just taken office under Diefenbaker. He expressed surprise that Canada's military had never promoted his former boss beyond major-general. Burns had been running two high-profile UN operations in the Middle East for four years. Burns, never a cheery chap, responded that he would never make it any further up the ladder. Bassett then had a word with the prime minister, and Burns soon happily found himself being moved up a rung to lieutenant-general.

After Burns's six years of UN peacekeeping service ended in late 1959 the Diefenbaker government appointed him to the position of principal disarmament negotiator with the rank of ambassador, a post he held until 1968. Just before he took the job, both superpowers had voted in favour of a UN resolution affirming that "the question of general and complete disarmament is the most important one facing the world today" and calling on "Governments to make every effort to achieve a constructive solution to this problem."[77] The disarmament negotiators would grope their way tentatively towards a partial nuclear test-ban treaty in 1963, and Burns continued to maintain his interest in peacekeeping. In 1964 Pearson gave a talk at the Dag Hammarskjöld Memorial Series at Carleton University, discussing his government's plans for reconsidering the ad hoc tendencies of the peacekeeping operations undertaken to date. For political and practical reasons the world's nations had seen neither a standing UN army nor a standby force as feasible. Based on his own experience in cobbling together a UN force in the Sinai and aware of the difficulties that his Swedish counterpart Carl von Horn had encountered in the Congo, Burns suggested that Canada host a meeting of countries active in UN peacekeeping.

With Pearson's support the Canadian-organized international conference took place in late 1964 in Ottawa. It was a modest, mid-level meeting. External Affairs was more keen on peacekeeping than was National Defence, where minister Paul Hellyer said he was "not overly-optimistic that any startling progress would be made." The alliance with the United States took top priority for the military. Indeed, the share of its budget spent for UN peacekeeping had never risen above one-half of 1 per cent. In the conference's informal discussions no one would have to make any commitments, although the ad hoc nature of peacekeeping was scrutinized. The issue of maintaining direct national command of forces deployed for peacekeeping was also front and centre. John MacFarlane, a historian employed by National Defence, concluded some forty years later, "When political sovereignty was in jeopardy there was resistance—particularly from Canada."[78]

Indeed, Canada's role at the meeting reflected its ambivalence. Ottawa inevitably tried to project a benign image as a helpful international fixer while simultaneously being locked into a rigid alliance. The imperial impulse that had immersed the country in the British suppression of upstart Boer colonists had shifted. The ties that bound Canada to the U.S. imperium were not as tight as those that had bound it to Edwardian England. Unlike Australia, Canada had not said "Ready, aye, ready" and sent combat troops to join the U.S. effort in Vietnam. A leader like Pearson had a tight balancing act between empire and independence to perform, and, as MacFarlane noted, Canada's commitment to peacekeeping was "not always clear." But one clear goal was "international recognition" as a leader on the issue: "Canadians increasingly saw themselves as selfless leaders of the multilateral peacekeeping ideal, and this conference added to that image." Canada was increasingly getting the international recognition it desired on an issue that was popular with Canadian voters across the country. Moreover, the country could set itself off as "being distinct from U.S. policy without angering its important neighbour and ally."[79]

By the 1960s Canada's image—and its own self-image—as a peacekeeping nation had come into sharp focus. Paradoxically, it had by this time maintained—for the first time in its history—a fully equipped standing army in peacetime. Peacetime rearmament meant support for a Royal Canadian Air Force and a Royal Canadian Navy, though separate services produced practical problems; navy and air force signallers could not be transferred to army tasks when the need arose during the Congo crisis. Such inefficiencies, coupled with the usual interservice rivalries, would give rise to a bitter struggle over unification of the armed forces. The military became "Canadianized," and the painful episode of Nasser excluding British-tinged Canadians would not soon be repeated—although over forty years after the "Royal" disappeared as a descriptor for Canada's navy and air force a government that had turned its back on peacekeeping and adored the monarchy would—in a salute to the old empire—restore the Royal designation. Still, when the forces were unified, the new uniforms (closely resembling those of the U.S. Air Force) meant that Canadian badges would, in the words of Desmond Morton, "be recognizable to Canada's new imperial protector."[80]

Most of its personnel and equipment were wrapped up in NATO, with the continuing fixation of Canada's military on a possible war with the Soviet bloc. Nevertheless, against the background of high-profile peacekeeping missions in the Middle East, Congo, and Cyprus—and the reflected glow from Pearson's Nobel Peace Prize—Canada had within twenty years after the end of the Second World War and in the depths of the Cold War emerged as a peacekeeping leader. It was, however, leadership of a rather qualified sort. Canada's activity in Vietnam, Congo, and Cyprus was in effect not a peaceable alternative to Cold War bullying, but rather its complement. To the outright coercion of applied U.S. imperialism in Vietnam and Belgian colonialism in the Congo, Canada would add the more consensual politics of investigation, invigilation, and mediation. The contradictions of Canada's position were apparent: a sovereign state that was also dependent and compliant. It was little comfort to Vietnam's napalmed villagers or the murdered rebels of Congo that Canadians were there to murmur soothing words of conciliation.

Canadian Airborne Regiment Chaplain Capt. Mark Sargent behind a group of bound and blindfolded Somali civilians, Somalia, 1993.

CHAPTER 6

"THE DECADE OF DARKNESS"

PEACEKEEPING AT A CROSSROADS

Canada, Canada.

– words cried by Shidane Abukar Arone,
lapsing into unconsciousness after being tortured
by Canadian soldiers in Somalia, March 1993

Prolonged peace is always a time of trial for any military.

– David Bercuson, *Significant Incident*, 1996

IN 1994 Brent Beardsley witnessed horrific crimes. During the genocide in Rwanda the capital city of Kigali was a charnel house, and Beardsley, a major in the Royal Canadian Regiment, was confronting the unspeakable on an almost daily basis. Once, entering a compound where terrified Hutus had taken refuge, he saw the ground littered with the bodies of people slaughtered with machetes. The flies had not yet arrived.[1] Some of the dead were women. Their clothing was at least partially removed, and Beardsley assumed they had been raped. Then he spotted a man standing with his trousers around his ankles and brandishing a machete. It was obvious what he had been doing.

Beardsley trained his weapon on the man. He immediately realized that he would not be able to arrest him. Kigali's roads were blocked by the checkpoints familiar to peacekeepers around the world. They were guarded by young men who were often drunk, and always unpredictable. Beardsley also knew that no one would ever know, or blame him, if he pulled the trigger. But he had second thoughts. "If I killed him, I would be not better than him," Beardsley later recalled, explaining why he chose to walk away. "You can't become a terrorist to stop terrorism. You cannot become a criminal to stop crime. And you cannot become a murderer to stop murder."[2]

Beardsley would go on to work from 2000 to 2002 as the chief instructor in the training of military observers at the Canadian Forces peacekeeping training centre in Kingston. Canada was starting to get out of the peacekeeping business, with the events of September 2001 as a catalyst for the shift. Back in 1993 Beardsley had been an infantry officer working on a draft of the Canadian military's peacekeeping manual when General Roméo Dallaire picked him to be his military assistant for a mission to Rwanda. Just before that the Canadian general had been "stunned" to learn that the Canadian government was not willing to supply a peacekeeping force to that troubled nation—that it would only send one officer (Dallaire himself) under a UN civilian contract. In the end Dallaire, who had no peacekeeping experience, was able to add Beardsley and got "the chance to learn first-hand what would work in the changing nature of conflict in the post–Cold War world."[3] Beardsley had spent time in Cyprus in the 1980s, but the situation on the Mediterranean tourist island had not prepared him for Rwanda. Nothing could have. Beardsley would go on to be co-author of Dallaire's painful account of the experience in *Shake Hands with the Devil*.

In speaking of the 1990s, people in Canadian military circles often repeat a "decade of darkness" story in which honest soldiers were sacrificed on the altar of political expediency. Their storyline is deeply ironic. After seven decades of world wars and the Cold War, a decade promising peace might, it seems, have been a refreshing change. For neo-conservatives, exactly the opposite was the case. In the United States many of them complained that a desk-bound military had lost its taste for blood; a softened and aimless population had lost its capacity for heroic virtue; and life, without the "sublimity" and nobility of war, had lost its meaning. Capitalism had triumphed over its Soviet enemy, yet in losing its indispensable enemy it had condemned westerners to lives that were pointless and boring.[4] Peacekeeping was a poor substitute for real wars in which real men could prove themselves against evil enemies. When neo-conservatives looked at the United Nations they saw in it not Pearson's noble experiment in reason, but a pathetic attempt by the weak to hobble the strong and manly. When they looked at peacekeeping, they could reluctantly accept it—it did, after all, provide a public rationale for militaries that suddenly found themselves bereft of an enemy—but only if it turned into something that looked a lot like war. Therein was the way in which the decade of darkness—dark because it seemed to presage a world without war—could be redeemed: by turning "peacekeeping" into its opposite, "war by other means."

At the time the official story had it that Canada's military was "rusted out," its personnel depleted by too many peacekeeping missions. Yet in 1993 the government seemed eager to send forces to an unfamiliar country threatened by famine and civil war. Perhaps, as Desmond Morton suggests, it was "an act of hubris" brought on in part by the eagerness of the military to get in on some action. An operation in Somalia would be just what they were looking for—"their chance to perform,"[5] in Morton's words—although before that they would have to contend with a confrontation at home, a brief war in the Middle East, and a controversy over a television program.

In the last decade of a century that had begun with the splendid patriotic fervour of the expedition to put down unruly Boers in South Africa, Canada's military faced a crisis of purpose. The two world wars, an inconclusive war in Korea, and the rise of the peacekeeping enterprise had changed Canada's view of the military. Rarely, after the bloody debacle of 1914–18, had English Canadians been seized with the notion that military prowess was integral to their identity as a nation. Quebec had never done so.

Canadians by and large did not embrace martial culture—they remained a stubbornly unmilitary people. Americans, although inheriting a different history in which both revolution and civil war were foundational, nonetheless continued to appraise the size and strength of the armed services "according to the security tasks immediately at hand," in the words of American historian and retired colonel Andrew Bacevich. "A grave and proximate threat to the nation's well-being might require a large and powerful military establishment," but in the absence of such a situation, "policymakers scaled down that establishment accordingly." In both the United States and Canada, founding fathers viewed overgrown military establishments with suspicion— "particularly hostile to republican liberty," said George Washington— and the notion that nations required permanent war machines to project their power throughout the world was widely viewed as a prejudice of the Old World that the New World had wisely jettisoned.[6]

The Cold War gave rise to sustained military spending in the four decades after Korea. NATO membership obliged Canada to maintain forces in Europe. But even that commitment was not pursued with any great enthusiasm by the Liberal governments under Pierre Trudeau (1968–79, 1980–84), a prime minister suspicious of both military alliances and the military (save when it came time to deploy soldiers against Quebec nationalists during the October Crisis of 1970). John de Chastelain, who was Chief of Defence Staff when the Berlin Wall came down, was like many Canadian military men: he had spent years positioned and practising in Germany for possible war with the Red Army. "You were able to do things there in a much more realistic manner than you had been able to do in Canada," he said, recalling the Cold War era's freewheeling war-game manoeuvres.[7] Between the 1950s and the 1990s thousands of Canada's military men and their families became veterans, not of war but of peacetime life on foreign soil.

With the collapse of the Soviet Union and the independence of its Eastern European satellite states, military boosters in Canada and other Western countries were left in the position of a tug-of-war team whose opponents have suddenly let go of the rope. As leading neo-con Irving Kristol lamented in the United States, conservatives like himself suddenly felt they had been deprived of an indispensable enemy— and "in politics, being deprived of an enemy is a very serious matter. You tend to get relaxed and dispirited." Morton summed up the question that confounded proponents of military spending. "What was the justification for spending over $12 billion a year to keep 83,000 men and women clothed, paid and equipped with ships, aircraft and tanks?"[8]

From the end of the Second World War until Canada's support for UN peacekeeping operations began to decline in 1997, the country was a leading contributor to all such ventures. The roles included everything from what are known as traditional interpositional forces (Cyprus, Ethiopia/Eritrea) to observer missions (Georgia/Abkhazia, Lebanon), transitional administrations (Eastern Slavonia and East Timor), and the most controversial and difficult multidimensional operations—Bosnia, Rwanda, Somalia, Haiti, Sierra Leone.[9] The work was routine enough that participation in an operation such as the United Nations Transition Assistance Group (UNTAG) went largely unnoticed in Canada.

In 1989 UNTAG supervised successful elections in Namibia, the newly independent Southern African country that had been victimized by decades of domination by Germany (the Europeans killed four out of every five of the territory's Herero people) and South Africa. The United Nations Observer Group in El Salvador (ONUSAL) in 1991–92 helped to bring an end to a civil war of unsurpassed brutality. It would be twenty years before the Salvadoran government apologized for the 1981 murder of a thousand peasants at El Mozote by the elite U.S.-trained Atlacatl Battalion. The victims included the village's smallest children, herded into a house where the soldiers emptied the magazines of their M16s into a roomful of kids. By the time the United Nations left, 90 per cent of the people in the tiny Central American country were still living in poverty.[10]

During the Cold War Canada sent more troops on UN peacekeeping operations than did any other country, suffering the highest number of fatalities. Efforts like the transition to Namibian independence were high points. Others, like the several efforts in Haiti over the years, had checkered records—with the Haiti project in particular wrestling with the contradictions of a desperately poor country tormented by decades of imperial meddling orchestrated by the United States.

The end of the Cold War led to talk of a "peace dividend." Globalization became a fashionable buzzword. The Canadians stationed in Europe for so long would soon come home for good. But if Canada no longer had Warsaw Pact enemies, what, then, was the purpose of its military? In response the Canadian Institute for International Peace and Security channelled Lenin. "What Is to Be Done?" the semi-official foreign-policy think tank asked when it convened a 1990 panel of liberal-minded academics to discuss Canadian military security in the decade to come. Denis Stairs set the tone, juxtaposing the idea of globalization with the reappearance of "very traditional forms of nationalism . . . a need for group cultural expression in political terms." At that time Bosnia and Rwanda were, to most Canadians, unknown spots on the world map. Participant Desmond Morton urged Canada to keep its forces in Europe because it was the only place they could see "first class conventional warfare practiced by their neighbours." He remarked, with a touch of irony, that peacekeeping had become "the great morale builder" for Canadians who wanted to see their country active in some kind of military endeavour. The "political reality" was that Canadians saw it as the first priority. "It satisfies," Morton said, "a kind of benign imperialist urge among Canadians—how good the lesser breeds are being kept in order by our lads in blue berets." One of peacekeeping's more acute critics, Sherene Razack, observes that Canadians frequently indulge the national fantasy that they "are of Anglo-Saxon origin, descendants of a Northern people who consider themselves innately given to civility," a "law-abiding, orderly, and modest people." A typical Canadian, she believes, sees "herself or himself as someone who comes from the nicest place on earth, as someone from a peacekeeping nation, and as a modest, self-deprecating individual who is able to gently teach Third World Others about civility."[11]

For his part Stairs was frank about the raison d'être for Canada's NATO presence in Germany.

> We have not in any sense been a decisive player in preserving the security of the West. So Canadian defence expenditures have been about buying access to multilateral institutions at which we like to express ourselves, hopefully to prevent other countries from making fools of themselves—on the assumption, of course, that we never make a fool of ourselves.[12]

Investments in the military guaranteed the survival of Pearsonian quiet diplomacy.

As for the purpose of the army, in 1990 Canadians got a reminder of how their country's forces had a long history of putting down strikes, protests, and insurrectionary efforts at home—"aid to the civil power." That summer's "Oka Crisis" was as old as Canada, indeed older. An indigenous community, the Kanesatake Mohawks west of

Montreal, claimed title to land that French aristocrats had granted to a group of Catholic priests 150 years before Confederation. The Mohawks refused to recognize the European claim to the place "where the sandy crust dunes are" beside the Lake of Two Mountains, a widening at the mouth of the Ottawa River. Canada's government and courts refused to recognize indigenous title to a spot where the nine-hole Oka Golf Club abutted a white pine forest and the Mohawk Pine Hill Cemetery. One particular golfer, the mayor of Oka, did not bother to consult the Mohawks in 1989 when he announced a golf course expansion and adjoining luxury townhouse development. It was a recipe for trouble. In April 1990 Mayor Jean Ouellette, having already told town council that "you can't talk to the Indians," let Quebec's minister of Native Affairs know how he would deal with the Mohawks. "There's only one way we're going to be able to build the golf course. That's with the army."[13]

Cemeteries are not all that often transformed into golf course condo developments. Not surprisingly, despite the shooting death of a Quebec Provincial Police officer as the armed standoff between the Mohawks and the forces of order began, the Mohawk cause garnered significant support across Canada. It was this indigenous solidarity that was perhaps the most remarkable aspect of the crisis, with spontaneous roadblocks and demonstrations in Manitoba, British Columbia, Alberta, Saskatchewan, Nova Scotia, Ontario, and Quebec itself. The dramatic standoff attracted international attention, with European human rights monitors descending on the Montreal area and the European Parliament condemning Canada and Quebec for their actions against the Mohawks occupying the Pines. It did not help Ottawa's public relations cause when the minister of Indian Affairs told a parliamentary committee that the Mohawks were "immigrants" to Canada.[14]

The Mohawks themselves were hardly united in the face of the crisis. Their traditional forms of self-government had been deeply democratic in comparison to the feudal Europeans who confiscated their land before deeding it to each other. But like many other indigenous peoples, their modes of self-rule were fractured when something calling itself Canada arrived. In 1868, when Kanesatake leader Joseph Onasakenrat wrote to the Sulpician Fathers demanding that they return the traditional lands, only white men of property could vote in Canada's new federation. Only a century later were Aboriginal Canadians admitted to the democratic circle. In the meantime the Mohawks were forced to struggle with the settler government's laws about band councils and elected chiefs. Not all Mohawks adhered to the imposed systems. Divisions emerged between Mohawks who adopted Christianity and those who did not. Although gambling and tobacco smuggling also divided Mohawk communities, they preserved traditions of autonomous self-rule that surprised one Canadian army officer dispatched to counter militant Mohawks who called themselves "warriors."

"The chiefs have no decision-making power whatsoever," said a surprised Lieutenant-Colonel Robin Gagnon, sent to command the soldiers confronting the nearby Kahnawake Mohawks, who had acted in solidarity with Kanesatake by blocking the busy Mercier Bridge. "They must constantly consult their people and reach a consensus." Gagnon regretted that all of his military training had taught him nothing about the people with whom he had to negotiate. "Their outlook is altogether different than ours."[15]

The Oka Crisis of 1990 and the October Crisis of 1970—when Ottawa also dispatched the army to deal with trouble in Quebec—were different affairs. Using six thousand troops to help round up artists, labour activists, students, and other nationalist malcontents during the October Crisis was simply a matter of using the time-honoured secret police tactic of hauling surprised people out of bed in the middle of the night. Confronting armed Aboriginal people, many of whom, at least in Kahnawake, had military training—including experience with the U.S. forces in Vietnam—was a different order of business for Canadian soldiers, brought in to provide "public security." For the Mohawks, armed resistance to colonial incursions on land that they had never ceded was part of a long tradition of resistance.

The Oka Crisis ended at the end of September, as it had begun, with bitter recrimination and violence. The state used the army's overwhelming power to push for the end of the Mercier Bridge blockade and the Oka occupation—managing, as it had in the past, to put down its domestic opponents in a show of force that the army had seldom been able to exert in peacekeeping operations abroad.

★

In August 1990, well before the Oka Crisis ended, the Iraqi dictatorship under former Western ally Saddam Hussein invaded Kuwait,
leading to the Gulf War of 1991. Following the principle of my
enemy's enemy is my friend, most Western nations had backed Iraq
and furnished Saddam with weaponry during his country's war with
Iran; but alliances shift, and yesterday's friend became Hitler-on-the-
Tigris. Despite the "smart" bombs, "surgical" strikes, and the novelty
of round-the-clock cable news coverage that allowed vast audiences
to watch the destruction of the ancient city of Baghdad in real time, the
war was essentially an old-fashioned matter of restoration aimed at securing the throne for Kuwait's Emir Jaber al-Ahmad al-Jaber al-Sabah.
In 1986 the Emir had unilaterally dissolved parliament and suspended
parts of the constitution, citing national security as his rationale. In
1990, within hours of the invasion, he fled to Saudi Arabia. To counter
the Iraqi invasion Washington secured UN support for a military
operation to restore the sheikh and secure his small Persian Gulf kingdom, described, inevitably, as "oil-rich."

In retrospect, Operation Desert Storm was a critical turning point
in the history of the militarization of North America. Since Hiroshima
and Nagasaki, military thinkers in the United States had pondered the
future of war in an atomic age; since the chastening experience of Vietnam, they had reconsidered doctrines of "limited war" that they had
hoped would provide a continuing rationale for the huge U.S. military.
In the 1970s and 1980s, they embraced with ever-greater enthusiasm
an assortment of precision-guided munitions that drew upon the latest
advances in microelectronics, data processing, and communications.
(This penchant would be repackaged and promoted as the "Revolution
in Military Affairs," a concept that captured the imagination of many a
Canadian militarist.) In the new American way of war, guided by the
marvels of technology, military intervention would take the shape not
of protracted and complicated campaigns like Vietnam, but precise
and, if necessary, pre-emptive strikes. "The scalpel was seemingly now
at hand," writes Bacevich, "making it possible to eliminate threats with
near-antiseptic efficiency."[16]

After the 1980 declaration of the "Carter Doctrine"—whereby any
attempt by "any outside force to gain control of the Persian Gulf
region" would be regarded "as an assault on the vital interests of the
United States of America, and such an assault will be repelled by any

means necessary, including military force"[17]—any such pre-emptive strike could be justified in terms of the very survival of a society dependent upon foreign oil. Having been so badly burned by the candid television reporting that turned Vietnam into the living-room war, the U.S. military reinvented its public relations apparatus to ensure that the pictures of war were as antiseptic, even beautiful, as the sleek aircraft and shimmering missiles by means of which the conflict was conducted. The alliance that forced Iraq out of Kuwait in 1991 was essentially a U.S. operation, but like the invasion of Afghanistan ten years later it included a band of allies. In the midst of considerable domestic controversy the government of Brian Mulroney dispatched ships and fighter jets at a cost of some $700 million (eight times the bill for Oka). It was the first time since Korea that the Canadian military had participated in offensive combat operations. The Iraqis were easily defeated, their ground forces decimated. The Emir returned from his Saudi Arabian exile. As a friendly gesture, Jaber had tipped his *ghutra* to his Western patrons with the promise to enfranchise Kuwaiti women. Meanwhile, the *status quo ante* prevailed as the flow of Kuwaiti petroleum gradually resumed after the devastating sabotage fires set by retreating Iraqi forces. It would be another fifteen years before Kuwaiti women secured the vote.[18]

By this time Canada's military was beginning to chafe at the popularity of peacekeeping—and the anxiety was rendered all the more acute by critics who questioned the scale of the country's participation in the Gulf War. J.L. Granatstein seemed particularly exercised about such criticism. "Canada took part" in the Gulf War, the historian wrote, "though rather more hesitantly than I would have wished; and, in what I have no hesitation in characterizing as a just war in every canonical and legal definition, Iraq was driven from Kuwait at a terrible cost to its military and its people." Although the Gulf War was not a peacekeeping mission, Granatstein bemoaned the controversy that Canadian participation generated and criticized those who had made peacekeeping "the *sine qua non* of Canadian nationalism." Canada's peace activists and much of the rest of the population liked the country's peacekeeping record and worried that the Gulf War could mark a shift in direction. Peacekeeping, argued Granatstein, was being used as code for anti-Americanism, and the peacekeeping impulse had to be checked with realism.[19]

Although the profoundly unpopular Mulroney government refrained from making major new cuts to the defence budget, the immediate future did not look promising for those who regarded it as entirely appropriate for Ottawa to be lavishing more money on the military. The country was at peace, and the principal threat had just disintegrated. As in the United States, Canadian citizens were not obliged to perform military service—which severed one major link between the armed forces and the population—and the elite largely excused themselves from any military duties.[20] Ottawa was already spending more on the military than on anything besides interest payments on the ballooning national debt.[21] Canada finally pulled its forces out of Germany in 1993 just as the Chrétien Liberals were elected. The military would not be spared by the looming budget axe of Finance Minister Paul Martin Jr.—but then again, Ottawa also slashed programs for the elderly, the unemployed, and the poor. Martin's 1995 budget met with loud applause from business and right-wing think tanks, cutting the military off from its traditional backers just as the Progressive Conservatives, traditionally friendly to the armed forces, were trying to regroup in the political wilderness, their support eroded by the far-right Reform Party. Bases were closed down, and it was even reported—and endlessly repeated by military spending boosters—that military personnel at the bottom of the hierarchy were being forced to join other low-wage Canadians in food bank lineups. Thus had arrived the period that the new warriors would later cite as their decade of darkness.

"The Canadian military was in crisis," lamented General Rick Hillier, "divorced from the population and being used as a punching bag by the government." One of novelist John le Carré's national security spooks, reflecting on the headaches suffered by warriors-without-an-enemy, would complain about "that unfortunate fallow period between the Berlin Wall coming down and Osama bin Laden doing us the favour of 9/11."[22]

In the vast libraries on war and in the academies devoted to the study of matters martial, the Prussian theorist Karl von Clausewitz figures prominently. His famous observation that war is a continuation of policy by other means is one of the most widely cited observations on the subject.[23] The dictum lends to war an instrumentalist cast. Nations fight wars to promote national interests. Indeed, another Clause-witzian preoccupation—strategy—had by the early twenty-first century become a throwaway word. Organizations no longer held planning meetings. They inevitably engaged in *strategic* planning sessions—implying that care and deliberation would provide a rational means to a particular end. Thus the Gulf War, according to its critics, was undertaken to ensure a steady supply of oil to the United States and Europe. It was certainly that. But it was also a conventional war in that it attempted, with mixed success, to persuade the citizenry that it was a noble struggle for justice, demanding loyalty to flag and country. Although some Canadians objected to the war, others became rather excited by the carefully controlled images of aerial bombing. The fervour did not begin to approach the war frenzy of the opening months of the First World War, but the signs were still there. The cause, it was said, was worthy. The enemy was abominable. A few yellow ribbons appeared. Our boys (and a few girls) were doing their bit.

Despite this enthusiasm, Canada's role in the war to restore the Emir of Kuwait was marginal. The memory of brief sojourns in faraway deserts quickly faded. In the following year a battle of a different sort seized the Canadian imagination. It was a war of words and images fought over the memory of the last world war, an engagement played out in the media and the public square, with the academic John Crispo deploying an artillery of alliteration. He denounced the granting of an award to a television series special about the Second World War—characterizing the opinions of those with whom he disagreed as deceitful, disgraceful, dishonest, desperate, and distorted. And those were only the adjectives beginning with the letter "d"; the list also included ignorant, malicious, and spiteful.[24]

At issue in this skirmish was a 1993 Gemini Award presented to the producers of a three-part Second World War television documentary, *The Valour and the Horror*, directed by Terence McKenna (co-written with his brother Brian) and aired by the CBC over three weeks in January 1992. The series, salted with dramatizations featuring professional actors, dealt with three specific events: the ill-fated Canadian defence of Hong Kong, the aerial bombing of Germany, and the 1944 Canadian army campaign in Normandy. The second and third episodes in particular made controversial points about the course of actions and the "hiding of truth." The subsequent intensity of debate over *The Valour and the Horror* reflected a common tendency to glorify war and pillory those who cast doubt on that glory—and especially cast doubt in general on the conduct of what is generally considered the most just of just wars.

Cliff Chadderton, a leading campaigner against the series, said he represented "375,000 veterans and widows" and congratulated Professor Crispo for his denunciation. At an inquisitorial 1992 Senate hearing into *The Valour and the Horror,* officer cum academic John English accused McKenna of being a "petulant flower child" who had indulged in "yellow journalism" that was "riddled with throwaway lines that contain half truths and blatant inaccuracies. A staff officer would consider it sloppy." McGill historian Robert Vogel said the series was "virtually incomprehensible."[25]

"These are extraordinarily dangerous people," countered Concordia University historian Graeme Decarie, speaking of the angry Senators who conducted the hearings. "They have power, they are irresponsible and they are ignorant of what a democracy is." Decarie attended the Senate hearings but was not invited to comment on *The Valour and the Horror*. For Toronto's Michael Bliss, another history professor who attended the hearings, the process smacked of McCarthyism: "What I saw this afternoon didn't seem very Canadian to me." One veterans' group went so far as to launch a libel action, claiming to have been defamed in "Death by Moonlight," the episode about the flyers of Bomber Command and their boss, Air Marshal Sir Arthur "Bomber" Harris, the commander singled out for criticism in the episode. Harris himself had described a 1945 air raid on Pforzheim that killed 17,600 people as "a deliberate terror attack." When the case went to court, smartly dressed Legion activists packed the room, heckling the creators of *The Valour and the Horror* as "Nazi lovers."[26] The judge dismissed the lawsuit.

That was not the end of it. Before the year was out two more historians weighed in with a book-length attack on *The Valour and the Horror*. David Bercuson and S.F. Wise together described the debate over the series as "without precedent." They maintained, "Canadians are not usually disposed to debate their history, and especially not those aspects that are military in nature." According to this telling, the battle line on one side featured "enraged veterans' groups . . . furious that the part they played in the war had been mocked or called into question." (McKenna had long insisted that his production was a testimony to the incredible courage of the air crews.) Ranged against the veterans and their backers in the Senate were "embattled writer-producers." The historians noted, with a flaccid attempt at irony, that the filmmakers were "joined by journalists and media persons of every description to defend the sacred causes of freedom of speech, freedom of the press, and freedom of expression."[27]

The snide tone stood in puzzling contrast to the many flyers who believed they had fought to defend those very freedoms. Wise proceeded to make a highly controversial statement: "The weight of scholarship on the issue [of the effectiveness of mass area bombing] is that bombing crippled the German war machine. . . . While it is true that German industrial production continued to rise until late in the war, it rose neither as far nor as fast as it would have had there been no bombing offensive."[28]

The argument about what would have happened to industrial production if bombing had not taken place is, as a hypothetical conjecture, impossible to prove. The argument that "bombing crippled the German war machine" is flimsy, as an official three-volume history of the Royal Canadian Air Force, published the same year, makes clear. The four authors of *The Crucible of War* describe the bombing of Hamburg that killed more than forty thousand Germans, many of them cowering in bomb shelters:

> From one perspective the raid was actually beneficial to the German war economy. Workers displaced from non-essential tasks were soon doing more important things, a fact that helps to explain why Hamburg lost only about two months' worth of war production as a result of these raids and why, within five months, total output had recovered to about 80 per cent of pre-raid levels.

Summarizing official British documents, the writers go on to cast a critical eye on claims of the effectiveness of the terror bombing.

> Although the Combined Bomber Offensive against Germany did not begin to meet its objectives—the progressive, if not sudden, decline in

enemy war production and, later, civilian morale—until the last months of 1944, four full years after it began in earnest, it is also true that, bit by bit, bombing at least played some part in slowing the rate of expansion in the German war economy, and so contributed to the Allies' already significant materiel superiority. Precisely by how much, however, is difficult to determine.[29]

This official history, published in conjunction with the Department of National Defence, includes the most thoroughly researched study of Canada's role in the bomber offensive. Granatstein—although normally a historian's historian with an almost reverential attitude to archival research—promptly dismissed its analysis of the ever-controversial terror attacks as "like nothing so much as [*The Valour and the Horror*] with footnotes."[30] Other critics of the television series included one Senator appalled by interviews with German survivors of Allied air attacks. During his questioning of Brian McKenna, Senator John Sylvain declared, "These Germans belonged to a regime that killed people in the Holocaust. Do you believe that the Holocaust occurred?" When the CBC caved in to the Senators and their backers among militant veterans, the *Globe and Mail* weighed in with some purple prose of its own, declaring that the network's journalistic reputation had been "slit wide and deboned like a fresh-caught trout. . . . And the spirit of free historical inquiry, especially where the sensitivities of organized pressure groups are concerned, [has] been dealt a further blow. There is enough of the horror in this. But where is the valour?"[31]

The Valour and the Horror clearly tweaked many a sensitive nerve. Who gets to tell the story of what is conventionally regarded as a "good war"? Which stories are told? Whose war was it? When you include the perspectives of those who had once been on the other side, is it a betrayal of those who fought? Is it possible, or even permissible, to describe the bravery of rank-and-file fighters while simultaneously asking disturbing questions about how their commanders organized the campaigns?

The creators of *The Valour and the Horror* risked violating the mythology of war, interwoven as it is with the notion of sacrifice. Those who comment on war without adequately invoking the sanctity of "the fallen" remain vulnerable to denunciation by vigilant patriots quick to defend the memory of the dead, invoking the official story of why they died. What was revealing about the storm in Canada was the extent to which militarism had ruled out of question *any* critical evaluation of Canadian war-making. And even though they went to great lengths to praise those who fought and died, the creators of the program were still pilloried.

Their experience was not new. In 1926 Canada's first woman MP, Agnes Macphail, had dared, in the House of Commons, to doubt whether those who perished in the Great War had died for lofty ideals, implying that they had died in vain. "Will the honourable member admit," Macphail asked another member, G.B. Nicholson, that "the prime cause of the war was an economic one, and that the protection of women and children was not part of it?" Nicholson invoked the issue of German tyranny, telling Macphail that those who fought did so to "save Canada."

> These men made the sacrifice in order to protect the homes of Canadians so that the mothers and wives, the sisters and sweethearts, the women of this country whom my honourable friend from southeast Grey represents, would never again be called upon to endure the tortures and go through the hell of the experience which the women of North France and Belgium could not escape in those years.

According to historian Jonathan Vance's account of this exchange, there "may well have been some truth" in what Macphail was saying to her Commons colleague, but "there was no room for her truth in Canada's myth." Vance sums up the controversy with the sweeping generalization that, from Nicolson's point of view, Macphail's words were "a prescription for spiritual desolation."[32]

Whether Macphail, a member of the Reorganized Church of Jesus Christ of Latter Day Saints who regularly demanded cuts to military spending and an end to the flogging of prisoners, held opinions on war and peace that left her spiritually desolated remains open to question. More certain is that war, as the U.S. public intellectual Barbara Ehrenreich argues, enlists emotions "eerily similar to those normally aroused by religion." In her study of the origins and passions of war, Ehrenreich recalls the career of the English historian Arnold Toynbee, who became so caught up in the excitement of the First World War that he wrote atrocity propaganda for his side. He later repented "that brief burst of militarism" and came to see war as a kind of religion that filled a gap created by the decline of traditional forms of worship. Toynbee, Ehrenreich points out, reasoned that "Man" requires "spiritual sustenance," and if he could not find it by going to church he would instead look to the secular state and the solace of "militant nationalism," with its glorification of war as "a fundamental article of faith."[33]

Merilyn Simonds worked on *The Valour and the Horror*—she and writer Merrily Weisbord produced a book that accompanied the film—and during the subsequent controversy she kept a diary that in retrospect casts the debate in a different light. Simonds had married a Canadian of German descent, which meant that the couple's two sons had two grandfathers, one Canadian and one German. One grandfather had trained Canadian flyers who went on to bomb German cities in the Second World War; the other had worked defusing unexploded bombs in those cities until his leg was blown away. Simonds's boys grew up writing essays about their grandfathers' war experiences, hoping for a Legion prize for the best story about the war. They also heard a story their grandmother told them about pushing a baby carriage containing her son and all her possessions from Leipzig to Schweinfurt, all the while trying to avoid the cities where the bombs were falling.

After the television series was aired and the discussion took over, "My sons would come home with tears and anger and fear in their eyes," she wrote in her diary. "'Was Opa a bad man?' they would ask. 'Opa was a Nazi, wasn't he?' They saw war from a child's perspective. They couldn't understand why they felt so ashamed of their Opa."[34]

Having faced shouts of "Nazi-lover" for her part in the project, Simonds was left to struggle with contradictory feelings about what it means to remember. She thought the book she co-authored treated veterans like her father with reverence, but it had been denounced by veterans who urged that it be banned from public libraries. It had sought to explore the entirety of war, the courage and the terror and the lies. Like the films on which it was based, it was written as the Gulf War unfolded on Canada's television screens. The book's epilogue quoted the journalist principally responsible for the project. "What most people remember from the 1991 Gulf War is the 'smart' bomb," said Brian McKenna. "Yet only 7 per cent of the bombs were 'smart' or accurate. The other 93 per cent were conventional iron bombs—and three out of every four missed their military targets. They killed civilians. Women and children, blew them to smithereens."[35]

Simonds's diary entries concluded with a reflection on the old soldiers who came to her children's classrooms around Remembrance Day, with their suits and berets and medals. She reminded herself that she had to remember "the individual gallantries and honour them." Most of all, she wanted to remember "the stupidity, the ineptitude, the deception, and ultimately the horror that is war."

Critics of *The Valour and the Horror* clung stubbornly, in the face of compelling evidence, to the claim that the area bombing of German cities was a good thing because it hastened the end of the war, and that the thousands of Canadians killed in the campaign died as part of a rational plan. Bercuson and Wise, the editors of *The Valour and the Horror Revisited*, go so far as to abandon any pretence of analysis in blithely attacking the four historians who wrote *The Crucible of War*: "The *whole thrust* of volume 3 of the official history is that the bomber offensive was a misguided failure and that the deaths of 9919 Canadians in Bomber Command were essentially meaningless in the total picture of the war."[36] Yet nowhere in *The Crucible of War*, a painstakingly researched account of Canada's part in the bomber offensive, do the authors argue that the deaths from flak, Messerschmitt attacks, or fiery crashes were "meaningless," as if anyone's death anywhere, anytime, can be so described. Moreover, the militant historians argue that the terror attacks disciplined the German people, teaching them a lesson that they would not soon forget. They seem oblivious to the evidence of the Blitz, which, while undoubtedly terrorizing many Londoners, taught them many lessons, though not the ones the German High Command intended; or to proof of the more recent mass bombings of Korea and Vietnam, which killed millions but did not lead the bombed-out peoples to accept defeat.

Bercuson and Wise also draw an extraordinary connection between the aerial bombing and one of the best-known and most controversial campaigns of that war. "No event other than the final surge of the Red Army into Berlin," they say, "brought the war home more crushingly to the German people than the long-sustained bomber offensive with its terrible casualties and its immense damage." But that "surge" into Berlin involved what Anthony Beevor describes as "carnal booty" exacted by Soviet troops whose political officers had instructed them in "the honour and dignity of the Red Army warrior." In total an estimated two million German women, at the very least, were raped in that campaign; a substantial minority of them suffered multiple rapes.[37] According to the sterile account of Bercuson and Wise, this "final surge" was, together with the terror bombing, simply part of a salutary punishment for German misdeeds. In other words, Germans were learning the stern lessons of history.

"Out of this realization came the Schuman Plan of 1950, the European Economic Community of 1957, and the European Community of today," state Bercuson and Wise. "Out of it also came the emergence of a democratic and responsible Germany in full partnership and alliance with the states that once had bombed it." Apparently, then, according to these historians, a direct line of causality exists between the horrors of mass rape and indiscriminate bombing and the rise of the European Coal and Steel Community and, ultimately, European Union.[38]

Perhaps the most telling and temperate assessment of *The Valour and the Horror* came from Leonard Johnson, an air force pilot who went on to command Canada's National Defence College. For Johnson, the documentary series provided "a fair depiction" of the mass bombing campaign. He did think the production's suggestion that the air crews were being somehow deceived was wide of the mark.

> I cannot imagine a commander opening a briefing with 'Gentlemen, your target tonight is the women and children of Germany!' even if that was the inevitable outcome of what they were being briefed to do. The psychological burden of flying operations was heavy enough without compounding it with guilt, and it would have been easy to dismiss the victims when they were behind and below, unseen and unheard. Crews fighting for their lives, in searchlights, flak and fighters night after night, could not be expected to question the morality of their actions, especially when refusal to fly meant public disgrace and stigmatization for cowardice.

Still, for Johnson the "Death by Moonlight" episode offered broader lessons relevant to the recent Gulf War. "The film stripped away comforting rationalizations and brought its audience face to face with the human cost of aerial bombardment, then and since. . . . The film did nothing whatever to diminish the courage and sacrifice of the aircrews, whose valor continues to be an inspiration to Canadian airmen."[39]

More than the history of the 1940s was at stake in these violent battles over *The Valour and the Horror*. Not only did the series offend by suggesting that the sacralized Second World War, like all complex human events, was open to a variety of responsible critical interpretations, but it also potentially disturbed North Americans' new-found fascination and celebration with aerial warfare. Avoiding the emphasis on war's filth, violence, and inherent toxicity—in such films as *Apocalypse Now* (1979), *Platoon* (1986), and *Full Metal Jacket* (1987)—Hollywood in *An Officer and a Gentleman* (1982) and *Top Gun* (1986) constructed intriguing, glittering, even sexy images of techno-warfare, in which American derring-do, technical savvy, and inherent decency prevailed.[40] In the 1990s, across North America, people were encouraged to recover from the "Vietnam Syndrome" and fall in love again with war and warriors. President Ronald Reagan had endorsed such efforts, and soon President George W. Bush re-enacted a scene from *Top Gun* in declaring "Mission Accomplished" in Iraq. There was no room in this budding techno-romance on either side of the border for naysayers and spoilsports.

Even as the vitriolic controversy over one television treatment of Canada's role in the Second World War was still simmering, the challenge of revising the past to suit the needs of the present would arise once again. A 1993 incident in the Horn of Africa exposed Canada's military to the glare of public scrutiny—something to which the forces were unaccustomed—as officers scrambled to cover up the details of the torture and murder of a Somali child and the fatal shooting of a young, unarmed man as he ran away. The "Somalia Affair," as it came to be known, led both to media probes of the army (and stumbling attempts by the military to hide the facts) and to an official investigation that the Chrétien Liberals would abruptly terminate before it could complete its mandate.

For over a century Somalia, nicely positioned for commercial interests shipping oil and other commodities through the Suez Canal, served as a geopolitical pinball for Europe's great powers. The Italian government established its control over *Somalia Italiana* in the 1880s. Mussolini's fascists later used the arid territory as a springboard to attack independent Ethiopia in 1935 and British Somaliland (the northern part of present-day Somalia) in 1940. The Italians lost the territory in the Second World War but regained it afterwards as a trust territory when the United Nations granted them administrative control. Somalia became independent in 1960, and its predominantly nomadic and pastoral people lived under a succession of authoritarian regimes, backed by various Cold War patrons seeking to control their territory. Siad Barre, an Italian-trained military man, seized power in a 1969 coup and proved adept at talking the Marxist-Leninist talk as Somalia became a Soviet client state. It received weapons and aid in return for a naval and missile base at the port of Berbera. Barre, a devious Machiavellian, was adept at manipulating clan rivalries and encouraging regional resentments. But the state was still not well entrenched in Somali society by the time his Soviet patrons transferred their favours to an equally dubious regime in neighbouring Ethiopia. Even before the Soviet invasion of Afghanistan in 1980, the United States was implementing a "counterforce strategy" to support any opposition to Soviet allies in the Third World. In keeping with that goal, the Cambodian Khmer Rouge and the Afghan Mujahedin were beneficiaries of U.S. aid, and Barre soon joined that select company.[41]

By the late 1980s Barre was enmeshed in brutal campaigns against his opponents. In 1990 the United Somali Congress spearheaded a final assault on the capital, and Barre fled in early 1991. Somalia had begun its descent into the chaos of a "failed state" (in the newly popular expression of some international relations specialists). By 1992 the capacity of Somalis to feed themselves had been depleted by years of conflict, and their country was awash with imported weaponry. A complex, clan-based society was fractured and people began to flee the country, with Canada a destination of choice. The Red Cross estimated that 4.5 million people faced starvation and issued a warning:

"Only a global approach can prevent a disaster on an unprecedented scale." The Red Cross found itself spending 20 per cent of its total worldwide budget on emergency aid to Somalia. Estimates of malnutrition reached "horrifying levels" in the area around Belet Huen and in the refugee camps near Merca.[42]

When the gravity of the situation in Somalia percolated into global consciousness in 1992, Canada's military was already heavily involved in UN peacekeeping operations in what was by then being described as the former Yugoslavia. In the years following the collapse of the Soviet Union an upsurge in UN peace operations began to take place in fractured states, including Croatia and Bosnia, where the UN's massive peacekeeping effort in the 1990s was a "Chapter 6" operation. Based on the UN Charter's Chapter 6, intended to deal with conflict through investigation and mediation, peacekeeping troops from contributing countries can go into service under Security Council resolutions. Lightly armed Chapter 6 peacekeepers can use force only to defend themselves and are not allowed to take direct action when people are murdered at random. Soldiers dispatched on Chapter 6 deployments to the former Yugoslavia, Rwanda, and other war zones found the constraints appallingly frustrating. Unlike the "interpositional" efforts of the Suez Crisis of 1956 and the ups and downs of the years in Cyprus, where uneasy ceasefires prevailed, the fighters in the Balkans just kept on fighting. There was, according to the common refrain, no peace to keep.

Brent Beardsley, who witnessed the depravity of the Rwandan genocide first-hand and became "particularly adept at rescuing nuns," reflected on the frustrations that would become commonplace among peacekeepers. Operations in places such as the Balkans, he said, were not based on any clear and enforceable mandate or mutual consent of the belligerents. The principals were still engaged in combat. They might have said okay to the outside forces coming in, but that was about it. Their attitude was: "You gotta stay out of our way. If not, you take your risks." In Beardsley's experience it was a matter of European countries intervening "out of their own self-interest . . . trying to sort out a problem so they don't have a bunch of refugees on their doorstep." The peacekeepers were in the position of "watching ethnic cleansing taking place"—without either the authority or the mandate to do anything about it.[43] The upshot of the Balkan peacekeeping—

which eventually entailed bombing campaigns that went far beyond conventional "just war" thinking and diplomatic ventures that in effect perpetuated ethnic cleansing by other means (based as they were upon simplistic prejudices about Balkan primitivism and tribalism)—was a cruel revelation of the limitations of war conducted in the name of peace.[44]

Somalia was different. Launched in early 1992 when the Security Council imposed a complete arms embargo on the country, the campaign was not a Chapter 6 peacekeeping operation. By year's end the UN Operation in Somalia (UNOSOM) had a Chapter 7 authorization, which included military force—"real soldiering," said one military man pleased to be in a "non-blue-beret fight" in Somalia.[45] The Council "welcomed the United States' offer to help create a secure environment for the delivery of humanitarian aid in Somalia and authorized, under Chapter 7 of the Charter, the use of 'all necessary means' to do so." The U.S. military leadership, aglow after its Gulf War victory over the brutal but incompetent Saddam Hussein, had been wary of intervening in the Balkans but now agreed to what strategists assumed would be a tidy little effort in Somalia—"We do deserts, we don't do mountains."[46]

Canada's military leadership responded promptly. Chief of Defence Staff John de Chastelain, who had a close relationship with the U.S. Joint Chiefs of Staff chairman Colin Powell, immediately contacted his opposite number at the Pentagon, suggesting that Canada also send troops to Somalia. As he explained, "A role that was seen to be secondary would not sit well with the troops, with me, with the Government or with Canadians."[47] But Somalia was not Iraq, even though it had lots of desert. The U.S. intervention, using troops with no experience in peacekeeping, turned into a massive debacle as the Americans essentially ignored the wider UN operation.

A degree of imperial hubris was involved in the North American assumption that the unelected policemen of the world from Canada and the United States could simultaneously intervene in both an escalating Balkan conflict and in the equally complicated situation in Somalia. In March 1993 soldiers from the Canadian Airborne Regiment, conventionally described in media accounts as an "elite" outfit, gunned down Abdi Hamdare and Ahmad Aruush, allegedly for breaching their compound's security fence, or "perimeter" in soldier-speak.

Hamdare and Aruush were shot from behind as they fled; Aruush was finished off at close range. Captain Michel Rainville was charged in connection with the incident but acquitted on the grounds that he was following orders. He stated that when local Somalis breached the wire border the act "clearly" constituted "an act of sabotage or an act of terrorism." (The Canadians, it later came out, were putting out food and water as bait to attract intruders.) Rainville's superior, Lieutenant-Colonel Carol Mathieu, congratulated his man on his performance. Army commanders in Somalia apparently saw the shootings as part of the hard work of peacekeeping. Mathieu was also acquitted after being charged with negligence. Capt. Rainville's defence lawyer told the court that Somalia had a lot of heat and sand but lacked order.[48]

Army physician Major Barry Armstrong examined the dead and wounded Somalis after the shooting and wrote to his wife about "a very big racist thing going on here." Major Armstrong was clearly in violation of the all-for-one/one-for-all esprit de corps that lies at the heart of the military culture's incestuous camaraderie. After his letter was leaked to the press he told military police that he had come under increasing pressure to leave Somalia. Lt.-Col. Mathieu noted at the time: "He is a doctor. I don't tell him how to perform operations."[49]

On March 16 sixteen-year-old Shidane Abukar Arone was caught in an abandoned U.S. compound where military functionaries had jettisoned many materials, valueless to them but of potential worth to the desperately poor population in the area. Canadian peacekeepers found Arone hiding in a portable toilet and then proceeded to torture the boy to death. While the ordeal was going on some eighty soldiers, according to one estimate, could hear his screams. One soldier compared Arone's cries to an experience he remembered from his rural childhood when animals were slaughtered on the family farm. "If an animal was not put down properly then as they were finished off they would still be alive and conscious and that sound was very close to what I heard."[50]

Most of the facts eventually came to light due to Major Armstrong's refusal to go along with the military's attempted cover-up, and to the persistence of a handful of journalists. The military hierarchy attempted to stymie the release of information, destroying documentation along the way, with journalists salivating all the more over the possibility of a Watergate-style story in which the cover-up threatens to overshadow the actual crimes. Only two days after the army attempted to showcase its "hearts and minds" humanitarian effort at Belet Huen by opening a school it had rebuilt, the CBC reported the first allegations of a cover-up in the murder of Shidane Arone. The two years that followed saw a steady drip-drip of revelations that prolonged public interest in the Somalia Affair. CBC-Radio's Michael McAuliffe received altered documents related to the issue. Several soldiers—but no one over the rank of major—were convicted in relation to the killings in Somalia, although no one would serve over two years in prison. McAuliffe received more documents that had been illegally altered to appear to fit with the altered documents he had already received. By January 1995 the CBC was broadcasting videotapes of the Airborne Regiment's hazing rituals. Together with the photos of a bloodied Shidane Arone and his torturers, the tapes foreshadowed the infamous Abu Ghraib photos that would, a decade later, expose U.S. atrocities in Iraq. The Airborne tapes showed simulated sodomizing, a black soldier smeared with shit spelling out "KKK," and a soldier declaring that Somalis were not starving but that "they never work, they're lazy, they're slobs, and they stink."[51]

By March 1995 the Somalia affair was attracting so much attention that the Chrétien Liberals disbanded the Canadian Airborne Regiment and appointed a three-person Commission of Inquiry to look into the Somalia Affair. The Commission was stonewalled by Department of National Defence delays in the face of orders to produce all documentation related to the scandal. A nervous government ordered it to complete its work immediately. An election was looming. "There would be no hearings into the March 16 murder of Shidane Arone or allegations of subsequent cover-up in Ottawa," wrote veteran journalist Peter Desbarats.[52] In his book *Somalia Cover-Up: A Commissioner's Journal*, Desbarats pointed to signs that a reliable old boys' network was making a comeback, citing hurry-up reports from "official experts" commissioned by Defence Minister Doug Young just as the minister cashiered the Somalia inquiry. One such expert was J.L. Granatstein, who referred to the proceedings as a "kangaroo court." The historian "continued to take pot shots at us even as he pocketed his contract from the minister," wrote Desbarats. Granatstein referred to the inquiry chair, Judge Gilles Létourneau, as the "Grand Inquisitor" and came to the defence of General Jean Boyle, the Chief of Defence Staff who was forced to resign in disgrace, but quickly moved on to become vice-president of "business development" for Boeing International.[53]

The main victims of the Somalia affair were, of course, the Somalis who suffered at the hands of the Canadian military. But according to one line of thought it was the military itself that was victimized by the 1993 events in the Horn of Africa. Perhaps the most striking single text of the decade of darkness was David Bercuson's *Significant Incident: Canada's Army, the Airborne, and the Murder in Somalia* (1996), which appeared even before the Somalia inquiry was terminated. "The Canadian army is in crisis," blared the back cover—raising a note of alarm that pervaded the book, in which Bercuson used the death of Shidane Abukar Arone as a springboard for a polemic against the moral rot of a welfare state whose complete destruction—"with gusto"—he had urged two years before.[54]

In *Significant Incident* Bercuson turned his attention to postwar Canada's most deformed offspring, the peacekeeping tradition. In his mind this tradition held a large measure of the responsibility for the Somali teenager's death. In a roundabout way, and with considerable chutzpah, Bercuson managed to associate war crimes committed by Canadians with the "peace-and-love" permissiveness of the detested 1960s. Shedding little light on the tragedy itself, the book provides a revealing glimpse into the troubled mind of a new warrior, a notable member of the far-right Calgary School and an academic linked to the Canadian Defence and Foreign Affairs Institute and the Centre for Military and Strategic Studies, both funded in part by the Department of National Defence via the Security and Defence Forum. *Significant Incident* was, indeed, an early new warrior manifesto for a new army and a new Canada. It not only celebrated the martial virtues of a bygone age, but also called out for a great leader capable of defending those values in the future.

Who should take responsibility for Arone's death? Not, said Bercuson, the members of the Canadian forces or, at least, not the vast majority of them. No, apart from the easily demonized men who carried out the killing—one of them depicted as an oddball "swag-gerer" and a "bully"—Bercuson laid most of the blame at the feet of Ottawa politicians and bureaucrats, inside and outside the military—functionaries who corrupted the military, and Canada itself, with their soft-hearted, soft-headed misapprehensions about the true nature of war and the martial heart of Canada itself. The men on the Somalia front were betrayed by a government that appointed to senior military positions men who had forgotten "that armies exist to fight wars." Arone died, in other words, because post-1960s Canadians and their leaders were far too inclined to peace. Managers on one side—pen-pushers who scurried for cover at the first sign of trouble—and staunch warriors on the other—valiant men who really understood both war and Canada—were locked in an epic struggle for the very soul of the army. And so far, Bercuson said in 1996, "the warriors are losing."[55]

In Canada, then, true soldiers have been sacrificed so that pam-pered politicians can prate on about rights, sanction "endless cycles of welfare," and blather on about bilingualism, multiculturalism, and peace. In doing so, these politicians offend not just Canada and its war-riors, but the human species. For war is a permanent, unchanging, and essential aspect of humanity, as "old as civilization itself," a constant "since the first dawn." To avert your eyes from this stern Darwinian truth (or to engage with the extensive anthropological counter-evidence that radically complicates it) is to engage in liberal daydreams. Aban-doning war means abandoning this fundamental evolutionary truth, and it threatens to rob true soldiers of their moments of transcen-dence. For the true soldier, war is majestic, enthralling, beautiful. What is it that he (far more rarely she) loves about war?

> It is the awful beauty of tracer fire at night, of a horizon lit by the gun flashes of a thousand field pieces, of a formation of hundreds of bombers droning through the sky despite bursts of anti-aircraft fire and the wanton attacks of enemy fighters. It is the experience of com-radely love so strong as to cause men to sacrifice their lives without a moment's hesitation to save their fellows.

Under fire men form deep bonds, experiencing a "sublime love for those who share the same fate and a deep hatred for the nameless and usually faceless enemy who opposes them."[56]

A Canada that turns its back on battle, a Canada that heeds the call of those who understand none of war's sensual and transcendent beauty, a Canada run by paper-pushing bureaucrats and civilian busybodies: here is the Canada that killed Shidane Abukar Arone. It takes real war to generate real warriors—no mere training exercises, no matter how realistic, can ever do the trick. Peace corrupts and corrodes martial virtues. The crimes committed by the Airborne can be partially accounted for (and to an extent implicitly exonerated) by lengthy descriptions of the taxing Somalia environment, but they are better explained, said Bercuson, by recognizing that the perpetrators were not real soldiers. They were products of a system that failed to weed out the unfit and incompetent and did not provide opportunities for soldiers to be *blooded*—brought under actual fire—a key concept in Bercuson's symbolic universe. Until a unit has been *blooded*, no one can know who are the fittest, who deserve to survive, and who are the unfit—or "misfits"—who deserve to be weeded out. Confronted with the murder of Arone, Bercuson said, in effect, "But no *true* Soldier would do such a thing!" Yet actually existing soldiers have done such things the whole world round. On other interpretations, the warriors were acting in the racist and brutal ways long familiar to students of empire.[57]

Bercuson constructed Somalia—the supposed subject of his book—as a purely deficient place, the exact opposite of the martial sublimity he extolled so ecstatically. Like many of the heroes in Somerset Maugham's stories, Bercuson's Canadians were driven near-crazy by the suffocating heat and dust of the Tropics. Here is a maddening place—and a maddening people. The Somalis encountered in Bercuson's text are not our fellow humans struggling, just like us, to get through the day without sickness or starvation. Instead, they are petty thieves, mired in corruption, the spawn of a squalid and failed state. The murder of poor Arone was one of the least significant, and the least thoroughly described, incidents in *Significant Incident*.

Although Bercuson and the new warriors want Canada to be a proud part of the projection of Anglo-American power throughout the world, their even more fundamental agenda is the moral and political redemption of this country itself. Canada's politics will be reformed only when war once again becomes the centrepiece of our military. A priestly caste of warriors—those who approach war "with solemnity and a strong sense of occasion, as a priest might approach an altar for a mass"—administer the sacrifice of the blood through which the nation is both solidified and purified. It is this caste that is called upon to defend the country's virtues, even its very survival, in the dog-eat-dog world of perpetual war.[58]

For this new warrior there is a "greater scandal" than the torture and murder of a Somali teenager: it is that "thousands of Canadian soldiers" were sent into a place where "their lives were recklessly risked by politicians who appear not to have cared for their welfare." Rather than focusing on the Somalia scandal, to which they were "treated" by the ever-prying and irresponsible media, Canadians should learn to get behind their troops and appreciate how, "for over a hundred years," such men and women had uncomplainingly defended the true values of the nation. Canadians must be shaken out of their stupor. They must see through the "pious cant about being an honest broker in an evil world" and realize that "all international relations, including trade, rest on a foundation of military power."[59]

Like U.S. neo-conservatives who championed the return of martial ideals (and the imperial efforts in Iraq and Afghanistan as noble experiments that would allow martial virtues to flourish once again), Bercuson called for a revolution in values. A social welfare state must be replaced by one in which "the old-fashioned, but necessary, virtues of honour, integrity, professionalism, dedication to the military as a vocation, and acceptance of the unlimited liability of soldiers will once again form the core values of the Canadian army."[60] Only then will the army of Vimy Ridge be redeemed, and only then will Canada as a whole be in touch with its past and destiny as a Warrior Nation.

Significant Incident is an early outline of the arguments that would later become the new common sense of politics: that massive rearmament is imperative, even in a time of peace; that Canada, founded on war, must elevate warriors to the status of permanent heroes; that coddled Canadians need their leaders to give them a psychological and cultural makeover—even an extreme makeover—to purge them of pacifism and indecision; and that questioning this program is an act of disloyalty to the country and its values. At the heart of the crisis gripping the army in 1996, and by extension the country, was the search for true leaders, "true warriors," those whose excellence and courage in battle will "set the tone for the entire chain of command."[61] As early as 1996, the armed forces could be heard, by Bercuson at least, crying out for their Caesar.

Indeed, all the media attention to the fate of women like Sandra Perron was a distraction from the matter at hand—the moral regeneration of army and nation through a decisive new leadership. In 1996 a photo leaked to the press showed a 1992 training exercise in which Perron, Canada's first female infantry officer, had been tied to a tree, barefoot in the snow, as a supposed "prisoner of war." A report of the incident said she had been punched in the stomach by a superior officer. She resigned from the army in 1996. Incidents such as these went to show, said one military analyst, that "political correctness" was incompatible with "effective combat forces."[62]

Military culture is all about war stories and places with evocative names: Dieppe, the Somme, Paardeberg. Medals are hugely important, as are cenotaphs, triumphal arches, and mass graveyards. Parades abound. Stories—the tales that have from time immemorial provided social glue to clans, families, and nations, also provide vitality to the military. Canadians maintain an apparently unquenchable thirst for books and museums dealing with war. One Canadian journalist managed to squeeze an entire book out of a skirmish in the Medak Pocket in Croatia, an incident that in other conflicts would have gone unreported. When Canadian troops got into that firefight, *The Ghosts of the Medak Pocket* became *The Story of Canada's Secret War.* There were heroes: "Drew was the kind of stuff that great Canadian soldiers are made of . . . from Vimy Ridge to Kap'yong." There were emotions: the exchange went "well beyond the scope of peacekeeping. . . . But the soldiers of Eight Platoon knew one thing: it felt good."[63]

The UN Protection Force in the former Yugoslavia (UNPROFOR) exemplified the limitations and frustrations of the peacekeeping enterprise. Some twenty-five hundred Canadians were at one time serving with UNPROFOR when it was operating at full strength in the period from 1992 to 1995—the fourth-largest force among thirty contributing countries. But its very name, Protection Force, reflected a reality that would have been ironic had it not been so tragic. Along with the 1994 Rwanda massacres, the 1995 slaughter of eight thousand Bosniacs (Bosnian Muslims) at Srebrenica put an indelible stain on the UN peacekeeping record. The Security Council had declared Srebrenica a safe area over two years before Serb forces carried out the systematic murder of Bosniac men and boys. Dutch peacekeepers, restricted by tight rules of engagement, could do nothing to stop the bloodletting. It took seven years for an agency in the Netherlands to issue a report, after which the Dutch government accepted partial responsibility. The finger-pointing would continue. In 2010 the U.S. general who had been NATO's top soldier at the time of the massacre blamed Europe's military shortcomings for the outrage. Echoing Canadians like Bercuson who blamed their country's lack of an appetite for combat for problems with the military, U.S. Marine Corps General John Sheehan was forthright about European milquetoasts: "They declared a peace dividend and made a conscious effort to socialise their military—that includes the unionisation of their militaries, it includes open homosexuality. That led to a force that was ill-equipped to go to war. The case in point that I'm referring to is when the Dutch were required to defend Srebrenica against the Serbs."[64]

To Brent Beardsley's ethical dilemma in Kigali could be added the experience of Patrick Rechner, an unarmed Canadian military observer who ended up being tied to a Serb ammunition dump as a human shield against NATO air attacks. One 1992 letter from a Canadian assigned to UNPROFOR described his voyage through Croatia. At first he had seen a countryside littered with dead livestock. Later those views of rotting cattle were replaced by "the sight of dead humans who litter the gutters and river which flows through the main city." People regardless of their age or sex were being gunned down in the streets.[65]

Like much else in the Balkan civil war, the images were caught on camera and broadcast around the world. Peacekeeping can be a dangerous, frightening business. In a typical incident, three Canadian soldiers had their jeep crushed when a Serbian army truck attempted to pass on a blind curve. Jim De Coste was killed, and Rick Turner and Stacey Bouck were badly injured. When Serb soldiers pulled Bouck out of the jeep, both of her legs had been broken and a lung punctured. Instead of providing further assistance, the Serb soldiers stole her money and clothing. In *Tarnished Brass: Crime and Corruption in the Canadian Military*, soldier-turned-gadfly-journalist Scott Taylor denounced the military command for accepting the blame for the incident and even paying for the damage to the Serbian truck.[66]

The one time that Canadian troops did get to cut loose with their weapons—during the skirmish in the Medak Pocket in Croatia—Ottawa chose not to publicize the dust-up. That decision caused much angst among men who supported a warrior ethos. It would take nearly ten years for the Department of National Defence to come up with an award ceremony and medals "for the soldiers who had fought to stop ethnic cleansing."[67]

The deaths at Srebrenica represented the worst act of mass murder in Europe since the Second World War. Together with Rwanda, the Balkan debacle did much to prompt increasingly critical scrutiny of the whole concept of peacekeeping. Although the term would remain fixed in popular parlance, discussions among the cognoscenti at the United Nations and in foreign policy circles would increasingly refer to "peace operations" and "peace support operations." The term "peacebuilding" referred to postwar situations, which meant peace enforcement with armed intervention that was usually accompanied by the adjective "robust." As Michael Riordon remarks, in this world of spin, "peace" could now mean almost anything, including war.[68]

Shifts in terminology and complexity were accompanied by a gradual expansion of the number of peacekeeping operations in the period after 1990, which was also marked by the emergence of a unipolar world in which the United States, its economic dominance fading, emerged unchallenged as the sole remaining military superpower. This new-model peacekeeping was itself a contradiction. The early, first-generation missions—numbering thirteen between 1956 and 1978—meant, according to Sandra Whitworth, "establishing an interposition force between belligerent groups that had given their consent to the establishment of a peacekeeping mission." In principle if not always in reality, this meant respecting the sovereignty, competence, and dignity of each of the parties in the conflict. The second-generation missions—totalling twenty-nine between 1988 and 1996—"involved a whole host of tasks, including military and police functions, the monitoring of human rights, the conduct of elections, the delivery of humanitarian aid, the repatriation of refugees, the creation and conduct of state administrative structures, and so on."[69]

More recently, in what amounts to third-generation missions, the United Nations is often either marginalized or quietly complicit; and, as in the cases of Lebanon, Afghanistan, Iraq, Haiti, and Libya, regime change in the interest of Western interests is undertaken by armed force, once again often in the name of peace. Over the 1990s, peacekeeping was transformed into something more closely resembling imperial policing. The enterprise entailed not respect for sovereignty but often—in the name of the "responsibility to protect"—its systematic abrogation.

In the process, the most promising and even implicitly subversive element of Pearsonism—the imperfectly developed implication that westerners should respect the competence, national identities, and complexities of Others—was progressively lost. Instead of a partial acknowledgement that a conflict might have at the very least two sides—something that peacekeepers should keep in mind—the new model of peacekeeping rediscovered the old Empire's habits of imperial superiority and denigration, now redecorated in an unctuous language of liberal universalism and human rights. An obvious, if infrequently observed, contradiction of the new missions that were promiscuously dubbed "peacekeeping" was the obvious tension between, on one side, training young men to fight and kill and, on the other, the diplomatic, social, and cultural skills required to build peace. "If we only prepare people for war," one critic mused, "it is far more likely that this is what we will get."[70]

The twentieth century was surely the most violent and war-ravaged in the history of humankind. At century's end the signals for a shift to a more peaceful world were decidedly mixed. Apostles of globalization trumpeted the ways in which open borders and the liberation of capital from wage-earners and welfare states would promote freedom. Capitalism's victory and the triumph of self-regulating markets, following so soon after the demise of the Soviet Union, came to be equated with an upsurge in liberty. Freer markets, less government, more prosperity, more freedom, more peace.[71]

Yet Russia, though it had embraced free markets with a vengeance, was rapidly turning into a horror show of corruption and declining life expectancy. It also turned out that those countries experiencing the most success were, as economist Joseph Stiglitz noted in 2001, regulated by governments that "took an unabashedly central role, and explicitly and implicitly recognized the value of preserving social cohesion, and not only protected social and human capital but enhanced it."[72] Stiglitz was referring to East Asia's success stories. Some eight years earlier the *Financial Times* had been moved to the editorial admission that globalization was still "an imperfect force. . . . About two thirds of the world's population have gained little or no substantial advantage from rapid economic growth. In the developed world, the lowest quartile of income earners have witnessed trickle-up rather than trickle-down."[73]

In Canada the laissez-faire approach was accompanied by respectable economic growth and increasing social inequality and poverty. Elected in 1993, the Chrétien Liberals appointed Lloyd Axworthy as minister of Human Resources Development. A charter member of the fast-fading leftish rump of a Liberal Party that had embraced the gospel of globalization, Axworthy spent the next three years reforming the unemployment insurance system by making it harder for jobless workers to qualify for benefits, and even indulging in bromides about breaking "the cycle of dependency" faced by the poor.[74] Paul Martin's 1995 budget marked the final triumph of business liberalism and a reversal of postwar welfare-state programs. The military's self-proclaimed decade of darkness was certainly gloomy for the country's most vulnerable people. The loyalist Axworthy, having served in the ministry trenches under both Trudeau and Chrétien, finally got his reward in 1996 when Chrétien appointed him to the plum political appointment of the Department of Foreign Affairs and International Trade (DFAIT).

Axworthy, faced with a department reduced through cutbacks, tried to make a virtue out of necessity by embarking on an agenda emphasizing "human security" and "soft power." Canada's foreign policy would, he argued, reflect its "profoundly attractive values, democracy, bilingualism, multiculturalism, tolerance and respect for diversity, the rule of law, a market economy tempered by unifying social programs, and flexible federalism."[75] Even though Canadian aid was being slashed, Axworthy pulled off something of a coup by actively backing the efforts of citizens' groups pushing for an international treaty to ban land mines. The so-called Ottawa Process took advantage of momentum from below as Axworthy played a key role in persuading most of the world to sign a convention banning the manufacture, use, and export of one of the most deadly and insidious tools. (The United States, China, and Russia gave the treaty a pass.) Axworthy also had Canada actively backing the International Criminal Court, making efforts to curb small arms, and promoting the rights of children.

None of this posed a threat to the hegemony of let-the-market-decide thinking, but it unsettled orthodox foreign policy types. In 1998 Kim Richard Nossal explained that soft power was a "buzzword," even a "squishy notion . . . next to useless." He insisted that Canada needed "the expensive tools of traditional hard power—highly skilled diplomats, an honourable development program, war-ready armed forces, and long-reaching intelligence services."[76] More and more, the new warriors equated Canadian and U.S. national interests. That there could be any underlying conflict of interest between the two countries, on any substantive issue, came to be considered far-fetched. Their annexationist nationalism identifies the meaning and essence of Canada to be its assimilation within a U.S.-led North America and, beyond that, a world-changing Anglosphere.

When Axworthy backed non-governmental organizations (NGOs) in carving out a niche for what he saw as an activist foreign policy, he was seemingly moving away from this narrow conception of Canada. Yet he challenged almost nothing in the Anglosphere's stance towards the world. Axworthy went nowhere near the economic arrangements of the North American Free Trade Agreement (NAFTA) and the World Trade Organization (WTO), which had been established to enforce the neo-liberal Washington Consensus. As political scientist Stephen Clarkson pointed out, in a nice distillation of the realities of life within the Anglosphere, Axworthy "could pull an occasional feather from the American eagle's tail. But any resulting contretemps with the United

States had to be on the high road of multilateralism, not the low roads along which the continental political economy travelled."77

The Ottawa Process that culminated in the international agreement to ban land mines reflected the limitations and strengths of this approach. Some of the main producers and users of land mines failed to sign onto a multilateral agreement that moved in the direction of a global regulatory regime. That said, the challenge to the imperative of armies to deploy whatever weapons they want, wherever and whenever their commanders feel it necessary, was an accomplishment that cannot be discounted. It was not an achievement of what international relations specialists like to describe as "statecraft." It was, on the other hand, the result of a global social movement that encompassed both big NGOs and sprawling, informal networks of citizens in some of the world's poorest countries.

This was not the same sort of high-level diplomacy that had won Pearson the Nobel Peace Prize in 1956. But it did win, for the International Campaign to Ban Landmines (ICBL) and its co-ordinator Jody Williams, the same prize in 1997. Other groups (Amnesty International and International Physicians for the Prevention of Nuclear War) that had come to be described as part of "civil society" had already received the Peace Prize, a reflection of the recognition that history is not simply shaped by great men but by people acting collectively, often with the aim of improving the common good.78 The attack on land mines and their devastation of innocents had its roots in the peace movement of the 1980s. In 1992 Handicap International, Human Rights Watch, Medico International, Mines Advisory Group, Physicians for Human Rights, and Vietnam Veterans of America Foundation launched the ICBL. The global networking effort soon gathered dozens of national campaigns and hundreds of groups worldwide, including crucial efforts by people in the countries most affected. By the time the prize was awarded, the network included "human rights, humanitarian, children's, peace, veteran's, medical, development, arms control, religious, environmental, and women's groups in over 60 countries."79

There was something in the new fashionability of civil society, it seemed, to furrow the brow of right-wingers and give cheer to peaceniks—but appearances were somewhat deceiving. Just as they transformed peacekeeping into war-making, the new warriors embraced "civil society" by changing its meaning. Confirming Jenny Pearce's 1997 contention that civil society denotes an "arena of contestation" reflecting the "social divisions of society as a whole,"[80] the new warriors effectively mobilized so that, over time, the cry for a new warlike Canada seemed to emanate spontaneously from the Canadian people themselves.

In the arena of matters military, the Conference of Defence Associations, founded in 1932, is not as old as the Royal Canadian Legion, but is better organized. An old boys' club of retired officers, it offers up a coterie of military retirees as press contacts, supporting the war in Afghanistan, holding an annual Vimy Dinner, sponsoring a Vimy Award, publishing Vimy Papers, and generally extolling all things military. It does all of this with the support of weapons manufacturers and the Department of National Defence.[81] In other words, the Defence Department funds military retirees to urge Ottawa to spend more money on the Defence Department. According to Morton's impish analysis of the CDA, it is a group that meets to hear papers and "tell each other how wonderful they were. How the infantry is the Queen of Battle while others stand around while we win the war. The artillery says they win the wars. And the engineers say you would not get to war if you didn't have roads. The air force association says 'We need more planes.'"[82]

Such organizations seldom advertise themselves as lobbyists for the arms industry. Rather, the emphasis is invariably on something called "security." Indeed, national security is a notion so vague that the government can use it to justify the targeting of its political enemies and increasingly to deploy the most despicable abuses of power. Security and national security: the easy jargon often masks the ways in which liberties are stripped away. Much mischief—and far, far worse—can be rationalized under the national security umbrella, a grim truth that would be brought home to Maher Arar in 2002. Just as importantly for wannabe warriors, invoking the vague issue of security, along with the spectre of rusting equipment and insufficient investment in soldiery, can be a bracing tonic for institutional budgets.

Defining security is like trying to nail jelly to a wall. For militarists, it means the security of the state and the existing social order. It has little if anything to do with security in the sense of secure access to food, clean water, or health. The 1990s brought an international sanctions regime aimed at the pariah regime under Saddam Hussein in Iraq. The sanctions decimated the country's social infrastructure, which was already reeling from the aerial bombing of the Gulf War. Some commentators calculated that hundreds of thousands died as a result of sanction-related hardships; others said the statistics were inflated by the regime. What both sides could acknowledge was that one undeniable result of the new world conflict was a blurring of the distinction between war and politics. Without declaring war on Iraq, the U.S. government and its allies could, through "coercive diplomacy," guarantee dire consequences for the Iraqi people. Even the age-old democratic principle of civilian control over the military became meaningless, as civilians themselves became leading proponents of military coercion.[83] One 1999 U.S. Congressional staff report cited a discussion with Anupama Rao Singh, head of UNICEF in Iraq:

> She urged the delegation to look at the situation facing children now, and how these economic problems caused by sanctions will have a major impact on their future. She pointed to examples of civil unrest in Africa and elsewhere, usually caused by disaffected youth with no hope of education, job, or a future. There is just such a generation of Iraqis growing up now ... and that will be very dangerous.[84]

The United States would learn the extent of the danger in the wake of the Bush regime's disastrous 2003 decision to invade Iraq.

The desperate conditions faced by the people of Iraq had become widely recognized by 1998. At the end of that year, Canada's leading peace and disarmament organization made an appeal to the government that underlined the ideals of a different notion of *security*. Project Ploughshares, an ecumenical Christian organization that had its own understanding of just what is meant by peace, told the prime minister about other conceptions of security that go far beyond the military understanding of the idea.

> The relevant security doctrine, embraced by Ottawa and by the growing international peacebuilding community, is characterized as "human security"—the idea that the safety and welfare of persons (even, one might dare to hope, the people of Iraq), rather than the survival or defeat of regimes, must be the primary focus of international security strat-

egy. . . . Military prowess cannot be relied on to implement human security, or to maintain either stability or the containment of weapons of mass destruction. The only insurance against tyranny and the tyrant's pursuit of weapons of mass destruction is an emboldened indigenous civil society that claims the right and acquires the capacity to give direct expression to the principles of justice, political participation, and basic economic well-being.[85]

No one seemed more awed—or, to use his term, "enthralled"—by U.S. might than Rick Hillier, an ambitious Canadian officer assigned in 1998 to the largest military base in the world. The "assets were incredible," noted Hillier, recalling the envy he felt living at Fort Hood, Texas, home to 250,000 people. "Family was all-important to the U.S. Army," he said of the sprawling base, seventy-five of whose personnel would commit suicide in the wake of wars in Iraq and Afghanistan between 2003 and 2009. By this time the U.S. government was spending over $300 million annually on military bands alone. The Canadian could not contain his praise for being "at the cutting edge of military technology," where he could meet up with commanders from around the world. He learned about U.S. military public relations tactics, "getting celebrities onside and using them, in the most positive sense, to achieve things for your country." Hillier was made an honorary citizen of Texas. To top it all off, he even got to talk to Governor George W. Bush on a conference call.[86]

According to Rick Hillier, commander of Canada's military when the Afghan detainee scandal was exposed, Canadians concerned about the fate of insurgents captured by his soldiers "were just interested in promoting their own agendas." Editorial cartoon by Brian Gable, *The Globe and Mail*, April 25, 2007.

CHAPTER 7

YELLOW RIBBONS AND INDIAN COUNTRY

NEW WARRIORS ON THE MARCH

The drift of modern history domesticates the fantastic and normalizes the unspeakable.

– Paul Fussell, 1975

O N JULY 25, 2006, Canadian Major Paeta Hess-von Kruedener was stationed at Patrol Base Khiam, a long-established UN observation post in south Lebanon. He and three other UN peacekeepers were killed when a 500-kilogram GPS-guided Joint Direct Attack Munition hit the base during an Israeli attack on Hezbollah forces. The bunker, built to withstand conventional artillery fire, was destroyed by the "bunker-busting" bomb.

A Human Rights Watch report issued within weeks of the attack said that the tragic event was part of a pattern of "systematic failure" by the Israeli Defence Forces (IDF) "to distinguish between combatants and civilians." Since the start of the Israel-Hezbollah war, Israeli forces had "consistently launched artillery and air attacks with limited or dubious military gain but excessive civilian cost." The timing and intensity of the attacks, the lack of military targets, and the return strikes against rescuers, the human rights NGO concluded, "suggest that Israeli forces deliberately targeted civilians." Intentionally killing innocent civilians has long been part of the tit-for-tat pattern of Israeli-Arab warfare. In this case Hezbollah fighters had launched poorly aimed missiles at northern Israel, killing 18 civilians. The IDF had in turn attacked Lebanon, killing 153 civilians, including 7 Canadian citizens at the village of Aitaroun.[1] Now they had deliberately killed UN peacekeepers.

The killing of Major Hess-von Kruedener raised eyebrows in Canada. To have a Canadian soldier on UN duty killed by a Canadian ally was surprising at best, unconscionable at worst, particularly because many Canadians had long regarded peacekeeping as a national vocation. A Canadian military Board of Inquiry, with which the Israelis refused to co-operate, reflected the Human Rights Watch conclusion that the IDF was intentionally killing non-combatants. "Considering that on previous occasions the IDF had halted fire when protests [from the United Nations] were received," the Board of Inquiry concluded, "no indication has been offered as to why protests of this nature and severity did not result in the halting of fire."[2]

On the release of this conclusion General Rick Hillier, by this time Canada's top military officer, issued a statement that contradicted his own institution's report. He described the major's death as a "tragic accident." The Canadian commander, or more likely one of his public relations minions, went on to offer up the usual boilerplate about "the young men and women who proudly wear our uniform. Major Hess-Von Kruedener did not die in vain and we shall never forget his ultimate contribution in the pursuit of peace."[3]

More telling was the reaction of Canada's prime minister. Immediately after the aerial assault on Patrol Base Khiam, having previously described Israeli attacks on Lebanon as "measured," Stephen Harper said he doubted that the bombing that killed the Canadian soldier was deliberate. His concern, rather, was about why peacekeepers had stayed in a war zone—why they had not withdrawn: "We want to find out why this United Nations post was attacked and also why it remained manned, during what is, more or less, a war, during obvious danger to these particular individuals."[4]

Cynthia Hess-von Kruedener responded to the official story about her husband's death on a peacekeeping mission with surprise and anger. "I'm shocked that Harper doesn't know why Paeta was there." She thought her husband had indeed died in vain. "What is being done by our government? Nothing. . . . What we've done is send a really clear message: If you kill UN observers or attack a UN patrol base, we will do nothing about it." She requested a verbal apology—an "eye-to-eye" meeting with the Israeli prime minister and the head of IDF, but had no illusions that such a meeting would come to pass. Her only solace, she said, was her "UN family" and the engaged sympathy of the Canadian public.[5]

The response of the recently elected Conservative government also came as a shock to some veterans. Retired Major Bill Porter lined up with those using the term "rusted out," arguing that Ottawa had been neglecting the military. The peacekeeping veteran had commanded the UN peacekeeping forces in the area of southern Lebanon that included the Khiam post. He had run patrols out of the post and in retirement was donning his medals and dressing in a blue blazer to visit Ottawa elementary schools on Remembrance Day to talk to children about war and peace.

"What did Harper not understand when he said 'Why didn't they withdraw?' *Goddamit!* Once they start to shell, the drill is to go into the goddamn bunker. That's why they call it a bunker."[6]

During the 1982 Israeli invasion of Lebanon, Porter recalled, Khiam had been shelled for seventeen straight days by the Israeli proxies of the South Lebanon Army—an organization that later established a torture centre nearby. Recalling how 155-millimetre artillery shells were falling along the approach roads to the UN observation post, he explained that when the shelling starts, a soldier does not jump into a jeep and go for a ride. "I'm a Conservative and all the rest of that but when I hear Harper say, 'Why didn't they withdraw?' I really got pissed off because that was fucking ignorant! What made it wrong this time is that the Israelis used a precision-guided bunker-buster bomb. They said it was due to a map error. I think that's bullshit."

The ignorance of Canada's war-boosting prime minister about the realities of peacekeeping may have been troubling to those familiar with the nitty-gritty reality of UN operations; but it marched in lock-step with the historians and other commentators who had little use for the notion of peacekeeping. It also dovetailed nicely with the UN-phobia of the far right in the United States, inspired in some cases by the conviction that the body was interfering with the religious destiny of Israel to fulfil its role in the End Times, and in other cases by a neo-conservative hostility to any attempt to place limits on the exercise of American power. In the first decade of the twenty-first century, as the country's contribution to peacekeeping dwindled, Canada would stop saying "Yes" to UN requests for peacekeeping forces.

The September 2001 attacks on New York and Washington were carried out by a group led by an Egyptian and made up mainly of Saudi Arabians. The reactionary, fundamentalist al-Qaeda militants had been given a safe haven by the governing Taliban in Afghanistan, where many of them had previously participated in the struggle against the occupying Soviet army in the 1980s. During that war Osama bin Laden and his followers had initially allied themselves not with the Taliban but with the Gulbuddin Hekmatyar—a ruthless favourite of the Saudis, the CIA, and the Pakistani spy agencies that were funnelling foreign money into Afghanistan. On bin Laden's return to Afghanistan after the 1996 Taliban takeover, some Taliban leaders believed that they owed him a debt of honour and gave him refuge. The al-Qaeda zealots directed their violence against the United States with the same fanatical zeal they had brought to the anti-Soviet struggle. After their 9/11 attacks on the United States, the term "blowback" gained popularity as a way of describing how former allies had turned against the Americans.

As late as the Second World War, according to Andrew Bacevich, "The United States itself had been the world's Saudi Arabia, producing enough oil to meet its own needs and that of its friends and allies." In the 1980s, he points out, the Cold War was winding down but a "successor war"—already begun but only partially understood—was underway: the war for the Middle East. On four occasions in the 1980s the Reagan administration intervened militarily in the Islamic world: it inserted U.S. Marine "peacekeepers" into Lebanon, which culminated in a devastating bombing of its base in Beirut in October 1983; it clashed with Libya, with air strikes against targets in Tripoli and Benghazi starting in April 1986; it engaged in the "tanker war" of 1984–88 to protect the flow of oil from the Persian Gulf; and it extended U.S. aid to the Afghan resistance movement, which ended in the ouster of the Soviet army by early 1989.[7]

Despite simple-minded bromides employed by Western leaders and militarists about how the Islamists simply hated freedom, bin Laden and his coterie had rather more specific grievances. The Gulf War of 1991 marked a substantial increase in the U.S. military presence in the region, with the United States establishing city-sized bases in Saudi Arabia, the birthplace of Islam, after the war. As English security analyst Paul Rogers explains, "For convinced jihadists, a profound motive for fighting Soviet forces in Afghanistan in the 1980s had been the intense desire to evict occupying forces from an essentially Islamic state. For such people, the basing of US forces in the Kingdom of the Two Holy Places was a far greater affront." Before the Gulf War, Rogers points out, there had been "virtually no uniformed U.S. military presence" in Saudi Arabia.[8]

Over ten years and two major wars later, September 11, 2001, had taken on the status of a world-historical event. Both bin Laden and Saddam Hussein, another former U.S. ally, had been killed. The United States had been bled white, with the Iraq war alone consuming up to $11 billion a *month* by 2007.[9] Beyond its shattering impact on the U.S. treasury and American self-confidence, the effects of this latest effort at the projection of power would prove to be incalculable. The Bush administration used the attacks as a rationale to save both the Afghans and Iraqis from themselves, enhance the U.S. geopolitical position vis-à-vis the Russians and the Chinese, and establish new bases in Central Asia, an important future source of petroleum reserves in a world in which debates over peak oil rivalled discussions of how quickly climate change was destroying the polar ice caps and glaciers.

By then it had become a cliché to point out that the United States had squandered the immense global good will generated by the attacks on New York and Washington. As part of his 2011 swan song, Robert Gates—U.S. defence secretary under both Bush and Obama—denounced European allies for being soft on defence, telling a NATO meeting that they were not spending nearly enough on armaments and armed men. His rebuke suggested that NATO, the precious alliance forged by Pearson and a handful of other Cold warriors, faced "military irrelevance," a future that was "dim if not dismal." The statement stunned the Pentagon chief's elite audience of diplomats and officers.[10] The problem was that many NATO allies, particularly outside the Anglosphere, had little or no appetite for combat operations in Afghanistan, a landlocked country far from the North Atlantic zone that the anachronistic military alliance had been established to defend.

As Gates was hectoring his allies, the recently retired British ambassador to Afghanistan, Sherard Cowper-Coles, came out with *Cables from Kabul*, an account of his years in a land scarred by thirty years of war. He recalled politicians and journalists getting the standard tour of the country. It was left to one Estonian diplomat to pose the relevant question, "What the fuck are we doing here?" There were also divisions, however subtle, within the Anglosphere. Cowper-Coles was "privately appalled" when Afghan president Hamid Karzai—who had engineered re-election using industrial-scale vote fraud—decided to make a spectacle out of the execution of a group of prisoners. When the execution party found the designated killing ground locked up, they drove the condemned men around Kabul before the authorities came up with a place to shoot them. "My American colleague," wrote Cowper-Coles, "told the President, without the slightest of irony, that the executions had been a 'beacon of hope for the future of Afghanistan.'"[11]

Describing the NATO effort as a "quasi-imperial expeditionary activity," Cowper-Coles went on to eviscerate the Western effort—so enthusiastically embraced by Harper, Hillier, and the rest of the Canadian brass—as a model of how not to proceed. It shattered all the "rules of grand strategy: getting in without having any real idea of how to get out . . . no coherent or consistent plan; mission creep on an heroic scale . . . military advice, long on institutional self-interest, but woefully short on serious objective analysis of the problems of pacifying a broken country with largely non-existent institutions of government and security."[12]

In 2001 the Taliban had been forced, literally, to head for the hills. The Americans handed formal authority to a coalition of war lords and drug dealers whose power had been sharply reduced by the Taliban. The Taliban's opponents in the Northern Alliance were still a force to be reckoned with. Along with India and Russia, Iran was a key Northern Alliance backer, an indication of intricate regional manoeuvring. Similar politics were at play in Western capitals. For its part, the Bush administration was making a series of major blunders. The first was to ignore its principal NATO allies, which had been willing to invoke their founding treaty to declare that the 9/11 attack on the United States was an attack on the alliance. But the Europeans were "totally unprepared for the policy of unilateralism that Washington now followed," with the NATO secretary general "abused" and "badly snubbed" by Bush's neo-conservative advisers. As Pakistani journalist Ahmed Rashid put it, "Only British Prime Minister Tony Blair seemed oblivious to the damage being done to the Atlantic Alliance as he accepted America's unilateralism without question."[13] The ideal of the Anglosphere gained significant adherents, with a host of historians—Niall Ferguson and Michael Ignatieff most prominently—tracing inspiring lines of liberal continuity between the British and U.S. empires, both seen as necessary guardians of humanity's centuries-old civilizing process.[14] Although the United States ousted the Taliban with the help of the Northern Alliance in late 2001, the stage had been set for a debacle of historic magnitude.

Back when the Taliban was on the run, war-weary Afghans were receptive to foreign troops and foreign aid. But the United States, led by a president who had once mistaken the Taliban for an all-girl pop group, had another war to fight. Iraq loomed large. Rashid, a veteran of regional reporting intimately familiar with the internal intrigues of Pakistani and Afghan politics, had broken with many colleagues when he initially suggested that the war in Afghanistan was not an imperial intervention. By the time he wrote *Descent into Chaos* in 2008, he was describing the war as a "tragedy" associated with "imperial overstretch." While Gates might excoriate his NATO allies for not pulling their weight, Rashid noted that although Afghanistan was supposedly a multilateral effort, the U.S. government would continue to make the big military and aid decisions on its own, without taking its partners seriously. "The Bush doctrine was also doggedly to sweep under the carpet any discussion or understanding of the 'root causes' of terrorism—the growing poverty, repression and sense of injustice that many Muslims felt at the hands of their U.S.-backed governments, which in turn boosted anti-Americanism and Islamic extremism."[15]

Some ten years after 9/11 and the apparent demise of the Taliban, Afghanistan was reeling from another decade of war. The Bush administration, turning its attention to Iraq, had handed security over to warlords and drug barons, and NATO responsibility for the Taliban heartland was left to Canada, whose military leaders were eager to get into a real war while boosting what Cowper-Coles recognized as their own institutional self-interest. The warlords had the same respect for women as did the Taliban, which had gradually made a dramatic come-back after its 2001 defeat. The Taliban insurgency spread to nuclear-armed Pakistan, with stability, that elusive goal of the West's political and military leaders, a distant chimera. A third of Afghanistan's people did not have enough to eat. Rashid referred to the entire Western effort, proudly trumpeted by Canada's political and military leaders, as incompetent and incoherent.[16]

In 2011, decked out in flak jacket and helmet, Harper addressed the departing Canadian troops. He was trying to perform a bit of political alchemy—to turn defeat into victory, or a victory of sorts. While admitting there had been "successes and failures" in Afghanistan, he went on to declare that the country was no longer what he termed "a geo-strategic risk to the world." He insisted that this outcome constituted "a tremendous accomplishment, one that obviously serves Canadian interests." A NATO air strike two days earlier had mistakenly killed twelve Afghan children and two women in neighbouring Helmand province. The battle for hearts and minds was continuing as Canada packed up to leave the southern combat zone.[17]

The prime minister had a solid track record for windy pontification while speaking to soldiers in Afghanistan. Immediately after his 2006 election he hurried to the sprawling U.S. base in Kandahar, where Pizza Hut, Burger King, and Tim Hortons stood as reassuring symbols of a way of life being protected. Harper listed a menu of war aims. It was the first time soldiers from rich countries would occupy poor countries so little girls could go to school and learn the same lessons as did children in Calgary.

> Before its liberation, under the Taliban regime, Afghanistan often served as an incubator for Al Qaeda and other terror organizations. . . . An unstable Afghanistan represents easy pickings for drug lords who would use the country as a safe haven for the production of heroin, which wreaks its own destruction on the streets of our country.
>
> Our Canada is a great place, but Canada is not an island. . . .
>
> [The Kandahar effort is] also about demonstrating an international leadership role for our country. Not carping from the sidelines, but taking a stand on the big issues that matter.
>
> You can't lead from the bleachers. I want Canada to be a leader. . . .

Finally, but no less important, is the great humanitarian work you're doing. Working with the Afghan government and Afghan people to enhance their security helps them. It helps them rebuild their country to make a better life for themselves and their children. . . .

Reconstruction is reducing poverty; millions of people are now able to vote; women are enjoying greater rights and economic opportunities that [sic] could have been imagined under the Taliban regime; and of Afghan children who are now in school studying the same things Canadian kids are learning back home. . . .

There may be some who want to cut and run.

But cutting and running is not your way.

It's not my way.

And it's not the Canadian way.

We don't make a commitment and then run away at the first sign of trouble.

We don't and we won't. . . .

Your work is vital to Canada.

To the free world. To the Afghan people. . . .

God bless Canada.[18]

Harper's closing call-out to the Almighty echoed his speech after the minority government victory of January 2006—words indicating that the religious right had finally achieved a new influence in Canada. One of the major impulses behind the construction of the Warrior Nation is religious: to "reclaim Canada for Christ" and to redeem a country that had been, in the words of one highly influential Christian warrior, "defiled to the core by an anti-God agenda for decades."[19]

As the examples of Methodists Lester Pearson and James Endicott suggest, Christians in Canada inherit a complicated history with regard to war. The "just war" tradition, the cornerstone of Christian thinking in this regard, holds that recourse to war is defensible only in cases of self-defence and as a last resort, after all peaceful avenues are exhausted. In the nineteenth century Christians, both Catholic and Protestant, often observed with something less than fondness the whoring and whisky-guzzling soldiers they encountered in the streets and read about in the police-court columns of their newspapers. During the Great War many patriotic ministers bent just war arguments into pretzels to incite their congregants to join up, but the postwar period saw a widespread Protestant revulsion against such bombastic militarism. Down to the 1960s, many regular churchgoers were sceptical about war and reluctant to revere its practitioners. Yet in the Cold War period, and especially after the 1960s, new Christian voices came to the fore. Evangelical Christians began to see soldiers as exemplars of virtue, fighting on behalf of Christianity against atheistic communism.

A minor nineteenth-century current of Protestantism, premillennial dispensationalism, found in Holy Scripture a prophecy of the Earth's last days, in which the Antichrist rises up, is defeated in a great battle at Armageddon, and is followed by the Second Coming of Christ. In this reading of Scripture, those who accept Christ as their personal saviour will be transported heavenward in the Rapture; those who do not will endure the horrific violence of the wars of the last days, before Christ once again mounts David's throne in Jerusalem. What was a minor and, for most Christians, off-the-wall heresy in the nineteenth century had become a formidable religious and political force by the twenty-first.[20]

Canada now outrivals the United States in its total commitment to whatever Israel does—even if this means turning an uncomplaining eye on the Israeli killing of a Canadian peacekeeper in a designated bunker. Israel plays an important role in practical geostrategic conceptions of the Middle East as "our" player in a volatile but economically crucial region—but it has symbolic religious importance for a significant slice of the Canadian population—between 10 to 15 per cent—who are born-again Christians. When these true believers look at Israel's many wars, they do not invoke Christianity's traditional just war theory. They draw instead upon the very different motifs of a crusade of good against evil. They go back to the old metaphors of the evil empire of communism, transmuting them into the evil empire of Islam. They confer a "presumptive moral palatability" upon any war waged by the United States in the Islamic world, and often go so far as to see these campaigns as necessary parts of the accomplishment of Christ's work on Earth.[21] For them, Christ—the Prince of Peace for most Christians—becomes the Minister of Perpetual War, at least until the Day of Rapture finally arrives.

When Canada's newly elected prime minister rushed to Afghanistan in 2006, his invocation not just of God but of the "free world," that rusty old Cold War theme, recalled the old days when Afghan freedom fighters (and their allies like Osama bin Laden) brought the Red Army to its knees. By 2006 it was a little much to make the case that the new evil had anything like Soviet-level fire power. In comparison to the massive campaigns of Canada's world wars, Afghanistan was a skirmish. There had not been such a technological mismatch between Canadian troops and their enemies since Ottawa deployed the Gatling gun against the poorly armed Métis in 1885 (the locals in Saskatchewan were reduced to firing pebbles from their rifles). Despite their prime minister's fervent attempts to connect the Afghanistan war to a grand crusade for democracy, freedom, Canada, and God, there remained a solid bloc sceptical of both the war and the Anglosphere on whose behalf it was being waged.

In April 2003 conservative zealot Tristan Emmanuel organized a "Canadians for Bush" rally to coincide with the U.S. invasion of Iraq.[22] He picked a strange spot—Brock's Monument in Queenston, Ontario—for a demonstration in support of a foreign war, in this case a war being waged by the Americans against Iraqis. While the gathering might well have been called Their Country Right or Wrong, any irony seemed lost on the prominent politicians who attended. These included Ontario cabinet ministers Jim Flaherty and Tim Hudak and former Canadian Alliance leader and prime ministerial candidate Stockwell Day, whose new boss, Stephen Harper, really did want Canada to follow George W. Bush into a war that would be a murderous mistake. Harper had told a similar send-the-troops rally in Toronto that he supported "the liberation of the people of Iraq. Let us pledge today, that in the future, when our American and British friends and our friends around the world take on the cause of freedom and democracy, we will never again allow ourselves to be isolated."[23]

Emmanuel, inspired by a support-our-troops event that he had attended in New York, hoped that ten thousand people would show up at Brock's Monument in a similar show of sympathy for the cause.

One of the nine hundred who did turn up was literally wrapped up in an American flag and told reporters that the Chrétien government was wrong in giving a pass to the invasion. Canada's prime minister had "made the wrong choice, morally," said St. Catherines resident Doris Eaglesham. "I think it is a just war and I think it is a legal war."[24]

A few weeks earlier a global surge of protest against the impending invasion had culminated in the largest demonstrations in the history of the world. For the millions who turned out in some sixty countries, the looming war was not just, not legal, not moral. The largest Canadian rally took place in Montreal, where over a hundred thousand people turned out on one of the coldest days of the winter. A crowd of similar size assembled in New York, with the U.S. peace group Not In Our Name's "Pledge of Resistance" reflecting the feelings of many opposed to invasions associated with the "War on Terror."

> We believe that as people living
> In the United States it is our
> Responsibility to resist the injustices
> Done by our government, in our names ...
>
> Not in our name
> will you invade countries
> bomb civilians, kill more children
> letting history take its course
> over the graves of the nameless
>
> We pledge resistance
>
> We pledge alliance with those
> who have come under attack
> for voicing opposition to the war
> or for their religion or ethnicity.[25]

The ideals of justice and peace around which the global demonstrations were organized are represented in stone atop Canada's Vimy Memorial, commemorating the goals for which another disastrous war was ostensibly fought. That war ended officially on November 11, 1918, but the war against this new enemy promised no victory, no armistice, no peace treaty. No end. For terror is a feeling and terrorism a tactic.

It is difficult to wage war on emotions and tactics. Easy cynicism has it that one man's terrorist is another man's freedom fighter, implying that branding a person or organization as terrorist is simply a statement of opposition to their cause. There is, however, a more precise definition of terrorism as a means to an end. Terrorism is "the intentional use of, or threat to use violence against civilians, or against civilian targets, in order to attain political aims." This succinct definition was developed in 1998 by Boaz Ganor, an Israeli academic and security specialist. Canadian political scientist Jonathan Barker notes that Ganor's definition, unlike those promiscuously employed by governments and the media, applies as much to governments as to non-governmental organizations like al-Qaeda. Barker points to the relationship between violence and politics:

> People and organizations and strategies make use of terrorism often in conjunction with other kinds of political action. Can the organization be induced to abandon terrorism in favor of politics? If so, labeling the whole organization as terrorist may be a mistake. . . . The definition opens the door to fundamental questions about the circumstances under which people, groups and states adopt (and also abandon) terrorist methods.[26]

When the term "terrorism" is thrown around like confetti, it loses its political context. In militarist discourse the line between terror and non-terror—like the boundary between war and peace—becomes ever more obscure. New warriors often maintain that the only way of saving the innocent and safeguarding democracy is to bomb villages and shore up dictators. In *Empire Lite*, a revealing apology for liberal imperialism, Michael Ignatieff himself remarked that a core contradiction of the war in Kandahar was that winning any war on terrorism meant consolidating the power of the warlords who constituted the chief obstacle to state-building. He held out hope that, by making a "moral pact with the devil of war," the Allied forces would succeed in "using its flames to burn a path to peace." Derrick O'Keefe counters, "As everyone knows, nothing burns a path to peace like a war stoked by the fires of Hell."[27]

★

In December 2008 news arrived that the "butcher's bill" in Afghanistan had reached one hundred Canadians, with three more dead. The prime minister, in Petawawa for a Trees for the Troops event, declared, "It is because of them, now and throughout our history, that we are able to celebrate our Christmas in such peace and prosperity." New warrior historians were quick to fall in behind the prime minister. J.L. Granatstein told an Ottawa *Citizen* reporter that measurable progress had been made in Afghanistan: the local police and military were being trained, the national government strengthened, and the insurgents forced into a box, now unable to directly confront NATO forces. But the historian also insisted that the Afghan War's biggest advances were on the home front. "The Canadian Forces have found their raison d'être again. They are a military force; they are not a peacekeeping force," he said. "That is, to my mind, absolutely critical for the survival of the Canadian Forces, and I would say, the long-term survival of the country. Peacekeeping has failed, except in the minds of the Canadian people."[28]

Granatstein had long been railing against peacekeeping and the way it had sapped the potency of Canada's soldiery. In 2004 he had made the claim that it had become a "flaccid military." Now a dose of war-on-terror Viagra had stiffened the resolve of armchair warriors and superannuated officers and historians who believed that spending more treasure and lives in Afghanistan was exactly the right thing to do. A leading government patriot was Harper's first defence minister, Gordon O'Connor, who had retired from the military to work peddling weapons systems for General Dynamics and other war-machine manufacturers. Questioned by the parliamentary opposition over the Afghan War, O'Connor specialized in facile rejoinders. "I don't want to go back to World War II, but they don't want the military to be involved in anything," O'Connor said in response to NDP leader Jack Layton. "Does this party support our mission in Afghanistan or not?"[29]

General Dynamics probably did. It was offering funding support to outfits like the Canadian Defence and Foreign Affairs Institute (CDFAI)—a policy soapbox from which militarist academics declaimed on the need for more money for "Our Troops." The U.S. arms dealer had been a consistent donor to the CDFAI since 2004, soon after the Institute was established as a well-heeled backer of the new warrior mentality. By the time that Canada's war in Afghanistan was in full swing, the government's approach was clear. Those asking hard questions about why more Canadians were being killed and wounded in support of a corrupt dictatorship would be tarred with the support-our-troops brush. O'Connor was eventually cashiered from his Defence portfolio for chronic fumbling during the 2007 Afghan detainee scandal, during which *Globe and Mail* reporter Graeme Smith revealed that the Canadian military was routinely turning over Afghan prisoners to torture.[30] O'Connor, eventually demoted to the lowly Revenue portfolio, was a fan of Donald Rumsfeld, the man in charge during the Abu Ghraib torture outrages and the key architect of the Iraq war. O'Connor saw Rumsfeld as a visionary fellow whom Canadians should surely emulate. He wrote to the U.S. secretary of defense congratulating him for a job well done: "You have helped transform the armed forces of the United States to meet the threats of the 21st century. Your vision in recognizing and responding to these new threats has set the standard for forward-looking defence planning in an uncertain world."[31]

O'Connor's letter was sent off just as the extent of the disaster in Iraq was becoming clear. It was equally evident that Canada's war in Afghanistan was on the same trajectory. O'Connor's top soldier, Rick Hillier, was also committed to the *Their Country, Right or Wrong* leitmotif. The Chief of Defence Staff had embraced as Canadian military doctrine the notion of a "three-block war" that had briefly been a popular metaphor in the U.S. Marine Corps in the late 1990s. Though never adopted either by NATO or the U.S. military as a whole, the three-block-war model imagined a conflict situation (an imaginary urban battlefield, hence the "block" construct) in which the military would be involved simultaneously in combat, peacekeeping, and humanitarian work. In an approach that sounded very much like the military version of Canada's much-touted (but soon lamented) three-D policy prescription for Afghanistan—Defence, Diplomacy, Development—the three-block-war idea appealed to Hillier, anxious to get Canada into a combat role in Afghanistan. In 2005, just as he was telling the Liberal government under Paul Martin that the Canadian military would be able to handle the deployment to the Taliban heartland of Kandahar, Hillier waxed enthusiastic about the concept.[32] "Preparing for the three-block war will be the foundation of all our training. Leaders at all levels must ensure that our soldiers are set up for success in all aspects of the three-block war." A new Alberta military training centre featured a boosterish gateway sign. "Forging Masters of the Three Block War." The thinking, if it can be so described, even made it into Canada's 2005 foreign policy statement.[33]

Canada's three-D policy would fail in Kandahar, where diplomacy and development took a back seat to military operations, otherwise known as "defence." The war effort, or "mission" as its backers commonly called it, soon became an essentially military approach run by Forces.ca. The Canadian International Development Agency (CIDA) and Foreign Affairs and International Trade Canada (DFAIT) had nowhere near the resources available to the military. Clashes of institutional culture and interdepartmental turf wars broke out. There was also the bedevilling problem of having heavily armed soldiers looking very much like the forces of an alien empire—dressed as they were in bulky flak jackets and heavy boots, sporting goggles and microphones and masses of high-tech kit—driving around a poverty-stricken, war-torn country whose language they could not speak. These soldiers were expected to perform diplomatic functions and deliver humanitarian assistance. The approach was, according to one Canadian military official interviewed in Kabul in 2007, "never anything more than Chris Alexander [Canada's first ambassador to Afghanistan] and General Andrew Leslie tearing around town in a jeep." Hillier, responsible as much as anyone for Canada's Afghanistan misadventure, apparently regarded a transformed Afghanistan as something that you could establish courtesy of Canada Post. "CIDA delivers development. We deliver security and reconstruction." The general, fond of the mess-hall braggadocio central to his appeal to the rank and file—and Canada's media—later wrote a memoir freighted with instances of him recalling how he had been "fucking pissed off," along with similarly creative metaphors. For Hillier, NATO, most of whose non-English-speaking members were not as keen on the Afghan War as were the United States, United Kingdom, and Canada, was a "decomposing corpse" in need of somebody "to perform a Frankenstein-like life-giving act by breathing some lifesaving air though those rotten lips into those putrescent lungs." As early as 2007 Hillier had wondered about the United Nations and its failure to provide that elusive quality called "governance" to Afghanistan. "Who delivers governance? We don't have a toolkit for governance."[34]

Should Canada have expected Hillier, Canada's first superstar soldier of the twenty-first century and a self-proclaimed expert on the
need for decisive leaders, to grapple successfully with elusive notions
of development and governance? Perhaps not. But what about the
three-block-war concept that the general employed to sell the Liberals
on the war? Writers Janice Stein and Eugene Lang make its centrality
clear:

> Hillier claimed that the biggest threat to global peace and security for
> the foreseeable future would be failed and failing states. Afghanistan
> was a taste of the future. . . . Hillier used the phrase 'Three-Block War'
> to describe the types of missions Canada's military (read 'army') had
> performed in recent years in Bosnia, Somalia and Afghanistan. . . .
> This, Hillier argued, was the present and the future. Canada's military
> needed to be properly equipped and organized to meet the challenges
> of a Three-Block War. Blue-helmeted peacekeeping operations sepa-
> rating one-time combatants along a ceasefire line were, Hillier insisted,
> a thing of the past for the Canadian Forces.

The simplicity of the argument appealed to the Liberals as well as to
liberal analysts like Stein and Lang, who saw it as "a logical and compelling articulation of the international security challenges in the
post–Cold War period."[35]

The problem with the three-block-war construct was that it turned
out to be simpleminded and wrong. Influenced by what C. Wright
Mills once called a "military metaphysics,"[36] that is, a tendency to see
complex social and cultural issues as military problems, and more
specifically by the hubristic vision of the revolution in military affairs,
with its beguiling dream of technology as panacea, the three-block war
helped some apprehensive Canadians reconcile themselves to the
Afghanistan campaign's blatant departure from the traditional ideals
of the just war or Pearsonian peacekeeping. They could tell themselves that, even though Canadians and their allies were safeguarding a
narco-state and bombing villagers, they were still part of a uniquely
benign imperium because they were providing schools, food, and
medicine to the locals—defined, as always, by what they lacked.
"'They' are understood insofar as they are different from 'us,'" Sandra

Whitworth suggests, "and 'we' can be reassured that the kinds of ir-rational barbarism currently defining 'their' lives will never come to define 'ours.'" For all its seeming up-to-the-moment modernity, there was much about the Afghan War that recalled the age-old patterns of British imperialism and colonization. As early as 2003 Canadian reporter Chris Wattie, later Hillier's ghostwriter, had noticed that Royal Canadian Regiment troops in Afghanistan had started to call all of the territory outside their control "Indian country."[37]

Yet the three-block concept was easy to communicate and could be used to sell the idea of war in a poor and conflicted country such as Afghanistan. It was useful in "imparting a sense of purpose and confidence," but did "not allow specificity of mission mandate, which is critical for mission clarity, both for Canadian Forces personnel and local populations." Moreover, according to analysts Walter Dorn and Michael Varey, the theory lacked a firm intellectual footing. "The three-block war's simplicity is most problematic when the concept makes the jump from tactical description of the reality on the ground to a strategic vision, as it did when it was introduced in Canada."[38] But the three-block war had one distinct advantage: it was all about war.

Dorn, a faculty member at the Royal Military College and the Canadian Forces College, was favourably disposed to peacekeeping. Just as Canada's Kandahar effort was gearing up in early 2006, he pub-lished an article ("Canada Pulls out of Peacekeeping") in the *Globe and Mail*, pointing to the country's retreat from its traditional commit-ment to UN peace operations. Dorn's logic ran contrary to the Harper government's belief that a muscular military was the key to winning friends and influencing people around the world. Dorn figured that a return to operations aimed at maintaining peace was the right way to "secure a continuing place of pride and influence in the world." He was, however, marching into a stiff political headwind. As he pointed out at the time, a Canadian colonel had just prevailed in a tough com-petition for the top chief of staff job at the Department of Peacekeep-ing Operations at UN headquarters. But the officer's superiors refused to let him serve at the United Nations.[39]

Meanwhile, in Afghanistan, Canada was preparing for Hillier's three-block war. "It's like a hockey team changing lines," explained Lieutenant-Colonel Ian Hope, speaking of the Canadian takeover from the U.S. Task Force Gun Devil in Kandahar that winter. "The sticks haven't left the ice. It's the same team, just different players."⁴⁰

In 2007 the army dropped the three-block-war concept, which had never gained traction with other branches of the military. It was not even mentioned in "Land Operations 2021," the army's doctrinal design for the future. But it had served its purpose as a selling point. For the new warriors, the real goal of the Afghan War was not good governance, peace, and prosperity in Afghanistan. It was about promoting an image of the Canadian Forces as a combat outfit that was no longer "risk averse"—the implication was that too much peace and peacekeeping had turned Forces.ca into something other than real soldiers. The mission was not so much about taking democracy to a faraway country as it was about nurturing warriors in Canada, about building a country that was not afraid to go to war.

It did not matter that with respect to war in Afghanistan, as Dorn and Michael Varey warned in 2008, "It is unclear whether it is even possible to carry out peacekeeping and play a humanitarian role while at the same time fighting a war against a determined enemy who can readily sabotage such efforts . . . [where] it is near impossible to tell a Taliban 'terrorist' from a civilian 'supporter.'" One thing that was clear was that the precipitous deployment of Canadian soldiers in Kandahar was taking its toll. Canada's 2006 and 2007 fatality rates were more than double the rates of those of the U.S. and U.K. forces in Afghanistan.⁴¹

Dorn's critique of the entire rationale for the war was unconscionable for the new warriors. He was an insider who could ask disturbing questions. But his was a lonely voice inside both the military and the academic institutions that provided intellectual underpinnings for the new commitment to "realism," America's wars, and the hard business of fighting the foreigners, bad people stirring things up in failed states.

In March 2007 the House of Commons Standing Committee on Foreign Affairs and International Development met to hear from Dorn and Douglas Bland, who chaired the military-funded Defence Management Studies Program at Queen's University. Bland, a retired lieutenant-colonel, echoed the party line by invoking the "appalling state of the Canadian armed forces." He worried that Canadians did not "have much stomach for an international role beyond rhetoric" to fight for people "who wish to be free." Bland's testimony, itself largely rhetorical, admonished the assembled politicians for not spending enough on the military. He praised NATO's support for the Afghan War, warning of "ungoverned spaces" in the Third World. Grasping for a historical parallel, Bland attempted to link the war and its Defence-Development-Diplomacy policy rationale to the Second World War and Canada's part in the liberation of the Netherlands, where his father had been with the artillery. He reminisced about how the old man would tell his Legion chums about what were essentially "Three D operations." When the Canadians took a break from the "defence"—from firing at German positions—they took up the diplomacy and development: feeding the locals, handing out candies, and building schools. This, apparently, is the Canadian way. "Our soldiers do it particularly well all over the world," said Bland, citing the Somalia effort as a case showing that "the three-D notion is ingrained in our traditions of foreign policy and military operations."[42]

For his part, Dorn told the Committee that Canada was at an all-time low in its contribution to UN peacekeeping during a period in which international peacekeeping efforts had reached a historic high. He reiterated what he saw as the key peacekeeping principles of impartiality, consent, and minimum use of force, criticizing the new deployment in Kandahar for contradicting all three. It was an offensive operation in which the consent of the local population was in doubt— not surprising because they were often casualties during large-scale combat offensives. Dorn testified that in September 2001 he had heard George Bush proclaim that the United States would make no distinction between terrorists and those who harboured them. "At the time I recognized this as a recipe for expanding an endless war." Displaying an understanding of Afghanistan's internal dynamics that seemed to elude Bland, he stressed that international forces truly interested in justice and peace had to serve the local population and always be ready to negotiate with those using violence by offering everyone except the most egregious war criminals a way out. Finally, he suggested that it was crucial to appreciate the complex motivations of the people who actually call southern Afghanistan home. "This means recognizing that not all those who oppose the Canadian presence are Taliban terrorists. There are many former mujahedeen from various clans that the West once supported during the war against the Soviet invaders. They are motivated by the defence of their country, not love of the

Taliban. They long to live and die like the heroes of their folklore, whether it be heroes from the time of the British colonizers or Soviet occupiers."

All of which seemed to make Col. Bland a little cross. "I'm a little surprised that Dr. Dorn would be praising the Taliban as a liberating and helpful Boy Scout organization in Afghanistan," he immediately replied.

"Don't put words in my mouth," Dorn said, though he could not stop Bland's bluster.

"They are hardly the people to hold up to the Afghan people. It's why the government invited Canadians to make war on these criminal elements."

The exchange typified the fault lines between the new warrior position on the need for a large, combat-ready military to go after bad guys and a nuanced understanding of the nature of the armed conflicts that plague countries caught up in civil strife. For Bland, as for the Harper conservatives and the militarist intellectuals supporting increases in spending on Forces.ca, endless war was, after the turn of the century, a given. Bland stated plainly, "We're in an era now of what I call continuous warfare." He offered no indication of his thoughts as to whether this was in any way tragic or even an unfortunate state of affairs.[43]

Along with the Afghans and foreign troops killed and maimed, one of the tragedies that would mark the sordid Afghan War was the torture of prisoners handed over to the local authorities by Canadian forces. In May 2007 Hillier visited Kandahar, where he was forced to backtrack on his previous claims, acknowledging that a 2005 deal he had signed opened the door to torture of prisoners by Afghan authorities. The normally media-friendly commander evaded questions about why it had taken so long for the torture revelations to surface, saying only that "perhaps that deal was not sufficient." Kandahar governor Asadullah Khalid, praised by General Hillier for his "phenomenal work," would eventually be fired after months of pressure from an embarrassed Canadian government that—for reasons of "national security"—blanked his name from official reports of prisoner torture. Khalid consistently claimed that torture stories were Taliban lies. For his part, the commander of Forces.ca would dismiss the torture scandal as a "massive kerfuffle." The army had learned the lessons of Somalia, he added modestly, because of "the excellent leadership in place."[44]

Just as the war was intensifying, Hillier was photographed indulging in some manly horseplay, wrestling a Saskatchewan corporal into a headlock. The general had a chunky timepiece on his wrist, a reminder of an old saying that local people often repeat when soldiers from rich countries undertake operations against ragged local insurgents: "They have the watches, but we have the time."

Monuments and memorials to past wars dot Canada's urban landscape. Statues, plinths, cairns, arches, and obelisks. Decorated with angels, swords, and crosses, they assure the citizenry about the thousands killed (or, most always, "sacrificed") in wars—that the cause was just, the sacrifice noble. In London, Ontario, the First World War memorial designed by Walter Allward (he of Vimy Memorial fame) portrays Civilization triumphant over Barbarism, opposing ideas so often invoked in support of Canada's war in Afghanistan.

People gather at monuments to sanctify the nation and the cause for which its soldiers once fought. The cause could be the defence of a British colony against U.S. attack or the defence of a U.S. attack on a faraway land. It could be a war in Belgium or in Korea. The ceremonies are usually militarized, complete with the old parading and the young firing guns into the air. The formalities are so commonplace as to convey the message that war itself will always be with us, that all we can do—the best we can do—is to simply remember the steadfast commitment of those killed. Writing as the Vietnam War was drawing to a close, Paul Fussell recalled English poet Ivor Gurney, who died in a mental hospital in 1937 and was at the time still writing war poetry, still convinced the war was going on. Noting a contemporary headline, "U.S. Aides in Vietnam See an Unending War," Fussell went on to list the nightmare wars that had come and gone after Gurney's death, concluding, "The drift of modern history domesticates the fantastic and normalizes the unspeakable."[45]

But how to memorialize and normalize what U.S. military planners would, after 2001, call the Long War—or what Andrew Bacevich would describe nine years later as "not really war but something akin to imperial policing combined with systematic distribution of alms"?[46]

One answer can be found in a new suburb named Garrison Green. It is in many ways an antidote to conventional real-estate development in Calgary, where urban sprawl is the norm. The project took shape after the closure of Canadian Forces Base Calgary, a military post that dated from 1911. The member from Calgary West, Stephen Harper, demanded that the Chrétien government keep the base open, and much local muttering occurred about a base in Edmonton, home of two Liberal MPs, that did survive the cuts of the mid-1990s. In the end Ottawa's Canada Lands Company controlled the type of housing that replaced CFB Calgary. Garrison Green, with densities higher than the suburban norm, represents the new urbanism in action, with garages off lanes behind the houses, ample parks, and fifty-year-old trees left in place.

"Garrison Green hearkens to a simpler, friendlier era," says a developer's website. "A time when neighbours congregated on front porches, when your morning coffee was savoured at home, not on your long commute, when your family's safety and security extended beyond your front doorstep. At Garrison Green, 'home' means an escape to yesteryear in the most modern of urban settings."[47] The nostalgia-sodden pitch has a positive tinge, a none-too-subtle hint that there may well be something amiss with today's big city life that is both threatening and stressful.

Back *then* was when Canada dispatched peacekeeping forces to the Sinai, Gaza, and the Congo. Garrison Green has streets named for these places, as it does for well-known Canadians who have worked as peacekeepers. In the same way that, after 1918, Canadian streets were named for battles like Ypres, Lens, and Vimy, in the new Calgary suburb Cyprus Green gives onto Buffalo Park, with its tot lot and plaque and propeller from a Buffalo aircraft—this last commemorating the nine Canadian peacekeepers killed in 1974 when their Buffalo was shot down by the Syrian military, the largest single-incident loss of life, including Afghanistan, involving Canada's military since Korea. Dallaire Avenue runs along one side of Peacekeeper Park, adjacent to Peacekeepers Way. Tom Hoppe Mews and John Gardham Avenue are nearby.

The naming and renaming of streets can be controversial, as in the case of Montreal's Boulevard René Lévesque, formerly named for the English colonial aristocrat Sir Guy Carleton, First Baron of

Dorchester and still called Dorchester Boulevard in the Anglophone enclave of Westmount. But Montreal did not rename the street until after the death of Quebec's first sovereignist premier, whereas many Garrison Green streets were named for people who were still alive at the time. Commemorating the living is unusual, but Garrison Green exemplifies Canada's official efforts to cultivate its familiar blue beret image as a country committed to UN peacekeeping, an era that was largely over by the time the project was completed. The neighbour-hood's 1950s nostalgia hearkens back to what has been called the "golden age" of Canadian diplomacy, a time when Canada, rather than being pointedly excluded from the Security Council, as it was in 2010, was a central player at the United Nations. Peacekeeping, though a lapsed Canadian enterprise, remains fixed in the Canadian imagina-tion as a peculiarly Canadian specialty. Historian Colin McCullough notes, "Ideas of peace, justice, international co-operation and altruism are commonly used to describe peacekeepers, and Canadians as a peo-ple as well."[48]

The most strikingly emblematic feature of Garrison Green is Peacekeeper Park. The well-tended green space features a Wall of Honour, a low, curving structure that recalls the Vietnam Memorial in Washington, allowing passersby and people attending the annual August 9 Peacekeepers' Day ceremony to read the inscriptions etched into the stone. When the wall was inaugurated in 2004 it included the names of the dead and the UN peacekeeping operations on which they had served. In accordance with the ongoing effort to designate anyone who dies on military duty as a hero, the Canadian Association of Veterans in UN Peacekeeping planned the Wall of Honour to list "our 186 heroes who have paid the ultimate sacrifice whilst deployed on international peace support operations."[49]

Don Ethell, who has a nearby street named for him and is described on a plaque as the former director of Peacekeeping Opera-tions for the Department of National Defence, was a key organizer of the commemorative space at Peacekeeper Park. A retired colonel, Ethell shares the view that the term peacekeeping is "passé." Canada's military, he insisted in an interview, had long been neglected by "the Liberal dictatorship." Sitting beside the Wall of Honour, he explained proudly how things had changed by 2009. "The first thing Harper did when he took over the government, the first speech he gave, was in

Kandahar. He immediately flew to Kandahar and said, 'We're here and we're going to support you.'"

Ethell was pleased with the resulting military spending binge, the evidence of which he had seen in Edmonton. "You drive through the base and see some of the equipment they've got. Just mind-boggling. . . . Canadians will say, seeing a C-17 or a Leopard 2 roll by, 'Jesus! Finally we've got pride in this.' There will always be the one asshole who'll say 'That's costing us a lot of money and why are we doing it?' Well, if you're gonna play on the international stage, you gotta be able to sit at the table."[50] While the prime minister would not, at least for the foreseeable future, be saluting a Soviet-style Red Square May Day parade of tanks and missiles, the sentiment was clear enough. In 2010 the government appointed Col. Ethell lieutenant-governor of Alberta.

In the years following the inauguration of the Calgary park as a memorial to peacekeepers, Canada's military posture continued to shift. Using the death rate of the previous fifty-five years, the designers calculated that one wall had sufficient space to last another sixty years. But then Canadians started to be killed in Afghanistan, a conflict that new warriors insisted enthusiastically was a *real* war—not a UN peacekeeping operation. Yet the Calgary organizers did not hesitate to put the names of those killed in the Afghan War on their peacekeeping monument. They soon ran out of room and began construction of another wall behind the first. The ambivalence that is peacekeeping took on physical shape. Paeta Hess-von Kruedener, intentionally killed by a staunch Canadian ally, is commemorated on the same space as those killed by Taliban attacks during a combat operation. The organizers of the monument have made a conscious effort to connect the Afghan War with peacekeeping and the values it represents for many Canadians. Proclaimed Ethell, "All of the Fallen shall be so recognized!"[51]

The lines between peacekeeping and war-making are also blurred in statues adjacent to Calgary's Wall of Honour. Two larger than life figures in bronze stand facing one another. A soldier sporting a beret is depicted handing a small stuffed toy to a ragged-looking young girl, intended to represent a refugee. The scene is rendered ambivalent by the soldier's posture, his automatic weapon brandished conspicuously. Ethell explained that peacekeeping can be violent, and so the aggressive posture was deliberately chosen. "We intentionally went this way to indicate that, 'Yes there's a humanitarian side but it requires that they're prepared to fight.' As they are doing in Afghanistan."⁵²

The theme of Canada as Warrior Nation runs through Calgary's Peacekeeper Park alongside tributes to peacekeepers and recognition of peacekeeping missions. The relationship is ambiguous, uneasy, a variation on a theme. That is, peacekeeping is part of a national military history very much aligned with fighting imperial wars as part of a system of Western—and more specifically Anglo-American—alliances.

When the 1988 Nobel Peace Prize was awarded to UN peacekeeping forces, the chair of the Norwegian Nobel Committee explained that it was the first time that the prize for peace had been given to a primarily military organization. Shortly after the Peace Prize award, Canada's Department of National Defence initiated plans to erect a monument dedicated to the eighty thousand men and women from the Canadian military who had by that time followed Tommy Burns by working on Blue-Helmet operations. The military brass was aware that their political masters were fond of Canada's middle-power image as a helpful fixer on the international stage and that the units they commanded had become leaders in UN peacekeeping. The 1990 Competition Guidelines for interested sculptors and designers stated explicitly that this was not to be a traditional commemorative monument. It would be "a tribute to the living, not a memorial to the dead." Moreover, the planners wanted "to recognize and celebrate through artistic, inspirational and tangible form Canada's past and present peacekeeping role in the world." They wanted, the guidelines said, to "represent a fundamental Canadian value: no missionary zeal to impose our way of life on others but an acceptance of the responsibility to assist them in determining their own futures by ensuring a non-violent climate in which to do so."⁵³

Retired army colonel John Gardham was an energetic moving force behind the project. Although his role as project manager ended with the monument's 1992 inauguration, the veteran of the United Nations Emergency Force in the Sinai continued on as its unofficial curator. Col. Gardham exhibited the same soldier's pride in the Ottawa monument that Don Ethell expressed when applauding a parade of

shiny new tanks. A former Canadian representative on the Commonwealth War Graves Commission and long-time board member of
Ottawa's Perley and Rideau Veterans' Health Centre, Gardham conducted tours for diplomats, royalty, and anyone else who displayed
an interest in a monument that was clearly the culmination of a life's
work. He unearthed the Suez Crisis quotation from Lester Pearson
that is eternalized, in heavily edited form, on the concrete.[54] He
scolded young skateboarders caught using the structure for their tricky
manoeuvres.

Gardham's operating guideline vaguely stipulated that if the Government of Canada approved an operation intended to restore peace,
that project became eligible for inclusion on the monument. "That's
how Afghanistan is on here." Gardham insisted that Canada is much
less involved in peacekeeping "only because of Afghanistan. . . .
Afghanistan is a goddamn war." Still, he remained hopeful that the
peacekeeping enterprise was not dead. Although Canada had lost
global influence because of the Afghan War, many countries in conflict
would accept Canada-as-peacekeeper "but they won't accept the U.S.
or the U.K."[55] It remained uncertain when the completion date for the
war would finally be chiselled into a monument dedicated to peace.

Peace has seldom dominated memorials erected as part of the
British tradition that set the pattern for Canada's efforts after 1918.
The English art historian Paul Gough, a student of the aesthetics of
conflict and the iconography of commemoration, examined the nature
of various peace parks and war memorials before turning his attention
to Ottawa's Peacekeeping Monument in 2002. Peace is conventionally
portrayed as a consequence of victory, he says, "not as a separate or
distinct entity." After the Second World War a shift occurred in this
realm of public art, much of which attempted to "promote peace,
rather than celebrate its achievement." These "heavily politicized
activities" often involved not totemic structures but ever-changing,
open-ended works of art such as designed landscapes, preserved ruins,
and cairns to which people could contribute, thus promoting direct
public involvement.[56]

According to Gough, "Reconciliation . . . At the Service of Peace"
is different, symbolically and aesthetically, yet again. It is dedicated to
the maintenance of peace through official military and political intervention. Its two smooth outer walls and inner corridor of symbolic

ruins—the rubble-like chunks of concrete representing the Green Line separating Greek and Turkish Cypriot forces in Cyprus—are somewhat overwhelmed, physically if not symbolically, by Moshe Safdie's gleaming National Gallery of Canada to the north and, to the south, the foreboding mass of the new U.S. Embassy. In some ways the structure is a peacekeeping monument subservient to its surroundings.

With its depiction of three soldiers, only one of them with a weapon, and one of them a woman, "Reconciliation"—the name strongly suggests peace over war—sits in sharp contrast to Ottawa's official National War Memorial a few hundred metres to the south. That older monument, unveiled in May 1939 and known as "The Response," features First World War soldiers bristling with weaponry, triumphantly struggling to haul a small artillery piece through an archway. The newer Peacekeeping Monument, more ambiguous, more complex, symbolizes war's wreckage and waste. Its three soldiers are on different levels, looking in different directions. They stand still, observing, communicating. The monument stands as neither a bold statement in favour of peace nor a traditional effort to invoke the heroism and sacrifice of the dead.

"Unlike most 'war' memorials," Gough writes, Canada's national Peacekeeping Monument "makes no attempt at closure or the resolution of private or public suffering. It does, however, record the historic involvement of Canadian troops in peacekeeping. And, with sufficient space available for 30 future campaigns, it projects a confidence that Canadian participation in such ventures will endure." Gough adds a caveat. Recent developments, including the intervention in Afghanistan, he speculates, "might even suggest that the preoccupation with peacekeeping evoked by the monument may come to be seen as representative of only a certain phase in Canadian military and foreign policy, to be supplanted by something else, the contours of which are only now beginning to take shape."[57]

In 2008 the Canadian government passed a law proclaiming August 9, the day in 1974 on which Syrian military forces shot down the Buffalo airplane carrying Canadian peacekeepers, as Peacekeepers Day. Veterans Affairs explained that the occasion had become an "official day." The August 9, 2009, ceremony at "Reconciliation" honouring Canadian peacekeepers featured the wife of a soldier killed in Afghanistan. An official pamphlet available at the 2009 ceremony—

which was also an occasion on which the Ottawa chapter of the Canadian Association of Veterans in UN Peacekeeping was named after John Gardham—listed the names of those killed in Afghanistan. After much saluting and martial music, Chief of Defence Staff Walt Natynczyk invoked hockey and peacekeeping in addressing the ranks of veterans in blue berets and a modest crowd of spectators. When it comes to peacekeeping, he asserted counterfactually, "we're second to none."

The conflation of peacekeeping with the new militarism puzzled some of Canada's veteran military leaders. Paul Manson, Chief of Defence Staff when the plans for Calgary's Peacekeeping Monument were laid, said he was "astounded" that the names of the Canadian dead in Afghanistan had found their way onto the monument. One of Manson's successors as Canada's top soldier, on learning that the Peacekeepers' Day ceremony had come to include the publication of the names of individual soldiers killed in Afghanistan, remarked that their names had been "kidnapped."[58]

"This is *not* a memorial to the dead," insisted Gardham, the monument's most fervent supporter, echoing its original intent. "It is a memorial to the very spirit of peacekeeping and our ongoing missions."[59]

Like so much of the new militarism, the peace-is-war/war-is-peace dynamic that transformed the Afghan War into a peace operation, at least for the purposes of historical memory, smacks of the world that Orwell imagined in *1984*. Big Brother consigned history to a memory hole, into which inconvenient facts just vanish. Other inconvenient facts, such as how Canadian veterans are treated in the aftermath of war when they are forced to sue the government for decent benefits, also disappear. Even as loyal a military patriot and volunteer as Gardham experienced this first-hand. In 2008, just as the Warrior Nation drumbeat was becoming more intense, the Perley and Rideau Veterans' Health Centre noted that the retired officer had been "a fixture" there for fourteen years, "instrumental in raising the health centre's profile by helping to raise funds for a variety of important projects while sitting on three Perley Rideau boards." Despite his service, should he need a bed in the long-term care facility, he would not qualify.

Gardham said he intended to donate his war medals to the War Museum. Those medals indicate that he served the country for forty-two years, but that was not enough to make him eligible to get into the

Veterans' Health Centre. "I did not serve in the Korean War and I did not serve in the Gulf War. I was a peacekeeper."[60]

★

"It is with profound sadness that we announce that two Afghan children . . . were killed in this incident," explained the Canadian army, employing the passive voice. Defence Minister Peter MacKay sounded equally sober about the "horrible decision that had to be taken." The 2008 event was, it seemed, shrouded by a sense of inevitability. MacKay blamed it on "the despicable tactics used by the Taliban, hiding among the civilian population."[61]

Regrettable but inevitable. The children were in a vehicle whose driver had not heeded warnings to stay away from the Canadian military convoy. The reports did not explain whether the 25-millimetre round came from a Bushmaster autocannon, a standard NATO weapon developed by McDonnell-Douglas. Nor did they specify whether the light armoured vehicle that the Canadian gunner was using was one of the LAV-25 series built by General Dynamics Land Systems Canada. It was clear, however, that the cucumber-sized projectile tore through the four-year-old girl's skull before it left a gaping hole in her two-year-old brother's chest. A police officer at the Kandahar hospital reported hearing the grieving mother scream, "My innocent children have been killed by foreigners—for no reason!"[62]

It was an incident tragically typical of NATO's Afghan War. One Afghan at the Red Cross hospital claimed angrily that, had his own children suffered the fate of the others, he would don a suicide vest and join the ranks of the suicide bombers whose gruesome tactics so concerned the Canadians. Another Kandahar man, merchant Din Mohammed, was also visiting the Mirwais Hospital, funded and staffed by the Red Cross, the only international aid organization with foreign staff still permanently based in the war zone that was Kandahar. "They must stop this," said the shopkeeper. "Otherwise the day will come when everybody will stand up against the foreigners in a holy war, a *jihad*." That had happened once before, he said, with the Soviets. "If things continue like this, history will repeat itself."[63] The history of shell shock, combat fatigue, and post-traumatic stress disorder, the syllables multiplying with the twentieth century's wars, repeated itself among Canadians returning from Afghanistan. The effects on the young soldier who fired on the children would remain unknown to all but the man himself and those close to him.

The history of many another insurgency was, as the Kandahar shopkeeper warned, being repeated in Afghanistan. The ruthless Taliban, a brutal crew by any measure, hanged compatriots suspected of collaborating with the "foreigners," just as the American insurgents of 1776 lynched compatriots who remained loyal to the colonial cause. Francis Marion, a much-eulogized Carolina militia leader known as the "Swamp Fox," had a dozen U.S. municipalities named for him. After helping with an ethnic cleansing operation that pushed the Cherokee people from their lands before the Revolution, Marion organized what his heirs in the U.S. military would come to call asymmetric warfare against the British. The South Carolina Air National Guard, with the image of a fox painted on its jet fighters, calls its base the Home of the Swamp Fox. American nationalists know of him as a "determined and dangerous warrior." In the wake of a 2000 movie loosely based on his life, *The Patriot*, one British commentator labelled Marion a terrorist, "not at all the sort of chap who should be celebrated as a hero."[64]

Heroes and villains. Freedom fighters and terrorists. These claims and counterclaims are as old as war, as puzzling as Canadians being exhorted in 1914 to believe that the Great War was a fight for Christian civilization when the men firing from the other side of no man's land were Lutherans and Catholics.

What James Laxer tellingly called Canada's "Mission of Folly" in Afghanistan was marked by important milestones: the first overseas fight against local guerrillas since the Boer War; the longest war in the country's history; the first time that the country's military had quit the battlefield while the enemy was still fighting and, despite claims by generals and politicians, was gaining the upper hand.[65] But the misadventure in Afghanistan was consistent in one important respect: wars big and small have always been breeding grounds for government lies. The state attempts, with mixed success, to bolster public support for the bloodletting. So it was here: a war that began with the invasion of an impoverished country to dislodge its government in order to get at those who had planned the attacks of September 11, 2001, was turned into a struggle for freedom and democracy in Central Asia. Canadian war promoters, previously AWOL from the front lines of feminist struggles, also posited that the intervention was all about liberating Afghan women from their fundamentalist shackles and allowing little girls to go to school. (No matter that the warlords, grifters, and dope dealers amongst Canada's allies in the Karzai government were themselves hard-shell misogynists.)[66]

As defeat loomed, the shape-shifting war aims became more modest. It was all about stabilizing the country and "training" men how to fight—men, just incidentally, brought up in a culture steeped in a warrior ethos. Or, at the very least, the men had to be persuaded to fight with sufficient enthusiasm to bring the Taliban to the negotiating table. A war that began as a campaign to defeat the Taliban became an effort to make a deal with them. Just as Canada's Kandahar operation was ending, U.S. defense secretary Robert Gates confirmed that the United States was involved in "very preliminary" negotiations with the Taliban.[67] NDP leader Jack Layton had endured the vitriolic "Taliban Jack" campaign for merely suggesting this sort of thing.

Canada's Afghan War was, in many ways, typical of so many that preceded it—an exercise in imperial overstretch, a tragic waste of life, a misuse of resources that could have been directed to pressing needs at home and abroad. Undertaken by a Liberal government and picked up with zeal by a Conservative regime, the Kandahar mission lacked clear aims and was, given the history of foreign interventions in Afghanistan, doomed to failure. Any strategist who examined the situation should have clearly recognized that a campaign involving a divided NATO alliance and an enemy with safe havens across the border in Pakistan did not bode well. But the Canadian military, led by a general who by his own account saw his job as puffing up his institution's image and budget, was apparently not seriously pondering the nature of the Pashtun resistance and the cagey games of Pakistan's Inter-Services Intelligence, the inefficiencies and corruption of its Afghan allies, and the preoccupation of its principal ally with the disastrous occupation of Iraq.

There were no indications that Canada's top brass had digested the historical lessons set out in Norman F. Dixon's classic analysis *On the Psychology of Military Incompetence*. With respect to Afghanistan, Dixon cited the First Afghan War of 1842, in which a British army of 4,500 dispatched to support a puppet ruler was decimated by poorly equipped

Afghans. Nor were the Canadian militarists and the politicians who agreed to send troops to Kandahar apparently aware of Dixon's insights into examples of strategic incompetence, including an inability to learn from past experience and the deployment of a force without clear objectives.[68]

But if Canadian war aims in Kandahar were fuzzy, suffering from a lack of appreciation of regional history, the war at home had clear intentions. This revanchist struggle was a propaganda assault promoting the notion of Canada as Warrior Nation. The military, flush with cash, energetically updated its image, rebranding itself as "Forces.ca." The effort transformed recruiting tactics. Gone was "There's no life like it." Young Canadians watching televised hockey began to see ads commanding them to "Fight!"—"Fight Fear. Fight Distress. Fight Chaos. Fight with the Canadian Forces." The new marketing pitch, according to Howard Fremeth, "showcased aggressive weaponry and borrowed cinematic techniques from American war films, video games and geopolitical thrillers to show the seductive allure of modern warfare." Low-angle shots using handheld cameras and grainy grey colours echoed war epics such as Steven Spielberg's uber-patriotic *Saving Private Ryan*. Some of the new warrior marketing borrowed from video games such as *Call of Duty*, with first-person camera shots displaying guns in the foreground, positioning the spectator as combatant. Thumping, heartbeat-style background music emulated U.S. television's political thrillers like *24* and *NCIS*.[69]

Rick Hillier, never able to restrain the fountain of superlatives about the members of Forces.ca, called the effort "Recruit the Nation." Picking up on the propaganda primer that Hillier had absorbed at Fort Hood, Texas, the military launched an assault on Canadian consciousness and the military's own self-image. It aimed to be what the general himself described as a "cultural revolution." David Bercuson's peculiar reveries about war's sublime beauty—"the awful beauty of tracer fire at night"—became standard televisual fare. Any public event, particularly those involving televised sports, could expect an onslaught of martial images: "Celebrities were a way to reach audiences we could never hope to influence, no matter how many recruiting commercials we aired. All we had to do was introduce them to our people and let the celebrities do the rest. There was no doubt a good story would follow, because our people were so impressive."[70] The use of "personalities" proliferated, particularly when those people had something to do with hockey. Forces.ca was apparently no longer at risk of having its gear rusted out. Indeed, after 2008 Hillier's successor Walt Natynczyk spent nearly $1.5 million on exclusive flights aboard government jets to get to professional hockey and football events celebrating the military. He also managed to squeeze in one such flight for a Caribbean vacation. One short jaunt from Ottawa to a Maple Leafs hockey game that was also a military appreciation event cost $23,231.30.[71]

Hockey was, not surprisingly, the main focus of military efforts to emulate hometown-style boosterism. The Stanley Cup was shipped to Kandahar, with press reports chronicling its arrival aboard a military aircraft "making a tactical combat landing." One panting Canwest reporter had it that Canada's francophone commander at the time looked like the Montreal Canadiens great Henri Richard, and somehow imagined the fluid guerrilla war as a replay of the Somme. "Canadian battle lines have been buzzing for weeks with news of the impending visit of the Cup."[72]

The home front was the principal target for the attempts to link the national game with militarism. This has long been a common trope in the United States, where football, that game of territorial possession and "field generals," has been a primary vehicle for this sort of propaganda. Canada's best-known hockey personality, Don Cherry, occupies a high-profile bully pulpit on CBC-TV's *Hockey Night in Canada*. An honorary member of the Legion, Cherry took pride in supporting the troops as well as Prime Minister Harper ("a grinder and a mucker") and being the embodiment of military values. [73] "I never seen such a vicious hate series. It's great!" he intoned during the 2011 Stanley Cup final. That the public broadcaster would allow Cherry to keep airing ethnic slurs and partisan political rants had for years been a subject of controversy, with critics attributing it to the CBC's financial situation (the network depended on hockey ad revenues) and steady rightward drift. In 2010, when Cherry was made an "honorary Patricia" by the Princess Patricia's Canadian Light Infantry, the televised spectacle drove television critic John Doyle to exclaim: "Cherry is as constant as a canal horse, following the same straight path relentlessly, pulling a barge of barking patriotism and notional Canadian authenticity."[74]

Canada's "home game," the title of the insightful book by Ken Dryden and Roy MacGregor—a study linking hockey to what it means to be Canadian—was a natural vehicle for conscription into the campaign to persuade Canadians to identify their wintry country with the military and all its works.[75] The image of a swaggering Warrior Nation, however, was also inspired by the cultural role-model south of the border, where militarized patriotism and football march hand in hand. Canada's military gained the full co-operation of the Canadian Football League, a corporation itself struggling to rebuild and rebrand. The military launched Operation Connection in 2006, just after the Harper Conservatives first came to office and the first Canadians headed for Kandahar. It was a prototype of things to come as the military began showing up at community events, big and small, across the country.

The first big splash came at the CFL's annual Grey Cup festivities in Winnipeg. Canadian pro football's championship game had long featured low-key political photo opportunities of Paul Martin tossing the pre-game coin, Pierre Trudeau in a floppy hat and fur coat, or John Diefenbaker performing the ceremonial kickoff. In the fall of 2006, however, the Grey Cup week featured an unprecedented military marketing blitzkrieg. The operation included a lot of escorting, with soldiers accompanying the burly players from the airport, the shiny Grey Cup to the Forks, and the cheerleaders all around town. Parachutists jumped. Tanks and heavy artillery rolled by. "Support the Troops" paraphernalia were showcased. Recruiting tents popped up. The Grey Cup parade included armoured vehicles—Leopards and Bisons. In an inadvertent comment on automotive culture, Forces.ca staged a draw for a children's hospital. The winner got to ride in an actual tank as it obliterated an old vehicle, the culmination of a "charity car crush." The championship game itself became a hypermilitarized spectacle featuring the Canadian Forces "tri-service colours," howitzers firing after each touchdown, and even a message from General Hillier himself on the Jumbotron.[76] In 2011 Winnipeg fans, their aspirations to big-league status long confined to the local CFL franchise (the Blue *Bombers*), received the happy news that their old NHL franchise would soon be returning to town. The Winnipeg Jets would have the same name as the previous incarnation. The chosen logo, however, was no longer the generic airplane of old but the sharp-edged image of what was clearly a military fighter jet.

Everything old was new again. It all hearkened back to the drum and bugle patriotism marshalled to support the First World War carnage. Although twenty-first-century propaganda was underpinned by polling and focus groups, benefiting from slick advertising techniques, the messages from what Jeffrey Keshen described as "Canada's Great War of deception" were eerily echoed ninety years later. Newspaper magnate Maxwell Aitken had described the disaster of Second Ypres, where Canada lost fifty times more soldiers in one battle than it did in ten years in Afghanistan, as a place where the seeds of a proud Canadian nationalism were sown. The Dominion's stalwart warriors, Aitken's readers learned, had "saved the day" so that "the mere written word Canada" would thereafter shine "with a new meaning before all the civilized world."[77] The story retailed by Afghan War backers may have been slightly more subtle, but the message resonated. Our soldiers became heroes, every one—models of what it means to be a real Canadian. Their war was a triumph for Canada on the world stage.

Just as Canada's Kandahar war got started, Rudyard Griffiths, the co-founder of the Dominion Institute, started to agitate for a state funeral for John Babcock, the last surviving Canadian veteran of the Great War. Even though Babcock had yet to die and had not actually fought in the war (on Nov. 11, 1918, when the war ended, he was under arrest for a dance hall brawl in Wales), Griffiths apparently believed that the veteran deserved a hero's funeral. According to this new warrior, Babcock needed remembering because "the duty not to forget now falls on a generation who has never known war." Journalist Andrew Cohen eulogized the aged man, who had moved to the United States soon after the First World War. "As John Babcock lived and breathed he reminded us, by virtue of his service, that Canada didn't just arrive here yesterday.... His message: We built. We sacrificed. We came from somewhere." Babcock's own modest message was that he "really didn't accomplish very much" in the war and he thought it would be "nice if all the different people in the world could get along together so we weren't having wars."[78]

Once Canada quit Kandahar a new story was put about. *Everyone* who had worn a uniform there was a hero. At least this was the claim made by military booster and Canadian Football League television commentator Glen Suitor, who saluted "37,000 Canadian heroes" during the broadcast of a game on Sept. 11, 2011. Those killed, said the football man, made "the ultimate sacrifice in defence of our freedom." That year an Edmonton dentist was trying to get the city to rename a street "Heroes Boulevard" in honour of everyone in the military. Explaining that he wanted to do more than stick a flag decal on his car, he faced a roadblock in the form of city officials who explained that it would be too expensive to change all those signs and addresses. Officials at CFB Edmonton added that many of its personnel thought of themselves as people doing their jobs rather than as heroes. They also apparently feared that the move might dilute Ontario's better-known Highway of Heroes.[79]

The support-our-troops campaign, together with the notion of every-soldier-a-hero, became impossible to ignore after 2006. The effort included an attempt to designate "red Fridays" by having Canadians wear special red shirts with yellow-ribbon logos as a gesture of support for the troops. More successful—and much easier to organize—was the mass distribution of yellow-ribbon flag decals that could be affixed to the backs of vehicles. Most conspicuous in communities with military bases, the effort generated support from civic authorities who agreed to place yellow-ribbon decorations on fire trucks, police cars, and ambulances. To oppose the support-our-troops loyalty display was politically risky, making the yellow-ribbon campaign useful in attempts to silence opposition to the war or even to question skyrocketing military spending. Politicians who criticized the Afghan War were vilified as Taliban sympathizers. The new Caesar was not interested in informed criticism.

Canada's war boosters set the tone in 2006 during a visit by Afghan president Hamid Karzai. A support-the-troops crowd gathered in the shadow of the Peace Tower to cheer Stephen Harper and his Afghan counterpart. A sceptical Trevor Haché quietly held up a sign reading "Support the troops, bring them home." The staffer for the Non-Smokers' Rights Association and one-time NDP candidate was attacked by a group that *Espirit de Corps* publisher Scott Taylor described as "red-shirt-wearing zealots." They tore up Haché's sign and threw him to the ground. Two years later another peace activist and NDP candidate was protesting a Halifax trade show featuring companies selling new ways of killing. Tamara Lorincz shouted, "This is a racket and it should be shut down. We need a peace economy, not a military economy." Although Lorincz was not accosted directly, when Peter MacKay heard about her protest he bravely stepped into the breach. He told reporters that he "felt physically ill" and that it was "one of the most disgusting things" he had heard in a long time. The defence minister added that Lorincz was "unfit for public office" and urged the NDP leader to pull "that woman's" nomination papers.[80]

The yellow-ribbon campaign became an emblem of those claiming political neutrality with respect to war, part of a conscious effort by military and political elites to reimagine the country in a way that elevated the military as an institution. As with the efforts to reimagine Canada as a nation-forged-in-fire, the campaign exalted martial values by placing war at the centre of the national memory and imagination.

The new warrior efforts represented an attempt at a state-orchestrated cultural revolution complete with newly reconfigured myths and symbols. The yellow ribbon is an American cultural import, with roots in an old folk song reputed to date from the Civil War: the story of a woman who wore a yellow ribbon to recall her lover who was "far, far away." In 1949 the great Hollywood director John Ford made a hit western starring, appropriately enough, John Wayne. *She Wore a Yellow Ribbon*, borrowing its imagery from the nineteenth-century American illustrator and sculptor Frederick Remington, depicts the U.S. Cavalry—with yellow stripes on the legs of their blue uniforms—not as a force conducting an ethnic cleansing campaign against the peoples of the Western frontier but as a benign outfit that somehow managed to round up the Cheyennes and Arapahos with very little violence. The film version of the traditional folk song was changed so that the female lead wore a yellow ribbon "for her lover in the U.S. Cavalry."[81]

The yellow ribbon was consolidated as a symbol of U.S. troops fighting imperial wars in 1973 when the pop group Tony Orlando and Dawn sang their hit song "Tie a Yellow Ribbon Round the Ole Oak Tree" to honour Vietnam veterans at the Cotton Bowl, a college football championship. By the end of the 1970s yellow ribbons were indicating support for Americans taken hostage by militants who had overthrown the Shah of Iran and his U.S. client regime. The symbolic ribbons then became support-our-troops signifiers during the U.S.-led war to restore the Emir of Kuwait, otherwise known as the 1991 Gulf War.[82] It was perhaps a logical step that once Canada became mired in Afghanistan the American yellow loyalty ribbon should become a semi-official symbol north of the border.

Symbols in support of the war were on conspicuous display along Ontario's Highway of Heroes, the section of Highway 401 that was renamed after people began to gather on overpasses to watch and salute as hearses carrying soldiers killed in Afghanistan drove from Canada's biggest air base at Trenton to Toronto. One of the main organizers of the Highway was Pete Fisher, a local newspaper photographer who recalled in 2007 that the Highway of Heroes was meant to "honour our soldiers who die so others can live a better life." Fisher claimed that Canadians were not "trying to conquer a country," insisting that the war was all about altruism. "They are trying to help the people of Afghanistan." The effort began modestly in 2002 when the bodies of four dead soldiers passed by, although Fisher's story about the origin of the Highway of Heroes did not mention that those four men had been killed by an overly zealous U.S. fighter pilot. He described the "sudden sea of arms waving Canadian flags" brandished by the patriots of Port Hope—the highway streams across its northern boundary—"wanting to let family members in the procession know we are there for them, that we share their pain and are proud to be Canadian." He also explained how it was a columnist for the Toronto *Sun*— a tabloid controlled by Quebec's right-wing Peladeau interests—who coined the Highway of Heroes label.[83]

The official designation of the highway marks one area in which Canada did part ways with its senior partner in the Afghan War. The U.S. military was wary of conspicuous displays of casualties in what had quickly become unpopular wars in Afghanistan and Iraq. The Canadian government's public relations strategy evolved differently. In a historically unprecedented effort, unknown in former wars where those killed were most often buried near the battlefield, the government eventually turned the dead into a spectacle. Canadian media in Kandahar recorded solemn rituals soon dubbed "ramp ceremonies." Similar rituals were repeated when the aircraft arrived at Trenton, where ceremonies sometimes included Governor-General Michaëlle Jean along with senior cabinet ministers. The importance accorded to these rituals—similar to the familiar convention of the mass police funeral, and reminiscent of Bercuson's invocations of a military priesthood—underscored the length to which the government was willing to go to project the image of soldiers as warrior heroes. How could any-one deign to cast doubt on the efforts—and implicitly the sacrifices—of "Our Troops"?

The support-our-troops rallying cry had a pernicious political effect that was played out in the cases of critics like Layton, Haché, and Lorincz. As cultural studies analyst A.L. McCready sees it, once soldiers are in "harm's way," the boundaries of public discussion shift. It is no longer about whether the war is just or even justifiable, but all about the sacrifices of soldiers and their families: "The yellow ribbon's function was and is to expedite this shift and, by extension, to imply that the time for 'politics' was over, and that it was now the time to rally around the flag."[84]

The tone of the political debate was reflected in 2010 during a dust-up over a new scholarship program called Project Hero, sponsored by Rick Hillier. The scholarship, administered by the federal government, was intended to provide support to the children of Canadian soldiers killed in the line of duty. At the University of Regina sixteen professors, alarmed by the growth of militarism as the Afghan War escalated, signed a public letter to the university suggesting it withdraw from Project Hero. Sociologist John Conway explained that Hillier's Project Hero was

> part of the ongoing propaganda offensive from the militaristic, pro-war cabal led by Prime Minister Stephen Harper and the former chief of defence, Rick Hillier. From the beginning this propaganda offensive sought to silence criticism of the war by equating it with a failure to support our troops. Efforts to turn this into a heroic battle will fail. Many Canadians are ashamed of Canada's role in a dirty, savage war which pits the random techno-barbarism of advanced warfare against a poorly armed insurgency. For this the blame lies with our government and our spineless Parliament, not our troops carrying out orders.[85]

The response was as belligerent as it was predictable. The Regina Sixteen were subjected to a torrent of abuse, typically "Shut up and teach." The official response was only slightly more civil. "No matter what one thinks of the mission in Afghanistan, there can be no doubt about the honour with which our soldiers carry out their duties," said local Conservative MP Andrew Scheer. "Attacking a scholarship for the children of our fallen service men and women is disgusting." Saskatchewan premier Brad Wall weighed in with a denunciation of his own. "Here we're talking about women and men—heroes, genuine heroes—who are serving our country, who have literally risked their lives and in some cases paid with their lives for the service of their country."[86]

One of the Regina Sixteen, Ken Montgomery, took the trouble to examine 346 responses to a single online CBC news story. Most of the postings were anonymous and abusive. One said, "These 16 special lil snowflakes should have their left leaning butts sent to embed with our soldiers for an upclose look at what our men and women do to protect our freedoms here at home." Montgomery politely framed another comment as "Orientalist discourse"—"You want Canada to pull out of its military obligations then start learning to speak some dialect from the middle east and start your conversion to become a Muslim before your head gets chopped off by these jackals and ghouls we are fighting for a reason."[87]

Aside from unalloyed racism and general hair-on-fire vituperation, the denunciations reflected a familiar militarist trope. Those protesting Hillier's scholarship scheme were repeatedly accused of abusing the freedom and democracy that had been brought to Canadians by the military. "It seems," responded John Conway caustically, "that our whole democratic system rests on the firm foundation of our military, not only the defenders of our freedoms but also the authors of our freedoms." This was, he continued, "simply historically untrue." In Canada democracy, freedom, justice, and dignity have been achieved from the bottom up, not thanks to the efforts of colonels and generals.

Conway listed the Patriotes of Lower Canada and the 1837 Reformers in Upper Canada fighting for responsible government; suffragists winning voting rights for women; Louis Riel and the Métis and Indian nations he twice led in struggles for the rights of westerners; the agrarian populists who took on the special interests dominating politics; workers fighting for the freedom to organize into trade unions. "Look at the historical record," Conway said. "What was the role of the military in this struggle for democracy and justice in Canada? As an arm of the state, the military was used, often with protests from its own ranks, as an instrument of control and repression." He came up with another list: repression of the 1837 rebels; the officers directing the

Gatling gun at Batoche; the use of the militia against strikers too numerous to mention; the 1917 conscription protesters shot down in the streets of Quebec City. He could have added the October and Oka crises in Quebec. "The list," he concluded, "is long."[88]

As the Highway of Heroes ceremonies gathered momentum, one resident of Port Hope watched the proceedings with a mixture of scepticism and alarm. Novelist Farley Mowat is perhaps the town's best-known citizen. Sitting in a cozy house overlooking the Ganaraska River and cluttered with the mementoes of a writer's life, he explained this latest round of patriotic militarism in organic terms. The author of a basketful of books on whales, wolves, and wilderness, Mowat had long drawn metaphorical inspiration from the natural world. He described the Highway of Heroes phenomenon as part of a "viral infection" that usually "lies dormant, festering in society, nurtured by boys' adventure stories of heroism in service to the nation." Mowat added, "You see it in the monuments we erect to the fallen and carefully scripted remembrances—until it slowly slouches back into respectability."[89]

By the time the Highway of Heroes had received official provincial government endorsement in 2007, finding its way onto roadside signs, Mowat had grown more disturbed. He recalled the patriotic fervour in 1939 when he joined the army. His enlistment had been "instinctive." But his months of terrifying combat experience, of watching friends being killed while fighting soldiers who were often better equipped, had left him with a deep distaste for war and its accompanying propaganda. "I didn't get into that war for love of fatherland, for God's sake. It was all about your primal need to feel affection for your primary tribe, your group, your band. But then that expands beyond reasonable limits to the point where anyone can get their finger in it and manipulate it and stir it up."

Mowat, ninety years old in 2011, explained that Canadian memory and identity were being exploited in a manner that he found both interesting and unpalatable. The Highway of Heroes was part of an effort that he compared to "a venus flytrap." It was, he believed, highly political. "I know the Conservative member of Parliament here is powerfully behind it and that is part of his role as the prime minister's *gauleiter* for this region."[90] Mowat had fought fascism in Italy and retained memories that did not dwell on noble warrior heroes. His thoughts focused, rather, on the historical legacy of war that went back far beyond Sicily and the battle for Ortona.

"We risk being sucked into a pathological state of mind where we will be helpless to defend ourselves against death and destruction. Just as the Spartans were. The Charge-of-the-Light-Brigade people—'Into the valley of death.' Any of the human beings who were lied to and manipulated to a point where they would willingly, happily advance into that valley. I lay a lot of the responsibility for this onto the Harper mentality. This sonofabitch is the scariest animal who has hit Canada in a long time."

A statue at Calgary's Peacekeeper Park makes a conscious effort to portray a soldier brandishing his weapon. As Don Ethell, a retired colonel and key organizer of the commemorative space, said: "We intentionally went this way to indicate that, 'Yes there's a humanitarian side but it requires that they're prepared to fight.' As they are doing in Afghanistan."

MILITARY FANTASYLANDS AND THE GATED PEACEABLE KINGDOM

War is peace. Freedom is slavery. Ignorance is strength.

– George Orwell, *Nineteen Eighty-Four*, 1948

Crisis has broken out in Zefra—that troubled and chaotic city in North Africa. Like Afghanistan as imagined by Canadian-military-man-turned-Conservative-politician Laurie Hawn ("an ugly place"), Zefra is "without hope, with no future." Worse, it has "literally millions of people knocking on its door for refuge" to escape situations that are even more dire. Images of Zefra evoke despair—the "cardboard shacks, filth-ridden alleys, places of casual rape and murder." The city's "baking streets" are jammed with "squabbling crowds." Its mosques are crumbling, its women wear burkhas. The place is a "vast, incoherent riot of humanity," gibber-jabbering crowds seized by one irrational emotion after another. Just visiting there can be a "nauseating ordeal." Zefra is a hopeless little eddy in humanity's otherwise fast stream of progress.[1]

Except that this painful place does not actually exist. Zefra was conjured up by consultant Karl Schroeder in a futuristic 2005 novel. The writer was working as part of a fourteen-man team within the Directorate of Land Strategic Concepts, a Kingston, Ont., security think tank that is in turn within Canada's Department of National Defence. Zefra is a figment of the National Defence imagination.

The Zefra story as delivered by the Canadian military consultant offers few other details about the location aside from its vision of a fantastical, nightmarish fog of weirdly dressed and unsanitary people. The main thing we need to know is that Zefra is a "failed state"—and a "trouble spot for Africa's ongoing water and oil wars."[2] It is prey to Islam, socialistic doctrines, despicable anti-Western conspiracies, and fanatics who hate the West for its freedoms. Indeed, this Zefra has no useful history from which other human beings might learn. Rather, it functions as Western civilization's static Other. While westerners were getting on with making world history, Zefra's vast, incoherent crowds were apparently spending centuries aimlessly milling around its ancient white towers. As the radical Caribbean-born intellectual Frantz Fanon might well have said, westerners arrive at a place like Zefra with a complete and satisfactory narrative of progress in their minds—with the colonized put to work in this framework as emblems of how low humanity can sink if it is not taken over by more evolved human beings.[3] Like us, for instance.

Crisis in Zefra does not directly announce that Anglos and their friends must prevail over their racial inferiors. Yet the discredited dogmas of race that once warmed the hearts of imperialists like William Stairs and John Buchan have not disappeared. They are merely couched in a more cautious language. Many of Zefra's likeable Canadian characters bear appropriately multicultural names, and none of them pronounces any alarming speeches about racial superiority. Yet the "African Orient" they visit is saturated with assumptions about the intrinsic and unchanging primitiveness of the locals. The book's illustrations crystallize a racialized vision. Hook-nosed, grimacing, slouching, yet intent; crafty-looking eyes topped with sinister eyebrows: the villains of this piece are depicted like the dastardly Arabs from Hollywood's Central Casting.[4]

If applied to any other ethnic groups, such officially published illustrations would spark outrage: against Arabs and Africans they can evidently pass muster. Zefra exemplifies, all too apparently, the non-Western world as at least parts of the Canadian Forces think they know it. For *Crisis in Zefra* is no mere novel: it is a kind of fictional training manual designed to help young Canadian soldiers imagine the brave new world of perpetual war for which the new warriors are preparing. *Crisis in Zefra* is that unusual creature, a state-orchestrated pedagogical novel liberally sprinkled with footnotes guiding us to the web pages of weapons dealers. Even the dialogue is interspersed with information-laden footnotes trumpeting the marvellous new toys on the military shopping list.

Zefra intends to instruct young Canadian soldiers, in particular, about the sort of enemies they might well be confronting in the not-too-distant future (perhaps c.2020). Although not nearly as captivating a character as *Prester John*'s Reverend John Laputa, *Zefra*'s villainous anti-Western conspirator, Mastan Nouria, could be plucked at random from any of Buchan's lesser works. Sly, superstitious, and unscrupulous, Nouria is a fanatical follower of Frantz Fanon, the real-life writer whose work on the psychopathology of imperial domination dissected the colonial mindset. Nouria has named his group the "Fanonist Irredentist Fellaheen." Like Laputa, Nouria is a disturbing mixture of old and new: a fanatic who surfs the Internet. His message is one of dire simplicity: kick out the foreigners and restore the homeland to its ancient traditions. Nouria's image floats above his followers like "some sort of dark religious icon."[5]

Despite the emphasis on Fanon, Schroeder and his team do not bother to explore the influential thinker's intriguing works: all you need to know about Fanon and the Fanonists is that they are rabid enemies of Western freedom. "They're Fanonists," one character explains. "They believe in an oppressive colonialism, one that's reinforced by media like language and technology. Think McLuhanites hostile to the global village." They are so unhinged that they happily undermine their own strategic position just to pursue their mad, sad dream of an Africa without Canadians. But no need to worry: the Canadians— the "good guys," according to the author—have landed.[6] To the sick they bring comfort. To the hungry they bring food. To a land trapped in superstition and tradition, they bring democratic practice and administrative efficiency. Equipped with superior morals and intelligence, Canadians grasp at once—seemingly in the absence of anything like an election—that the rebels are opposed by the "majority of the citizens." We Canadians are working in Zefra "to protect the people's newly established rights."[7]

The bad news is that these powerful Canadians imagine a future in which Canadian soldiers will be fighting an endless series of colonial wars. The good news is that our soldiers will subdue the world's unruly natives with an array of breathtaking things. Shiny things. Buzzing things. Magical things. Expensive things.

Networked up to their eyeballs, the brave men and women of our coalition are fighting a three-block war, just like in Iraq and Afghanistan. In the first block, we are *nice*—handing out treats to the children, helping pregnant mothers. In the second block, we are not quite so nice—here the "peace support operations" might entail some pretty heavy scenes. In the third block, soldiers get to be soldiers, fighting "high-intensity" fights. Take Warrant Officer Vadna Desai and her handy HMD (head-mounted display): "From her godlike perspective above the city, she already thought she knew it better than she'd known Montreal before leaving home. She could zoom through the model as if flying through the real city, penetrating the walls of houses and garages, automatic system agents counting vehicles and foot traffic as she went."[8]

The book serves up a sort of secular religion—a kind of "muscular Canadianism" in which the chosen people of the North deliver tough love to the decidedly unchosen people of the South. In the imaginary world of *Zefra*, the coalition of good guys is very nearly undone by the schemes of the bad guys. When the "commentators and cynical political flacks" in the wider world comment on "the possibility that the fragile North African peace was going to collapse," they were merely repeating "the propaganda and disinformation" of the enemy.[9] If ever Canadians did happen to shoot up a crowd of civilians—and, nice people that we are, we will work *ever* so hard not to do so—we can tell ourselves, as Defence Minister Peter MacKay told Canadians in 2008, that all the blame belongs to "the terrorists" who disguise themselves as non-combatants.

Much has changed since the African exploits of William Stairs, including the empire's name, which goes unmarked in this book. Yet, in another, more important way, nothing has changed at all. Armed with translation programs and pseudo-anthropological insights, the peacekeepers imagined in *Zefra* are less interested in the people they are dominating than was Stairs in the 1880s. But, like Stairs, we are still convinced that we have the right to impose our "sanity and sanitation" upon people whose history for us is a mishmash of Orientalist clichés and racist stereotypes. Like Stairs with his awesome Maxim gun, we remain as convinced as ever that for every world problem there is a

military solution. We preserve an unalterable sense of ourselves as
the steadfast servants of a Western civilization in whose name we have
every right to kill. The Victorian world of the *Boy's Own Annual*
appears, uncannily, to be up and running again in a freshly militarized
Canada.

Yet *Zefra* is, as a work of *government fiction*, also doing something
new. In the Warrior Nation, premised as it is on an anxious state of
perpetual emergency, the techniques of war propaganda are deployed
in a country still at peace. As the director general of Land Capability
Development explains, "The current security environment and anticipated future security challenges demonstrate that our Army must
be expected to operate anywhere, anytime, under any circumstances.".
Canadians must get used to this atmosphere of "permanent emergency." They must realize that, in purchasing new aircraft, security
systems, and eventually maybe even "smartdust," they are standing up
for Western civilization. We are invited to participate in building the
"Army of the Future."[10]

Although fictional, *Crisis in Zefra* "offers a glimpse of future possibilities—possibilities that could ultimately become real both in light
of ongoing trends and an inability (or unwillingness) on the part of the
international community to effectively manage (and hopefully contain) their potential impacts in the decades ahead." In an appendix to
the book Peter Gizewski—co-editor of the aptly named *Towards a
Brave New World: Canada's Army in the 21st Century*—solemnly warns
that failed states like Zefra may well proliferate in Africa: "With an
ethnically diverse, sparsely educated, and rapidly growing population,
a semi-modern (primarily agrarian) economy and highly dependent
on foreign aid, the nation maintains an uneasy existence in the years
following independence—all the while exceedingly vulnerable to the
whims of external actors and unfavourable climatic conditions."[11]

Under such conditions, bad actors—in this case, "a radical group
seeking massive redistribution of national wealth and espousing a
quasi-socialist, anti-western ideology"—are very likely to win influence.[12] Left unasked is whether the wretched of the earth—to use
Fanon's haunting phrase—might not quite reasonably aspire to a different future than one proclaimed by Canadian robocops from the sky.
Operating in a climate of dread and fear, sustaining crude visions of
cultural and racial superiority, entranced by technology as something

that will solve almost every problem, blind to the wider moral or political implications of the work they are doing, the team behind *Crisis in Zefra* reminds us that military adventure stories are not just for boys. They are for immature people of all ages.

Crisis in Zefra reflects what is old and what is original in Canada as Warrior Nation. Much of the DND's imagined Africa recalls the continent as seen by William Stairs and John Buchan. And although the story of the twenty-first-century Scramble for Africa, in which China and its Western competitors are in a new race for resources, remains to be written, many of its key campaigns will be couched in the vocabulary of military humanitarianism. Struggles over oil, coltan, copper, and water will be reshaped as crusades for humanity. As in Libya in 2011, where a UN resolution was creatively interpreted by NATO as a licence for an all-out bombing campaign, today's scramble will be sold as a campaign for democracy and freedom.

As a sub-imperial power integrated within the Anglosphere, Canada will be expected to play a helpful role in this new carving up of a continent. Whether any Africans will be liberated by the drone strikes, brand-new F-35s, or "boots on the ground" from Canada and NATO is as yet unknown. Yet, rather like Leopold II with his ersatz nineteenth-century philanthropies, those whose eyes are fixed on Africa will undoubtedly argue that they are only exercising their "responsibility to protect" innocent civilians. But follow the money—not just the subsidies that Canadian and U.S. citizens will be lavishing on bases and fancy new equipment, but the flow of cash onto the balance sheets of mining and petroleum interests. The twenty-first century's most destructive war to date, the Second Congo War, had cost some 5.4 million lives by 2008. It involved nine African countries, eight of them supplied with arms and military training by the U.S. government. UN peacekeeping and peace-building proved ineffectual. Canadian mining operations managed to prosper.[13]

Like conquistadores dreaming up elaborate natural-law justifications for slaughtering and enslaving indigenous peoples in the Americas, today's imperialists construct impressive bodies of historical and social theory to explain why they have the natural right to be lords of humankind. As in *Zefra*, the colonized (or those about to be colonized) are represented as unknowable and primitive, inscrutably inaccessible to our modes of reason, imprisoned in a static past. Today's indispensable Others are often Muslims living on or near energy resources or the pipelines and sea routes necessary for the secure passage of those resources to the West. Framing Muslims as civilizational enemies living in "failed" (or, if war is coming, "rogue") states gives soldiers and their political masters a comfortable way of explaining the need for more pricey hardware.[14]

As in the days of Stairs, the new warriors divide target populations living in areas of interest into the friendly and modern and the unfriendly and backward. Violence originates amongst the unfriendly denizens of foreign lands; peace and understanding come from us. Those Others are closed and strange; we are open and transparent. They are "developing" and we are "developed." As it happens, they are often "dark" and we are generally "light." We are sane, they are often lunatics. Through this binary lens, insanity can characterize entire countries. Why should Canadians involve themselves in keeping the peace between Iran and Iraq, asked J.L. Granatstein, given that they are "lunatic countries" ill disposed to any peace? Our modern-day villains are all recycled from the Empire: as early as the eighteenth century the "Mad Mullah" and "Cruel Turk" haunted the British imperial imagination.[15]

The debacle in Afghanistan revealed the extraordinary hold of such antique Kiplingesque assumptions. Media coverage seemingly never tired of describing a static, mysterious East: ancient tribes with primitive codes of hospitality and exotic costumes. That many objected to being invaded and bombed, even by decent soldiers bearing candies for the children, seemed further evidence of their unreachable, primitive natures. This crude anthropology rendered our "work" in Afghanistan resistant to critique. Anyone questioning the nature of the regime left in the wake of the war will meet up with the response, "Well, look at the awful people we had to deal with. They are trapped in the Middle Ages."[16]

NATO ostensibly ran the show in Afghanistan—which is revealing in itself. Fighting a war in Central Asia would appear to have little to do with the organization's original focus on defending the "North Atlantic" against the Soviets. But NATO, as everyone knows, is not an alliance of equals. Within it, and certainly in Afghanistan, Washington exercises the rights of leadership that devolve from its overwhelming military (though waxing economic) might. Ideologically, the Anglosphere gives the new warriors the indispensable sense of standing up for causes more exalted than the Barrick Gold Corporation, just as it inspired Stairs as he charged across Katanga in the service of Leopold II. That cause they would call "freedom," but it might better be termed "Anglo-globalization." It entails (in their minds) the worldwide spread of peace, order, and good government, with secure rights of private property and personal liberty under administrations that are stable, honest, and thrifty—and capable of enforcing business contracts.[17] As Tony Blair eloquently explained in 2002, addressing an American audience: "We do think the same, we do feel the same, and we have the same—I think—sense of belief that if there is a problem you've got to act on it." Stephen Harper—on the same wavelength, though characteristically rather less articulate—told the Council on Foreign Relations in 2007 that a rosy future for the world depended on "capable, committed, like-minded nations."[18]

Within the new paradigm, the market is far more than an incidental and useful mechanism for sorting out some economic transactions; rather, it is the Market, a name one does not take in vain. The wars that the new warriors project for our future will be fought in the name of rescuing women and children and avenging some enormity against civilization—but the regime's nastiness and the degree of Anglo hostility towards it have little if any correlation. Repressive regimes can be our friends, always provided that they accept free-market economics. Relatively non-repressive regimes can swiftly become our enemies if our own regime determines that they have been infringing, even in mild ways, upon the Market.

The practical military watchword of the Anglosphere is "interoperability." The term, in the sense of "standardization of programs," is nothing new; it dates back to the Second World War. Yet recent developments have, according to international relations theorist Srdjan Vucetic, "harmonized the militaries of core Anglosphere states to an unprecedented level," with new norms for multinational military co-operation and states increasingly fighting as one.[19] For Canada's General Andrew Leslie, in the "network-centred approach to operations" the Canadian Forces will be "JIMP-capable." That is, they will be ready to achieve wonders of interoperability through becoming "Joint, Interagency, Multinational and Public." Perhaps this might be better rendered as "JIMPUS"—"Joint, Interagency, Multinational, Public and U.S-directed."[20] With almost heart-breaking innocence, Canada's military men seem to think that they will have tangible influence over the conduct of the wars that our rulers would like us to fight alongside the Americans.

Canada's armed forces have become so deeply integrated with the U.S. military establishment that it is quite reasonable to wonder whether they really are this country's own armed forces. The armies of the two countries share training facilities. They participate in joint training exercises. Canadian military personnel are routinely placed in U.S. regiments on exchange with their counterparts. The careers of Rick Hillier and Walt Natynczyk illustrate that a stint in the U.S. military can work wonders for your CV: like many another Canadian soldier they became thoroughly at home in U.S. military culture. As the reconfigured ideals of empire take hold, the two militaries blend together. It is already rather difficult to tell them apart.

Many liberal-minded Canadians have grown up thinking that their country is characterized by certain continuing traits or values—multiculturalism, global peacekeeping and global citizenship, regionalism, commitment to a strong social safety net, and a consensual, collaborative, community-oriented approach to shared problems, to pick five traits from a 2010 survey of school texts.[21] Desmond Morton argues that "the great legacy of Canadian history is that it is a 'user's manual' for a Canada dependent on accommodation and compromise."[22]

The new warrior Canada is, by contrast, a crusading kingdom founded upon specific British and Christian traditions, militantly committed to the spread of specific notions of the market, and prioritizing military might over the peaceful resolution of disputes. Both imagined Canadas refer to myth-symbol complexes that spur the imagination, uniting citizens at some deeper level of belonging. Yet, similar in this respect, they are not equivalent in all ways. Drawing upon traditions of right-wing thought with well-established records of toxicity, new warrior nationalism leads us to different notions of national "interest" than does the model it seeks to displace. It rehabilitates powerful currents of Victorian imperialism—a sense of the superiority of Anglo-American institutions, a belief in rugged individualism, and a conception of a world in which states, like individuals, are necessarily caught up in a dog-eat-dog struggle to survive. Hence the need to travel in packs.

The meaning of war changes from one paradigm of Canadianness to another. In the first, war is at best a last resort, and Canada's general value to the species resides in its contribution to peace. In the second, war is an indispensable foundation of true Canadianism; Canada's honour and worth reside in its membership in an alliance that will dispense peace, order, and good government across the globe—by force if necessary (and it will be necessary). Both frameworks speak of "peace," but they are not talking about the same thing.

Canada's new myth-symbol complex entails an aggressive campaign to substitute the Warrior Nation for the peaceable kingdom—including a no-holds-barred attack on the "myth" of peacekeeping as a key component of the Canadian identity. Using a simplistic idea of "myth" as "that which did not actually take place," new warriors have targeted what they take to be the most pernicious myths and symbols of post-1960s Canada: the Charter of Rights and Freedoms, bilingualism, multicultural relativism, gender equality, and peacekeeping. In their place they promote religious fundamentalism, the military, manly sports, the special relationship with the United States and Britain, and the British monarchy—all now described as core attributes of Canada. Patrick Muttart, Prime Minister Harper's former deputy chief of staff and a key election strategist (he would move on to work for a Chicago public relations firm), explains, "What we're seeing is the emergence of a new patriotism or at the very least a small-c conservative alternative to the established Liberal narrative about Canada." As Harper reminded his British business audience in 2006, it was to the "British race" that humanity as a whole owed much of its joy, peace, and glory. His alternative to the "established Liberal narrative" will plainly revive, in all its moral ambiguity, the racializing imperatives of the Empire. It is the symbolic equivalent of undoing more than a half-century of democratic decolonization.[23]

Entirely missing in the new warrior universe is any understanding of Canadian history as a complex process involving forces, struggles, and movements that bring change over time. When new warriors speak of white settlers waging war on each other, they quickly push the fast-forward button to the "tradition of accommodation" that guaranteed "our shared traditions, identity and values." Even more radically, they whitewash such enormities as the country's painful treatment of the Japanese in the 1940s. Unsuspecting readers may imagine that the Conservative government's new guidebook for immigrants, *Discover Canada*, is just flatly reporting the facts on this question—first talking about the Japanese empire's acts of aggression and mistreatment of prisoners of war, then moving on to the relocation of Japanese Canadians and the forcible sale of their properties. Yet these sentences distil, and make official, the argument put forward by Granatstein in the 1986 book *Mutual Hostages*, in which he states that "both wartime Canada and Japan looked on the Japanese and Canadians under their control as mutual hostages"—drawing a direct (and seemingly exculpatory) parallel between the treatment of Canadian prisoners of war in Japan and the internment of Canadians of Japanese descent in Canada.[24] Granatstein's interpretation was roundly rejected by the professional consensus of the time. Critics observed that he was establishing a false parallel between the actions of a country against prisoners of war and the actions of our own state against its own people. *Discover Canada*, a classy handbook circulated by the federal state, is distinctly implying a historical thesis that is disturbingly redolent of doctrines of racial essence—in the same text that hails John Buchan, the concentration camp administrator who went on to argue for Canada as a "white man's democracy," as an exemplar of enlightened ethnic relations.

An attack on the "myth of peacekeeping" is central to the rebranding of Canada. For the new warriors, the peaceable kingdom, with peacekeeping as its centrepiece, is a myth; war-making on behalf of Empire and Dominion is the fount of spiritual truth. One mythology is invoked to cancel the other. Yet myths are much more complicated than this treatment allows. They generally do contain a kernel of truth. There really was a Robert the Bruce of Scotland and a George Washington in the United States; their respective spider-watching and cherry-tree-chopping exploits were subsequently added to their biographies to suggest sterling qualities of perseverance and honesty.

Exercising the power of cultural selection, elites often edit and alter cultural traditions as they hand them down, especially if they hold these traditions as being central to the definition of the nation. National narratives, sometimes taken up by people struggling to challenge power, can come to mean different things in different contexts. Louis Riel, for instance, was in one myth-symbol complex a traitor whose defeat and execution demonstrated the brilliance of the British Empire and the courage of its soldiers. In another he was a martyr-hero of the Western region, of the Métis nation, of the First Nations, and of a bilingual and bicultural Canada.[25] In this battle of mythologies, the facts about Riel might be consistent, but the meaning read into those facts can vary.

Many of the debates revolve around male heroes—and one of the traditional functions of the hero has been to serve as a role model for masculinity. For years hockey analyst Don Cherry managed to bind together a certain brand of hockey, a chilly disdain for Europeans and French Canadians, and a militantly macho stance towards the Afghan conflict. With his appearances, particularly in the first-intermission "Coach's Corner," *Hockey Night in Canada* became an extended info-mercial for war, with Cherry functioning as a kind of down-market Caesar, reiterating the martial virtues of manliness, hierarchy, and unswerving deference to authority, and applying them with equal populist vehemence to both hockey and foreign policy.

Women do have a place in the new warriors' muscular universe—generally as damsels in distress, crying out to be rescued. The new warriors' Canada is a nice country for women. Even the oil from the tar sands, evidence of environmental devastation notwithstanding, can be marketed as ethical oil because it comes from a land that is chivalrous to women and children, as opposed to oil that comes from the unethical (fanatical, Islamic) lands. New warriors are breaking new ground here, marketing dirty oil by advertising its moral cleanliness, but they are also cashing in on clichés and prejudices about the free women of the West and the unfree women of the East that go back to the Crusades. Like all crude binaries, this chivalric tale captures a few elements of reality on the way to its crude "us-versus-them" formulation. Its adherents repeat with gusto clichés that fire their followers, and our troops, with the sense that they are fighting wars on behalf of womankind. The unlikeliest of people—sworn enemies of reproductive choice and civil rights for homosexuals and affirmative action— become the most militant of feminists when they talk about the global South and Canada's innumerable Islamic enemies. One of the most powerful cards played by new warriors in talking Canadians into the Afghanistan debacle was that of the beleaguered Afghan women we would be betraying were we ever to "cut and run." This narrative seldom mentions that Western intervention since the early 1980s has dramatically worsened the position of women in Afghanistan.[26]

After more than a decade of conflict and over 150 Canadian dead, Afghanistan's regime is unlikely to be much better, or much worse, for women than was the government that Canada spent years supporting. But it may well prove tractable on the central pipeline issues that have long percolated beneath the surface of the conflict—and if it is, we can confidently expect to hear as little about Afghanistan's women and children in the future as we now hear about those in "friendly" states such as Colombia, Honduras, or Saudi Arabia.

As A.L. McCready observes, even if Canadians are still led to believe that they are the world's peacekeepers, now, in the post-9/11 world, they must follow this noble calling by "waging dubious wars of aggression in the interests of peace and (somehow) democracy."[27] What the Afghan War confirmed was a trend that had gradually become clear after the fall of the Soviet Union: Canada abandoned even the pretence of an independent foreign policy. On questions of climate change, Canada itself would become a "rogue nation," arrogantly opposed to even modest Kyoto-style measures of redress. From the 1990s on, Canada graduated from UN peacekeeping projects to NATO and U.S.-led "policing" projects—naval patrols in the Persian Gulf, a ground war in Afghanistan, and even a quiet but important supporting role in George W. Bush's 2003 invasion of Iraq.[28]

Canada stressed its benevolent role in Kandahar, yet the niche that Canadians filled there was part of an imperial strategy that differed in detail but not in substance from the U.S. war in Vietnam or from Britain's brutal pacification campaigns in Malaysia and Kenya. Behind the Canadian peacekeeper stood the NATO pacifier.

Yet Canada's invasion and occupation of Afghanistan could never be officially admitted. Any such candour went against the regime's newspeak. War is Peace. When Canadians make war, we really make peace. Mark Neufeld notes that Canadians have proved remarkably reluctant even to admit that they went to Afghanistan as an "invading and occupying force," largely operating under U.S. direction to achieve specific economic and political objectives.[29] They shielded themselves from acknowledging any responsibility for the chaos and suffering left behind—which can all be blamed on NATO, the Americans, or, better yet, on the Afghans themselves. The pianist playing hymns in a brothel may be admired for his piety only on condition that he is genuinely unaware of the raison d'être of the institution in which he plies his trade.

Even as Canada awaited the final bill for Afghanistan, the Harper regime announced a further bold new projection of Canadian power on the world stage: the creation of new military fixtures overseas, to defend the "national interest." As of June, 2011, the Canadian military was engaged in talks "to establish a permanent presence in up to seven foreign countries . . . marking the first time since the end of the Cold War that Canada has aimed to expand its military reach around the globe." Under the "Operational Support Hubs Network" concept, Canadian facilities may be established in Senegal, South Korea, Kenya, Singapore, Jamaica, Germany, and Kuwait. In the view of David Bercuson, in his capacity as the "senior research fellow" of the Canadian Defence and Foreign Affairs Institute, the aim is to establish "forward supply depots" near "parts of the world where Canadian Forces may be deployed in future." (Senegal should prove handy for Canadians fighting for multinational claims to Africa's oil.) Undeterred by the mixed record of a similar venture in the Middle East, surreptitiously conceived, expensively maintained and now embarrassingly concluded, the government was, then, contemplating the establishment of Canadian operations in many of the world's hot spots. Perhaps, in homage to both William Stairs and George Orwell, one of these bases could be named "Fort Peace." Although doing its bit at "force projection," Canada will never approach what Andrew Bacevich describes as an "empire of bases." The U.S. government maintains some 300,000 troops at 761 "sites" in at least forty foreign lands.[30]

Establishing foreign toeholds is just part of a colossal buildup of Canadian defence spending, which began under the Liberal administration of Paul Martin. Harper not only agreed to fulfil the outgoing government's promise to increase defence spending by over $12.8 billion over five years, but committed an additional $5.3 billion to an unprecedented increase in the military budget. Under Harper, Canadian military spending attained its highest level since 1945, exceeding even the levels attained in the Cold War.[31] The $492-billion *Canada First Defence Strategy: A Modern Military for the Twenty-First Century* (CFDS), first introduced in 2008, linked vastly enhanced military spending to an increasingly abstract notion of "Canadian values."

In all of this Canada is simply taking advantage of a continental arms bonanza after decades of modestly diverging from that stream. By 2009 the U.S. military budget was seven times as high as that of its nearest competitor, China; its military spending was roughly equal to that of the entire rest of the world combined. It has long been the world's biggest arms dealer. But the Canadian war machine itself is not inconsiderable. Although in both the United States and Canada it is difficult to obtain an exact account of military expenditures, one estimate pegged Canadian military spending at just over $21 billion in 2009. In that year Canada ranked thirteenth in the world for its military spending—the sixth highest in NATO.[32]

As *Zefra* so excitedly suggested, the new world of permanent war entails elaborate and wonderfully expensive networks, an entire hidden economy flourishing largely outside the purview of the public. The new-style wars are neither declared nor officially terminated. The battlefields are often no longer even identifiable places. In the new forms of "Network-Centric Warfare," in the words of U.S. Vice Admiral Arthur Cebrowski, victory will go to the side with the best "total information awareness." The wars following this new model will unfold within a world "in which communication systems, modes of production and transportation systems function as vectors redirecting war from the battlefield to the scientific and the military economy." Fighting the new wars will be a job for civilians, perhaps as much as, or even more than, it is a job for professional service men and women. WikiLeaks disclosures revealed that about six hundred "civilian" organizations in the United States have joined in the planning and execution of war.[33]

Iraq and now Afghanistan have introduced the world to a form of war not generally seen for two centuries: the mercenaries' war, fought by subcontractors and retailers pursuing profit wherever they can find it. Henceforth, the Anglosphere's exploits will be necessarily accompanied by such emblems of Western superiority as Tim Hortons, Pizza Pizza, and Subway, in addition to a host of more militarized firms such as Blackwater, since rebranded "Academi." The for-profit War on Terror, Naomi Klein points out, signals the arrival of a new "disaster capitalism complex," one with more far-reaching tentacles than the military-industrial complex denounced by Eisenhower: "This is global war fought on every level by private companies whose involvement is paid for with public money, with the unending mandate of protecting the United States homeland in perpetuity while eliminating all 'evil' abroad."[34]

This perpetual war economy, already extraordinarily expensive, will become more and more burdensome. "Redistributive militarism" entails increases in war spending along with tax cuts for the wealthy. Peace activist Matthew Behrens notes: "Slightly more than $63 million a day is spent on Canada's war machine. That's the daily equivalent of 420 affordable housing units or 3,000 four-year full-tuition grants for university students. Over the course of a month, that's 13,000 affordable housing units and 90,000 students going to university without massive debt load."[35] The welfare state is starved so that the warfare state might thrive. Canada as Warrior Nation means a stance of permanent aggression. It also signifies a hard, competitive society in which the weak go to the wall. We all become warriors—in a permanent struggle against each other.

Another feature of war in our times is greatly enhanced executive power. An ominous line was crossed when Harry Truman was able to mount a major war in Korea without congressional approval. In Canada, although both Laurier and King made the phrase "Parliament Will Decide" a hardy perennial in foreign policy debates, the principle that parliament should rule on any question of war and peace was never constitutionally enshrined. The executive—in the Canadian case, the prime minister and cabinet ministers—is extraordinarily powerful in the determination of foreign policy. It was a remarkable sign of the extent to which foreign policy is an executive privilege in Canada that Prime Minister John Diefenbaker, who doubled at the time as the secretary of state for External Affairs, could approve the signing of the North American Air Defence Command (NORAD) agreement after consulting only his defence minister. The implications for civil liberties of such executive authority are serious. An executive operating on the premise that it is acting in a "state of emergency" can do pretty much anything it likes.

In Canada this system has already locked up people for years, on suspicion of terrorism, without allowing them to confront the charges against them. Staring into the abyss of terror, much of it magnified far beyond its actual significance into a menace to Western civilization, we become very much like the monster we think we are confronting, dancing with a devil of our own design. In 2010 human rights specialist and author Erna Paris pointed out that the Afghan prisoner detainee scandal meant that the Canadian government stood accused of wilfully ignoring Geneva Convention war crimes; and that when new warrior politicians used the episode to smear Richard Colvin, the diplomat who corroborated the ugly episode, the occasion would perhaps "be seen by future historians as a marker moment when the thin underpinnings of Canadian identity began to unravel."[36]

The War on Terror is so imprecisely defined, conducted not against a country but an abstraction, that it can be used to justify almost any coercive policy. During the Cold War the "new normal" became an ambient sense of dread, and the War on Terror has intensified this atmosphere. When today's new warriors dream about Canada generating battalions of "peace warriors" to police the global South,[37] they are not being entirely original: one of Ronald Reagan's favourite missiles was even called the "Peacekeeper." Then and now all preparations to kill people can be represented as aspects of an armed peace.

The new warriors remained locked in Cold War patterns of thought. At times they even revert to thinking of Russia as the country's big enemy. In August 2010, for instance, in a grimly amusing tale of the enduring power of the Cold War, a Harper spokesperson sent reporters a breathless message detailing the thrilling exploits of two

of Canada's CF-18 fighter jets. The dauntless Canadian pilots, defending the country's sovereignty in the Arctic, forced Russian planes heading for Canadian airspace to turn around. This example of "staring
down Russian long-range bombers" demonstrated how wise the
regime was, and is, to invest in expensive military equipment, such as
the sixty-five F-35 fighters the government intended to buy, at a price
that ranged upwards, by some estimates *far* upwards, of $16 billion. It
was as though Igor Gouzenko walked again—until NORAD spokes-
people unhelpfully pointed out that such flights were purely routine
and that NORAD itself had conducted a joint exercise with Russia a
few weeks earlier.[38]

In this time of permanent war—so reminiscent of the Cold War—
we have entered an institutionalized "state of exception," in which
incarceration without trial has become a new court-sanctioned nor-
mality. In such a neo-liberal order, Nikhail Singh remarks, "Crime
and war blur in a zone of indistinction."[39] We learn to apply to troubled neighbourhoods and racialized minorities at home the same
absolute dichotomies we apply to Afghans and the fictional Zefrans.
Superprisons loom on the horizon.

An ominous continuity links the rhetoric applied to enemies without and enemies within. The almost infinitely elastic boundaries of
"war" were suggested by the Canadian Forces themselves. In recruiting campaigns, when Forces.ca urged youngsters to sign up to "Fight
Fear, Fight Distress, Fight Chaos," they were not asking the young
recruits to tackle the fearful policies of the World Bank or chaotic
short-selling on the London and New York stock exchanges. They
were instead advertising the romance of war itself, signalling the
debut of a new publicly funded military-entertainment complex.[40]

In what Henry Giroux calls the "permanent warfare state," the
public is kept in a constant state of apprehension.[41] With no declaration by Parliament, and no termination marked by the signing of a
treaty and general jubilation (at least among the victors), war becomes
the undertone of everyday life. Canada never "declared" war on
Afghanistan, and although most of its fighters were withdrawn in 2011,
many remained as "trainers" and "mentors," to instruct the Afghans in
the gentle arts of policing and army-building. So, were we in—or out?
Are we now at war? Were we ever? James Forrestal, an early Cold War
U.S. defense secretary, approvingly labelled this sense of permanent

crisis *semi-war*—a condition in which danger is ever present, always justifying the need for higher military spending.[42]

Executive privilege in the field of foreign policy was carried over into the government's rebranding effort, as though the entire country were its product to market to the world as it saw fit. Whole branches of government started to worry about reconstructing the "brand" of Canada, to be sold both to Canada and the world. Corporate tax cuts may be a difficult thing to sell in a time of austerity, but because such cuts have somehow come to be considered as a way of creating jobs, they should proceed as planned. Even more important, such cuts would inspire world confidence and provide, in the words of Finance Minister Jim Flaherty, "a way of branding Canada."[43]

Rebranding Canada as a Warrior Nation involved a substantial public relations investment on the part of the military itself. Operation Connection, launched on February 6, 2006, entailed a massive military onslaught: no hockey game was too minor, no charity dinner too obscure, no county fair too remote for this marketing exercise, orchestrated in the absence of any apparent link to the event in question. Veterans became regular visitors to classrooms, their way prepared by textbooks that present Canadian history as a succession of military achievements.

The presentation of war in Ontario high-school classrooms became focused on military life strictly speaking, rather than, for instance, on the politics surrounding war. The Canadian students learned that Canada "came of age" at Vimy Ridge and participated heroically in war; yet the Canadians were not, at the same time, responsible in any way for the causes or consequences of the hostilities. A basic, repeated story stressed Canada's global role, which purportedly leads to new recognition and respect from powerful nations. The Memory Project, begun in 2000, orchestrated by the Historica-Dominion Institute and indirectly funded by the state, mobilized veterans to visit classrooms and offered teachers online access to oral interviews, digitized archives, and memorabilia of Canadian soldiers who fought in the Second World War.[44] By focusing on the lives of rank-and-file soldiers, both textbooks and remembrance literature suggest that Canadians were caught up in an event they did little to shape. While students might learn to empathize with soldiers in the trenches, they do not come to know much if anything about the First World War's origins or its implications for the European state system.[45] In essence, the story goes, warriors, made us what we are today. Warriors led us in the past and should govern in the future; and, if you are lucky, you too might grow up to be a warrior.

In this social Darwinist universe, some countries—those with strong leaders, strong armies, strong corporations—will win. Weak countries—whose armies are burdened with peacekeeping, whose leaders are soft and ineffectual—will lose. Only a Canada that is not afraid to stand side by side with its partners in the United States and Britain can measure up to a world threatened as never before by cunning and cruel enemies whose ways are not our ways.

With this pattern of intensive indoctrination the country crosses a boundary separating militarism from militarization. In a narrow sense militarism means arguing for more money for arms, more respect for soldiers, and more muscularity in foreign policy. Militarization means the extension of martial values into completely new spheres. Politics, personal life, leisure, culture, and sports are couched in the language of war. Militarization, then, is a much more open-ended and total, indeed even totalitarian, phenomenon than militarism. Militarization is a process through which the state reorganizes society to realize a specific vision of Canada. Today's leaders preside over a "quasi-militarization of everyday life" (in the words of William Greider) that has the reciprocal effect of making them seem to be indispensable. They have rediscovered an old Machiavellian truth—that fear can be a powerful weapon in the hands of the rich and powerful, as they struggle to defend their privileges.[46]

For instance, where it was once common to speak of the "Canadian border," this term has been militarized (and continentalized) into the "North American security perimeter." Where it was once common to speak of "dissidents," we now more commonly speak of "terrorists" or "terrorist sympathizers." Words and images do not just provide us with a neutral way of depicting reality; in the case of militarization, they actively work to construct the reality that they represent. As historian Daniel Pick puts it, "Words, ideas, images constitute the discursive support for military conflict; they should be understood not as though they are mere froth without consequences, but as crucial aspects of the destructive reality of violent conflict itself."[47]

Military men are certainly aware of the power and significance of the webs of words and images that they spin around war. In the United States, major television networks air the views of retired generals, who become trusted figures on questions of defence and foreign policy. Left unmentioned, as a rule, is that many of these former generals sit on the boards of weapons manufacturers. In Canada the Department of National Defence tied funding for the Conference of Defence Associations, a military think tank, to that body's ability to generate press coverage for the military. Millions of dollars from Canadian taxpayers are funnelled through the DND to universities and platoons of pundits.[48] In effect the government is treating its own citizens much as an invading army might treat a country subject to a campaign of pacification. Very seldom, if ever, as they saturate newspaper columns or appear as seemingly disinterested experts on television news programs, do these pundits declare conflicts of interest.

In the relentless spinning of meaning, questions of peacekeeping are replaced by issues of global counterinsurgency—with insurgents defined as all those who reject, or impede, the full implementation of Anglo-globalization. Instead of a Pearsonian approach respecting the sovereignty of states, even those with which we disagree, a neo-liberal Geiger counter registers the political value and worth of various countries around the world. If they have market economies but lack certain traditions that we say we cherish, such as the rule of law or freedom of religion or a civil rights tradition, we tend to look the other way: there is no great inclination among new warriors to bomb China or rough up Colombia. But if we think such countries diverge dramatically from the rules of possessive individualism, we unflinchingly apply absolute standards. Lives within some sorts of states are worth defending, whereas lives within states that we deem to be threats to free-market order are slated for destruction. Military solutions are substituted for diplomacy, effective intelligence, and democratic institutions. The logic seems "inexorable."[49]

In Canada, publishers, academic and non-academic, have become more fascinated than ever with military history. J.L. Granatstein, for one, has been delighted with the state's direct role in guiding young people to forms of knowledge useful to the state. He salutes the emergence of "scores of academics" writing on matters military, many of them attached to "various university centres that are sometimes called strategic studies or policy research centres," financed by the powerful Security and Defence Forum, a grant program of the Department of National Defence. What appears to be a spontaneous increase in academic fascination with things military has been deliberately cultivated and funded by the state, whose funding, according to Granatstein, supports "some 230 courses" and helps to "educate 10,000 students each year. In addition, $1-million in research grants help academics and students work on their projects."[50] A relatively small investment has proved lucrative for those seeking to legitimize the culture of the new warriors. Some, like Barry Cooper and David Bercuson, argue for the demolition of the welfare state, at least as it applies to people other than themselves. Many of them regularly appear in the media, where, again, their links to DND funding are rarely disclosed.

While cash-strapped universities bring in military funding, the military acquires legitimacy through the academy. A ministerial directive in the crisis-ridden 1990s required officers to hold a recognized undergraduate degree; many keen on advancement also obtain graduate degrees in specialized areas. Former colonel Russell Williams, once the admired commander of CFB Trenton and later convicted of murder and sex crimes against women, obtained his Master of Defence Studies from Royal Military College in 2004 with a succinct thesis supporting the Harper position on the War in Iraq. Bernd Horn, the chief of staff of Strategic Education and Training Programs in the Canadian Defence Academy and adjunct professor of history at RMC, notes that the 1990s in particular required the Canadian Forces to "examine its anti-intellectual culture and make necessary changes to increase the importance of education to the Canadian profession of arms." Officers choose from a menu of courses on war-fighting, engage in research at a new Canadian Defence Academy, and read the DND-supported *Canadian Military Journal*, wherein the new "common sense" of permanent war underlies scores of specific replays of past campaigns and anticipates new ones. "Machines don't fight wars," muses Colonel John Boyd, who has clearly divined the ambition and scope of the new cultural regime. "Terrain doesn't fight wars. Humans fight wars." To that end, he concludes, "You must get in the minds of the humans. That's where the battles are won."[51]

Canadians of all ages watch television and movies, play video games, and go online, and in all three they will find almost endless images of war, many disturbingly beautiful. Art imitates life, and life imitates art. Meanwhile Canada's national broadcasters were featuring such series as *The Border* and *Afghanada*, which made the new "military normal" seem like obvious and common-sense aspects of reality. Many Canadian boys, even some in their thirties and forties, spend many a happy weekend massacring thousands of virtual people whose sole crime is obstructing the shooter's progress to the next level. Thanks to superb graphics, blood and guts explode entertainingly and believably all over the screen as virtual victims scream out in agony.[52]

Yet, as historian John R. Gillis points out, juvenile killers with joysticks are simply channelling the zeitgeist: everywhere around us we see the merging of violence, politics, and culture. Military metaphors and military ways are "so much a part of our lives" that we can hardly spot them anymore.[53] The Highway of Heroes, the ubiquitous yellow ribbons, the talk of coming of age at Vimy Ridge, Remembrance Day: all become politically charged elements of a military-entertainment complex extolling the new cult of the warrior hero. To an extent that would have seemed mind-boggling in 1990, the new warriors have shifted the very meaning of "heroism." In December 2009 thousands lined the Highway of Heroes to pay homage to the funeral cortège of a single Canadian soldier; there was no such commemoration for four Toronto construction workers who fell to their deaths in the same week.[54] They were not heroes, evidently, because they did not die in a state-sanctioned occupation of another country—an exercise sold to the Canadian public as peace-building. Rather, they died repairing a building.

Not two decades ago, Remembrance Day, as it was generally observed in public schools, was in good measure about peace. Little children recited poems about the horrors of war; school assemblies mourned the lives cut down in violent conflict—sometimes even Japanese and German lives. In the rebranded Canada as Warrior Nation, Remembrance Day is mainly about war, with proud homage paid to our valiant soldiers who, it is claimed, created Canada's freedom. In the cult of the soldier, all Canadians who died in the service of the Anglosphere—in the Crimea in the 1850s, Manitoba in the 1870s, the Congo in the 1880s, South Africa in 1900, Vimy Ridge in 1917—indiscriminately receive the "big hero" treatment. The truest and best Canadians become soldiers who fought for King and Country and the Empire. Remembrance Day has also become a preferred occasion to repeat the canard that the military has some connection to liberty, the curious but increasingly common claim typified by the retired Kingston colonel insisting to a November cenotaph assembly that soldiers not only brought press freedom to Canada but also provided the freedom of speech enjoyed by a grateful citizenry.

The new warrior project is sophisticated, and the regime is energetically promoting it. Yet it suffers from important contradictions—economic, military, ideological.

The core economic contradiction is manifested in the cuts to social programs and lavish giveaways for the military, the hope being that Canadians will "kill the beast" of the welfare state by overfeeding the monster of the warfare state. This contradictory stance will become difficult to defend in times of acute economic crisis. The world's largest debtor country, the United States, cannot indefinitely run huge deficits driven in large measure by military expenses.

The costs of an inconclusive War on Terror have been staggering. In 2011 the CIA advised that there might be no more than fifty to seventy-five "al-Qaeda" types in Afghanistan, yet crushing them was costing the U.S. government about $10 billion a month. As the wars in Iraq and Afghanistan began to wind down, the per person costs went up: in the case of Afghanistan from $507,000 per service member in fiscal 2009 to $667,000 the following year to an estimated $694,000 in 2011. The wars and their ripple effects have cost the United States $3.7 trillion, or more than $12,000 per American. In 2008 economists Joseph Stiglitz and Linda Bilmes estimated a slightly higher price tag—perhaps as high as $5 trillion—but they cautioned that even this figure is conservative because any full accounting of the war must also factor in the costs of treating returning troops, 50 per cent of whom were eligible to receive some level of disability payment.[55] The reason why such prominent economists allow for so much multi-trillion-dollar wiggle room in their estimates is that nobody really knows exactly how much the U.S. military spends. Admiral Mike Mullen, the former chairman of the Joint Chiefs of Staff, has called the U.S. national debt the biggest single threat to that country's national security.[56]

The signs of underlying U.S. economic weakness carry profound implications for Canada. Credible evidence from within the U.S. military-industrial complex itself collides with the new warrior campaigns for ever more investment in the military; and the menace of U.S. retaliation, should Canada step even slightly out of line, may well recede. The arguments of critics who championed a post–Cold-War peace dividend, maintaining that overinvestment in the military is a drag on capitalist development, become more and more plausible,[57] whereas the countervailing argument, that Canada must not reap such a dividend because doing so will risk U.S. displeasure, loses much of its credibility. Indeed, Janice Stein and Eugene Lang argue that, even in the run-up to Canada's war in Kandahar, Canada's defence and foreign policy establishment panicked after the Martin government decided not to back the Pentagon's loopy Ballistic Missile Defence (BMD) scheme. In *The Unexpected War* they discuss how surprisingly little official Ottawa, including the gung-ho Hillier, discussed actual conditions in Kandahar—a place about which Canada was forebodingly blasé. The military wanted, desperately but predictably, to prove themselves in combat. "Despite the evidence that the Canada-U.S. relationship had suffered little or no damage because of Canada's decision not to participate in BMD," conclude Stein and Lang, "Ottawa felt a renewed sense of urgency to do something significant to offset the negative consequences they feared. Afghanistan seemed a logical place to start."[58]

In early 2012 Canadians learned more about the shadow manoeuvring that led to Kandahar, and how the war was perhaps not all that unexpected. A study by Matthew Willis for the Royal United Services Institute, a London-based think tank, revealed that senior British and Canadian personnel had secretly planned, without the knowledge of the NATO command (which was, in theory at least, running the

Afghan War), to have the Canadians move into Kandahar. A senior NATO official told Willis, "The Canadians and the British hammered out the whole thing without NATO's assistance, behind closed doors." NATO had apparently been pressuring Hillier's predecessor to send Canadian forces to Herat or Chaghcharan. But the Canadian military wanted to play with the big boys, taking part in "mission-defining decisions." The report, based on insider interviews and confidential British records, casts light on "the contentious question" of "why the senior Canadian military leadership, and the defence and foreign affairs departments, persisted in pushing the mission forward." Willis's conclusion: "Ostensibly, the military was seeking redemption after a decade of unremarkable performances in unremarkable (read: peace-keeping) theatres; or perhaps it wanted to show the U.S., the Canadian public and other key allies that it really could do combat if called upon." *Globe and Mail* reporter Doug Saunders, who broke the story, asked how Canada could "avoid repeating the mistake" of a "five-year semi-colonial odyssey in Kandahar."[59] The answer would seem to have much to do with a foreign policy driven by something beyond the institutional well-being of Canada's officer class and what might go over in Washington.

Much depends on how Afghanistan, the largest Canadian conflict since Korea, is debated and remembered by Canadians. If new warriors succeed in making the Afghanistan campaign an uplifting moment—as they are plainly trying to do when they suggest having veterans of the Afghan campaign present at swearing-in ceremonies for new citizens—they might succeed in evading their due measure of responsibility for placing Canadian lives in danger. The news from Afghanistan will be parsed, as long as it is possible to do so, for any evidence, however slim, that Canada's objectives were even partially met. Yet over time, barring something truly unexpected, it will be more and more difficult to disguise defeat in Afghanistan as victory; and for that defeat, the country's political and military leadership must be held accountable.

In many respects the new warriors' sense of nation is essentially a rejection of Canada's post-1945 achievements—something that goes strongly against the grain of most Canadians and devalues past accomplishments. Unlike a Québécois nationalism exalting the survival of their people in a continent otherwise dominated by Anglos, and unlike a pan-Canadian nationalism hailing the democratic evolution of the country from colony to nation, new warrior nationalism nominates as its Canadian heroes—among them an assortment of non-Canadians—all those who played a great role in consolidating the empires they cherish. For them, the great events in Canadian history were those in which the British and American empires were built and defended. It is in the rush of Canadian soldiers to defend those empires that Canadians should find their national identity.

This approach is "annexationist" nationalism. It can only work through an acceptance of Canada's permanent annexation by one or the other of the empires or, better yet, both of them at once. Nothing achieved in Canada by a Canadian thus signifies nearly so much as the great deeds of the founding of an Anglosphere traceable back to 1215 and England's Magna Carta—as the *Discover Canada* guidebook emphasizes at the very beginning of its outline of the "Rights and Responsibilities of Citizenship."[60] Undoubtedly this emphasis does appeal to some Anglo-Canadians, but it gives almost nothing to others—to francophones, First Nations, and ethnic and racial minorities who might also like to see something of themselves in official narratives of the country's past.

While strongly reminiscent of the Victorian and Edwardian imperialism that so engaged many Canadians, the new warriors' Anglosphere nationalism fails to give Canada a role equivalent to the one it played in earlier times. As Pearson noted so vividly in the 1940s and 1950s, the U.S.-Canada relationship, unlike the past connection that many Canadians believed they had with London, was inextricably one of domination between a superior and inferior. Canada counts for much less in Washington than it ever did in London, and Canadians who embrace the Anglosphere as the source of their national identification are being asked to devalue all the halting and partial steps that Canadians once took towards self-determination. This decidedly subaltern version of "imagined community" revels in the return of the country's leaders to the status of choreboys for empire, either denigrating or erasing those who sought a measure of independence. J.L. Granatstein, perhaps awakening too late to the pronounced authoritarianism of the militarists he has steadfastly encouraged, remarked incredulously: "The idea of rolling back the national symbols to make them more British is just loony. Who does Harper think he's appealing to?"[61]

Harper is appealing, plainly, to those who vest their hopes and dreams in the Anglo Empire, whether ruled from London or Washington, and his project is not necessarily "loony." From a far-right perspective, it is all quite logical. The application of "Royal" to institutions left and right may seem comical, but one would be ill-advised to minimize the extent to which the British sovereign is a deeply meaningful symbol of whiteness, hierarchy, and authoritarian rule.

Yet a nationalism founded upon the celebration of empires based elsewhere is nonetheless somewhat counterintuitive. The last attempt to impose such a unitary imperial nationalism on the country reached its culmination with the imposition of conscription on Quebec under Borden. It came close to splitting the country permanently. If pursued and made a serious inspiration of policy—if, for instance, the treatment of Quebec as a mere "enclave" comes to be rooted in actual government practice—it will threaten to undo all the "reasonable accommodations" (pluralist multiculturalism, bilingualism, recognition of Quebec as a nation, among others) that have for pragmatic reasons been characteristic of Canadian statecraft.

Canadians live in intimate proximity to Americans and are deeply absorbed by many American happenings. So generations of nationalists have lamented. Yet, as Robert Teigrob points out, such nationalists often overlook how Canadians are also exposed to a wide range of opinions about the complexities of U.S. politics and the huge costs of the U.S. empire. Familiarity does not necessarily breed acquiescence.[62] Canadians hear from many American sources, not simply about NFL football and the Oscars but also about the downside of out-of-control military spending, increasing inequality, and the failure of the prison-industrial complex. Many—now over a million a year—can balance what they hear about Cuba-as-devil with the Cuba they experience first-hand on vacation. Canadians are often, as some Americans have complained over the years, inclined to a kind of agnosticism about the many causes that seize Washington's passions, from Cuba to Nicaragua to Iraq, in part because they have sufficient distance from the U.S. infotainment complex to regard it with a certain irony. Modern Canada, never its own country and always aware that any assertion of its sovereignty may entail untold sacrifices, often regards the succeeding senior managers of the condominium with a mixture of pragmatism and servility, wounded pride and resentment. Endless campaigns for empire may well engender, under the smiling face of acquiescence, seething sentiments of inner resistance. Instilling fervour for imperial adventurism in the hearts of pragmatic and complicated Canadians may turn out to be a tall order.

These contradictions offer positive possibilities for Canadians concerned about the hegemony of the new warriors. How far Canadians can push depends in large part on the extent to which the United States is truly losing its position as world leader. If the United States remains the hegemon, Canadians can only push so far. If it declines, Canada might want to seek out another senior imperial partner—or Canadians might even want to return to the interwar quest they generally abandoned after 1945, the quest for genuine independence.

That Canada is a small and helpless state whose position and history dictate that it be forever tied to an empire is a core assumption of Canadian history that merits re-examination. Some analysts have been surprised, when they add up the objective factors that should work to build up a country's strength and prestige, that Canada has not become a great power.[63] Perhaps they oversimplify the ways in which economic resources can be translated into effective political power—economic strength does not translate into political strength without an active and energetic leadership. They might also be oversimplifying the constitution of the national interest in a country made up of a variety of nations, whose interests may converge on some issues and diverge on others.

Militarily, the contemporary world teaches us that the resources of power are not easily converted from one context to another; many military technologies that seem overpoweringly effective in the abstract are underwhelming when they are put into practice. In other words, and despite the bloated numbers in defence budgets, there is no rock-solid certainty to the permanence of U.S. military domination. It is possible to outspend the rest of the world on armaments and still not have a well-functioning military. The Americans' characteristic penchant for unilateralism, crushing displays of military force, technological solutions to political problems, and unswerving commitments to problematic client states can all be taken as signs of historic weakness, especially given the corresponding neglect of traditional tools of statecraft, such as the recognition of the interests of subordinate but important players. Sheer military dominance does not automatically translate into a stable and successful hegemony—the capacity to exert global leadership culturally, economically, and politically.[64]

For new warriors, rapt devotees of military metaphysics, virtually every world conflict has an appropriate military solution. They tend to identify peacekeeping with saccharine sentimentalism and an age of bellbottom jeans. On the contrary, peacekeeping and the middle-power project generally exhibited a tough-minded realism—the precise correlate of passive revolution and Canada's ambiguous relationship with its guardian empires. The new warrior project is founded upon a shallow understanding of the underlying forces shaping Canadian history. The militarist zeal has marginalized the voices of hard-won experience.

After a fifty-year career of war-fighting, peacekeeping, and disarmament-negotiating, Tommy Burns voiced an exasperated view of military complacency. "The military should realize," he wrote in his 1966 book *Megamurder*, "that the greatest threat to the survival of democracy is no longer the Russians or the Chinese or any other country professing anti-democratic ideologies, but rather war itself." Burns underlined the role played by institutional and individual self-interest in justifying the perpetual need for more weaponry. Few soldiers would say they are opposed to peace or disarmament, but after that, he says, the discussion tends to break down into a series of "clichés"— for example, "There have always been wars, and there always will be," or "You can't change human nature." Burns offered advice about his friends in the military, men whom he did not consider mercenary cynics:

> No one would suggest that they would be so selfish as to think consciously to themselves, "Whether disarmament would be better for the country and make the lives of all its inhabitants safer or not, it would mean that I would be out of a job, and therefore I am against it." But every serving officer might well examine his conscience in this particular and ask himself the question, "Can my attitude to disarmament be affected, unconsciously, by my personal interest?"[65]

Burns's question might well haunt the many new warriors who have undertaken to transform Canada. Are they being guided purely by their personal interests—boosting military prestige, safeguarding lucrative pensions and post-retirement consultancies, selling books, putting down feminist adversaries, acquiring plum positions and securing yet more lavish state funding? Are academic new warriors still operating, in any significant sense, as free-standing intellectuals? Or have they sold their souls to a militarizing project which, in rewarding them with jobs and prestige, demands that they conform to an implicit party line? Has this position led them to espouse the ideologies of a zealous, at times even crazed, minority, utterly convinced that it has the right and duty to reprogram the country?

In 2000 an immensely popular beer commercial hit television screens across English Canada. In the ad a man named Joe appears and gives a short speech, more accurately a rant, about Canada. Joe is dressed in a checkered shirt open at the front to show a T-shirt beneath. As the musical score builds he talks with increasing passion. Explaining that he does not live in an igloo or eat blubber, he says, "I have a prime minister . . ." as the Peace Tower flashes behind him. The background image is quickly replaced by a picture of the White House as Joe adds, "not a president." He continues, "I can proudly sew my country's flag on my backpack," then adds, "I believe in peacekeeping." A white hand on screen makes a V for Victory sign. "Not policing." The hand changes to a pistol. He starts to wave his hands in the air, his voice rising. "It *is* pronounced zed, not zee, *zed*!!" The climax comes when he hollers, as Paul Henderson's famous 1972 Team Canada goal against the Soviets flashes behind him, that his country is "the first nation of hockey." He shouts, "I am Canadian!" The YouTube version of the minute-long performance soon accumulated 1.8 million views.[66]

This nationalist rant, directed by an American, premiered during the Academy Awards show from Los Angeles. The background music is Edward Elgar's "Land of Hope and Glory," a 1902 patriotic song extolling imperial Britain (and which ended up being the official anthem of the British Conservative Party). The beer being pushed was Molson Canadian, and the famous firm's "I am Canadian!" campaign finished when Molson was acquired by the U.S.-based Coors. (Molson's executive offices are now located in Montreal and Denver, Colorado.) Ironies abound. So too does the evidence that "Joe" articulated, in a way that perfectly reflected Canadian ambiguity, a widespread Canadian yearning for a distinctive identity in North America.

For the new warriors the most brazen and troubling instance of this yearning came with Canada's resistance to full entry into the invasion of Iraq. That refusal suggested a distancing of Canada from the Anglosphere and a dangerous and rival (because independent) form of nationalism. Joseph Jockel, a U.S. historian of Canada-U.S. defence relations, argues that peacekeeping became popular because it "fulfills a longing for national distinctiveness, especially vis-à-vis the United States." Norman Hillmer, former Defence Department historian, told a House of Commons committee that "peacekeeping is seen as an independent, distinctively Canadian activity and our internationalism as an antidote to too much continentalism." Jockel noted soon after Ottawa's national Peacekeeping Monument was unveiled that "recent Canadian enthusiasm for the country's role in international peacekeeping has sometimes crossed the line into mythmaking." Granatstein asserted that peacekeeping ("for too many Canadians . . . a substitute for policy and thought") became "a *sine qua non* of Canadian nationalism" in the 1960s because it was something that Canada did and the Americans did not. It was "Canada's *anti-military* military role." Business and management professor Henry Mintzberg stated in 2003, "We Canadians love to distinguish ourselves from Americans."[67] It is an article of faith among the new warriors that Canadians should *not* distinguish themselves from Anglo-Americans. We are of the same blood, share the same ideals, and fight the same enemies.

Here we are, then, in a country still stubbornly harbouring people dangerously addicted to peaceful, complicated, often slow-acting remedies for problems that new warriors think are amenable to military solutions. Again and again, the new warriors say of Canadians: "These people must be re-educated." Complaining of the media tendency to focus on those with politically unreliable views, the principal of the Royal Military College, John Scott Cowan, used his 2008 RMC convocation address to remind the new members of the officer class ("In the battles to come, you are our sword and shield") that "while war and national interest are complicated, sometimes so much so that they confound the media and their pollsters, we continue to hope that the key leaders of the profession of arms would be well prepared for such complexity." Cowan, who doubled as president of the Conference of

Defence Associations Institute, could not resist complaining about poor journalism, fingering CBC reporters who "stick microphones under the noses of whatever slack-jawed gum-chewing vagrants they can find on the street." Just before Canada headed to Kandahar, in a comment oddly reminiscent of Joseph Stalin talking about disciplining the false consciousness out of stubborn kulaks, one DND communications operative was calling for a sustained drive to repair a "conceptual gap in the Canadian psyche."[68]

The new warrior impulse to attack their critics, and their inclination to polarize every discussion, may well have the unintended consequence of creating the very radicalism they seek to repress. Indeed, the new warriors have solid reasons to fear social-democratic ideals that, along with peacekeeping, are part of the myth-symbol complex they seek to uproot. Many of these ideals have stubbornly rooted bases of support.

New warriors rightly point out that peacekeeping was often aligned with Cold War objectives; that Pearson in 1956 was largely acting from a script written by the United States; that there has been a sentimentalization of the peacekeeper at the expense of a realistic reconnaissance of his or her actual position; and that many of today's peacekeeping activities diverge radically from peacekeeping as defined in Pearson's time. Most Canadians want, somehow, to preserve what they have distilled from the Pearsonian moment—not its Cold War *realpolitik* but its idealistic sense of building institutions that offer the possibility of a more peaceful world. Even when operations are plainly not about peacekeeping in any technical sense—as the DND website advised its visitors with some asperity, Afghanistan was no peacekeeping operation because "there are no ceasefire arrangements to enforce or negotiated peace settlements to respect"[69]—many Canadians want to believe that, call it peace-building, peace-enforcement, peace-monitoring, peacekeeping, or just peace, our troops are not in the business of occupying countries and killing their inhabitants. "Re-educating" these Canadians will be no easy task.

New warriors are grandly missing the forest for the trees, and in doing so they open up yet another contradiction. A solid and substantial case can be made that Canadians have a coherent and historically founded set of interests in the peaceful settlement of conflicts. They strongly suspect, as William Lyon Mackenzie King knew, that warfare might well split the country, with unpredictable effects. Granatstein himself captured this sensibility in discussing Ottawa's divisive attempt to impose an absolute ideal of equity in the case of conscription in the Great War:

> The zealots who preached for equality of sacrifice were probably the same people who let the war bring out their visceral and racist responses, who let their latent hostilities emerge into the open under the tensions of the war. Those attitudes helped persuade other Canadians that this war was not theirs at all, and this natural response served only to feed the majoritarian fires.

With regard to this poorly conceived and badly applied top-down state strategy of militarism, Granatstein raised the prospect—writing here with J.M. Hitsman—of "another race war in Canada," with conscription having "divided French-speaking Canadians from their compatriots" and in the process "shattering the political system and fostering mistrust and division in the country."[70] Granatstein here astutely warns against the grave political consequences of any rigid application of a militarist formula to Canada. His solemn warning about war as an instigator of visceral racism has proved to be prescient.

Modern Canadians might on occasion be talked into dubious exercises of the War = Peace variety, if the case is seemingly sound and/or the propaganda is well executed; or, as in the cases of Iraq and Afghanistan, they might be divided fifty/fifty, despite relentless media pressure, with an anti-war majority slowly emerging over time. Canadians routinely select "peacekeeping" in a broad sense—that is, the promotion of world peace—when asked to identify the most positive contribution that Canada makes to the world; almost nine in ten Canadians tell pollsters that "promoting world peace" is the "most important policy objective for Canada."[71] Evidently millions of defective Canadian psyches are calling out for the urgent ministrations of new warriors—who clearly have their ideological reprogramming work cut out for them.

Peacekeeping as Pearson conceived of it in 1956—UN troops in blue helmets stationed at clearly designated ceasefire lines separating sovereign states agreeable to their presence—does not match up to twenty-first-century, post–Cold War political realities. Even the

UN monopoly over operations called "peacekeeping" has ended. With that the organization has become progressively less and less "pacific" and more and more "warlike."[72] Pearson himself was a bundle of contradictions—even his speech accepting the Nobel Prize, which opens with saccharine sentiments about peace worthy of Hallmark, ends with a sabre-rattling refusal to imagine a permanent détente with an unreformed Soviet bloc. Like all the achievements of post-1945 Canada, peacekeeping as policy was the messy and at times incoherent product of a passive revolution whereby Ottawa, intervening from the top and deeply concerned to safeguard the country's contribution to the modern world-system, deftly contained and transformed pressures from below.

As with the country's gap-infested welfare state, its half-hearted embrace of socio-economic planning, its slow and partial acknowledgement of the Quebec and indigenous nations within its borders, so it was with peace: "peacekeeping" was a far cry from the vision of Rev. Edwin Pearson, Lester's father, who had proclaimed in 1927 that since the "swords of men" had become so "scientifically destructive," they would of necessity be "beaten into ploughshares" or human civilization would perish.[73] Over time, in an autocratic and bureaucratic United Nations, peacekeeping missions came to resemble their passive-revolutionary Canadian equivalents: that is, they simply channelled and contained disputes in top-down exercises in crisis management without addressing the underlying conflicts and contradictions that generated them.

Often the missions created the semblance, but not the reality, of genuine peace. Often, as such scholars as Mark Neufeld, Sherene Razack, and Sandra Whitworth suggest, they were continuations of imperial and Cold War policies by different means. From the Congo to Vietnam to Bosnia, they often camouflaged old imperial agendas. Politicians and soldiers often spoke of peace, but they meant business as usual—and on terms congenial to the world's most powerful capitalist countries. There is no "golden age of peacekeeping" that can be invoked against the new warriors, as a spotless legacy they are defiling. Thinking creatively about a peaceful world in the twenty-first century requires breaking with patterns of Anglo colonizing superiority. It will ultimately require, for Canadians, a break with patterns inherited from the 1940s.

If indeed *Pax Americana* is in crisis—a proposition by no means proved—a question posed in the 1940s arises once again. Can Canada actually live without empire? Can it finally reconstruct itself, from the bottom up, in a grassroots form of politics? Can Canada itself become a political community rather than merely playing a part in another empire? Can Canada come up with new forms of peacekeeping that do not involve the curious proposition that soldiers trained to kill are always the best instruments of policies aimed at ending killing? Why are we still in NATO and NORAD, when the Cold War is long gone? With the end of the Cold War and the decline of the United States from a position of unquestioned hegemony, is there no possibility of a realignment of the country?

Kim Richard Nossal points out, very sanely, that alignments are inertial and intricate—once in place, they are very difficult to change.[74] Individuals cannot simply will such a moment into being. Yet in the 1940s there was something like a realignment, which a talented leadership turned in a particular direction—not, unfortunately, one of genuine independence, but of an even-deeper relationship of inferiority within a revamped condominium. It is too soon to tell if we are about to experience a similar moment, but the signs of a dramatic shift in world power relations are accumulating. They spell enormous dangers. They also contain great opportunities for a genuinely democratic renewal. If so, for the first time since the 1940s, and more radically if we understand and live the moment fully, Canadians would experience a genuine moment of independence. And for the first time since the 1840s, Canadians would face the possibility of creating a very different, and differently aligned, political order in northern North America.

However acutely flawed and even distorted have been the results of the translation into policy of the heartfelt abhorrence of war and drive for peace, that abhorrence and that drive have been, and still are, durable parts of life in northern North America. As both Nossal and Morton eloquently remind us, there is much about the notion of Canada as a relatively peaceful country that is demonstrably the case.[75] Many Canadians who support peacekeeping in a general sense are simply, if imperfectly, translating into a policy their realistic, well-grounded sense of what Canada is and what it should be. It is sheer hubris to describe as delusional or childish a scepticism towards imperialism and war that has influenced so many Canadians and their leaders for so many years, from Laurier through to Trudeau. The unrealistic romantics are those infatuated with the idea that empires headquartered in London or Washington can transform the world into a free-market utopia.

Since the War of 1812–14, Canada has not been subject to large-scale armed invasion; as a country it has never on its own account and in its own name invaded another country. When "Flanders Fields" asks us each Remembrance Day to "Take up our quarrel with the foe," most Canadians might be forgiven for wondering, "Whichever foe might that be?" The number of countries most Canadians would feel justified in invading, in order to right historic wrongs or pursue their ambition of world domination, is exactly zero. The "foes" we might more readily see as ones genuinely worth fighting—world hunger, injustice in the Middle East and throughout the global South, planetary climate change, capitalism itself—cannot be fought militarily. There is more to the ideal of the peaceable kingdom than just myth-making: it chimes with a good part of Canadians' past and present sense of reality.

That a Canadian "invented" peacekeeping, that Canada pursued peacekeeping for strictly altruistic reasons, and that peacekeeping is core to the Canadian identity—these are all highly debatable propositions. Yet that the country did come to be so identified, and is to this day, can be empirically demonstrated. It is not a "myth," then, in the sense of a wilful and ideological misrepresentation—that characterization fits far better the new warriors' toxic rehabilitation of empires past and present—but a selective rendition of a more complicated truth.

The new warriors have mobilized a formidable, long-term project which, if successful, could change the country beyond recognition. Mounting visceral campaigns of irrationalism and fear, in which their critics are shouted down and covered in epithets; appealing to atavistic and violent conceptions of blood and soil; proudly flourishing the age-old symbols of empires and cherishing as heroes their often violent partisans; targeting universities for full incorporation into an ever-expanding war-machine: the campaign aims to supplant any vestige of that modest, imperfect but promising experiment called Canada.

As historian Tony Judt observes, many other societies have gone through moments similar to the one through which we are passing.[76]

Cults of blood and soil; historical arguments privileging the superiority of people from certain backgrounds; celebrations of the triumph of the will and of virile masculinity; denigration of dissenters as enemies of the people: none of these are new devices for instilling anxiety into a population. For decades, twentieth-century Europe experimented with various regimes that made free use of such techniques of persuasion. None of them were rightly called democracies.

In late 2011 the government of Canada took the lead. Fulfilling its eagerness to be the new tough guy on the world stage, it poked a sharp stick in the eyes of the world's most vulnerable peoples. Ottawa became the first signatory to formally repudiate the modest goals of the Kyoto treaty, which had been the established political world's effort to mitigate the causes of climate change. With the collapse of Kyoto the planet appeared to be headed towards a shameful Hurricane Katrina future in which the poorest and weakest peoples are left behind, just as they were when New Orleans was devastated in 2005.[77] The decades to come will see the emergence of severe global food shortages, although peoples in northern latitudes, Canadians among them, should be able to feed themselves. Africa, including the Canadian military's fantasyland combat zone of Zefra, will probably be hardest hit by climate change. In many places food will simply not be available at any price. As the Canadian "security" pundits warned in the postscript to the Canadian military's Zefran dystopia, that benighted land was reeling from "unfavourable climatic conditions."

An understated analysis by Canada's Anglosphere partners in the British Ministry of Defence was straightforward. "Increasing demand and climate change are likely to place pressure on the supply of key staples," the study concluded. "Water stress will increase." The British defence ministry was hardly alone. A former Pentagon staffer and long-time observer of the impact of climate chaos on security pointed out that unless the world reduces greenhouse gas emissions, "We really have some frightening futures." The iconoclastic Canadian military analyst Gwynne Dyer concluded in his study *Climate Wars* that the world faced the real risk of triggering "massive population dieback," with climate change being *the* threat to planetary survival unless fossil fuel use declines dramatically. "What would that somewhat chastened end-of-the-century global society look like?" Dyer asked in 2008. "It would be a world with much greater equality of wealth between the old rich countries and the Majority World, because that is the precondition for making it through the crisis."[78]

This view of countries and peoples existing together in a world and acting for the common good reflects straightforward enlightened self-interest. Still, enlightened as it is, this direction is decidedly not the one in which Canada-as-Warrior-Nation is headed. Canada's regime views the world through a lens of anxiety and security. It offers up a Canada as energy superpower determined to provide petroleum corporations with the easiest possible access to some of the world's dirtiest fossil fuels from the tar sands. International agreements like Kyoto have no part in this. But a military poised to intervene by helping Canada's allies bomb oil-rich Libyans to freedom does. So too does the view of Canada and the United States working together to establish, not a border, but a "security perimeter" around North America.

A government that touts fear of crime, getting tough on all fronts, is also a government whose world view reflects what it sees as the anxieties of an older, white, middle-class constituency, many of whom are indeed attracted by the ostensible security of gated communities— known in South Africa as "security parks." The top Frequently Asked Question for one such fortified Ontario space, Grand Cove on Lake Huron, is, according to its developers, "How safe is the community?" The answer: "This is a gated community with restricted access. No unauthorized persons or peddlers are allowed."[79]

Within a culture of anxiety, security becomes a marketable commodity freely available from property developers whose favourite adjective is "exclusive." Neighbourhoods and nations become defensible spaces. Historian Mike Davis, a pioneer in examining an ecology of fear by "excavating the future," speaks of how we are witnessing a "residential arms race as ordinary suburbanites demand the kind of social insulation once enjoyed by the rich."[80]

The key to gated communities is the exclusion of poor and minority people. Reproduced on a global level, rich nations are transformed into gated communities writ large. A Warrior Nation's future is as part of a gated globe. Its citizens are separated, psychically at least, from the rest of the world just as people purchasing property at Grand Cove bought into the idea that they can isolate themselves from those bothersome peddlers. Canada's newly muscular military will be guarding the gates while also projecting its power to countries that are unstable or have important resources. Or both.

The separation of Canada from the rest of the world, argues Canadian anthropologist and ethicist Stephen Bede Scharper, is based on the notion that people can achieve contentment by keeping misery out of sight; and that the status quo of an unending spiral of fossil fuel consumption can somehow continue. Such ideas are not only "morally disquieting." They are also absurd. They suggest a world in which the need for security—and for the armed forces necessary to provide it—becomes a dominant worry. It is of a piece with the idea that Northern countries can enjoy climate prosperity while peoples of the Majority World, reeling from climate change, starve and—like the military's imaginary Zefrans—fight one another to survive.[81] Such is the new warriors' world. It need not be ours.

NOTES

pp. 1-2   Details of the Mons battle and the Currie libel trial are in Robert J. Sharpe, *The Last Day, the Last Hour* (Toronto: The Osgoode Society, 1988).

CHAPTER ONE — WAR AND PEACE AND PAPER CRANES

1   A.R.M. Lower, "The Character of Kingston," in *To Preserve and Defend: Essays on Kingston in the Nineteenth Century*, ed. Gerald Tulchinsky (Montreal and Kingston: McGill-Queen's University Press, 1974), pp.19-20, 30-31.

2   Ibid., pp.30-31.

3   Lower quoted in Jamie Swift, *Cut and Run: The Assault on Canada's Forests* (Toronto: Between the Lines, 1983), pp.33, 48.

4   J.L. Granatstein, *Whose War Is It? How Canada Can Survive in the Post 9/11 World* (Toronto: HarperCollins, 2007), pp.52n, 26, 153; Linda McQuaig, *Holding the Bully's Coat: Canada and the U.S. Empire* (Toronto: Doubleday Canada, 2007).

5   Granatstein, *Whose War Is It?,* p.149 (Quebec), p.202 (British political culture), p.203 (soul and survival). In the latter two instances, Granatstein is quoting from Australian prime minister John Howard and applying his words to the Canadian case.

6   Remembrance Day ceremony, City Park, Kingston, Ont., Nov. 11, 2008.

7   Veteran Affairs Canada, "50 Ways to Remember," www.veterans.gc.ca/eng/teach_resources/50ways_remember; Gerretsen quoted in *Whig-Standard* (Kingston), July 16, 2011.

8   Joanne Cochrane, "From Behind the Mic," *Whig-Standard*, Dec. 1, 2007. For military public relations, see Forces.ca, "Public Affairs Officer," www.forces.ca/en/job/publicaffairsofficer-136 and http://www.forces.ca/Content/transcripts/

00203_publicaffairsofficer_en.html: "More than ever, we live in a media-dominated world. Knowing how to get the real story of our soldiers out to the Canadian public through all that noise and clutter is a great challenge."

9   Stephen Harper, speech to the Canada-UK Chamber of Commerce, London, July 14, 2006, in The Monarchist League of Canada, "Memorable Quotations about Canada's Monarchy," http://www.monarchist.ca/en/quotes; Prime Minister of Canada Stephen Harper, "Prime Minister Harper Welcomes Australian Counterpart to Parliament," http://pm.gc.ca/eng/media.asp?id=1168.

10 "Tory Campaigner Resigns over Plagiarized Speech," *Globe and Mail* (Toronto), Sept. 30, 2008. "Many of the lines of Mr. Howard's speech were also used in editorials Mr. Harper submitted to newspapers such as the Toronto Star, National Post and Ottawa Citizen." The staffer, Owen Lippert, had worked for the Fraser Institute and written *Globe and Mail* editorials.

11 Barry Cooper, *It's the Regime, Stupid! A Report from the Cowboy West on Why Stephen Harper Matters* (Toronto: Key Porter Books, 2009), p.21. Immediately after the election, in a *Globe and Mail* op-ed article, former Harper strategist Tom Flanagan used the "ruler" discourse. Funding for the University of Calgary's Centre for Military and Strategic Studies is particularly cloudy, with its largest tranche ($291,000) of research support in 2009–10 coming from "anonymous donations." See Centre for Military and Strategic Studies, Annual Reports, http://cmss.ucalgary.ca/reports.

12 David J. Bercuson and Barry Cooper, *Derailed: The Betrayal of the National Dream* (Toronto: Key Porter Books, 1994), pp.21 (whiners), 16 (maternal order), 199 (collectivist housekeeping), 209 (welfare state of mind), 199 (superiority).

13 Postmedia News, July 2, 2011.

14 Rick Hillier, *A Soldier First: Bullets, Bureaucrats and the Politics of War* (Toronto: HarperCollins, 2009), p.470.

15 *Citizen* (Ottawa), July 6, 2011.

16 Citizenship and Immigration Canada, *Discover Canada: The Rights and Responsibilities of Citizenship, Study Guide*, 2010 edition (Ottawa: Minister of Public Works and Government Services Canada, 2009), pp.21, 15, 10. For an excellent rejoinder to the official guide, see Esylit Jones and Adele Perry, *People's Citizenship Guide: A Response to Conservative Canada* (Winnipeg: Arbeiter Ring Publishing, 2011).

17 Citizenship and Immigration Canada, *Discover Canada*, p.11.

18 John Buchan, *Canadian Occasions: Addresses by Lord Tweedsmuir* (Toronto: Musson Book Company, 1940), pp.99–100.

19 For the talk at McGill, Buchan, *Canadian Occasions*, p.22, 99; "Scotland writ large" in Andrew Lownie, *John Buchan, The Presbyterian Cavalier* (Toronto: McArthur & Company, 2004), p.244; John Buchan, *Prester John* (London, New York: T. Nelson, 1910), p.200.

20 Citizenship and Immigration Canada, *Discover Canada*, p.3.

21 Cited in Andrew Lownie, *John Buchan: The Presbyterian Cavalier* (Toronto: McArthur and Company, 2004), p.253. So devoted are the extreme right histo-

rians to Buchan's memory that they have named as the "hon. Patron" of their far-right *Dorchester Review* the Lord Tweedsmuir of Elsfield, Buchan's grandson, and boost a "handsome new edition" of Buchan's *The Thirty-Nine Steps*. See http://dorchesterreview.ca/The_Dorchester_Review/Home.html.

22 Edmund Burke, *A Philosophical Inquiry into the Origin of Our Ideas of the Sublime and Beautiful*, pt. ii, secs. ii–iii (1757), in *The Works of the Rt. Hon. Edmund Burke*, vol.1, p.34 (1834), http://harpers.org/archive/2008/01/hbc-90002245. For an analysis of the uses of fear in contemporary North America, see Corey Robin, *Fear: The History of a Political Idea* (Oxford and New York: Oxford University Press, 2004).

23 Canadian Press, March 27, 2011.

24 Frank Furedi, *Politics of Fear* (New York: Continuum, 2005), p.131; thanks to Craig Jones for underlining the implications of the fear agenda.

25 Although it publishes no annual report outlining the sources of its funding, the Conference of Defence Associations received an annual grant from the Department of National Defence: personal communication with Alain Pellerin, CDA Executive Director, Aug. 10, 2011. In recent years CDA has been receiving $100,000 per year from DND (see http://www.vcds.forces.gc.ca/sites/page-eng.asp?page=8420; see also http://www.espritdecorps.ca/index.php?option=com_content&view=article&id=570:its-time-to-end-the-conference-of-defence-associations-military-funding). It also typically receives the services of an intern paid by DND ($35,000 per year; see http://www.admfincs.forces.gc.ca/apps/dgca-dposc/ dgcaoqld-dposcstld-eng.asp?q=2&y=2011&id=113). The CDA's logo features a pentagon adorned with a maple leaf.

26 Daniel Gosselin, "Navigating the Perfect Wave: The Canadian Military Facing Its Most Significant Change in Fifty Years," *Canadian Military Journal*, Winter 2007–8.

27 Ibid.

28 Ibid.

29 Dexter Filkins, *The Forever War* (New York: Knopf, 2008), p.27.

30 QMI Agency, "War Wounds: Poll Suggests We Don't Feel Afghan Mission Was Worth It," Aug. 4, 2011.

31 CBC-Radio, *The Current*, Dec. 11, 2009.

32 "Using Our Military Muscle," *Globe and Mail*, Oct. 22, 2010.

33 The title of the classic book by Philip Knightly: *The First Casualty: From Crimea to Vietnam, the War Correspondent as Hero, Propagandist and Mythmaker* (New York: Harcourt, Brace, 1975); but also Deborah Harrison, *The First Casualty: Violence against Women in Canadian Military Communities* (Toronto: James Lorimer and Company, 2002).

34 *Star* (Toronto), Nov. 5, 2010.

35 CBC-Radio, *The House*, July 2, 2011.

36 *Star*, Nov. 7, 2010.

37 Desmond Morton, *A Military History of Canada*, 5th ed. (Toronto: McClelland and Stewart, 2007), p.167.

38 "The Canadian War Vet Is No Longer an Old Guy," *Globe and Mail*, July 15, 2011.

39 Murray Brewster, *The Savage War: The Untold Battles of Afghanistan* (Toronto: Wiley, 2011), pp.51–52.

40 Hillier, *Soldier First*, p.3.

41 Vice-Admiral Bruce Donaldson, Conference on Defence and Security, Ottawa, Feb. 25, 2011, CDA Institute, Seminar 2011, http://cda-cdai.ca/cdai/ defence-seminars/seminar2011.

42 Gosselin, "Navigating the Perfect Wave."

43 Quoted in Antony Beevor and Luba Vinogradova, eds., *A Writer at War: Vasily Grossman with the Red Army 1941-1945* (Toronto: Knopf, 2006), p.xv.

44 *Lord, make me an instrument of your peace.*
    Where there is hatred, let me sow love.
    Where there is injury, pardon.
    Where there is doubt, faith.
    Where there is despair, hope.
    Where there is darkness, light.
    Where there is sadness, joy.

CHAPTER TWO – PAX BRITANNICA AND THE WHITE MAN'S BURDEN

1 See James D. Frost, *Merchant Princes: Halifax's First Family of Finance, Ships and Steel* (Toronto: James Lorimer and Company, 2003); William James Stairs, *Family History: Stairs Morrow: Including Letters, Diaries, Essays, Poems, Etc.* (Halifax: McAlpine Publishing, 1906).

2 When the boys' rituals became a controversial topic in the 1890s, one culprit was the son of a justice of the Nova Scotia Supreme Court; another the son of the Bishop of Nova Scotia. When outsiders looked at RMC they noted that such a small largely rural country, lacking much in the way of a "leisure class," would never generate enough cadets committed to becoming professional soldiers. It was both efficient and practical to graft a course of instruction in civil engineering and practical mining onto a military course. Richard Arthur Preston, *Canada's RMC: A History of the Royal Military College* (Toronto: University of Toronto Press for the Royal Military College, 1969), p.150.

3 See Preston, *Canada's RMC*, p.12. On the "militia myth" in Canada, see James Wood, *Militia Myths: Ideas of the Canadian Citizen Soldier, 1896-1921* (Vancouver and Toronto: UBC Press, 2010).

4 *Speeches by Mr. Mulock in the House of Commons in the Session of 1894* (Toronto: Hunter, Rose and Co., 1894), p.31. The figure comes down to $90,153 when the fees realized by the college are taken into account.

5 Of RMC's first eighteen graduates, thirteen had careers that were primarily civilian; three spent their professional careers in the United States. Only five served in the armed forces of Canada or the British Empire. One 1883 estimate

of the career trajectories of the fifty-four RMC graduates was that eleven had entered the public service of Canada, twenty-three had gone into railway and engineer work, and only eleven had entered the British forces (Preston, *Canada's RMC*, p.92). J.L. Granatstein and Dean F. Oliver are off the mark when they say the college was opened to "train officers for the Canadian militia and frequently for the British army." See *The Oxford Companion to Canadian Military History* (Don Mills: Oxford University Press, 2011), pp.384–85. From the outset even RMC's staunchest backers conceded that the school, despite its name, could not be a strictly military college; it had to play a double function as both a military and civilian institution, one primarily devoted to the creation of engineers. Preston, *Canada's RMC*, p.ix.

6 See Michael Paris, *Warrior Nation: Images of War in British Popular Culture, 1850-2000* (London: Reaktion Books, 2000), p.41.

7 *Illustrated London News* and Palmerston quoted in Paris, *Warrior Nation*, p.21. The *News* was describing the Opium War in China, which the paper confessed was not really justified.

8 This preoccupation had a certain irony, as Paris points out: "Despite their professed love of 'fair play' and desire to 'play the game,' the Victorian officer corps made little concession to the Zulus at Ulundi or the Dervishes at Omdurman, for example, when they countered the enemy's assegais and swords with modern artillery and machine guns." Paris, *Warrior Nation*, p.78.

9 Preston, *Canada's RMC*, pp.52, 55, 136. Hazings had reached such a degree of brutality in the 1890s that entering cadets were obliged to take an oath that they would not physically coerce other cadets.

10 Preston, *Canada's RMC*, p.138.

11 Roy MacLaren, ed., *African Exploits: The Diaries of William Stairs, 1887-1892* (Montreal and Kingston: McGill-Queen's University Press, 1998) [hereafter *Stairs Diary*], July 19, 1891, pp.331–32, 335; "the feeling of pleasurable excitement" in Joseph A. Moloney, *With Captain Stairs to Katanga: Slavery and Subjugation in the Congo* (London: Sampson Low, Marston and Company, 1893; reprinted Jeppestown Press, 2007), p.31.

12 Preston, *Canada's RMC*, pp.118–19; Moloney, *With Captain Stairs to Katanga*, p.17.

13 Preston, *Canada's RMC*, pp.118–19.

14 See Roy MacLaren, *Canadians on the Nile, 1882-1898* (Vancouver: UBC Press, 1978).

15 Janina M. Konczacki, ed., *Victorian Explorer: The African Diaries of Captain William G. Stairs 1887-1892* (Halifax: Nimbus Publishing, 1994), p.43.

16 *Stairs Diary*, p.61.

17 Konczacki, *Victorian Explorer*, p.43.

18 *Stairs Diary*, p.46.

19 William Stairs, "From the Albert Nyanza to the Indian Ocean," *Nineteenth Century: A Monthly Review* 29 (June 1891), p.959.

20 Henry M. Stanley, *In Darkest Africa, Or, The Quest, Rescue, and Retreat of Emin,*

Governor of Equatoria (New York: C. Scribner's Sons, 1890), vol. 1, p.5; Nigel Fitzpatrick, "A Victorian Canadian in Africa," *Historic Kingston* 35 (January 1987), p.54.

21   Stairs, "From the Albert Nyanza," p.968.

22   *Stairs Diary*, pp.199, 302.

23   Ibid., pp.317, 270.

24   See Mary Louise Pratt, *Imperial Eyes: Travel Writing and Transculturation* (London: Routledge, 1992).

25   Stanley, *In Darkest Africa*, vol. 1, p.9.

26   Ibid., p.4.

27   Fitzpatrick, "Victorian Canadian in Africa," pp.54.

28   *Stairs Diary*, p.304.

29   Moloney, *With Captain Stairs to Katanga*, p.24.

30   For the letter to the Belgian officer, see Williams Stairs, "Report on Katanga Expedition in *Le Mouvement Géographique*," in *A Sketch of the Lives and Services of the Late Captains H.B. Mackay, W.H. Robinson, and W.G. Stairs*, by Captain A.H. Van Straubenzee, R.E. (Kingston: Select Papers from the Proceedings of the Royal Military College Club of Canada, no.1, 1893), p.29; Moloney, *With Captain Stairs to Katanga*, pp.186–87.

31   Ibid., p.22.

32   David Harvey, *The New Imperialism* (Oxford and New York: Oxford University Press, 2003), p.45.

33   Expedition member quoted in Fitzpatrick, "Victorian Canadian in Africa," p.50; commentator remarked, in *Truth*, April 11, 1889, cited in *Stairs Diary*, p.300; *Stairs Diary*, p.72.

34   Stanley quoted in Ruth Rempel, "Not a 'Cloth Giver': Entitlement, Hunger, and Illicit Transfers on the Emin Pasha Relief Expedition, 1886-1890," *International Journal of African Historical Studies* 39,1 (2006), pp.3, 5; see also Rempel, "'No Better Than a Slave or Outcast!': Skill, Identity, and Power among the Porters of the Emin Pasha Relief Expedition, 1887-1890," *International Journal of African Historical Studies* 43,2 (2010), pp.279–318. Both articles draw from her illuminating "Exploration, Knowledge and Empire in Africa: The Emin Pasha Relief Expedition, 1886-1890," Ph.D. thesis, University of Toronto, 2000. The various sources show slight discrepancies in the numbers devoted to the expedition.

35   Stairs, "From the Albert Nyanza," p.964.

36   Rempel, "Not a 'Cloth Giver,'" p.6.

37   *Stairs Diary*, p.52.

38   Ibid., pp.187, 198. With regard to the execution of children, the diary does not indicate for certain whether Stairs was directly responsible or merely complicit.

39   *Stairs Diary*, p.114.

40   Ibid., p.144.

41   Ibid., p.247.

42 Ibid., pp.198, 152.

43 Ibid., p.201.

44 Ibid., pp.337, 78, 207.

45 "Sceptic" in *Truth*, in *Stairs Diary*, p.300; Roy MacLaren, "Afterword," in *African Exploits*, ed. MacLaren, p.396.

46 Adam Hochschild, *King Leopold's Ghost: A Story of Greed, Terror, and Heroism in Colonial Africa* (Boston and New York: Houghton Mifflin, 1999).

47 Konczacki, *Victorian Explorer*, p.41.

48 *Stairs Diary*, pp.93, 201, 204.

49 Geoffrey Plank, *An Unsettled Conquest: The British Campaign against the Peoples of Acadia* (Philadelphia: University of Pennsylvania Press, 2001), p.78.

50 *Stairs Diary*, p.333.

51 Ibid. Stairs, although probably not conversant with any evolutionary theory specifically, was here seemingly influenced by a theme developed by both Charles Darwin and Herbert Spencer.

52 Rempel, "Not a 'Cloth Giver,'" p.7.

53 *Stairs Diary*, p.101. For a reflection on similar patterns of Western disparagements of patterns of "primitive warfare" followed by surreptitious borrowings of them, see Patrick Porter, *Military Orientalism: Eastern War Through Western Eyes* (New York: Columbia University Press, 2009).

54 *Stairs Diary*, p.176; Stairs, "From the Albert Nyanza," p.953.

55 *Stairs Diary*, p.339.

56 Ibid., p.151.

57 Ibid., p.224.

58 Ibid., pp.150–51, 224–25. Thanks to Rempel's pioneering work, it is now possible to discern the elements of working-class resistance to this kind of authority.

59 *Stairs Diary*, pp.335, 388.

60 Ibid., p.95.

61 Ibid., pp.87, 317, 293–94.

62 Ibid., pp.76, 142.

63 Ibid., pp.171–72n.

64 Drawing on Phillip Buckner, "Introduction: Canada and the British Empire," in *Canada and the British Empire*, ed. Phillip Buckner (Oxford: Oxford University Press, 2008), p.17.

65 *Stairs Diary*, p.304.

66 Timothy H. Parsons, *The British Imperial Century 1815-1914: A World History Perspective* (Lanham, Boulder, Col., New York and Oxford: Rowman and Littlefield, 1999), p.72.

67 Mark Neocleous, "War as Peace, Peace as Pacification," *Radical Philosophy* 159 (January/February 2010), pp.8–17.

68 For an excellent contemporary discussion, see Jean Bricmont, *Humanitarian Imperialism: Using Human Rights to Sell War* (New York: Monthly Review Press, 2006).

69 John Buchan, *Lord Minto: A Memoir* (London, Edinburgh and New York: Thomas Nelson and Sons, 1924), p.131.

70 Ibid., p.166.

71 Paul Maroney, "The Peaceable Kingdom Reconsidered: Attitudes toward War in English Canada, 1885-1914," Ph.D. thesis, Queen's University, Kingston, Ont., 1995.

72 Quoted in Peter Buitenhuis, *The Great War of Words: British, American, and Canadian Propaganda and Fiction, 1914-1933* (Vancouver: University of British Columbia Press, 1987), p.6.

73 Carman Miller, *Canada's Little War: Fighting for the British Empire in Southern Africa, 1899-1902* (Toronto: James Lorimer and Company, 2003), pp.14 (citing *Toronto Evening News*, March 11, 1899), 31.

74 Ibid., pp.14–15, 16, 50.

75 Ibid., p.58.

76 Ibid., pp.58–59, 78; Carman Miller, *Painting the Map Red: Canada and the South African War, 1899-1902* (Montreal and Kingston: McGill-Queen's University Press, 1993), pp.322, 344. Rapes, prisoner executions, and concentration camps are all curiously absent from the entry for the South African War in David J. Bercuson and J.L. Granatstein, *Dictionary of Canadian Military History* (Oxford: Oxford University Press, 1994), pp.201–2, which does find space to mention that four Canadians won the Victoria Cross for valiant wartime deeds.

77 Michael Redley, "John Buchan and the South African War," in *Reassessing John Buchan: Beyond the Thirty-Nine Steps*, ed. Kate Macdonald (London: Pickering and Chatto, 2009), p.68.

78 John Buchan, *Memory Hold-the-Door* (Toronto: Musson, 1940), p.108; Janet Adam Smith, *John Buchan: A Biography* (London: Rupert Hart-Davis, 1965), p.115.

79 Redley, "John Buchan," pp.68–69.

80 Smith, *John Buchan*, p.118.

81 John Buchan, *The African Colony: Studies in the Reconstruction* (Edinburgh: William Blackwood and Sons, 1903), pp.166–67.

82 Ibid., pp.260, 56, 60–61, 65, 66, 70, 67, 56, 338.

83 Ibid., pp. 309, 290–91.

84 John Buchan, *A Lodge in the Wilderness* (Edinburgh and London: William Blackwood and Sons, 1906), p.206.

85 J. Bartlet Brebner, *Canada: A Modern History* (Ann Arbor: University of Michigan Press, 1960), p.295. In Stairs's case, the entire Stanley expedition would have been unthinkable without the support of U.S. newspapers and the powerful (and profitable) cult of personality they had woven around the explorer, whose own troubled identity was Anglo-American. RMC, although "Royal," was more closely patterned after West Point than the British colleges. Many of its graduates went on to become engineers in the United States.

86 Quoted in MacLaren, "Introduction," in *Stairs Diary*, p.3. For discussion, see

Srdjan Vucetic, *The Anglosphere: A Genealogy of a Racialized Identity in International Relations* (Stanford, Cal.: Stanford University Press, 2011), p.3.

CHAPTER THREE – FROM WAR TO WAR TO WAR

1 *American Mercury*, August 1927.

2 Jeffrey Keshen, *Propaganda and Censorship during Canada's Great War* (Edmonton: University of Alberta Press, 1996), p.166.

3 E.L.M. Burns, *General Mud: Memoirs of Two World Wars* (Toronto: Clarke, Irwin, 1970), pp.38–47.

4 Pierre Berton, *Vimy* (Toronto: McClelland and Stewart, 1986), p.295.

5 Burns, *General Mud*, p.2. For the awarding of the Military Cross, see E.L.M. Burns file, Casualty Form Active Service, LAC, RG 9, No.92–93/166, quoted in D.E. Delaney, *Corps Commanders: Five British and Canadian Generals at War, 1939-45* (Vancouver: UBC Press, 2011), p.60.

6 *Star* (Toronto), April 10, 1967.

7 Ibid.

8 *Globe and Mail* (Toronto), April 10, 1967.

9 Quoted in B. Horn and M. Wyczynsky, "E.L.M. Burns: Canada's Intellectual General," in *Warrior Chiefs: Perspectives on Canada's Senior Military Leaders*, ed. B. Horn and S. Harris (Toronto: Dundurn, 2001), p.144.

10 The 1923 monument at RMC that celebrates the valour of Stairs and the many other cadets who were subsequently slain in battle has it right: "To the Glorious Memory of the Ex-Cadets of the Royal Military College of Canada Who Gave Their Lives for the Empire."

11 Hew Strachan, "John Buchan and the First World War: Fact into Fiction," in *Reassessing John Buchan: Beyond the Thirty-Nine Steps*, ed. Kate Macdonald (London: Pickering and Chatto, 2009), p.78.

12 Janet Adam Smith, *John Buchan: A Biography* (London: Rupert Hart-Davis, 1965), p.201.

13 Peter Buitenhuis, *The Great War of Words: British, American, and Canadian Propaganda and Fiction, 1914-1933* (Vancouver: University of British Columbia Press, 1987), p.109.

14 Ian McKay, "The 1910s: The Stillborn Triumph of Progressive Reform," in *The Atlantic Provinces in Confederation*, ed. E.R. Forbes and D.A. Muise (Toronto and Fredericton, N.B.: University of Toronto Press and Acadiensis Press, 1993), pp.192–229.

15 For a superb exploration of this pattern, see Daniel T. Rodgers, *Atlantic Crossings: Social Politics in a Progressive Age* (Cambridge, Mass. and London: The Belknap Press of Harvard University Press, 1998).

16 As one soon-to-die soldier wrote, in words that Buchan placed in his scrapbook of Great War memorabilia, "Try and not worry too much about the war. . . .

Remember, we are writing a new page of history. Future generations cannot be allowed to read the decline of the British Empire and attribute it to us. We live our little lives and die." Quoted in Keith Grieves, *"Nelson's History of the War*: John Buchan as a Contemporary Military Historian 1915–22," *Journal of Contemporary History* 28,3 (July 1993), pp.536–37.

17   Paul Fussell, *The Great War and Modern Memory* (New York: Oxford University Press, 1975), pp.174–87.

18   See, for a softer statement of this critique, Jeet Heer, "Remembrance Day: The Great War and Canadian Mythology," Sans Everything, http://sansevery-thing,wordpress,com.2010/11/11/remembrance-day-the-great-war-and-cana-dian/mythology.

19   Quoted in Buitenhuis, *Great War of Words*, p.95.

20   He was noteworthy among his contemporaries for resisting the spreading of stories he knew to be unfounded about the Germans—a scrupulosity for which he paid dearly in the British war propaganda bureaucracy.

21   Parker quoted in Buitenhuis, *Great War of Words*, p.30; Kipling quoted in Harold D. Lasswell, *Propaganda Technique in World War I* (Cambridge, Mass.: MIT Press, 1971 [1927]), p.91, drawing from the *Morning Post* (London), June 22, 1915. For Bryce, see Phillip Knightley, *The First Casualty: The War Correspondent as Hero, Propagandist, and Myth Maker from Crimea to Vietnam* (London: André Deutsch, 1975), pp.83–84; for Law, Knightley, *First Casualty*, p.83.

22   Canon Frederick George Scott, C.M.G., D.S.O., *The Great War As I Saw It* (Toronto: F.D. Goodchild Company, 1922), pp.76–77; Tim Cook, "The Politics of Surrender: Canadian Soldiers and the Killing of Prisoners in the Great War," *Journal of Military History* 70,3 (2006), p.651.

23   Robert Graves, *Goodbye to All That*, quoted in *The Book of War: 25 Centuries of Great War Writing*, ed. John Keegan (New York: Penguin Books, 1999), p.297.

24   Ibid.

25   Charles Yale Harrison, *Generals Die in Bed* (New York: William Morrow, 1930); Currie quoted in Cook, "Politics of Surrender," p.663.

26   Cook, "Politics of Surrender," pp.655, 658. Killing them was justified on the grounds that the men required to take them back to prisoner-of-war cages could not be spared from the fighting.

27   The 3,598 Canadians killed and the 7,004 wounded in this bloody battle on April 9, 1917, merely contributed to a short reprieve from a dismal failure of the Allies to dislodge the Germans. It was a great victory mainly in the eyes of Canadians; historians of the war from other countries give it short shrift.

28   Jonathan Vance, *Death So Noble: Memory, Meaning, and the First World War* (Vancouver: UBC Press, 1997), p.263.

29   See especially Will R. Bird, *And We Go On* (Toronto: Hunter-Rose, 1930).

30   The Vimy Foundation, www.vimyfoundation.ca.

31   Quoted in Jean Martin, "Vimy, April 1917: The Birth of *Which* Nation?" *Canadian Military Journal* 11,2 (2011). See also Barbara Ehrenreich, *Blood Rites: Ori-*

gins and History of the Passions of War (New York: Henry Holt, 1997). Ehrenreich (p.19) shows how the sacralization and religiosity of war help to make it "impervious to rebuke."

32 The Editors, "Afterthoughts," in *Vimy Ridge: A Canadian Reassessment*, ed. Geoffrey Hayes, Andrew Iarocci, and Mike Bechthold (Kitchener, Ont.: Wilfrid Laurier University Press, 2007), p.316.

33 Vance, *Death So Noble*, pp.56, 260. Vance is not directly quoting Dafoe.

34 Martin, "Vimy, April 1917," pp.37–38.

35 Benjamin Isitt, "Mutiny from Victoria to Vladivostok, December 1918," *Canadian Historical Review* 87,2 (June 2006), pp.223–64.

36 Desmond Morton, *A Military History of Canada*, 5th ed. (Toronto: McClelland and Stewart, 2007), pp.152, 156.

37 See James William Gibson, *Warrior Dreams: Paramilitary Culture in Post-Vietnam America* (New York: Hill and Wang, 1994); Andrew Bacevich, *The New American Militarism: How Americans Are Seduced by War* (Oxford: Oxford University Press, 2005), chs.1, 2; *Whig-Standard* (Kingston), Aug. 19, 1938, reprinting *New York Journal and American*.

38 Quoted in Morton, *Military History of Canada*, p.169.

39 J.L. Granatstein, *The Generals: The Canadian Army's Senior Commanders in the Second World War* (Toronto: Stoddart, 1993), p.118.

40 Burns, *General Mud*, pp.85–86.

41 Marion Elizabeth Rodgers, *Mencken: The American Iconoclast* (New York: Oxford University Press, 2005), p.259.

42 Burns, *General Mud*, p.88.

43 *American Mercury*, June 1924. See also p.75 here. The Freudian appeal of the bayonet would persist long after the weapon had been consigned to the museum; when, many decades later, Rick Hillier started his crusade to convince Canadians that their country was all about war and the army all about killing, he said, "You go out and bayonet somebody. We are not the Public Service of Canada." Quoted in Janice Gross Stein and Eugene Lang, *The Unexpected War: Canada in Kandahar* (Toronto: Viking, 2007), p.196.

44 *American Mercury*, June 1924.

45 Vance, *Death So Noble*, pp.193–94.

46 George Orwell, "Looking Back on the Spanish War," and "Politics and the English Language, in *The Collected Essays, Journalism and Letters of George Orwell* (New York: Harcourt, Brace, 1968), vol. 2, pp.252, and vol.4, p.139.

47 Keshen, *Propaganda and Censorship*, p.xvii.

48 *American Mercury*, July 1925.

49 *American Mercury*, September 1932.

50 *American Mercury*, March 1937; Delaney, *Corps Commanders*, p.73.

51 Granatstein, *Generals*, p.121.

52 Burns, *General Mud*, p.90.

53 Churchill quoted in Richard Toye, *Churchill's Empire: The World That Made Him and the World He Made* (London: Macmillan, 2010), pp.22, 54.

54 Burns, *General Mud*, pp.92–93.

55 Ibid., pp.95, 98.

56 L.B. Pearson, *Mike: The Memoirs of the Right Honourable Lester B. Pearson*, vol.1, *1897-1948* (Toronto: University of Toronto Press, 1972), pp.171–72.

57 *Globe and Mail*, June 21, 1943. For "star of the Permanent Force," see Delaney, *Corps Commanders*, p.63. For Crerar's opinion, see Granatstein, *Generals*, p.127.

58 Quoted in Granatstein, *Generals*, pp.128–29. The controversial letter went unmentioned in his memoir.

59 Morton, *Military History of Canada*, p.203.

60 For evidence of his critical abilities, see Delaney, *Corps Commanders*; S.J. Harris, *Canadian Brass: The Making of a Professional Army 1860-1939* (Toronto: University of Toronto Press, 1988), p.203; Harris cites M. Pope, *Soldiers and Politicians: The Memoirs of Lieutenant-General Maurice Pope* (Toronto: University of Toronto Press, 1962), p.53; and Burns, "A Division That Can Attack," *Canadian Defence Quarterly*, April 1938, quoted in Harris, *Canadian Brass*, p.204.

61 Burns, *General Mud*, p.133.

62 Delaney, *Corps Commanders*, p.80.

63 *Globe and Mail*, June 21, 1943.

64 Burns, *General Mud*, p.150.

65 Mark Zuehlke, *The Liri Valley: Canada's WW II Breakthrough to Rome* (Toronto: Stoddart, 2001), p.71.

66 Zuehlke, *Liri Valley*, pp.418, 429–30.

67 D.G. Dancocks, *The D-Day Dodgers: The Canadians in Italy, 1943-1945* (Toronto: McClelland and Stewart, 1991), p.288.

68 Burns, *General Mud*, p.173.

69 W.J. McAndrew, "Eighth Army at the Gothic Line: Commanders and Plans," *RUSI*, March 1986, quoted in Dancocks, *D-Day Dodgers*, p.289.

70 Crerar papers, in Granatstein, *Generals*, p.137; Stacey, *A Date with History*, Ottawa, 1982, quoted in Dancocks, *D-Day Dodgers*, pp.289–90. For details of the affair, see Mark Zuehlke, *The Gothic Line: Canada's Month of Hell in WW II Italy* (Vancouver: Douglas and McIntyre, 2003), ch.2; D.F. Delaney, *The Soldiers' General: Bert Hoffmeister at War* (Vancouver: UBC Press, 2005), pp.155–56; Dancocks, *D-Day Dodgers*, ch.13; and Granatstein, *Generals*, ch.5.

71 G.W.L. Nicholson, *The Canadians in Italy, 1943-1945* (Ottawa: Queen's Printer, 1957), p.681. One of Burns's underlings on the northward push through Italy was John Bassett, who would become a notable Toronto media mogul (Toronto *Telegram*, CTV) and professional sports entrepreneur (Toronto Argonauts and Maple Leafs); years later the connection made on that march north would prove helpful to Burns's stalled climb up the military ladder.

72 Zuehlke, *Liri Valley*, p.461; McCreery quoted in Granatstein, *Generals*, pp.141–42.

73 Interview with Desmond Smith, quoted in Dancocks, *D-Day Dodgers*, p.385.

74 Delaney, *Corps Commanders*, pp.60, 79–80.

75 For Burns to Crerar, see Granatstein, *Generals*, p.143; for Burns, "serve the country," see Burns, *General Mud*, p.220.

76 Will Lofgren, "In Defence of 'Tommy' Burns," *Canadian Military Journal*, Winter 2006–7; personal communication, Feb. 7, 2011. Lofgren's *CMJ* analysis did not make it into Delaney's 2011 profile of Burns.

77 Adam Chapnick, *The Middle Power Project: Canada and the Founding of the United Nations* (Vancouver: UBC Press, 2005), p.9.

78 Morton, *Military History of Canada*, pp.227–30.

79 Tony Judt, *Postwar: A History of Europe Since 1945* (London: Penguin, 2005), p.18.

80 E.L.M. Burns, *Manpower in the Canadian Army, 1939-45* (Toronto: Clarke, Irwin, 1956), pp.5–6; Power quoted in Dancocks, *D-Day Dodgers*, p.376.

81 For historians, see Bliss, Granatstein, and Neary cited in Jeffrey A. Keshen, *Saints, Sinners, and Soldiers: Canada's Second World War* (Vancouver: UBC Press, 2004), p.3; Angus Calder, *The People's War: Britain 1939-1945* (London: Jonathan Cape, 1969).

82 Keshen, *Saints, Sinners, and Soldiers*, p.280.

83 Quoted in Granatstein, *Generals*, p.144.

84 Quoted in Chapnick, *Middle Power*, p.121.

85 John English, *The Worldly Years: The Life of Lester Pearson*, vol.1, *1949-1972* (Toronto: Knopf Canada, 1992), pp.12, 22.

86 For "instrument of unimaginative militarism," see English, *Worldly Years*, p.22. Quotations regarding Acheson appear in Donald Creighton, *The Forked Road: Canada, 1939-1957* (Toronto: McClelland and Stewart, 1976), p.168, apparently citing Pearson, *Mike*, vol.2, p.56.

87 Robert Teigrob, *Warming Up to the Cold War: Canada and the United States' Coalition of the Willing, from Hiroshima to Korea* (Toronto: University of Toronto Press, 2009), p.57.

88 Robertson quoted and summarized in English, *Worldly Years*, p.15; Pearson quoted in Reginald Whitaker and Gary Marcuse, *Cold War Canada: The Making of a National Insecurity State, 1945-1957* (Toronto: University of Toronto Press, 1994), p.265.

89 Public opinion polls revealed consistently high support (80–90 per cent) for NATO in the 1950s—levels that persisted into the 1980s. See David Cox and Mary Taylor, eds., *A Guide to Canadian Policies on Arms Control, Disarmament, Defence and Conflict Resolution, 1985-86* (Ottawa: Canadian Institute for International Peace and Security, 1986), cited in Whitaker and Marcuse, *Cold War Canada*, p.281. In one amusing Gallup Poll of 1952, the pollsters were nonplussed to discover that 43 per cent of Canadians had never heard of NATO. Of the remaining 56 per cent, 16 per cent could not explain what it was, and 3 per cent described it in terms that the pollsters labelled "wrong completely." The

pollsters concluded that Canadians were not really sure what NATO was, although about 75 per cent still thought NATO was a good thing.

90 English, *Worldly Years*, p.108; Whitaker and Marcuse, *Cold War Canada*, p.280.

91 Kim Richard Nossal, *The Politics of Canadian Foreign Policy*, 2nd ed. (Scarborough, Ont.: Prentice-Hall Canada, 1989), p.33.

92 Quoted in English, *Worldly Years*, p.24.

93 David Jay Bercuson, *True Patriot: The Life of Brook Claxton 1898-1960* (Toronto: University of Toronto Press, 1993), p.40.

94 John W. Warnock, *Partner to Behemoth: The Military Policy of a Satellite Canada* (Toronto: New Press, 1970); Bercuson, *True Patriot*, p.227.

95 Bercuson, *True Patriot*, pp.167–68. The initial targeted reductions represented a budget cut of almost 55 per cent in one year. Brooke Claxton, the minister of defence, resisted their full implementation, but, Bercuson argues (p.169), he "had not been able to stop the budget slashing."

96 Morton, *Military History of Canada*, pp.237–38.

97 Quoted in Pierre Berton, *Marching as to War: Canada's Turbulent Years, 1899-1953* (Toronto: Doubleday Canada, 2001), p.578.

98 Teigrob, *Warming Up to the Cold War*, p.3.

99 Quoted in English, *Worldly Years*, pp.53–54.

100 Canada's involvement began in 1947 when the country's delegates to the UN agreed to join the United Nations Temporary Commission on Korea (UNTCOK).

101 Teigrob, *Warming Up to the Cold War*, p.183, paraphrasing *Time* magazine and Calgary *Herald*.

102 Ibid., pp.195–96, 191.

103 Pearson quoted in Whitaker and Marcuse, *Cold War Canada*, p.392; "of no military significance," ibid. Subsequent documents revealed that, for the United States, UN sanctions on North Korea came after Washington had already decided to move against the Communists, and the country would have launched the war with or without the UN. Not for the first time, the image of a "coalition of the willing" was misleading.

104 Pearson quoted in Whitaker and Marcuse, *Cold War Canada*, p.396.

105 For the reports documenting problems, including sexual assaults, see David J. Bercuson, *Blood on the Hills: The Canadian Army in the Korean War* (Toronto: University of Toronto Press, 1999), pp.173–77; Claxton cited in Whitaker and Marcuse, *Cold War Canada*, p.390. Bercuson (p.176) describes the views of some officers as "rampantly racist" and observes that among Canadian troops in general, links with Koreans were based on "need, not underlying respect for a different culture." He notes (p.177) that during the Korean War, "Canadian soldiers were tried and convicted for thirteen crimes of violence: four of rape or attempted rape, two of shooting (but not killing) Korean civilians, three of killing Korean civilians by a variety of means, three of killing ROK [Republic of Korea] soldiers, and one of the shooting death of a Canadian soldier." Although

there was no cover-up of such crimes in Korea, in every case but one, as historian Chris Madsen documents (cited by Bercuson), soldiers were treated leniently "after their cases were reviewed in Ottawa by a panel of legal experts and civilian judges."

106 The warring parties have never signed a peace treaty, which means that technically the war is still on, as intermittent crises on the peninsula remind us.

107 Berton, *Marching as to War*, pp.552–53.

108 Ibid., pp.575–76.

109 E.L.M. Burns, *A Seat at the Table: The Struggle for Disarmament* (Toronto: Clarke, Irwin, 1972), pp.12–13.

CHAPTER FOUR — PEARSON, ENDICOTT, AND THE COLD WAR

1 Robert Wright, *A World Mission: Canadian Protestantism and the Quest for a New International Order, 1918-1939* (Kingston and Montreal: McGill-Queen's University Press, 1991).

2 Stephen Endicott, *James G. Endicott: Rebel out of China* (Toronto: University of Toronto Press, 1980), p.99.

3 David Lenarcic, "Where Angels Fear to Tread: Neutralist and Non-Interventionist Sentiment in Interwar English Canada," Ph.D. thesis, York University, Toronto, 1992.

4 Quoted in Victor Huard, "Armageddon Reconsidered: Shifting Attitudes towards Peace in English Canada, 1936-1953," Ph.D. thesis, Queen's University, Kingston, Ont., 1996, pp.65–66; the general discussion here relies upon this text. Huard cites J. Lavell Smith, Clarence Haliday, and J.C.M. Duckworth, "A Protest," *New Outlook* 12 (August 1938), p.763.

5 Patrick Brennan, *Reporting the Nation's Business: Press-Government Relations during the Liberal Years, 1935-1957* (Toronto: University of Toronto Press, 1994).

6 The contradiction is explored in John English's illuminating, sympathetic two-volume biography, to which this account is greatly indebted. See John English, *Shadow of Heaven: The Life of Lester Pearson*, vol.1, *1897-1948* (Toronto: Lester and Orpen Dennys, 1989), and *The Worldly Years: The Life of Lester Pearson*, vol.2, *1949-1972* (Toronto: Alfred A. Knopf Canada, 1992). For a critique of Pearson as peacekeeper, see Yves Engler, *Lester Pearson's Peacekeeping: The Truth May Hurt* (Black Point, N.S.: Fernwood Publishing, 2012).

7 Quoted in English, *Shadow of Heaven*, pp.36, 34. The "seeds of his internationalist vision," English writes of Pearson (p.94), "germinated in the rich soil of liberal imperialism."

8 Quoted in English, *Shadow of Heaven*, pp.87, 169; "college friends were falling" in L.B. Pearson, *Mike: The Memoirs of the Right Honourable Lester B. Pearson*, vol.1, *1897-1948* (Toronto: University of Toronto Press, 1972), p.28.

9 English, *Shadow of Heaven*, pp.130, 136, 205.

10 Massey quoted in English, *Shadow of Heaven*, p.140; L.B. Pearson, *Mike: The*

Memoirs of the Right Honourable Lester B. Pearson, vol.2, *1948-1957* (Toronto: University of Toronto Press, 1973), p.76.

11 Quoted in Kim Richard Nossal, *The Politics of Canadian Foreign Policy*, 2nd ed. (Scarborough, Ont.: Prentice-Hall Canada, 1989), p.90.

12 Quoted in ibid., p.110.

13 English, *Shadow of Heaven*, p.209.

14 Quoted in ibid., p.161. Overall, Pearson contributed relatively little to postwar projects of disarmament and was an enthusiastic proponent of supplying Canadian arms to Israel, a proposition all the more attractive because the Israelis were willing to pay cash. See Joseph Levitt, *Pearson and Canada's Role in Nuclear Disarmament and Arms Control Negotiations, 1945-1957* (Montreal and Kingston: McGill-Queen's University Press, 1993); English, *Worldly Years*, p.122.

15 English, *Shadow of Heaven*, p.198.

16 See Ian McKay, "The Canadian Passive Revolution, 1840-1950," *Capital and Class* 34,3 (2010), pp.361–81.

17 Pearson and Keenleyside quoted in Denis Smith, *Diplomacy of Fear: Canada and the Cold War 1941-1948* (Toronto: University of Toronto Press, 1988), pp.21, 16.

18 Quoted in English, *Shadow of Heaven*, pp.248–49.

19 Pearson and Massey quoted in Shelagh D. Grant, *Sovereignty or Security: Government Policy in the Canadian North 1936-1950* (Vancouver: University of British Columbia Press, 1988), pp.76, 70, 71.

20 C.P. Stacey, *Canada and the Age of Conflict*, vol.2, *The Mackenzie King Era, 1921-1948* (Toronto: University of Toronto Press, 1981), pp.334, 324–26.

21 For an overview, see David A. Wolfe, "The Rise and Demise of the Keynesian Era in Canada: Economic Policy, 1930-1982," in *Modern Canada 1930-1980's*, ed. Michael S. Cross and Gregory S. Kealey (Toronto: McClelland and Stewart, 1984), pp.46–78.

22 Endicott, *James G. Endicott*, p.158.

23 Robert Teigrob, *Warming Up to the Cold War: Canada and the United States' Coalition of the Willing, from Hiroshima to Korea* (Toronto: University of Toronto Press, 2009), pp.23, 25.

24 Lester Pearson to Mackenzie King, Nov. 12, 1946, in English, *Shadow of Heaven*, p.300.

25 English, *Shadow of Heaven*, p.262.

26 Mark Kristmanson, *Plateaus of Freedom: Nationality, Culture, and State Security in Canada, 1940-1960* (Toronto: Oxford University Press, 2003), pp.xvi, 77, 82.

27 English, *Worldly Years*, p.172.

28 Reginald Whitaker and Gary Marcuse, *Cold War Canada: The Making of a National Insecurity State, 1945-1957* (Toronto: University of Toronto Press, 1994), p.7; Gary Kinsman and Patrizia Gentile, *The Canadian War on Queers: National Security as Sexual Regulation* (Vancouver: UBC Press, 2009), p.77. This is a detail banished, in English's biography, to one inconspicuous footnote: English, *Worldly Years*, p.104.

29 Gordon Barrass, *The Great Cold War: A Journey through the Hall of Mirrors* (Stanford, Cal.: Stanford University Press, 2009), p.34.

30 Quoted in Whitaker and Marcuse, *Cold War Canada*, p.9.

31 Barrass, *Great Cold War*, p.39.

32 Quoted in Teigrob, *Warming Up to the Cold War*, p.77, citing *New York Times*. Whether and to what extent foreign powers constructed the spy scare is as yet difficult to ascertain. Many of the most relevant documents remain under wraps or have mysteriously disappeared. Mackenzie King's diaries for the period have gone missing.

33 Quoted in Huard, "Armageddon Reconsidered," p.35. The general atmospheric description comes from Teigrob, *Warming Up to the Cold War*, p.20, and Whitaker and Marcuse, *Cold War Canada*.

34 Endicott, *James G. Endicott*, pp.15, 16.

35 Quoted in English, *Shadow of Heaven*, p.141.

36 Endicott, *James G. Endicott*, pp.95, 97.

37 Ibid., p.119.

38 Ibid., p.130.

39 Ibid., pp.129, 131.

40 Ibid., p.143.

41 Ibid., pp.161–63; Whitaker and Marcuse, *Cold War Canada*, p.367.

42 Endicott, *James G. Endicott*, pp.225, 271.

43 Ibid., p.217.

44 Quoted in ibid., p.265. For the petition signing, see Victor Huard, "The Canadian Peace Congress and the Challenge to Postwar Consensus, 1948-1953," *Peace and Change* 19,1 (January 1994), p.38. The government conceded that the estimate of signees was accurate, but in a secret memorandum one commentator dismissed 75,000 of the signatures as those of "Communists or fellow travelers" and the remaining 225,000 as those of "dupes."

45 Endicott, *James G. Endicott*, p.270.

46 Quoted in Huard, "Canadian Peace Congress," pp.37–38.

47 Endicott, *James G. Endicott*, p.342. The quotation is an early slogan of the peace movement.

48 Whitaker and Marcuse, *Cold War Canada*, pp.381, 376.

49 Ibid., p.372.

50 Endicott, *James G. Endicott*, p.167.

51 Ibid., p.191.

52 Ibid., pp.239–40, 217.

53 Ibid., p.254.

54 Ibid., p.3.

55 Quoted in Whitaker and Marcuse, *Cold War Canada*, p.273.

56 Quoted in ibid. See also Michiel Horn, *Academic Freedom in Canada: A History* (Toronto: University of Toronto Press, 1999), pp.186–88.

57   Endicott, *James G. Endicott*, p.275.

58   Whitaker and Marcuse, *Cold War Canada*, p.375.

59   Endicott, *James G. Endicott*, pp.276, 277, 286.

60   Quoted in Huard, "Canadian Peace Congress," p.41; Endicott, *James G. Endicott*, pp.269, 295, 342. For new evidence on the question of germ warfare in Korea, see Stephen Endicott and Edward Hagerman, *The United States and Biological Warfare: Secrets from the Early Cold War and Korea* (Bloomington and Indianapolis: Indiana University Press, 1998).

61   Whitaker and Marcuse, *Cold War Canada*, p.367.

62   Endicott, *James G. Endicott*, p.298; Whitaker and Marcuse, *Cold War Canada*, p.370. There was the additional complication, characteristic of life in the condominium, that Endicott's "treason," if that was what a court found his activism on the question of germ warfare to be, involved statements made not about Canada but about the United States. According to Teigrob, *Warming Up to the Cold War*, p.370, "sensitive information . . . might well have come forward in evidence at the trial" and "the Americans wanted no public forum to be opened for the charges to be tested. No wonder the Canadian cabinet stepped back from the brink."

63   Endicott, *James G. Endicott*, p.226. Endicott associates this argument with Reinhold Niebuhr, *Moral Man and Immoral Society* (1932).

64   Whitaker and Marcuse, *Cold War Canada*, p.366.

65   Teigrob, *Warming Up to the Cold War*, p.33; Madison quoted in Andrew Bacevich, *The New American Militarism: How Americans Are Seduced by War* (Oxford: Oxford University Press, 2005), p.7.

66   Endicott, *James G. Endicott*, p.266.

67   Frances Early, "Canadian Women and the International Arena in the Sixties: The Voice of Women/La Voix des femmes and the Opposition to the Vietnam War," in *The Sixties: Passion, Politics, and Style*, ed. Dimitry Anastakis (Montreal and Kingston: McGill-Queen's University Press, 2008), pp.25–41.

68   Kristmanson, *Plateaus of Freedom*, ch.2.

69   Quoted in English, *Worldly Years*, p.95.

70   Pearson, *Mike*, vol.1, p.233.

71   Whitaker and Marcuse, *Cold War Canada*, p.388.

72   Srdjan Vucetic, *The Anglosphere: A Genealogy of a Racialized Identity in International Relations* (Stanford, Cal.: Stanford University Press, 2011), p. 24; Churchill quoted, p.1.

73   J.L. Granatstein, and R.D. Cuff, *Ties That Bind: Canadian-American Relations in Wartime from the Great War to the Cold War*, 2nd ed. (Toronto and Sarasota: Samuel Stevens, Hakkert and Company, 1977).

74   Around some of the groups that Endicott was familiar with from the 1950s—such as the Canadian Committee for the Control of Radiation Hazards (later Canadian Committee for Nuclear Disarmament) and Combined Universities Campaign for Nuclear Disarmament, both founded in 1959 and modelled after

the Campaign for Nuclear Disarmament in Britain; the Voice of Women, created in 1960; and the Canadian Peace Research Institute, formed in 1961—would coalesce a broad-ranging movement that made the Canadian 1960s, 1970s, and 1980s a dynamic time of peace activism and war resistance.

CHAPTER FIVE — PEACEKEEPING AND THE MONSTER OF IMPERIALISM

1 E.L.M. Burns, *Between Arab and Israeli* (Toronto: Clarke Irwin, 1962), p.8.

2 Ibid. For an impressive overview of the broad spectrum of U.S. military thinkers and planners who viewed war in this way after 1945, see Andrew Bacevich, *The New American Militarism: How Americans Are Seduced by War* (Oxford: Oxford University Press, 2005), ch.2.

3 Burns, *Between Arab and Israeli*, pp.7–8.

4 Richard H. Immerman, *The CIA in Guatemala: The Foreign Policy of Intervention* (Austin: University of Texas Press, 1982), pp.167–72.

5 Rebecca Grant, "Dien Bien Phu," airforce-magazine.com, http://www.airforce-magazine.com/MagazineArchive/Pages/2004/August%202004/0804dien.aspx.

6 Caroline Elkins, *Imperial Reckoning: The Untold Story of Britain's Gulag in Kenya* (New York: Henry Holt, 2005), pp.xv, 233–74.

7 Alistair Horne, *A Savage War of Peace* (London: Macmillan, 1987), p.538.

8 Christopher Hitchens, *Cyprus* (London: Quartet Books, 1984), p.31.

9 The description of Burns comes from Sean Maloney, "The Forgotten: Lieutenant General E.L.M. 'Tommy' Burns and UN Peacekeeping in the Middle East," *Canadian Army Journal* 9,2 (Summer 2006).

10 Burns, *Between Arab and Israeli*, p.5.

11 Historian Benny Morris notes the paradox of competing Zionist and Palestinian nationalisms, with the former—its self-consciousness in full flower—dispossessing indigenous Arabs who in turn gained national self-awareness. "Paradoxically, it was in large part the thrust and threat of Zionism that generated this consciousness of collective self . . . a distinct Palestinian identity and nationalism. The Zionist leaders and settlers were only vaguely aware that the movement was having this effect. Indeed, to a very large extent they managed to avoid 'seeing' the Arabs. . . . It was as if the Jewish colony was a separate, self-contained universe, with nothing around it." Morris places this tendency in the context of a broader colonial tendency—"the routine European colonist's mental obliteration of the 'natives'; colonists tended to relate to the natives as part of the scenery, objects to be utilized when necessary, and not as human beings with rights or legitimate aspirations." Benny Morris, *Righteous Victims: A History of the Zionist-Arab Conflict, 1881-1999* (New York: Knopf, 1999), p.654.

12 Major General Carl von Horn, *Soldiering for Peace* (London: Cassell, 1966), p.62.

13 Burns, *Between Arab and Israeli*, pp.56, 68.

14 Ibid., p.70.

15 Ibid., pp.17–18; Benny Morris, *Israel's Border Wars: 1949-1956* (Oxford: Clarendon Press, 1997), p.350. The Egyptian regime had just executed members of the Muslim Brotherhood, and apologists for Nasser claimed that he was in no position to show mercy to Israeli agents.

16 Morris, *Israel's Border Wars*, chs.10, 11.

17 Eden quoted in Issandr El Amrani, "Why Tunis, Why Cairo?" *London Review of Books*, Feb. 17, 2011; and in John English, *The Worldly Years: The Life of Lester Pearson*, vol.2, *1949-1972* (Toronto: Alfred A. Knopf Canada, 1992), p.128; Robert Fisk, *The Independent*, Aug. 28, 2010; Richard Toye, *Churchill's Empire: The World That Made Him and the World He Made* (London: Macmillan, 2010), p.303

18 English, *Worldly Years*, ch.4.

19 Burns, *Between Arab and Israeli*, pp.182–84.

20 Morris, *Righteous Victims*, p.295.

21 Quoted in English, *Worldly Years*, p.138.

22 Lodge, a Boston brahmin who subsequently served as ambassador to South Vietnam, would superintend the initial escalation of that war and the coup that resulted in the murder of the country's president, Ngo Dinh Diem.

23 Michael G. Fry, "Canada, The North Atlantic and the UN," in *Suez 1956: The Crisis and Its Consequences*, ed. William Roger Louis and Roger Owen (London: Clarendon Press, 1989), pp.310–11. Fry (pp.314, 286) added a caveat to the usual paeans of praise for Canada's efforts with respect to the Suez crisis; just as "Israeli behaviour was often exasperating to its friends," Canada's role also caused ruffled feathers. "Pearson's efforts were well motivated and not without effect, but one should neither exaggerate the Canadian role not ignore the irritation it caused. Canada tried to serve many causes and mend several fences; her officials seemed to see all sides of every issue. They were not always applauded for doing so." Dulles apparently admired Pearson but saw him as being "torn between loyalty to NATO and the United States and his desire to be the West's problem solver."

24 Benedict Anderson, *Imagined Communities: Reflections on the Origin and Spread of Nationalism* (New York: Verso, 1983), p.149n16.

25 Donald Creighton, *The Forked Road: Canada 1939-1957* (Toronto: McClelland and Stewart, 1976), pp.281, 274–75.

26 English, *Worldly Years*, p.142.

27 Ibid., p.144.

28 Burns, *Between Arab and Israeli*, pp.188–89.

29 Ibid., pp.198–200.

30 L.B. Pearson, *Mike: The Memoirs of the Right Honourable Lester B. Pearson*, vol.2, *1948-1957* (Toronto: University of Toronto Press, 1973), pp.261–63.

31 Pearson, *Mike*, vol. 2, p.262; English, *Worldly Years*, p.141.

32 Brian Urquhart, *A Life in Peace and War* (New York: Norton, 1991), p.293.

33 Burns, *Between Arab and Israeli*, p.150.

34 Diem had had a chequered career, having been offered the premiership of the country by the retreating Japanese in 1945. During the independence war with the French he retreated to the United States, where he threw his lot in with the unreconstructed reactionary Cardinal Joseph Spellman and became popular in right-wing Catholic circles. The future quisling toured the United States, urging his hosts to save the country for the "free world" by supporting a government independent of the Viet Minh and the French, who regarded him as incompetent.

35 Victor Levant, *Quiet Complicity: Canadian Involvement in the Vietnam War* (Toronto: Between the Lines, 1986), p.118.

36 Pearson, *Mike*, vol.2, pp.116, 118.

37 Pearson quoted in Levant, *Quiet Complicity*, p.13; Lett in Ramesh Thakur, *Peacekeeping in Vietnam: Canada, India, Poland and the International Commission* (Edmonton: University of Alberta Press, 1984), p.286.

38 After 1968 the second cry was amended to *Nix-on, ass-ass-in! Tru-deau, complice!* The two books on Vietnam are Levant, *Quiet Complicity*, and James Eayrs, *Indochina: Roots of Complicity*, vol. 5 of Eayrs, *In Defence of Canada* (Toronto: University of Toronto Press, 1983).

39 J.L. Granatstein, "Canada: Peacekeeper (A Survey of Canada's Participation in Peacekeeping Missions)," in *Peacekeeping: International Challenge and Canadian Response*, ed. Alastair Taylor, David Cox, and J.L. Granatstein (Toronto: Canadian Institute of International Affairs, 1968), p.113.

40 Eayrs quoted in Levant, *Quiet Complicity*, p.194.

41 Gwynne Dyer, "Foreword," in Levant, *Quiet Complicity*, p.i.

42 Charles Taylor, *Snow Job: Canada, The United States and Vietnam 1954-1973* (Toronto: Anansi, 1975), p.188.

43 Ibid., p.17.

44 Ball to Lodge, May 30, 1964, Diplomatic Section, "Pentagon Papers," quoted in Taylor, *Snow Job*, p.51.

45 Taylor, *Snow Job*, p.52. Pearson's biographer John English explicitly challenges Taylor's interpretation of Pearson, Canada, and Vietnam, choosing to emphasize instead the prime minister's famous 1965 Philadelphia speech, during which he offered the mild advice that the United States make a tactical pause in its bombing of North Vietnam.

46 Mark Neufeld, "'Happy Is the Land That Needs No Hero': The Pearsonian Tradition and the Canadian Intervention in Afghanistan," in *Canadian Foreign Policy in Critical Perspective*, ed. J. Marshall Beier and Lana Wylie (New York: Oxford University Press, 2010), p.130; Johnson incident cited in English, *Worldly Years*, p.364. Other reports of the comment vary the wording slightly; Pearson's note in *Worldly Years*, p.369.

47 Levant, *Quiet Complicity*, p.1.

48 Quoted in Stephen J. Rockel, "Collateral Damage: A Comparative History," in

Inventing Collateral Damage: Civilian Casualties, War, and Empire, ed. Stephen J. Rockel and Rick Halpern (Toronto: Between the Lines, 2009), pp.12–13.

49 *Maclean's*, July 1967, quoted in Granatstein, "Canada: Peacekeeper," p.114.

50 Project Anti-War, *How to Make a Killing: A Preliminary Report Concerning Canadian Economic Involvement with the Pentagon and the War in Indo-China* (Montreal: Presse Solidaire, 1972); the researchers included Jamie Swift, Victor Levant, Paul Duchow, Myron Galan, Margaret McGregor, Sam Noumoff, Perry Shearwood, and Bill Worrell.

51 Cited in Levant, *Quiet Complicity*, p.218.

52 Lewis MacKenzie, *Peacekeeper: The Road to Sarajevo* (Vancouver: Douglas and McIntyre, 1993), pp.49–57.

53 Interview, Ottawa, August 10, 2009.

54 Ibid.

55 Quoted in Odd Arne Westad, *The Global Cold War* (Cambridge: Cambridge University Press, 2007), p.99.

56 Thomas Turner, *The Congo War: Conflict, Myth and Reality* (London: Zed Books, 2007), esp. p.26 regarding Lumumba's tenuous hold on power.

57 *Star* (Toronto), Jan. 9, 1959, quoted in Colin McCullough, "'No Axe to Grind in Africa': Violence, Racial Prejudice, and Media Depictions of the Canadian Peacekeeping mission to the Congo, 1960-64," mimeo, 2009. See also McCullough's article of the same title in *New World Coming: The Sixties and the Shaping of Global Consciousness*, ed. Karen Dubinsky, Catherine Krull, Susan Lord, Sean Mills, and Scott Rutherford (Toronto: Between the Lines, 2009), p.232. Such insights were not simply the product of another day. The militarist historian Sean Maloney allowed that the Congo had been a "placid Belgian colony . . . turned into a slaughterhouse." The huge, complex country was simply "a steaming tropical hell." Sean M. Maloney, *Canada and UN Peacekeeping: Cold War by Other Means, 1945-1970* (Toronto: Vanwell Publishing, 2002), pp.110, 104.

58 Robertson quoted in Kevin A. Spooner, *Canada, the Congo Crisis and UN Peacekeeping 1960-64* (Vancouver: UBC Press, 2009), p.37.

59 Spooner, *Canada, the Congo Crisis and UN Peacekeeping*, p. 28; for internal diplomatic correspondence, see pp.122–23.

60 Hébert and Reid quoted in ibid., pp.18–19.

61 Ludo De Witte, *The Assassination of Lumumba* (London: Verso, 2001), pp.17–22.

62 Georges Ngonzola-Ntalaja, *The Congo from Leopold to Kabila: A People's History* (London and New York: Zed Books, 2002), pp.109–10; see also De Witte's exhaustive treatment of the Lumumba murder in *Assassination of Lumumba*.

63 Spooner, *Canada, the Congo Crisis and UN Peacekeeping*, pp.112–13.

64 Ibid., p.147.

65 *Washington Post*, May 27, 2007.

66 Spooner, *Canada, the Congo Crisis and UN Peacekeeping*, pp.107–8.

67 Quoted in ibid., p.116.

68 Ibid., p.109.

69 Roméo Dallaire, *Shake Hands with the Devil: The Failure of Humanity in Rwanda* (Toronto: Vintage, 2004), p.318.

70 Hitchens, *Cyprus*, pp.10, 22; Perry Anderson, "The Divisions of Cyprus," *London Review of Books* 30,8 (April 24, 2008).

71 Quoted in Maloney, *Canada and UN Peacekeeping*, p.197.

72 Ibid., p.201; Martin's memoir, vol. 2, quoted in Maloney, *Canada and UN Peacekeeping*, p.200.

73 L.B. Pearson, *Mike: The Memoirs of the Right Honourable Lester B. Pearson*, vol.3, *1957–1968* (Toronto: University of Toronto Press, 1975), pp.134–35.

74 Pearson quoted in Maloney, *Canada and UN Peacekeeping*, p.216.

75 Pearson quoted in ibid., p.208.

76 Roy Thomas, "Re-evaluating the UN Effect on Cyprus," *Vanguard (Canada's Premier Defence and Security Magazine)*, March-April 2007.

77 E.L.M. Burns, *A Seat at the Table: The Struggle for Disarmament* (Toronto: Clarke, Irwin, 1972), p.7.

78 J. MacFarlane, "Sovereignty and Standby: The 1964 Conference on UN Peacekeeping Forces," *International Peacekeeping* 14,5 (November 2007).

79 Ibid.

80 Desmond Morton, *A Military History of Canada*, 5th ed. (Toronto: McClelland and Stewart, 2007), p.252.

CHAPTER SIX – "THE DECADE OF DARKNESS"

1 The Rwandan government had recently imported three-quarters of a million dollars' worth of machetes from China; its army was supported and trained by France, which, along with Canada's closest allies, the United States and the United Kingdom, opposed the more robust peacekeeping force for which the UN force commander Dallaire was pleading.

2 Interview, Kingston, Ont., July 13, 2009.

3 Roméo Dallaire, *Shake Hands with the Devil: The Failure of Humanity in Rwanda* (Toronto: Vintage, 2004), p.44.

4 Corey Robin, *The Reactionary Mind: Conservatism from Edmund Burke to Sarah Palin* (Oxford and New York: Oxford University Press, 2011), pp. 48, 123, 128, 162, 173, 192–93.

5 Desmond Morton, *A Military History of Canada*, 5th ed. (Toronto: McClelland and Stewart, 2007), pp.279–80.

6 Andrew Bacevich, *The New American Militarism: How Americans Are Seduced by War* (Oxford: Oxford University Press, 2005), p.16.

7 Interview, Ottawa, Nov. 16, 2010.

8 Kristol quoted in Robin, *Reactionary Mind*, p.60; Morton, *Military History of Canada*, p.271.

9   Walter Dorn, "Canadian Peacekeeping: Proud Tradition, Strong Future?" *Canadian Foreign Policy* 12, 2 (2005). Peacekeeping supporter Dorn, an RMC professor of defence studies who served with the United Nations in Ethiopia and East Timor, compiled a list of all UN peacekeeping operations to 2004.

10 Mark Danner, "The Truth of El Mozote," *The New Yorker*, Dec. 6, 1993, http://www.markdanner.com/articles/show/127?class=related_content_link; Margaret Popkin, *Peace Without Justice: Obstacles to Building the Rule of Law in El Salvador* (University Park: Pennsylvania State University Press, 2000). According to Danner, the Reagan administration "denied that any credible evidence existed that a massacre had taken place; and the Democratic Congress, after denouncing, yet again, the murderous abuses of the Salvadoran regime, in the end accepted the Administration's 'certification' that its ally was nonetheless making a 'significant effort to comply with internationally recognized human rights.' . . . For most Americans, El Salvador had long since slipped back into obscurity. But El Mozote may well have been the largest massacre in modern Latin-American history . . . a central parable of the Cold War."

11 Morton in "What Is to Be Done? Canada's Military Security in the 1990s," *Peace and Security* 5,2 (1990), Ottawa: CIIPS; Sherene Razack, *Dark Threats and White Knights: The Somalia Affair, Peacekeeping, and the New Imperialism* (Toronto: University of Toronto Press, 2004), pp.13, 9.

12 Quoted in "What Is to Be Done? Canada's Military Security in the 1990s."

13 Quoted in Geoffrey York and Loreen Pindera, *People of the Pines: The Warriors and the Legacy of Oka* (Toronto: Little, Brown, 1991), pp.45, 68.

14 Ibid., p.415.

15 Ibid., p.305.

16 Bacevich, *New American Militarism*, p.162.

17 Quoted in ibid., p.181.

18 *New York Times*, Jan. 16, 2006.

19 J.L. Granatstein, "Peacekeeping: Did Canada Make a Difference? And What Difference Did Peacekeeping Make to Canada?" in *Making a Difference? Canada's Foreign Policy in a Changing World Order*, ed. John English and Norman Hillmer (Toronto: Lester Publishing, 1992), pp.232–34.

20 Bacevich, *New American Militarism*, p.27. He remarks (p.27): "Even after 9/11, writes one acute observer, 'patriotism among the affluent classes has amounted to sticking an American flag decal on the tax-deductible Hummer.'"

21 Morton, *Military History of Canada*, p.283.

22 General Rick Hillier, *A Soldier First: Bullets, Bureaucrats and the Politics of War* (Toronto: HarperCollins, 2009), p.130; John le Carré, *Our Kind of Traitor* (Toronto: Viking Penguin, 2010), p.151.

23 Clausewitz is analysed in Azar Gat, *A History of Military Thought: From the Enlightenment to the Cold War* (Oxford and New York: Oxford University Press, 2001), pp.158–265, 382–402. Gat's measured interpretation can be compared to the uses of Clausewitz by many of the Canadian new warriors, who interpret him, simplistically, as an apostle of the "cult of the offensive" and the enemy of

any moderation or restraint in the conduct of war. See, for example, David Bercuson, *Significant Incident: Canada's Army, the Airborne, and the Murder in Somalia* (Toronto: McClelland and Stewart, 1996), pp.21–22, which claims that Clausewitz argues that all wars, regardless of context, must be based on the total destruction of the enemy's ability to wage war: "He has been proven correct time after time." As an interpretation of Clausewitz, this is dangerously one-sided; as advice to a nuclear age, it is merely dangerous.

24 John Crispo, "The Valour, the Horror, the Travesty," *Star* (Toronto), March 9, 1993.

25 Cliff Chadderton, "Gemini Can't Be Given for Accuracy," letter to the *Star*, March 13, 1993; testimony to the Standing Senate Committee on Social Affairs, Science and Technology, Sub-Committee on Veterans' Affairs, June 25, 1992, unrevised transcript; *Gazette* (Montreal), June 26, 1992.

26 Decarie quoted in *Globe and Mail* (Toronto), June 26, 1992; Bliss in *Gazette*, June 26, 1992; Harris in Randall Hansen, *Fire and Fury: The Allied Bombing of Germany, 1942-1945* (Toronto: Anchor Canada, 2009), p.246; courtroom information from personal communication with defendant Merilyn Simonds, Jan. 12, 2012.

27 David J. Bercuson and S.F. Wise, S.F., eds., *The Valour and the Horror Revisited* (Montreal and Kingston: McGill-Queen's University Press, 1994), pp.3, 5.

28 Wise in Bercuson and Wise, eds., *Valour and the Horror Revisited*, p.28.

29 Brereton Greenhous, Stephen J. Harris, William C. Johnston, and William G.P. Rawling, *The Crucible of War 1939-1945: The Official History of the Royal Canadian Air Force*, vol.3 (Toronto: University of Toronto Press with Department of National Defence and Canadian Government Publishing Centre, Supply and Services Canada, 1994), pp.698, 866–67. Another Canadian study of the bombing campaign, published in 2008, also contradicts Wise's claim. Hansen argues that mass killing in cities like Hamburg would have been justified had it quickened the end of the war; but concludes that after 1943 it was increasingly clear the strategy was not working and area bombing "not only failed to win the war, it probably prolonged it." Hansen, *Fire and Fury*, pp.270–71.

30 J.L. Granatstein, "Warring Aloft 50 Years On," *Quill and Quire*, June 1994.

31 *Globe and Mail*, Nov. 12, 1992; Sylvain quoted in A. Collins, "The Battle over 'The Valour and the Horror,'" *Saturday Night*, May 1993.

32 Jonathan Vance, *Death So Noble: Memory, Meaning, and the First World War* (Vancouver: UBC Press, 1997), pp.262–63.

33 Quoted in Barbara Ehrenreich, *Blood Rites: Origins and History of the Passions of War* (New York: Henry Holt, 1997), p.15.

34 Simonds diary, uncatalogued records, Queen's University archives, Kingston, Ont.

35 Merrily Weisbord and Merilyn Simonds Mohr, *The Valour and the Horror: The Untold Story of Canadians in the Second World War* (Toronto: HarperCollins, 1991), pp.169–70. See also Paul Walker, "U.S. Bombing: The Myth of Surgical Bombing in the Gulf War," http://deoxy.org/wc/wc-myth.htm.

36 Bercuson and Wise, eds., *Valour and the Horror Revisited*, p.185, emphasis added.

37 Ibid., pp.185, 326–27, 410. See also Antony Beevor, *The Fall of Berlin* (New York: Penguin, 2002), pp.326–27, 410. Aside from Hansen's exhaustive study, which relies on extensive interviews with German survivors but suffered none of the attacks levelled at *The Valour and the Horror's* area bombing for doing so (although Hansen did receive his fair share of abusive correspondence), English philosopher A.C. Grayling's work stands out among recent examinations of already well-tilled fields. Grayling, *Among Dead Cities: The History and Moral Legacy of the WW II Bombing of Civilians in Germany and Japan* (New York: Walker, 2006), pp.273–74.

38 Bercuson and Wise, eds., *Valour and the Horror Revisited*, p.185. For a rather more nuanced probe of the complexities of European and particularly German public memory of the war and Holocaust, and especially Hannah Arendt's observations on a 1950 trip to her native Germany, see Tony Judt, *Postwar: A History of Europe Since 1945* (New York : Penguin, 2005), p.810.

39 *Whig-Standard* (Kingston), June 5, 1993. *The Valour and the Horror* suffered from empirical problems, and its implicitly ahistorical stance of passing swift moral judgments on figures in the past did merit criticism.

40 Bacevich, *New American Militarism*, pp.111–16.

41 Odd Arne Westad, *The Global Cold War* (Cambridge: Cambridge University Press, 2007), pp.331–32.

42 Quoted in Africa Watch and Physicians for Human Rights, "Somalia: No Mercy in Mogadishu, the Human Cost of the Conflict and the Struggle for Relief," *Africa Watch*, March 26, 1992.

43 Dallaire, *Shake Hands with the Devil*, p.340; interview with Beardsley, July 13, 2009, Kingston, Ont.

44 For the extent to which partition proposals overrode any consideration of what the Bosnian government wanted or what non-nationalist groups demanded, and instead bought into unexamined stereotypes about Balkan ethnicity, see David Campbell, *National Deconstruction: Violence, Identity, and Justice in Bosnia* (Minneapolis and London: University of Minnesota Press, 1998); for the hypocrisies and brutalities of the bombing campaigns, see Noam Chomsky, *The New Military Humanism: Lessons from Kosovo* (Vancouver: New Star, 1999). For a more general critique, see Jean Bricmont, *Humanitarian Imperialism: Using Human Rights to Sell War* (New York: Monthly Review Press, 2006).

45 Quoted in Sandra Whitworth, *Men, Militarism, and UN Peacekeeping: A Gendered Analysis* (Boulder and London: Lynne Rienner Publishers, 2007), p.100.

46 United Nations, Department of Public Relations, "Somalia—UNOSOMI, Mission Backgrounder," http://www.un.org/Depts/DPKO/Missions/uno-somi.htm, 23/5/11; "We do deserts . . ." is quoted in (and is the title of an article by) Alex de Waal, *London Review of Books*, Nov. 11, 1999.

47 Interview, Ottawa, Nov. 16, 2010; testimony to Commission of Inquiry into the Deployment of Canadian Forces to Somalia, quoted in Razack, *Dark Threats and White Nights*, p.67.

48 Razack, *Dark Threats and White Nights*, pp.80–84, citing "Information Legacy: A Compendium of Source Material/Commission of Inquiry into the Deployment of Canadian Forces to Somalia," 1997.

49 "Information Legacy," in Razack, *Dark Threats and White Nights*, pp.82–83.

50 *Citizen* (Ottawa), June 21, 1997, and "Information Legacy," both in Razack, *Dark Threats and White Nights*, pp.97–98.

51 Quoted in Peter Desbarats, *Somalia Cover-Up: A Commissioner's Journal* (Toronto: McClelland and Stewart, 1997), pp.343–49; Razack, *Dark Threats and White Nights*, pp.4–5.

52 Desbarats, *Somalia Cover-Up*, p.210.

53 Ibid., p.248.

54 Bercuson, *Significant Incident*; David Bercuson and Barry Cooper, *Derailed: The Betrayal of the National Dream* (Toronto: Key Porter Books, 1994), p.209.

55 Bercuson, *Significant Incident*, pp.9, vii, 106.

56 Ibid., pp.242, 32, 28–29. For a useful overview of anthropological counter-evidence, see Gopal Balakrishnan, "The Role of Force in History," *New Left Review* 47 (September-October 2007), pp.23–56.

57 Razack, *Dark Threats and White Knights*; Whitworth, *Men, Militarism, and UN Peacekeeping*. Throughout, whenever confronted with evidence of "soldiers behaving badly," Bercuson responds with a version of the fallacy that some logicians call the "No-True-Scotsman" move. For a discussion of this fallacy, see Antony Flew, *Thinking about Thinking* (London: Fontana, 1975), especially p.47.

58 Bercuson, *Significant Incident*, p.114.

59 Ibid., pp.240, 157, 97.

60 Ibid., p.242.

61 Ibid., p.114.

62 Ibid., pp.88–89; Desbarats, *Somalia Cover-Up*, p.212.

63 Carol Off, *The Ghosts of the Medak Pocket: The Story of Canada's Secret War* (Toronto: Random House, 2004), pp.238, 195.

64 "US General: Gay Dutch Soldiers Caused Srebrenica Disaster," *Guardian* (London), March 19, 2010.

65 Letter to Jane Snailham, July 16, 1992, in Jane Snailham, *Eyewitness to Peace: Letters from Canadian Peacekeepers* (Clementsport, N.S.: Canadian Peacekeeping Press, 1998), p.12

66 Scott Taylor and Brian Nolan, *Tarnished Brass: Crime and Corruption in the Canadian Military* (Toronto: Lester, 1996), pp.3–4.

67 Dorn, "Canadian Peacekeeping."

68 Michael Riordon, *Our Way to Fight: Peace-Work under Siege in Israel-Palestine* (Toronto: Between the Lines, 2011), p.1.

69 Whitworth, *Men, Militarism, and UN Peacekeeping*, p.12.

70 A. Betts Fetherston, as quoted in ibid., p.152.

71 It was sometimes urged that democracies generally do not make war on each other, a proposition that relied upon loaded and question-begging definitions

of "democracy." For a useful critique and analysis, see Srdjan Vucetic, *The Anglosphere: A Genealogy of a Racialized Identity in International Relations* (Stanford: Stanford University Press, 2011), pp.33–35.

72 Joseph Stiglitz, Foreword, in Karl Polanyi, *The Great Transformation: The Political and Economic Origins of Our Time* (Boston: Beacon, 2001), p.xiv.

73 Quoted in Eric Hobsbawm, *Age of Extremes: The Short Twentieth Century 1914–1991* (London: Abacus, 1995), p.574.

74 Jamie Swift, *Wheel of Fortune: Work and Life in the Age of Falling Expectations* (Toronto: Between the Lines, 1995), p.181.

75 Quoted in Stephen Clarkson, *Uncle Sam and Us: Globalization, Neoconservatism, and the Canadian State* (Toronto: University of Toronto Press, 2002), p.394.

76 *Citizen*, April 28, 1998.

77 Clarkson, *Uncle Sam and Us*, p.397.

78 The Nobel Committee's recognition of NGOs, civil society organizations, or whatever one chooses to call them did have historical precedents even if individuals had dominated the recipient list. Over the course of the twentieth century the Committee recognized the Quakers, the Red Cross (twice), and international groups supporting refugees and international law.

79 Nobelprize.org: The official web site of the Nobel Prize, www.nobelprize.org.

80 Jenny Pearce, "Civil Society, the Market and Democracy in Latin America," cited in Jamie Swift, *Civil Society in Question* (Toronto: Between the Lines, 1999), p.149.

81 Conference of Defence Associations, http://cda-cdai.ca/cda. See J.L. Granatstein, "Keynote Address: On Military Education," to 1998 CDA graduate student symposium, http://cda-cdai.ca/cdai/symposia/1998-graduate-student-symposium.

82 Interview, Montreal, Dec. 4, 2009.

83 Bacevich, *New American Militarism*, p.58. For an excellent analysis, see Michael Mann, *Incoherent Empire* (London and New York: Verso, 2003), pp.252–68.

84 Joy Gordon, *Invisible War: The United States and the Iraqi Sanctions* (Cambridge, Mass.: Harvard University Press, 2010), epigraph.

85 Ploughshares Research and Action for Peace, "Project Ploughshares Responds to Military Assaults on Iraq," Waterloo, Ont., Dec. 18, 1998, http://www.ploughshares.ca/content/project-ploughshares-responds-military-assaults-iraq.

87 Hillier, *Soldier First*, ch.11; Harper's Index, May 2011; *Washington Post*, Nov. 6, 2009.

CHAPTER SEVEN – YELLOW RIBBONS AND INDIAN COUNTRY

1 Human Rights Watch, *Fatal Strikes: Israel's Indiscriminate Attacks against Civilians in Lebanon*, New York, Aug. 2, 2008, http://www.hrw.org/en/reports/2006/08/02/fatal-strikes 17.

2 *Whig-Standard* (Kingston), Feb. 2, 2008.

3 National Defence and the Canadian Forces, "Major Paeta Hess-Von Kruedener Board of Inquiry Released," Ottawa, Feb. 1, 2008, http://www.cefcom-comfec.forces. gc.ca/pa-ap/nr-sp/doc-eng.asp?id=2530.

4 *Globe and Mail* (Toronto), July 26, 27, 2006; interview, Kingston, Ont., Sept. 16, 2009.

5 *Globe and Mail*, Feb.9, 2008.

6 Interview, Ottawa, Nov. 10, 2009. The following quotations from Porter are from this interview.

7 Andrew Bacevich, *The New American Militarism: How Americans Are Seduced by War* (Oxford: Oxford University Press, 2005), p.184.

8 Paul Rogers, *Why We're Losing the War on Terror* (Cambridge: Polity Press, 2008), pp.37, 42; see also Ahmed Rashid, *Taliban: Militant Islam, Oil and Fundamentalism in Central Asia*, 2nd ed. (New Haven, Conn.: Yale University Press, 2009); and Odd Arne Westad, *The Global Cold War* (Cambridge: Cambridge University Press, 2007).

9 Congressional Budget Office, in Ahmed Rashid, *Descent into Chaos: The U.S. and the Disaster in Pakistan, Afghanistan and Central Asia* (New York: Viking Penguin, 2009), p.lvii.

10 Ian Traynor, "US Defence Chief Blasts Europe over NATO," *Guardian* (London), June 10, 2011.

11 Julian Glover, "The Afghan War Is Lost. So Now Who'll Take the Blame?" *Guardian*, June 12, 2011.

12 Sherard Cowper-Coles, *Cables from Kabul: The Inside Story of the West's Afghanistan Campaign* (London: Harper Press, 2011), pp.277, 289–90.

13 Rashid, *Descent into Chaos*, p.65.

14 Niall Ferguson, *Empire: The Rise and Demise of the British World Order and Lessons for Global Power* (New York: Basic Books, 2002); Niall Ferguson, *Colossus: The Price of America's Empire* (New York: Penguin, 2004); Michael Ignatieff, *Empire Lite* (Toronto: Penguin Canada, 2003). For an impassioned manifesto for the new world order, see James C. Bennett, *The Anglosphere Challenge: Why the English-Speaking Nations Will Lead the Way in the Twenty-First Century* (Lanham, Md.: Rowman and Littlefield, 2004); for a more balanced conservative appraisal, see Charles S. Maier, *Among Empires: American Ascendancy and Its Predecessors* (Cambridge, Mass.: Harvard University Press, 2006).

15 Rashid, *Descent into Chaos*, p.lv.

16 Ibid., pp.xxxvii–lviii.

17 "PM's Farewell to Kandahar: 'Afghanistan Is No Longer a Threat to the World,'" *Globe and Mail*, May 30, 2011.

18 Prime Minister of Canada Stephen Harper, "Address by the Prime Minister to the Canadian Armed Forces in Afghanistan," Ottawa, March 16, 2006, http://pm.gc.ca/eng/media.asp?id=1056.

19 Faytene Kryskow ("reclaim Canada for Christ") quoted in Marci McDonald,

The Armageddon Factor: The Rise of Christian Nationalism in Canada (Toronto: Random House Canada, 2010), p.151. McDonald's book is a disturbing study of the rapid rise of the religious right in Canada. The following paragraphs draw on her work. For another cogent study of the same phenomenon, see Tom Warner, *Losing Control: Canada's Social Conservatives in the Age of Rights* (Toronto: Between the Lines, 2010), especially pp.222, 249.

20 See McDonald, *Armageddon Factor*, p.26, citing the Statement of Faith of the Christian and Missionary Alliance. That this practice is, to put it charitably, an inventive and imaginative reading of the Bible is explored by Barbara Rossing, *The Rapture Exposed: The Message of Hope in the Book of Revelation* (New York: Basic Books, 2005). Nowhere in the Old or New Testaments is there a direct reference to the Rapture, nor is there any scriptural warrant for reading a theological significance into the establishment of a Jewish state in the Middle East.

21 Bacevich, *New American Militarism*, p.146.

22 Emmanuel, a former Christian Heritage Party candidate, had advocated the return of corporal punishment in schools and the execution of children as young as eleven convicted of murder. *Spectator* (Hamilton, Ont.), June 14, 1996.

23 Greg Bonnell, "Eves, Harper, Stir Pro-U.S. Rally," Canadian Press, April 4, 2003.

24 *Standard* (St. Catherines), April 12, 14, 2003; *Review* (Niagara Falls), April 5, 2003.

25 Not In Our Name, www.notinourname.net. This national U.S. project has since announced that it has come to an end.

26 Jonathan Barker, *The No-Nonsense Guide to Global Terrorism*, 2nd ed. (Toronto: NI Publications and Between the Lines, 2008), pp.27, 29.

27 Ignatieff, *Empire Lite*, p.73; Derrick O'Keefe, *Michael Ignatieff: The Lesser Evil?* (New York: Verso Books, 2011), p.81.

28 *Citizen* (Ottawa), Dec. 6, 2008.

29 *Whig-Standard*, Feb. 15, 2008.

30 Smith, whose first-hand coverage of Afghanistan from 2006 to 2009 was the most comprehensive available to Canadians, did not receive the CDFAI/CDA Ross Munro Award for "significant and outstanding contribution to the understanding, by the general public, of Canada's defence and security issues." He did, however, receive three National Newspaper awards, the Michener Award for public service journalism, and, in the United States, an Emmy Award.

31 *Citizen*, June 21, 2007.

32 An early recounting of this crucial episode can be found in Janice Stein and Eugene Lang, *The Unexpected War: Canada in Kandahar* (Toronto: Viking Canada, 2007), ch.10; Hillier's memoir tells the story differently, although he does explain how keen he was to have Canada go to Kandahar because Herat in western Afghanistan "would have been costly and given us little visibility, credibility or impact internationally." General Rick Hillier, *A Soldier First: Bullets, Bureaucrats and the Politics of War* (Toronto: HarperCollins, 2009), p.343. In 2011 a British security researcher published a detailed look at the forces that led

Canada to Kandahar: Matthew Willis, "Canada in Regional Command South: Alliance Dynamics and National Imperatives," Whitehall Paper no.77, 2011.

33 Walter Dorn and Michael Varey, "Fatally Flawed: The Rise and Demise of the 'Three-Block War' Concept in Canada," *International Journal* 63,2 (Autumn 2008).

34 Duane Bratt, "Canada's 3D Approach in Afghanistan: Defence, Defence, Defence," *Development Forum* 1,1 (2008); military official quoted in Stein and Lang, *Unexpected War*, pp.279; Hillier quoted in Stein and Lang, *Unexpected War*, p.275; Hillier, *Soldier First*, pp.349, 477. Hillier's book benefited from the creative ministrations of *National Post* journalist and army reservist Chris Wattie, himself the author of a book about how the Canadian army saved Afghanistan. On May 19, 2006, the *Post* ran a prominent front-page story by Wattie claiming that Iranian Jews were to be forced to wear special insignia designating their faith. Even though Prime Minister Harper immediately commented that Iran was "very capable" of such a move and the story began circulating on the internet, the *Post* was forced to back off, removing the story from its website. The paper was subsequently forced to run a lengthy apology by its editor-in-chief. *National Post* (Toronto), May 19, 24, 2006.

35 Stein and Lang, *Unexpected War*, p.147.

36 C. Wright Mills, *The Power Elite* (1956; reprinted New York: Oxford University Press, 2000), p.222.

37 Sandra Whitworth, *Men, Militarism, and UN Peacekeeping: A Gendered Analysis* (Boulder and London: Lynne Rienner Publishers, 2007), p.39; for Wattie, see "We'll Be Your Friends, Troops Tell Villagers," Afghanistan News Centre, Sept. 16, 2003, www.afghanistannewscenter.com/news/2003/september/sep162003.html.

38 Dorn and Varey, "Fatally Flawed."

39 Walter Dorn, "Canada Pulls out of Peacekeeping," *Globe and Mail*, March 27, 2006.

40 Canadian Army, "Patricias Take Charge of Kandahar Province," http://www.army.forces.gc.ca/land-terre/news-nouvelles/story-reportage-eng.asp?id=982.

41 Dorn and Varey, "Fatally Flawed."

42 House of Commons, *Debates*, Standing Committee on Foreign Affairs and International Development, March 22, 2007.

43 Ibid.

44 *Globe and Mail*, May, 3, 2007, Feb. 1, 2, and March 13, 2008; Hillier, *Soldier First*, p.461.

45 Paul Fussell, *The Great War and Modern Memory* (New York: Oxford University Press, 1975), p.74.

46 Andrew Bacevich, *Washington Rules: America's Path to Permanent War* (New York: Henry Holt, 2010), p.201.

47 See Albi Homes, "The Measure of Craftsmanship," http://www.albihomes.com/community-about.asp?CommunityCode=GAR.

48 "Escape to Yesteryear," paper submitted to the Canadian Historical Association Annual Meeting, Ottawa, May, 2009.

49 Canadian Association of Veterans in UN Peacekeeping (CAVUNP), "Peacekeeper Park," http://cavunp.ab.ca/home2.html.

50 Interview, Calgary, Sept. 30, 2009.

51 Peacekeeper Park, http://cavunp.ab.ca/home2.html. A Peacekeeper Park in Ontario's Middlesex County also includes those killed in "Task Force Afghanistan." See www.peacekeeperpark.com.

52 Interview, Calgary, Sept. 30, 2009.

53 "Competition Guidelines," National Capital Commission and Dept. of National Defence, in Paul Gough, "Peacekeeping, Peace, Memory: Reflections on the Peacekeeping Monument in Ottawa," *Canadian Military History* 11,3 (2002).

54 "We need action not only to end the fighting but to make the peace. My own government would be glad to recommend Canadian participation in such a United Nations force, a truly international peace and police force."

55 Interview, Ottawa, Dec. 5, 2008.

56 Gough, "Peacekeeping, Peace, Memory," p.68.

57 Ibid., p.73.

58 Interviews, Ottawa, Nov. 11, 2009, Aug. 10, 2009.

59 Interview, Ottawa, Dec. 5, 2008.

60 Quoted in Brant Scott, "Colonel John Gardham Retiring as Perley Rideau Foundation Chairman," *Between Us*, Spring 2008; interview, Ottawa, Dec. 5, 2008.

61 Canadian Press, "Canadian Troops Kill 2 Children When Car Approached Convoy in Afghanistan," July 28, 2008; *Guardian* (Charlottetown, P.E.I.), July 28, 2008; CTV News, July 28, 2008, http://www.ctv.ca/CTVNews/CTVNews At11/20080728/afghan_children_080728. As Fussell (*Great War and Modern Memory*, p.177) puts it, "The troops became masters of the use of the passive voice common among the culturally insecure as a form of gentility . . . only they used it to avoid designating themselves as agents of nasty or shameful acts."

62 Canadian Press, "Canadian Troops Kill 2 Children When Car Approached Convoy in Afghanistan," July 28, 2008.

63 Ibid.

64 "Mel Gibson's Latest Hero: A Rapist Who Hunted Indians for Fun," *Guardian*, June 15, 2000.

65 See James Laxer, *Mission of Folly: Canada and Afghanistan* (Toronto: Between the Lines, 2008). As an important segment of the mission ended in 2011, the Canadian military claims, together with those of the Afghans they called their partners, continued to be bafflingly counterfactual. "I don't believe that since the Second World War, any nation has been faced with such a large challenge—and done it as well as Afghanistan," said Major-General D. Michael Day, discussing the bright future of training the Karzai government forces. His Afghan counterpart Afghan Brigadier-General Ahmad Habibi added, "The enemy is on its

knees and very weak." *Globe and Mail*, July 6, July 5, 2011. By early 2012 NATO was entering into serious negotiations with Taliban emissaries that are almost certain to return politicians linked to the Taliban to power. Karzai, our "ally," was himself once a minor Taliban functionary. The country's economy and society had been devastated but opium exports were flourishing.

66 For an excellent first-person and critical antidote to such "situational chivalry" disguised as feminism, see Malalai Joya with Derrick O'Keefe, *A Woman Among Warlords: The Extraordinary Story of an Afghan Who Dared to Raise Her Voice* (New York: Scribner, 2009).

67 *Economist* (London), June 25, 2011.

68 Norman F. Dixon, *On the Psychology of Military Incompetence* (London: Futura, 1976), p.71.

69 Howard Fremeth, "Searching for the Militarization of Canadian Culture: The Rise of a Military-Cultural Memory Network," *Topia: Canadian Journal of Cultural Studies* 23/24 (2010), p.69n3.

70 Hillier, *Soldier First*, p.371.

71 *Globe and Mail*, Sept. 18, 2011.

72 Canwest News Service, March 19, 2008.

73 "Past Remarks by CBC Hockey Personality That Caused Uproar," Postmedia News, Oct. 11, 2011, Canada.com CTV.

74 *Globe and Mail*, Oct. 12, 2010.

75 Ken Dryden and Roy MacGregor, *Home Game: Hockey and Life in Canada* (Toronto: McClelland and Stewart, 1989).

76 "Military Is Front and Centre at Grey Cup Game," http://www.army.forces.gc.ca.

77 Aitken in Jeffrey Keshen, *Propaganda and Censorship during Canada's Great War* (Edmonton: University of Alberta Press, 1996), pp.27, 31–33.

78 Quoted in Noah Richler, "What We Talk about When We Talk about War," *Queen's Quarterly*, Summer 2011.

79 "Canada's 157th Afghan Casualty Travels the Highway of Heroes," *Globe and Mail*, June 29, 2011. Suitor's comment was heard on the Sept. 11, 2011, broadcast.

80 Esprit de Corps website, www.espritdecorps.ca/index.php?option=com_content&view=article&id=256:our-troops-and-peter-mackays-true-colours&catid=37:politics&Itemid=97.

81 Afghanistan News Center, Sept. 16, 2003, www.afghanistannewscenter.com/news/2003/september/sep162003.html July 15, 2011.

82 See A.L. McCready, "Tie a Yellow Ribbon 'Round Public Discourse, National Identity and the War: Neoliberal Militarization and the Yellow Ribbon Campaign in Canada," *Topia* 23/24 (2010).

83 *Evening Guide* (Port Hope), July 13, 2007.

84 McCready, "Tie a Yellow Ribbon," p.43.

85 John F. Conway, "Regina 16 Say Common Folk Won Freedoms," *Herald* (Calgary), April 6, 2010.

86 *Globe and Mail*, March 26, 2010.

87 Ken Montgomery, "'Shut Up and Teach': Collisions of Nationalism, Militarism, and Racism in Public Education," International Conference on Educational Sciences, Famagusta, North Cyprus, June 2011.

88 J.F. Conway, "The Project Hero Controversy: How War, Propaganda and Pit Bull Politics Are Wrecking Our Country," *Prairie Dog*, April 8, 2010.

89 Interview, Port Hope, April 13, 2011.

90 During the Nazi period Germany was divided into administrative regions called Gaue, overseen by members of the governing Nazi party called gauleiters. Each was appointed by Hitler and reported to him.

CHAPTER EIGHT − MILITARY FANTASYLANDS AND·THE GATED PEACEABLE KINGDOM

1 Directorate of Land Strategic Concepts (DLSC), *Crisis in Zefra* (Ottawa: Department of National Defence, 2005), Story Author Karl Schroeder, pp. 44, 46, 11, 5, http://issuu.com/philipboyle/docs/crisis_in_zefra_e; Lawrie Hawn, interview, "The Current," CBC Radio, Dec. 11, 2009.

2 DLSC, *Crisis in Zefra*, p.10.

3 See, for instance, Frantz Fanon, "On National Culture," in *The Wretched of the Earth* (London: Penguin, 1963).

4 See the illustrations in DLSC, *Crisis in Zefra*, pp.8, 21, 52. Hollywood's stereotyping of the Arabs can be traced back to Rudolph Valentino's performances in *The Sheik* (1921) and *The Son of the Sheik* (1926). For an excellent documentary exploring this phenomenon, see Sut Jhally, dir., *Reel Bad Arabs: How Hollywood Vilifies a People* (2006).

5 DLSC, *Crisis in Zefra*, p.73.

6 Ibid., p.102. For Karl Schroeder's artistic vision, and this expression, see his website, http://www.kschroeder.com/foresight-consulting/crisis-in-zefra.

7 Ibid., p.10.

8 DLSC, *Crisis in Zefra*, p.10.

9 Ibid., pp.55, 53.

10 Ibid., p.xi.

11 Ibid., Peter Gizewski, "Anatomy of a Failed State," p.123; Lt.-Col Bernd Horn and Peter Gizewski, eds., *Towards a Brave New World: Canada's Army in the 21st Century* (Kingston, Ont.: Army Publishing Office, 2003).

12 DLSC, *Crisis in Zefra*, p.124.

13 See Conn Hallinan, "The New Scramble for Africa," *Dispatches from the Edge*, Sept. 14, 2011. For an exploration of the United Nations' disappointing record in the DRC, see Séverube Aytesserre, *The Trouble with the Congo: Local Violence*

and the Failure of International Peacebuilding (New York: Cambridge University Press, 2010). For the Canadian mining projects, see Todd Gordon, *Imperialist Canada* (Winnipeg: Arbeiter Ring, 2010); Mining Watch, www.miningwatch.ca. In 2010 MiningWatch, a Canadian advocacy group, pointed out that after Parliament rejected a law that would have placed some modest safeguards on the activities of Canadian mining companies operating in the global South, the victims of predatory corporate practices began legal actions against such companies in the Canadian courts.

14 See Peter Morey and Amina Yaqin, *Framing Muslims: Stereotyping and Representation after 9/11* (Cambridge, Mass., and London: Harvard University Press, 2011).

15 J.L. Granatstein, in *Globe and Mail* (Toronto), Aug. 11, 1988, p.A1. As Markus Kienscherf remarks, "The military deployment of cultural knowledge juxtaposes an Orientalist space, which is construed as illiberal, violent and crisscrossed by multiple divisions, with an occidental space that is by default liberal, unitary and peaceful." Markus Kienscherf, "Plugging Cultural Knowledge into the U.S. Military Machine: The Neo-Orientalist Logic of Counterinsurgency," *Topia: Canadian Journal of Cultural Studies* 23/24 (2010), pp.135–36.

16 Ironically, by Orientalizing their enemy, the NATO occupiers actually blinded themselves to the clear indications that the Taliban were far from static, grasped quickly the strategic and tactical requirements of fighting on Afghan terrain, and were obviously not the product of a fixed and eternal cultural system. By freezing and distorting the people against whom they fought, both the warriors and the politicians failed to understand the war they were fighting. See Patrick Porter, *Military Orientalism: Eastern War through Western Eyes* (New York: Columbia University Press, 2009).

17 Drawing upon the distillation of David Landes, as reported in Ferguson's impassioned defence of the new world order: Niall Ferguson, *Empire: The Rise and Demise of the British World Order and the Lessons for Global Power* (London: Allen Lane, 2002), p.307.

18 Blair quoted in Srdjan Vucetic, *The Anglosphere: A Genealogy of a Racialized Identity in International Relations* (Stanford, Cal.: Stanford University Press, 2011), p.101; Harper in Mark Neufeld, "'Happy Is the Land That Needs No Hero': The Pearsonian Tradition and the Canadian Intervention in Afghanistan," in *Canadian Foreign Policy in Critical Perspective*, ed. J. Marshall Beier and Lana Wylie (Don Mills, Ont.: Oxford University Press, 2010), p.127.

19 Vucetic, *Anglosphere*, p.145.

20 Neil Balan, "A Corrective for Cultural Studies: Beyond the Militarization Thesis to the New Military Intelligence," *Topia: Canadian Journal of Cultural Studies* 23/24 (2010), pp.160–61.

21 Susan W. Hardwick, Rebecca Marcus, and Marissa Isaak, "Education and National Identity in a Comparative Context," *National Identities* 12,3 (2010), pp.253–68, especially p.258.

22 Desmond Morton, "Teaching and Learning History in Canada," in *Knowing,*

Teaching and Learning History: National and International Perspectives, ed. Peter
Stearns, Peter Seixas, and S. Wineburg (New York: New York University Press,
2000), p.55. We were drawn to this reference by Lisa Y. Faden, "History Teach-
ers 'Think the Nation': Narratives of Citizenship in Wartime Canada and the
United States," paper presented to the Annual Meeting of the American
Educational Research Association, Teaching History Special Interest, New
Orleans, April 2011.

23 Jane Taber, "Harper Spins a New Brand of Patriotism," *Globe and Mail*, Aug. 9,
2011; Stephen Harper, speech to the Canada-UK Chamber of Commerce,
London, July 14, 2006, in The Monarchist League of Canada, "Memorable
Quotations about Canada's Monarchy," http://www.monarchist.ca/en/quotes.

24 Citizenship and Immigration Canada, *Discover Canada: The Rights and Responsibilities of Citizenship, Study Guide*, 2010 edition (Ottawa: Minister of Public
Works and Government Services Canada, 2009), p.23; Patricia Roy, J.L.
Granatstein, Masako Iino, and Hiroko Takamura, *Mutual Hostages: Canadians
and Japanese during the Second World War* (Toronto: University of Toronto Press,
1990), p.x. Although the other contributors add empirical insights, the book's
contentious core concept would seem to be Granatstein's. Canadian citizenship
did not exist as a legal category before 1947. Technically, in international law,
nobody was a citizen of Canada before 1947. If the formal category of citizenship had existed, the Japanese Canadians in question here would, like all other
Canadians, have been "citizens."

25 See Jennifer Reid, *Louis Riel and the Creation of Modern Canada: Mythic Discourse
and the Postcolonial State* (Albuquerque: University of New Mexico Press, 2008);
Ramon Hathorn and Patrick Holland, eds., *Images of Louis Riel in Canadian Culture* (Lewiston, Queenston, and Lampeter: Edwin Mellen Press, 1992).

26 It was never apparent how the rights of women were actually being furthered by
bombing Afghan villages, and the right-wing case suffered serious damage
when Afghan MP Malalai Joya, who brought to the argument the pertinent
experience of being an Afghan feminist, demanded the immediate withdrawal
of occupation forces and pointed out that the rhetoric of women's liberation
was being systematically abused when it was put to the purpose of whipping up
war fever. Balan, "Corrective for Cultural Studies," p.147. By almost every
measure the position of women declined in Afghanistan after the early 1980s—
that is, since the United States and its allies decided to back Islamic fundamen-
talists as part of a Cold War agenda.

27 A.L. McCready, "Tie a Yellow Ribbon 'Round Public Discourse, National
Identity and the War: Neoliberal Militarization and the Yellow Ribbon Campaign in Canada," *Topia* 23/24 (2010), p.34; see also James Compton, "Fear and
Spectacle on the Planet of Slums," *Topia: Canadian Journal of Cultural Studies*
23/24 (2010), p.349, for a discussion of the phrase "post-9/11 world."

28 Canadians were involved especially in multinational naval group Task Force
151, which patrolled the Persian Gulf region. Other Canadians worked at U.S.
Central Command in Qatar. Canadian Air Force pilots flew combat missions
with the U.S. Air Force.

29   Neufeld, "'Happy Is the Land That Needs No Hero,'" p.133.

30   Andrew Bacevich, *Washington Rules: America's Path to Permanent War* (New York: Henry Holt, 2010), p.25; Tristin Hopper, "Canada to Expand Military Reach with New Facilities across the Globe," *National Post* (Toronto), June 2, 2011. Camp Mirage, a semi-secret logistics facility in the United Arab Emirates, was established to support Canada's Afghan operations. It was subsequently used as a bargaining chip by the U.A.E. in a dispute over airline landing rights. The ultimate price tag of this misadventure was an estimated $300 million. Defence Minister Peter MacKay proudly announced that Canada had become the "go-to" country for military missions. Overseas bases will complement the C-17 "Globemaster" transport aircraft (price tag: $3.4 billion) that the military has already purchased. In *The New American Militarism: How Americans Are Seduced by War* (Oxford: Oxford University Press, 2005), Bacevich notes (p.229n20) that one source indicates that U.S. troops are stationed in 150 foreign countries, although the Pentagon openly acknowledges having bases in only 40.

31   For a superb distillation, see Stephen Staples, "Harper, the Military, and Wedge Politics," in *The Harper Record*, ed. Teresa Healy (Ottawa: Canadian Centre for Policy Alternatives, n.d. [2008]), www.policyalternatives.ca.

32   Canadian Centre for Policy Alternatives, *Canadian Military Spending 2009* (Ottawa, 2009), http://www.policyalternatives.ca/publications/reports/canadian-military-spending-2009. For U.S. military spending, see Bacevich, *Washington Rules*.

33   For "civilian" organizations and war, Jody Berland and Blake Fitzpatrick, "Introduction: Cultures of Militarization and the Military-Cultural Complex," *Topia: Canadian Journal of Cultural Studies* 23/24 (2010), pp.15–16; for the new model, ibid., p.14, drawing upon the work of Paul Virilio; Vice Admiral Arthur Cebrowski quoted in ibid., p.18.

34   Naomi Klein, *The Shock Doctrine: The Rise of Disaster Capitalism* (Toronto: Alfred A. Knopf Canada, 2007), p.14. See Jeremy Scahill, *Blackwater: The Rise of the World's Most Powerful Mercenary Army* (New York: Nation Books, 2007). A shift in Blackwater ownership produced the collegial sounding "Academi" moniker, the new proprietors claiming to be inspired by Plato's Academy and hoping to suggest a caste of disciplined warriors who are thinkers as well as fighters.

35   Ismael Hossein-zadeh, as quoted in McCready, "Tie a Yellow Ribbon," p.31; Matthew Behrens, "Canada's Massive Military Budget Is off the Table in Federal Election," Rabble.ca, April 29, 2011, http://rabble.ca/news/2011/04/canadas-massive-military-budget-table-federal-election.

36   Erna Paris, "The New Solitudes," *The Walrus*, March 2011.

37   See, for "peace warriors," Balan, "Corrective for Cultural Studies," p.146. He cites a recent piece by David Bercuson, "There's a New 'Peace Warrior' in Town," *Globe and Mail*, March 1, 2010.

38   "Canada's Armed Forces: Fighting to Keep Fighting," *The Economist*, Sept. 9, 2010, http://www.economist.com/node/16994606.

39 Nikhail Singh, "The Afterlife of Fascism," *South Atlantic Quarterly* 105,1 (Winter 2006), p.85.

40 This useful term is introduced by Tim Lenoir and Henry Lowood in a recent account of war game simulation technology. See Howard Fremeth, "Searching for the Militarization of Canadian Culture: The Rise of a Military-Cultural Memory Network," *Topia: Canadian Journal of Cultural Studies* 23/24 (2010), pp.52–76, quotation on p.58.

41 Henry Giroux, "War Colleges," *Counterpunch*, June 29, 2011, http://www.counterpunch.org.

42 M.J. Hogan, *A Cross of Iron: Harry S. Truman and the Origins of the National Security State, 1945-1954* (Cambridge: Cambridge University Press, 1998), p.74, quoted in Bacevich, *Washington Rules*, pp.27–28.

43 Karen Howlett, "Corporate Tax Cuts Don't Spur Growth," *Globe and Mail*, April 6, 2011.

44 Faden, "History Teachers 'Think the Nation.'" See The Memory Project (Historica-Dominion Institute), http://www.thememoryproject.com/home.aspx.

45 See Jeet Heer, "Remembrance Day: The Great War and Canadian Mythology," http://sanseverything,wordpress,com.2010/11/11/remembrance-day-the-great-war-and-canadian/mythology.

46 William Greider, "Under the Banner of the 'War' on Terror," *The Nation*, June 21, 2004, p.14. For a sophisticated reflection on the politics of fear in the contemporary world, see Corey Robin, *Fear: The History of a Political Idea* (Oxford: Oxford University Press, 2004). In Canada the deliberate inculcation of a climate of fear is apparent in the regime's attempts to create a moral panic about a supposed crime wave despite Statistics Canada data revealing that crime levels are declining. The Harper Conservatives could rely upon the Macdonald-Laurier Institute, which issued a report disputing the official statistics, enabling the regime to argue that it had science on its side when it brought in eighteen crime bills, at a cost of $631 million, on top of a $2.1-billion makeover of Canadian prisons, which will come to resemble more and more the maxi-prisons of the United States. Donald Gutstein, "Harper's Crime Floggers: Macdonald-Laurier Institute, Key Accomplice in the Tories' Assault on Truth," *The Tyee*, March 21, 2011, http://thetyee.ca/Opinion/2011/03/21/CrimeFloggers.

47 Daniel Pick, *War Machine: The Rationalization of Slaughter in the Modern Age* (New Haven, Conn.: Yale University Press, 1993), p.14.

48 Stephen Chase, "Think Tank's Funding Tied to Getting Good Press," *Globe and Mail*, May 16, 2008. In one case a former general appeared numerous times to denounce any attempt to scale down the war in Afghanistan. The viewing public never learned that about 53 per cent of the profits of the general's company depended upon the Afghan War. Laura Bassett, "Networks Still Hosting Military Analysts without Identifying Massive Conflicts of Interest," *Huffington Post*, Dec. 11, 2009, http://www.huffingtonpost.com/2009/12/11.

49 Giroux, "War Colleges."

50 J.L. Granatstein, "Fort Fumble on the Rideau: Just Say No to Military Acade-

mics," *Globe and Mail*, Aug. 22, 2011. The $492-billion, twenty-year program outlined in the Harper government's pivotal *Canada First Defence Strategy: A Modern Military for the Twenty-First Century* (CFDS) blatantly depended upon the wit and wisdom of Granatstein, whose shrill rhetoric in *Whose War Is It? How Canada Can Survive in the Post-9/11 World* (Toronto: HarperCollins, 2007) is directly echoed in the government's text.

51 Bernd Horn, "A Rejection of the Need for Warrior Scholars?" *Canadian Military Journal* 11 (Jan. 2, 2011), www.journal.dnd.ca/vo11/no2/08-horn-eng.asp.

52 Fremeth, "Militarization of Canadian Culture," p.69n23; McCready, "Tie a Yellow Ribbon," p.33. See also David A. Clearwater, "Living in a Militarized Culture: War, Games and the Experience of U.S. Empire," *Topia: Canadian Journal of Cultural Studies* 23/24 (2010), p.262.

53 John R. Gillis, *The Militarization of the Western World* (New Brunswick, N.J.: Rutgers University Press, 1989), p.9.

54 See Brian Osborne, "Commemorating the Nation's Workers: The Case of the 'Reesor Siding Incident,'" Dept. of Geography, Queen's University, Kingston, Ont., forthcoming.

55 Joseph Stiglitz, "The Price of 9/11," *Project Syndicate*, Sept. 1, 2011, http:// readersupportednews/org/off-site-opinion-section/56-56/7320-the-price-of-911. New U.S. research also suggests that many (perhaps 20 per cent) of the returned soldiers from Iraq and Afghanistan—war zones in which the improvised explosive device (IED) is often the insurgents' weapon of choice—suffer from mild traumatic brain injuries (mTBI), a misleading term for a condition that can entail such serious consequences as personality disorders and depression. Nowhere near enough military psychologists are available to treat the problem, and many civilian psychologists refuse to take on soldiers as patients. See Conn Hallinan, "The Wars Come Home: The Traumatic Brain Injury Epidemic," *Dispatches from the Edge*, June 18, 2011, dispatchesfromtheedgeblog.wordpress.com.

56 Nancy A. Youssef, "True Cost of US Wars Unknown," McClatchy Newspapers, Aug. 16, 2011, http://readersupportednews.org/news/news-section2/323-95/7054.

57 See especially Paul Kellogg, "Arms and the Nation: the Impact of 'Military Parasitism' on Canada's Place in the World Economy," Ph.D. thesis, Queen's University, Kingston, Ont., 1990; Paul Kellogg, "From the Avro Arrow to Afghanistan: The Political Economy of Canada's New Militarism," unpublished paper presented to the Society for Socialist Studies, Vancouver, 2008.

58 Janice Stein and Eugene Lang, *The Unexpected War: Canada in Kandahar* (Toronto: Viking, 2007), pp.177, 184, 195.

59 Doug Saunders, "Canada Picked Its Kandahar Moment" *Globe and Mail*, Jan. 7, 2012.

60 Citizenship and Immigration Canada, *Discover Canada*, p.8.

61 Taber, "Harper Spins a New Brand of Patriotism."

62 See Robert Teigrob, *Warming Up to the Cold War: Canada and the United States'*

Coalition of the Willing, from Hiroshima to Korea (Toronto: University of Toronto Press, 2009), p.228.

63 Kim Richard Nossal, *The Politics of Canadian Foreign Policy*, 2nd ed. (Scarborough, Ont.: Prentice-Hall Canada, 1989), pp.54–59.

64 For important works that develop this insight, see Stephen Gill, ed., *Gramsci, Historical Materialism and International Relations* (Cambridge: Cambridge University Press, 1994); Robert W. Cox with Timothy J. Sinclair, *Approaches to World Order* (Cambridge: Cambridge University Press, 1996); Mark McNally and John Schwarzmantel, eds., *Gramsci and Global Politics: Hegemony and Resistance* (London and New York: Routledge, 2009).

65 E.L.M. Burns, *Megamurder* (Toronto: Clarke, Irwin, 1966), pp.37, 179–80.

66 "Joe Canada Rant," YouTube, http://www.youtube.com/watch?v=pnpVH7kIb_8.

67 Hillmer cited in Joseph T. Jockel, *Canada and International Peacekeeping* (Toronto: Canadian Institute of Strategic Studies and Washington, Centre for Strategic and International Studies, 1993), p.19; J.L. Granatstein, "Peacekeeping: Did Canada Make A Difference? And What Difference Did Peacekeeping Make to Canada?" in *Making a Difference? Canada's Foreign Policy in a Changing World Order*, ed. John English and Norman Hillmer (Toronto: Lester Publishing, 1992), pp.232, 231; H. Mintzberg, "Foreword," to Harvey Schachter, ed., *Memos to the Prime Minister: What Canada Could Be in the 21st Century* (Toronto: Wiley, 2003).

68 John Scott Cowan, "War and National Interest," *On Track* (Conference of Defence Associations) 13,2 (Summer 2008), p.12; Lane Anker, "Peacekeeping and Public Opinion," *Canadian Military Journal* 6,2 (2005), p.24.

69 Quoted in McCready, "Tie a Yellow Ribbon," p.39.

70 J.L. Granatstein and J.M. Hitsman, *Broken Promises: A History of Conscription in Canada* (Toronto: Oxford University Press, 1977), pp.268, 269.

71 Anker, "Peacekeeping and Public Opinion," p.24.

72 For work reflecting on the United Nations' changing character, see Jocelyn Coulon, *Soldiers of Diplomacy: The United Nations, Peacekeeping and the New World Order* (Toronto: University of Toronto Press, 1998); Mark Mazower, *No Enchanted Palace: The End of Empire and the Ideological Origins of the United Nations* (Princeton, N.J.: Princeton University Press, 2009).

73 Quoted in John English, *Shadow of Heaven: The Life of Lester Pearson*, vol.1, *1897–1948* (Toronto: Lester and Orpen Dennys, 1989), p.141.

74 Nossal, *Politics of Canadian Foreign Policy*, p.7.

75 Ibid., pp.63–65; Desmond Morton, "Defending the Indefensible: Some Historical Perspectives on Canadian Defence, 1867-1987," *International Journal* 42 (Autumn 1987).

76 Tony Judt, "The New World Order," *New York Times Review of Books*, July 14, 2005.

77 See, for example, Michael Eric Dyson, *Come Hell or High Water: Hurricane Katrina and the Color of Disaster* (New York: Basic Civitas Books, 2006); Chris Rose, *One Dead in Attic: After Katrina* (New York: Simon and Schuster, 2007).

78 Gwynne Dyer, *Climate Wars* (Toronto: Random House, 2008), p.242; United Kingdom Ministry of Defence and Pentagon staffer quoted pp.6–8.

79 "Grand Cove—The Great Escape," www.grandcove.ca.

80 Mike Davis, *City of Quartz: Excavating the Future in Los Angeles* (London: Verso, 1990), p.246.

81 Stephen Scharper, "Rich Nations Retreat behind Gated Ecology," *Star* (Toronto), Dec. 4, 2011.

ILLUSTRATION CREDITS

INDEX

historical, 245; and identity, 258; national, 254
Memory Project, 279
Mencken, H.L., 80–81
Mennonites, anti-militarism of, 108
Methodism, 107, 111, 122, 225
Métis, 257; use of Gatling gun against, 227, 257–58
Middle East: injustice in as foe worth fighting, 297; unrest in, 142–43; war for as "successor war" to Cold War, 220. *See also* Suez Crisis
Middlesex County (Ontario): Peacekeeper Park in, 332n51
Mi'kmaq, 49
mild traumatic brain injuries (mTBI), 339n55
militarism: advances in British, 92; conflation of with peacekeeping, 245; and criticism of war-making, 192; disillusionment with, 108; enduring postwar danger of, 137; German, 70; growth of, 256; in Israel, 145; maelstrom of, 129; new, 245; new secular religion of, 72; patriotic, 258; Protestant revulsion against, 226; redistributive, 276; resistance to permanent, 92; sport and, 250–53; state strategy of, 294; vs. militarization, 280
militarization, vs. militarism, 280
military, Canadian: academy and legitimacy of, 282; boosterism of, 250–52; Canadianization of, 174; crisis of purpose, 179, 187; cuts to, 187, 236; desire to prove itself in combat, 285; elevation of as institution, 254, 270; glorification of, 13; increased spending on, 241, 275–76; integration of with U.S. military, 269; investments in and survival of Pearsonian quiet diplomacy, 182; neglect of, 219; overinvestment in as drag on capitalist development, 285; prioritization of over peaceful dispute resolution, 269; priority of alliance with U.S., 173; prompt response of to Somalia, 199; public scrutiny of, 196; rebranding of, 249; resources of power, 289; as "rusted out," 179, 219; suspicious view of overgrown, 180; top-heaviness of, 93; unification of forces, 174
military complacency, 290
military culture, war stories and, 206
military-entertainment complex, 278, 283
military history, fascination with, 281–82
military metaphors, 283
"military metaphysics," 233, 290
military service, lack of, 187
"militia myth," 304n3
Mill, John Stuart, 133
Miller, Carmen, 57
Mills, C. Wright, 233
Mines Advisory Group, 212
Minh, Ho Chi, 154, 157
mining projects, 334n13
Minto, Lord, 55, 58
Mintzberg, Henry, 292
Mobutu, Joseph, 161, 164, 166–67

Mohammed, Din, 246–47
Mohawks, and Oka Crisis, 182–85
Molson, Hartland de Montarville, 79–80
Molson Canadian, 291
Monarchist League of Canada, 11
monarchy, British, 270; adoration of, 174; as symbol of whiteness, hierarchy, and authoritarian rule, 288
Monroe Doctrine, 55–56
Mons (Belgium), capture of, 1–2
Montgomery, Ken, 257
Montreal: anti-war riots in, 58; Holy Trinity Cathedral, 57; labour unrest in, 117; socialist movement in, 57; street names in, 239–40
Morocco, 166
Morris, Benny, 146, 148, 319n11
Morrison, Edward, 1
Morton, Desmond, 88, 174, 179, 180, 182, 213, 269, 296
Mossadegh, Mohammad: overthrow of, 141
Mouvement National Congolais, 161
Mowat, Farley, 258–59
Msiri, subjugation of, 40–41, 47, 52
Mubarak, Hosni, 142
Mujahedin, U.S. aid to, 197
Mulock, William, 31
Mulroney, Brian, 186–87
multiculturalism, 269, 270, 288
Munich Agreement (1938), 110
Muslim Brotherhood, Egyptian execution of members of, 320n15
Muslims: Bosnian, 207; as civilizational enemies in "failed" states, 267; fanatical, 39, 43
Mussolini, Benito, 164, 197
Muttart, Patrick, 270
myth-symbol complex, 269–70, 293; nationalist, 136; right-wing, 69, 94

Nagasaki, 98, 117, 140, 185
Namibia, 55; independence of, 181; UNTAG in, 181
Nasser, Col. Gamal Abdel, 143, 151, 152, 161, 166, 170, 174; Burns's negotiations with, 144; Churchill and, 147; epithets used to describe, 147; goal of destroying, 147; visit to Gaza, 146
nation: from colony to, 116, 287; new warriors' sense of, 286
National Defence College, 195
National Film Board (NFB), purge of dissidents from, 118, 134
National Gallery of Canada, 244
nationalism: Anglosphere, 287; annexationist, 211, 287; and celebration of empires, 288–89; Congolese, 163; democratic, 117; flourishing of, 116–17; new warrior, 270, 287; pan-Canadian, 286; peacekeeping and, 159, 292; Québécois, 286, 288; and Suez Crisis, 149
national narratives, 272
National Policy, 56
National Post, 331n34